Mastering OpenLDAP

Configuring, Securing, and Integrating Directory Services

Matt Butcher

BIRMINGHAM - MUMBAI

Mastering OpenLDAP

First published: August 2007

Production Reference: 1230807

Published by Packt Publishing Ltd.
32 Lincoln Road
Olton
Birmingham, B27 6PA, UK.

ISBN 978-1-847191-02-1

www.packtpub.com

Cover Image by Ronald R. McDaniel (rmcdaniel@indata.us)

Credits

Author

Matt Butcher

Reviewers

Aaron Richton

George K Thiruvathukal

Quanah Gibson-Mount

Development Editor

Douglas Paterson

Assistant Development Editor

Nikhil Bangera

Technical Editor

Ved Prakash Jha

Editorial Manager

Dipali Chittar

Project Manager

Patricia Weir

Project Coordinator

Abhijeet Deobhakta

Indexer

Bhushan Pangaonkar

Proofreader

Rebecca Paterson

Production Coordinator

Shantanu Zagade

Cover Designer

Shantanu Zagade

About the Author

Matt Butcher is the principal consultant for Aleph-Null, Inc., a systems integrator that specializes in Free and Open Source solutions. He is also a member of the Emerging Technologies Lab at Loyola University Chicago, where he is currently finishing a Ph.D. in philosophy. Matt has written two other books for Packt: *Managing and Customizing OpenCms 6 Websites* (ISBN: 978-1-904811-76-3), and *Building Websites with OpenCms* (ISBN: 1-904811-04-3). Matt has also contributed articles to Newsforge.com, TheServerSide.com, and LinuxDevices.com.

Anyone who actively works with Free and Open Source software knows that any good project is the result of the contributions of a wide variety of people. I hope it is evident in this book that I have taken this lesson to heart. I would like to thank Bob Krumland for introducing me to LDAP in 1997. I owe a great debt of gratitude to Quanah Gibson-Mount and Aaron Richton, who both generously lent their technical expertise to make this a better book. I would like to thank Jon Hodge for his time and assistance. Also, I'd like to thank Mark Patterson, Paul Beam, George Peavy, Ed Mattson, and Kevin Reilly. And thanks to the members of the Emerging Technology Lab at Loyola University, especially George Thiruvathukal for his comments. The members of the OpenLDAP mailing list have been tremendously helpful, especially Kurt Zeilenga, Howard Chu, Pierangelo Masarati, and Aaron Richton. And, of course, thanks to Claire, Anna, and Angie for their continual support, encouragement, and crayon-colored pictures.

About the Reviewers

Aaron Richton is a Systems Administrator for the Rutgers University campus in New Brunswick/Piscataway, NJ. He has used OpenLDAP since the 2.1 series. The OpenLDAP servers he administers are responsible for the authentication of over 60,000 accounts. Richton holds degrees in Electrical and Computer Engineering and Computer Science from the Rutgers University School of Engineering.

George K. Thiruvathukal Ph.D. is an associate professor of computer science at Loyola University Chicago, where he directs the departmental computing and infrastructure. He has held positions in industry (at Fortune 500 companies such as R.R. Donnelley and Sons and Tellabs, both in the Chicago area) and in academia, including the Illinois Institute of Technology and Argonne National Laboratory. He has co-authored two books on advanced software development for Prentice Hall PTR and Sun Microsystems press, including *High-Performance Java Platform Computing: Threads and Networking* (see `http://hpjpc.googlecode.com`) and Web *Programming in Python* (see `http://slither.googlecode.com`). His research interests include parallel/distributed systems, programming languages/paradigms/patterns, and experimental computing. His teaching interests include most of the modern computer science curriculum and computing history. For more information, see `http://www.cs.luc.edu/gkt`.

Quanah Gibson-Mount graduated from the University of Alaska, Fairbanks with a B.S. in Computer Science. Quanah has been working with OpenLDAP since the early stages of the OpenLDAP 2.1 release. He is currently a Principal Software Engineer with Zimbra, Inc, where he focuses on OpenLDAP configuration and Release Engineering. He is also the release engineer for the OpenLDAP project, and in his spare (paid for) time teaches classes on LDAP and OpenLDAP for Symas Corp. Prior to his employment with Zimbra, Quanah worked at Stanford University, where one of his primary tasks was that of Directory Architect.

I'd like to thank my wife Karen for all of her support in these many endeavors.

Table of Contents

Preface

The OpenLDAP directory server is a mature product that has been around (in one form or another) since 1995. All of the major Linux distributions include the OpenLDAP server, and many major applications, both Open Source and proprietary, are directory aware, and can make use of the services provided by OpenLDAP. And yet the OpenLDAP server seems to be shrouded in mystery, known and understood only by the gurus and hackers. This book is meant not only to demystify OpenLDAP, but to give the system administrator and software developer a solid understanding of how to make use, in the practical realm, of OpenLDAP's directory services.

OpenLDAP is an Open Source server that provides network clients with directory services. The directory server can be used to store organizational information in a centralized location, and make this information available to authorized applications. Client applications can connect to OpenLDAP using the Lightweight Directory Access Protocol (LDAP). They can then search the directory and (if they have appropriate access) modify and manipulate records in the directory. LDAP servers are most frequently used to provide network-based authentication services for users. But there are many other uses for an LDAP, including using the directory as an address book, a DNS database, an organizational tool, or even as a network object store for applications. We will look at some of these uses in this book.

The goal of this book is to prepare a system administrator or software developer for building a directory using OpenLDAP, and then employing this directory in the context of the network. To that end, this book will take a practical approach, emphasizing how to get things done. On occasion, we will delve into theoretical aspects of LDAP, but such discussions will only occur where understanding the theory helps us answer practical questions.

What This Book Covers

In *Chapter 1* we look at general concepts of directory servers and LDAP, cover the history of LDAP and the lineage of the OpenLDAP server, and finish up with a technical overview of OpenLDAP.

The next set of chapters focus on building directory services with OpenLDAP, and we take a close look at the OpenLDAP server in these chapters.

Chapter 2 begins with the process of installing OpenLDAP on a GNU/Linux server. Once we have the server installed, we do the basic post-installation configuration necessary to have the server running.

Chapter 3 covers the basic use of the OpenLDAP server. We use the OpenLDAP command-line tools to add records to our new directory, search the directory, and modify records. This chapter introduces many of the key concepts involved in working with LDAP data.

Chapter 4 covers security, including handling authentication to the directory, configuring Access Control Lists (ACLs), and securing network-based directory connections with Secure Sockets Layer (SSL) and Transport Layer Security (TLS).

Chapter 5 deals with advanced configuration of the OpenLDAP server. Here, we take a close look at the various backend database options and also look at performance tuning settings, as well as the recently introduced technology of directory overlays.

Chapter 6 focuses on extending the directory structure by creating and implementing LDAP schemas. Schemas provide a procedure for defining new attributes and structures to extend the directory and provide records tailor-made to your needs.

Chapter 7 focuses on directory replication and different ways of getting directory servers to interoperate over a network. OpenLDAP can replicate its directory contents from a master server to any number of subordinate servers. In this chapter, we set up a replication process between two servers.

Chapter 8 deals with configuring other tools to interoperate with OpenLDAP. We begin with the Apache web server, using LDAP as a source of authentication and authorization. Next, we install phpLDAPadmin, a web-based program for managing directory servers. Then we look at the main features, and do some custom tuning.

The appendices include a step-by-step guide to building OpenLDAP from source (Appendix A), a guide to using LDAP URLs (Appendix B), and a compendium of useful LDAP client commands (Appendix C).

What You Need for This Book

To get the most from this book, you will need the OpenLDAP server software, as well as the client command-line utilities. These are all freely available (as Open Source software) in source code form from http://openldap.org. However, you may prefer to use the version of OpenLDAP provided by your particular Linux or UNIX distribution.

While OpenLDAP will run on Linux, various versions of UNIX, MacOS X, and Windows 2000 and so on, the examples in this book use the Linux operating system.

Since the basic LDAP tools are command-line applications, you will need basic knowledge of getting around in a Linux/UNIX shell environment. The book does not cover the network protocol in detail, and it is assumed that the reader has a basic understanding of client-server network models. It is also assumed that the reader has a basic understanding of the structure of web and email services.

Conventions

In this book you will find a number of styles of text that distinguish between different kinds of information. Here are some examples of these styles, and an explanation of their meaning.

There are three styles for code. Code words in text are shown as follows: "The telephoneNumber attribute has two values, each representing a different phone number."

A block of code will be set as follows:

```
########
# ACLs #
########
access to attrs=userPassword
        by anonymous auth
        by self write
        by * none
```

When we wish to draw your attention to a particular part of a code block, the relevant lines or items will be made bold:

```
directory /var/lib/ldap
# directory /usr/local/var/openldap-data
index objectClass sub,eq
index cn sub,eq
```

Any command-line input and output is written as follows:

```
$ sudo slaptest -v -f /etc/ldap/slapd.conf
```

New terms and **important words** are introduced in a bold-type font. Words that you see on the screen, in menus or dialog boxes for example, appear in our text like this: "Clicking the **Advanced Search Form** link at the top of the simple search screen will load a search screen with more options".

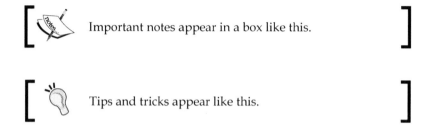

Important notes appear in a box like this.

Tips and tricks appear like this.

Reader Feedback

Feedback from our readers is always welcome. Let us know what you think about this book, what you liked or may have disliked. Reader feedback is important for us to develop titles that you really get the most out of.

To send us general feedback, simply drop an email to feedback@packtpub.com, making sure to mention the book title in the subject of your message.

If there is a book that you need and would like to see us publish, please send us a note in the **SUGGEST A TITLE** form on www.packtpub.com or email suggest@packtpub.com.

If there is a topic that you have expertise in and you are interested in either writing or contributing to a book, see our author guide on www.packtpub.com/authors.

Customer Support

Now that you are the proud owner of a Packt book, we have a number of things to help you to get the most from your purchase.

Downloading the Example Code for the Book

Visit http://www.packtpub.com/support, and select this book from the list of titles to download any example code or extra resources for this book. The files available for download will then be displayed.

Errata

Although we have taken every care to ensure the accuracy of our contents, mistakes do happen. If you find a mistake in one of our books—maybe a mistake in text or code—we would be grateful if you would report this to us. By doing this you can save other readers from frustration, and help to improve subsequent versions of this book. If you find any errata, report them by visiting http://www.packtpub. com/support, selecting your book, clicking on the **Submit Errata** link, and entering the details of your errata. Once your errata are verified, your submission will be accepted and the errata are added to the list of existing errata. The existing errata can be viewed by selecting your title from http://www.packtpub.com/support.

Questions

You can contact us at questions@packtpub.com if you are having a problem with some aspect of the book, and we will do our best to address it.

1
Directory Servers and LDAP

In this first chapter, we will cover the basics of LDAP. While most of the chapters in this book take a practical hands-on approach, this first chapter is higher-level and introductory in nature. We will get introduced to directory servers and LDAP, including commonly-used directory terminology. We will also see how the OpenLDAP server fits into the directory landscape, where it came from, and how it works. Here are the main topics covered in this chapter:

- The basics of LDAP directories
- The history of LDAP and the OpenLDAP server
- A technical overview of the OpenLDAP server

LDAP Basics

The term **LDAP** stands for **Lightweight Directory Access Protocol**. As the name indicates, LDAP was originally designed to be a network protocol that provided an alternative form of access to existing directory servers, but as the idea of LDAP—and the technologies surrounding it—matured, the term LDAP became synonymous with a specific type of directory architecture. We use the term LDAP when referring to directory services that comply with that architecture, as defined in the LDAP specifications.

 LDAP is standardized. The body of LDAP standards, including the network protocols, the directory structure, and the services provided by an LDAP server, are all available in the form of RFCs (Requests For Comments). Throughout this book, I will reference specific LDAP RFCs as authoritative sources of information about LDAP.

The current version of LDAP is LDAP v.3 (version 3), a standard developed in 1997 as RFC 2251, and widely implemented throughout the industry. The original specification has recently (June 2006) been updated, and RFCs 4510-4519 provide a clarified and much more cohesive specification for LDAP.

While directories in general, and LDAP directories in particular, are by no means novel or rare in the information technology world, the driving technologies are certainly not as well understood as near relatives like the relational database. One of the goals of this chapter (and of this book in general) is to introduce and clarify the function and use of an LDAP directory.

In this section, we will introduce some of the concepts that are important for understanding LDAP. The best place to start is with the idea of the directory.

What is a Directory?

When we think of a directory, we conjure images of telephone directories or address books. We use such directories to find information about individuals or organizations. For instance, I might thumb through my address book to find the phone number of my friend Jack, or skim through the telephone directory looking for the address of Acme Services.

A **directory server** is used this way, too. It maintains information about some set of entities (entities like people or organizations), and it provides services for accessing that information.

Of course, a directory server must also have means for adding, modifying, and deleting information, as well. But, even as a telephone directory is assumed to be primarily a resource for reading, a directory server's information is assumed to be read more often than written. This assumption about the use of a directory server is codified, or summarized, in the phrase "high-read, low-write". Consequently, many applications of LDAP technology are geared toward reading and searching for information.

 While many directory servers have been optimized for fast reading at the expense of fast modification, this is not necessarily the case with OpenLDAP. OpenLDAP is efficient on both counts, and it can be used for applications that require frequent writing of data.

Some sorts of directory servers (envision a simple server-based implementation of an address book) simply provide a narrow and specific service. A single-purpose directory server, such as an online address book, might store only a very specific type of data, like phone numbers, addresses, and email information for a set of people. Such directories are not extensible. Instead, they are *single-purpose*.

But LDAP (and its X.500 predecessor) was designed to be a *general-purpose* directory server. It has not been designed with the purpose of capturing a specific type of data (like telephone numbers or email addresses). Instead, it was designed to give implementers the ability to define—clearly and carefully—what data the directory should store.

Such a generic directory server ought to be able to store many different kinds of information. For that matter, it should be able to store different kinds of information about different kinds of entities. For example, a general purpose directory should be able to store information about entities as diverse as people and igneous rock samples. But we don't want to store the same information about people as we do about rocks.

A person might have a surname, a phone number, and an email address, as shown in the following figure:

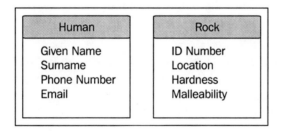

A rock sample might have an identification number, information about its geographical origin, and a hardness classification.

LDAP makes it possible to define what a person's entry would look like, and what a rock's entry would look like. Its general architecture provides the capabilities needed for managing large amounts of diverse directory entries.

In the remainder of this section we will examine how information in an LDAP directory is structured. We will start by looking at the idea of a **directory entry**, with a **distinguished name** and **attributes**. Then, we will look at how entries are organized within the **directory information tree**. By the end of this section, you should understand the basic structure of information within an LDAP directory.

The Structure of a Directory Entry

Let's continue with our comparison of a directory server and a phone book. A phone book contains a very specific type of information, organized in a very specific way, and designed to fulfil a very specific purpose. Here's an example phone book entry:

```
Acme Services
123 W. First St.
Chicago, IL 60616-1234
(773) 555-8943 or (800) 555 9834
```

As mentioned earlier, this sort of directory has specific information, organized in a specific way, designed to fulfill a specific purpose: it is information about how to contact a specific organization (Acme Services) organized in a familiar pattern (address and phone number). And it is designed so that a person, having a particular name in mind, can quickly scan through the directory (which is ordered alphabetically by organization name), and find the desired contact information.

But there are a few things to note about the phone book entry:

- The data is arranged for searching by only one value: the name of the organization. If you should happen to have the phone number of the organization, but not the name, searching the phone book for the matching telephone number in order to ascertain the name would be a taxing, and probably futile task.

- The format of the entry is sparse, and requires that the reader will be able to recognize the format and supply auxiliary information required for making sense of the data. One accustomed to reading phone book entries will be able to extrapolate from the previous entry, and identify the information this way:

```
Organization Name: Acme Services
Street Address: 123 West First Street
City: Chicago
State: Illinois
Postal Code: 60616-1234
Country: USA
Phone Number: +1 773 555 8943
Phone Number: +1 800 555 9834
```

In this example, the meaning of the information is made more explicit. Each value is preceded by a name that identifies the type of information given. Acme Services is now identified as the name of an organization. Information is also broken up into smaller chunks (city and state on separate lines), and some information which was implicit in the previous entry (such as the country) has been made explicit. And where two pieces of information (the two phone numbers) were initially compressed onto one line, they have now been separated, making the information more explicit.

This form of entry is closer to the way a record would look in an LDAP directory. But there is still another issue to address. How can we distinguish between two very similar records?

For example, say we have a telephone directory for the entire state of Illinois. And in Illinois, we have a company called Acme Services located in the city of Chicago, and another company named Acme Services located in the city of Springfield.

Simply knowing the company name alone is not sufficient information to isolate just one entry in the phone book. To do that, we would need some sort of unique name—a name that exists only once in the entire directory, and which can be used to refer to *one specific entry*.

A Unique Name: The DN

One way of distinguishing between two very similar records is to create a unique name for each record in the directory. This is the strategy adopted by LDAP; each record in the directory has a **distinguished name**. The distinguished name is an important LDAP term; usually it is abbreviated as **DN**.

In an LDAP directory, the directory designer is the one who decides what components will make up a DN, but typically the DN reflects where the record is in the directory (a concept we will examine in the next part), as well as some information that distinguishes this record from other near records.

A DN then, is composed of a combination of directory information, and looks something like this:

```
dn: o=Acme Services, l=Chicago, st=Illinois, c=US
```

This single identifier is sufficient to pick it out from the Springfield company by the same name. The DN of the Springfield company named Acme Services would, according to the previous scheme, look something like this:

```
dn: o=Acme Services, l=Springfield, st=Illinois, c=US
```

As may be evident from this example, when defining what fields will compose a DN, it is necessary to make sure that these fields will be fine-grained enough to distinguish between two different entries. In other words, all it takes to break the DN syntax is for another Acme Services to appear in Chicago.

DNs are not case sensitive

Some parts of LDAP records are case sensitive, and others are not. DNs, for example, are not case sensitive.

The DN is one important element in an LDAP entry. Next, we will take a closer look at the idea of an LDAP entry, and the components that make up an entry.

An Example LDAP Entry

Let's take a specific look at what an **LDAP entry** looks like.

An LDAP **entry**, or **record**, is the directory unit that stores information about an individual item in the directory. Again, drawing on ideas found in other directories is useful: an entry in a telephone directory describes a specific unit of information in that directory. Likewise, a record in an LDAP directory contains information about a specific unit, though (since LDAP is generic) the exact target of that unit is unspecified. It might be a person, or a company, or a rock, or some virtual entity like a Java object.

Originally, the LDAP specification stated that an entry had to have a correlate in the real world. While this may have been the intention of early directory server developers, there is no reason why, in practice, a directory server entry must correlate with anything external to the directory—real or virtual.

An entry is composed of a DN and one or more **attributes**. The DN serves as a unique identifier within an LDAP directory information tree. Attributes provide information about that entry. Let's convert our previous telephone directory entry into an LDAP record:

```
dn: o=Acme Services, l=Chicago, st=Illinois, c=US
o: Acme Services
postalAddress: 123 West First Street
l: Chicago
st: Illinois
```

```
postalCode: 60616-1234
c: US
telephoneNumber: +1 773 555 8943
telephoneNumber: +1 800 555 9834
objectclass: organization
```

The first line is the DN. All other lines in this record represent attributes.

Note that the main difference between this example and the previous telephone directory examples we have examined is the names of each field in the entry; these are now compacted into a form that the directory can easily interpret.

These attribute names, like o and postalAddress, refer to well-defined attribute definitions contained in an LDAP schema. They cannot be "invented" on the fly, or made up as you go. Creating new attributes requires writing a schema. Schemas are covered in Chapter 6 of this book.

An attribute describes a specific type of information. There are eight attributes here in our example, representing the following:

1. Organization Name (o)
2. Mailing address (postalAddress)
3. Locality (1), which may be the name of a city, town, village, and so forth
4. State or Province (st)
5. Postal Code or ZIP Code (postalCode)
6. Country (c)
7. Telephone Number (telephoneNumber)
8. Object Class (objectclass), which specifies what type (or types) of record this entry is

An attribute may have one or more attribute names, where these names are synonyms. For example c and countryName are both names for the attribute type that identify a country. Both identify the same information, and LDAP will treat the two names as describing the same type of information.

In any given record, an attribute may have one or more values (assuming the attribute's definition allows more than one value). The record above has only one attribute that contains more than one value. The telephoneNumber attribute has two values, each representing a different phone number.

Attributes are defined in *attribute definitions*, which will be discussed at length in Chapter 6. These definitions provide information about the syntax and length of the information stored in values, all of the attribute names that apply to that attribute, whether or not the attribute can have multiple values, and so on. Records stored in LDAP directories must adhere to the attribute definitions.

For example, the attribute definition for a country name gives the following information:

- The names c and countryName can refer to this object. The default name is c.
- A country name is stored as a string.
- When doing matches on the attribute values, case can be ignored.
- Matching can be done on either the entire string (for example Canada) or using substrings (Ca*).
- A country name cannot be longer than 32768 characters.
- Only one country name is allowed per record.

All of this information is packed into a compact schema definition that the directory server reads when it starts.

Attribute names are not case sensitive. The attribute name o is treated as synonymous with the name O. Likewise, GivenName, givenname, and givenName are all evaluated as the same attribute name.

As for the values of attributes, case sensitivity depends on the attribute definition. For example, the values of DNs and objectclass attributes are *not* case sensitive, but a URI (labeledURI) attribute value *is* case sensitive.

The Object Class Attribute

The last attribute in the given record is the objectclass attribute. This is a special attribute that provides information about what type of record (or entry) this is.

An object class determines what attributes may be given to a record. The object class, organization, indicates that this record describes an organization. According to this object class's definition, an organization record can contain a locality (1), and a postal code (postalCode), and all of the other attributes present in the record.

One of the fields, the organization name (o), is required for any entry with an organization object class.

The object class also allows several other attributes that are not present in our record, like description and facsimileTelephoneNumber.

Given the object class attribute, which is required for any entry, the directory can determine what attributes must, can, and cannot be present in the entry.

As with other attributes, the `objectclass` attribute may have multiple values, though which values may be given are subject to the **object class definition** and **schema definition** — the rules about what attributes belong to what object classes, and how these object classes can be combined.

 An **LDAP Schema** consists of rules that define the types of records in a directory, and how those records might relate to each other. The main two items stored in a schema (though there are others) are attribute type definitions and object class definitions. Chapter 6 of this book is devoted to schemas.

While a record may have multiple object classes, one of these object classes must be the **structural object class** for the record. A structural object class determines what type of object the record is. We will talk about structural object classes later in the book.

The LDAP record then, is composed of a single DN, and one or more attributes (remember, `objectclass` is required). The attributes contain information about the entity that is identified by the DN.

An LDAP directory contains an aggregation of entries, arranged in one or more hierarchies in a tree structure.

Operational Attributes

In addition to regular attributes, the directory server may also attach special **operational attributes** to an entry. Operational attributes are used by the directory server itself to store information about entries. Such attributes are not designed for use by end users (though on occasion they can be useful), and are usually not returned during LDAP searches.

At various points in this book, we will make use of operational attributes. But most of the time, when we talk about attributes, we are talking about regular attributes.

The Directory Information Tree

So far, we have been comparing an LDAP directory to an address book or a telephone directory. But now I am going to introduce one of the primary differences between the structure of the data in an LDAP directory server, and that of many other forms of directories.

The information in a telephone directory is typically stored in one long alphabetical list. But in an LDAP directory the organizational structure is more sophisticated.

Information in an LDAP directory is organized into one or more hierarchies where, at the top of the hierarchy, there is a **base entry**, and other entries are organized in tree-like structures beneath the base entry. Each node on the hierarchy is an entry, with a DN and more than one attributes.

This hierarchically organized collection of entries is called a **directory information tree**, sometimes referred to simply as a directory tree or **DIT**.

To understand this method of organizing information, consider the organizational chart of a company.

The top of the hierarchy is the company itself. Beneath this, there are a number of departments and organizational units, and beneath these are the employees, contractors, and other individuals with a formal affiliation to the company. We can draw this as a hierarchy:

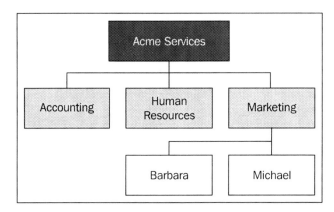

LDAP directories store data in hierarchical relationships, too. At the top of the directory information tree is the root entry. Beneath that is a **subordinate entry**, which, in turn, may have its own subordinate entries. Each of these records has its own DN, and its own attributes.

A File System Analogy

Most modern file systems represent data in hierarchies too.
For example, the directory /home may have multiple subdirectories: /home/mbutcher, /home/ikant, /home/dhume. We can say that /home has three subordinates, but that each of those has one superior (the /home directory). When thinking about LDAP directory trees, it may help to compare them to the layout of a file system.

Adapting this to the previous example, we could easily create an LDAP directory information tree that represented the organizational chart:

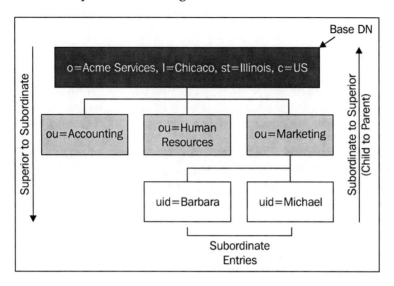

Note that the DN of each entry contains information about its **superior entry** (the record above it). In fact, a DN is composed of two parts: the first part is the **relative DN (RDN)**, and contains one or more attributes from the entry. The second part is the *full* DN of the superior entry. We will look at this relationship further in Chapter 3.

When we create our directory in the next few chapters, we will create a tree-like structure of records.

You should now have a basic idea of how a directory is represented in a directory information tree. Records, consisting of a DN and some attributes, are organized in a hierarchy. At the top of the hierarchy is the base entry, and beneath that entries are organized into branches.

What to Do with an LDAP Server

I've given a description of what an LDAP directory is, but it is also helpful to look at what an LDAP directory is used for. What is the function of an LDAP server? What problem is it intended to solve?

The first, and most obvious, answer is that LDAP is designed to provide a digital directory—an online presentation equivalent to a telephone directory or address book. Of course, there is some truth to this, and LDAP servers can indeed be used in this way. But so can relational databases and even more basic data structures.

We could expand on this answer, and point out that LDAP provides a robust layer of services—searching with complex filters, representing complex entities with attributes, allowing fine-grained access to data, and so on—that provide sophisticated directory services.

A more classical explanation, one rooted in the historical development of LDAP out of the X.500 directory, would be that LDAP is designed to represent organizations, including their structure, their physical assets, and their personnel. LDAP, by this account, isn't so much a fancy telephone directory as it is an enterprise management tool. In fact, this is one of the more common ways to use LDAP directories.

The most common use of an LDAP, a use based on a conception of LDAP as a narrow type of enterprise management tool, is as a central authority on network users, groups, and accounts. An LDAP directory stores information on each user account for the network—information like username, password, full name, and email address. Other services on the network, from workstations to email servers to web applications, can use LDAP as an authoritative source of user information. Applications can authenticate users against the directory. A single user account can be shared across multiple (perhaps all) enterprise applications.

Finally, there is a more generic, or abstract, view of the function of LDAP services. LDAP is nothing other than a special sort of database that organizes data into tree structures, like a file system hierarchy. This view is more easily seen by comparing an LDAP directory to a relational database (RDB) system.

Relational databases store information in tables, and tables are composed of records. Relationships, in RDBs, are established between records in different tables, and there are numerous forms of relationship: one to many, one to one, many to one, and so on. RDBs support reading and writing operations on data, typically implemented through some version of SQL (Standard Query Language), and they typically listen on network connections, making data available to other applications on the network.

Compared to an RDB, LDAP can also be seen as a storage system. Rather than presenting data in tabular structures, though, LDAP stores entries in a hierarchy (like a file system). The basic relationships in an LDAP consist of the superior-to-subordinate relation (one to many), and the subordinate-to-superior relation (one-to-one), though other relationships can be used.

Other Relationships in LDAP

While the superior/subordinate relationships are the most commonly used, they are not the only ones supported. Relationships among arbitrary entries within the database are often modeled by linking DNs together using attributes. We will examine this use in detail when talking about groups in Chapter 4.

Reading and writing to the database are supported through LDAP operations with sophisticated filters and data structures like **LDIF (LDAP Data Interchange Format)**. And LDAP directories, like their RDB counterparts, often listen on network sockets to provide services to other applications.

I have suggested some different views of the purpose of LDAP. Is any one of these the *correct* answer? No. Each of these uses of LDAP is legitimate, and LDAP directories can be used to address a broad range of problems.

The History of LDAP and OpenLDAP

At first glance, the term LDAP seems misleading. When we talk, for instance, about the primary protocol for the web, HTTP (HyperText Transfer Protocol), we are talking about the way that web applications transfer information across the network. We are not talking about the format of the data that is moved across the network, nor are we talking about how that data is stored on or retrieved from the server.

But when we talk about LDAP, we are usually talking not only about the network protocol, but about a particular kind of server that stores data of a well-defined format inside of a special database. There is a historical reason for this seemingly misleading name.

Originally, LDAP was just a network protocol used to get data out of an X.500 directory (a directory server architecture, designed in the 1980s and standardized in 1988). This was the intent of Yeong, Howes, and Killie when they initially drafted the LDAP specification as RFC 1487 in 1993.

About RFCs

RFCs (Requests for Comments) are a series of technical documents, usually specifying standards. Each RFC is identified by number, which are organized sequentially — earlier RFCs have lower numbers. There are many websites that make the RFC database, in whole or in part, available. One exemplary source is the RFC Editor (http://www.rfc-editor.org), which is used in this book.

The first LDAP servers were gateways to X.500 directories, but these servers quickly evolved into full-fledged directory servers. Tim Howes and his colleagues at the University of Michigan created the Open Source *University of Michigan LDAP Implementation*, which became the reference implementation for other LDAP servers.

Historical information on the University of Michigan LDAP project is still available online:
http://www.umich.edu/~dirsvcs/ldap/ldap.html

As the University of Michigan's LDAP server matured, a wealth of new standards was created. LDAP picked up industry momentum. Tim Howes was hired by Netscape, and LDAP went mainstream.

By the late 1990's, Netscape, Novell, Oracle, and Microsoft (among others) all touted LDAP offerings. RFC 2251, released in 1997, standardized LDAPv3, which made vast improvements to the earlier LDAP standards.

The market for LDAP servers matured, but the University of Michigan project lost momentum. Key developers had left the university to move along to other projects.

In 1998 the OpenLDAP project was started by Kurt Zeilenga. Soon after, Howard Chu (formerly of the University of Michigan, and the current architect of the project) joined. They rescued the University of Michigan's code base, beginning development anew. The result, OpenLDAP 2.0, was highly successful, and made its way into almost every major Linux distribution.

[A complete list of OpenLDAP contributors, from the project's inception to the present, can be found at `http://www.openldap.org/project/`.]

Since the late '90's, OpenLDAP has continued to mature, overseen by the OpenLDAP Foundation, and supported by contributions from industry sponsors. As of this writing, version 2.3 is the stable release, and version 2.4 is in the beta stages.

As was the intent with the University of Michigan LDAP server, OpenLDAP still adheres closely to the LDAP standards. In fact, Kurt Zeilenga is responsible for many of the updates made to the LDAP standards in June 2006.

But in addition to its high degree of standards compliance, OpenLDAP is also one of the fastest directory servers in the market, far outpacing offerings from other Open Source directory server implementations.

A Technical Overview of OpenLDAP

This book is a practically oriented technical book. It is designed to help you get OpenLDAP up and running, and to help you integrate LDAP into your own applications.

We will now begin this transition from the high-level material presented earlier to a more practical examination of the OpenLDAP suite of packages. First, let's take a brief look at the technical structure of OpenLDAP.

The OpenLDAP suite can be broken up into four components:

- Servers: Provide LDAP services
- Clients: Manipulate LDAP data
- Utilities: Support LDAP servers
- Libraries: provide programming interfaces to LDAP

In the course of this book, we will look at all four of these categories. Here, we will just get an overview:

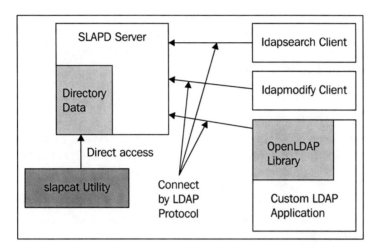

This diagram explains how these four elements relate to each other.

The Server

The main server in the LDAP suite is **SLAPD** (the **Stand-Alone LDAP Daemon**). This server provides access to one or more directory information trees. Clients connect to the server over the LDAP protocol, usually using a network-based connection (though SLAPD provides a UNIX socket listener, too).

A server can store directory data locally, or simply access (or proxy access) to external sources. Typically, it provides authentication and searching services, and may also support adding, removing, and modifying directory data. It provides fine-grained access control to the directory.

SLAPD is a major focus of this book, and we will discuss it in detail in the chapters to come.

Clients

Clients access LDAP servers over the LDAP network protocol. They function by requesting that the server performs operations on their behalf. Typically, a client will first connect to the directory server, then bind (authenticate), and then perform zero or more other operations (searches, modifications, additions, deletions, and so on) before finally unbinding and disconnecting.

Utilities

Unlike clients, utilities do not perform operations using the LDAP protocol. Instead, they manipulate data at a lower level, and without mediation by the server. They are used primarily to help maintain the server.

Libraries

There are several OpenLDAP libraries that are shared between LDAP applications. The libraries provide LDAP functions to these applications. The clients, utilities, and servers all share access to some of these libraries.

Application Programming Interfaces (APIs) are provided to allow software developers to write their own LDAP-aware applications without having to re-write fundamental LDAP code.

While the APIs provided with OpenLDAP are written in C, the OpenLDAP project also provides two Java APIs. These Java libraries are not included in the OpenLDAP suite, and are not covered in this book. Both however, can be retrieved from the OpenLDAP website: `http://openldap.org`.

As we move on through this book we will examine each of these components of the LDAP architecture in detail.

Summary

In this chapter we have covered the basics of LDAP directories in general, and of the OpenLDAP server in particular. We have covered the history of LDAP, the important terminology, and some of the high-level technical aspects of OpenLDAP. Now we are ready to start applying this knowledge.

In the next chapter we will turn our attention toward the process of installing and configuring OpenLDAP.

Installation and Configuration

2

In this chapter we will walk through the process of installing and configuring the OpenLDAP suite of tools. Here we will only cover basic configuration of the SLAPD server. This will serve as a base for subsequent chapters (particularly Chapters 4 to 7), where we will explore advanced configuration options. The specific topics that we will cover include:

- Installing binary OpenLDAP packages
- Configuring the LDAP server with the `slapd.conf` file
- Verifying the `slapd.conf` configuration with `slaptest`
- Starting and stopping the server
- Configuring client tools with the `ldap.conf` file
- Fetching the root DSE entry from the directory with `ldapsearch`

Before Getting Started

OpenLDAP is maintained by the OpenLDAP Foundation. The foundation maintains a suite of tools that we will call as OpenLDAP suite. As we saw in Chapter 1, the OpenLDAP suite includes the following classes of tools:

- Daemons (`slapd` and `slurpd`)
- Libraries (notably `libldap`)
- Client applications (`ldapsearch`, `ldapadd`, `ldapmodify`, and others)
- Supporting utilities (`slapcat`, `slapauth`, and others)

The official OpenLDAP source distribution includes all of these in one download. Various binary versions however, may break these out into sub-packages. Commonly the suite is split into three packages: *libraries*, *clients*, and *servers*.

OpenLDAP compiles and runs on a wide variety of operating systems. However, the OpenLDAP project itself does not provide binary versions of their software. As a result, different vendors and operating system maintainers compile and provide their own binary versions. There are versions of OpenLDAP compiled for most UNIX variants (including Mac OS X), as well as versions for the Windows operating system. Some binary distributions even come with commercial support.

OpenLDAP Binaries for Operating Systems

In this book, we will be using **Ubuntu Linux** as the operating system of choice. Ubuntu is a GNU/Linux distribution based on the venerable **Debian Project**. Like Debian (and the multitude of other Debian-based distributions) Ubuntu uses the Debian package format. Thus, if you are using another Debian-based distribution, the installation process should be largely familiar.

 Ubuntu is a user-friendly Linux distribution. You can learn more about Ubuntu at http://www.ubuntu.com/. To learn more about the Debian Project, on which Ubuntu is based, visit http://debian.org/.

Almost every major Linux and BSD distribution includes official support for OpenLDAP. You may want to consult the documentation for your chosen distribution to find out more information on getting and installing OpenLDAP. In some cases, OpenLDAP is installed with the base operating system.

For Windows, Mac, and other variants of UNIX, the best way to find a list of available binary packages is by perusing the list of distributions maintained in the **OpenLDAP Faq-O-Matic** (http://www.openldap.org/faq/data/cache/108.html).

Commercial OpenLDAP Distribution

If you need a commercially supported OpenLDAP distribution, you may want to consider the offerings from **Symas**. Symas (http://www.symas.com/) is owned and operated by many of the same folks who contribute to the OpenLDAP suite. They provide a commercial binary version of the OpenLDAP suite, distributed as **Connexitor Directory Services (CDS)**.

Several different CDS editions are available, with each edition tuned and optimized for specific organizational needs. Their *Platinum Edition*, for instance, is optimized for directories with more than 150 million records! Symas also provides LDAP training, maintenance and support services, and consulting.

Source Code Compilation

Instead of installing a binary file, you may wish to simply compile the OpenLDAP source code yourself. This process is outlined in simple steps in Appendix A of this book.

The primary advantage of building from source code is that you will benefit from many improvements long before these revisions are made available in mainstream packages. The focus of development on the stable branch of OpenLDAP is bug fixes. Thus, building from source generally improves OpenLDAP stability.

A Quick Note on Versions

Currently, the stable branch for OpenLDAP is *2.3 branch* (2.4 is in early beta). However, some Linux distributions still use the aging 2.2 version, originally released in 2003. If the latest package for your chosen operating system is still in the 2.2 branch, you may want to consider looking for *unofficial* versions of 2.3 for your platform, or even compiling a custom binary (see Appendix A).

Installation

In this section, we will walk through the process of installing on a system running Ubuntu Linux 7.04. Later, Ubuntu distributions will likely follow the same installation pattern.

Dependencies

The basic OpenLDAP configuration in Ubuntu requires a few extra libraries and packages. These are as follows:

- The Berkeley Database (bdb4) version 4.2 (but *not* 4.3, which has stability issues): In the Ubuntu default configuration, OpenLDAP stores the directory inside a BDB database. The Berkeley Database is often simply called BDB.
- The OpenSSL libraries: These provide SSL and TLS security. SSL and TLS provide encryption for network connections to the directory.
- The Cyrus SASL library: This provides support for secure SASL authentication.
- The Perl programming language: This can provide custom back-end scripting.
- The iODBC database connectivity layer: OpenLDAP can store the directory in a relational database (RDBMS). The iODBC library is used to connect to the RDBMS.

OpenLDAP also relies on some standard system library packages (such as `libc6`) that are installed on all UNIX/Linux distributions. In its default installation, Ubuntu includes BDB, OpenSSL, and Perl. Installation of other dependencies is handled automatically by the package manager, so don't worry about manually installing any of these.

Installing OpenLDAP

Like many other distributions, Ubuntu breaks OpenLDAP up into small packages. The daemons (`slapd` and `slurpd`) are packaged in the `slapd` package. The clients are packaged in `ldap-utils`, and the libraries are packaged in `libldap-2.3-0`. When Ubuntu 7.04 was released, OpenLDAP version 2.3.30 was provided. As security fixes are made, Ubuntu may release newer versions via online updates. While legacy 2.2.26 packages are still available, they should be avoided.

To install Ubuntu we can use the **Synaptic** graphical installer or any of the command-line package management utilities. For the sake of simplicity, we will use **apt-get**. This will download all of the necessary packages (including dependencies) from the official Ubuntu repository and install them for us. Note that installing this way will require access to the Internet (or, alternatively, to some other form of Ubuntu distribution media, such as a CD-ROM). We need to run the following command.

```
$ sudo apt-get install libldap-2.3-0 slapd ldap-utils
```

It may take a little while for the packages to download and install.

Once `apt-get` is done, the LDAP server and all of its clients should be installed. Next, we will begin the process of configuring the SLAPD server.

Configuring the SLAPD Server

There are two daemons that come packaged with OpenLDAP: SLAPD server and SLURPD server. **SLAPD**, sometimes called the **OpenLDAP server**, handles client requests and directory management, while **SLURPD** manages replicating changes to other directories. SLURPD is now deprecated in favor of a newer, more robust replication process, and will be removed from future versions of OpenLDAP.

In the next chapter we will talk more about what these two daemons do. Right now we are only concerned with getting the SLAPD server up and running so we can start connecting to (and using) our directory.

SLAPD has one main configuration file and any number of auxiliary configuration files. In this section we are going to edit the main configuration file. It is called slapd.conf, and in Ubuntu's distribution it is located at /etc/ldap/ (if you built from source, the default location is /usr/local/etc/openldap/).

Use find . -type f -name slapd.conf or if the locate service is enabled, you can use locate slapd.conf.

While Ubuntu provides a good basic slapd.conf file that you can work with, if you choose, we will not use it. For our purpose, we will start with an empty file and create a slapd.conf configuration from scratch. You may want to make a backup copy of the original slapd.conf file before we begin. You can do this from a terminal by running:

```
$ sudo mv /etc/ldap/slapd.conf /etc/ldap/slapd.conf.orig
```

This will rename the file from slapd.conf to slapd.conf.orig.

By default, Ubuntu does not activate the root account. Any time you want to perform a function as the superuser, you should use sudo. However, if you need to become root (to run, for instance, several commands in sequence), you can type sudo su.

Now we are ready to create our new slapd.conf file. Open the text editor and create a basic slapd.conf file:

```
# slapd.conf - Configuration file for LDAP SLAPD
##########
# Basics #
##########
include /etc/ldap/schema/core.schema
include /etc/ldap/schema/cosine.schema
include /etc/ldap/schema/inetorgperson.schema

pidfile /var/run/slapd/slapd.pid
argsfile /var/run/slapd/slapd.args
loglevel none

modulepath /usr/lib/ldap
# modulepath /usr/local/libexec/openldap
moduleload back_hdb

#########################
# Database Configuration #
#########################
```

```
database hdb
suffix "dc=example,dc=com"
rootdn "cn=Manager,dc=example,dc=com"
rootpw secret
directory /var/lib/ldap
# directory /usr/local/var/openldap-data
index objectClass,cn eq

########
# ACLs #
########
access to attrs=userPassword
        by anonymous auth
        by self write
        by * none

access to *
        by self write
        by * none
```

There are three headings in the file (**Basics**, **Database Configuration**, and **ACLs**), and we will now see each heading in detail.

 If you built from source, the paths in the above file need to be adjusted (or, alternately, you can relocate files on your file system). Look in the /usr/local portion of your file system to locate the correct location (for example, modulepath is in /usr/local/libexex/openldap/).

Basics

The first section of the configuration file, labeled *Basics*, contains a variety of configuration parameters:

```
##########
# Basics #
##########
include /etc/ldap/schema/core.schema
include /etc/ldap/schema/cosine.schema
include /etc/ldap/schema/inetorgperson.schema
pidfile /var/run/slapd/slapd.pid
argsfile /var/run/slapd/slapd.args
loglevel none

modulepath /usr/lib/ldap
# modulepath /usr/local/libexec/openldap
moduleload back_hdb
```

First note that all lines that start with a hash (#) are treated as comments, and ignored by SLAPD.

The first three functional (non-comment) lines all begin with the `include` directive. The `include` directive should always be followed by a full path to a file on the file system. When SLAPD finds the `include` directive it will attempt to load the indicated file. Those files will then be treated as part of the current configuration file. So, when SLAPD reads these three lines, it will try to load the three schema files (`core.schema`, `cosine.schema`, and `inetorgperson.schema`).

The `include` directive can be used to load any configuration parameters (in the next chapter, we will use it to include a file that contains ACLs). Traditionally, the schema information is stored separately from other configuration directives, and loaded (using `include` directives) at server startup. This improves the readability of the code and helps prevent the accidental modification of the schema information.

Schemas

Schemas provide definitions of (amongst other things) the different object classes and attribute types that OpenLDAP should support. Using these, OpenLDAP can determine what entries it is allowed to store, whether any given entry is valid, and how entries should optimally be stored.

The three schemas loaded here contain the most frequently used options. `core.schema` contains all of the attribute and object class definitions from the LDAP v.3 specification. The `cosine.schema` and `inetorgperson.schema` files contain schema definitions for commonly used standardized extensions (see RFCs 4524 and 2798). There are a host of other schemas available with OpenLDAP, and we will look at some of those in Chapter 6.

More Directives

After the schemas are included the next two directives, `pidfile` and `argsfile`, tell SLAPD where to store (and look for) files that contain information on:

- The process ID for the SLAPD server process
- The arguments that were passed into the `slapd` command at startup

Since SLAPD needs to write to these files, the user that runs `slapd` needs to have permissions to `read` from and `write` to these files. Since the files are removed when the SLAPD server shuts down, the user that runs `slapd` will also need write permissions on the directory where these files are stored (`/var/run/slapd/`, in this case).

Next, the `loglevel` directive is set to `none`. The `loglevel` directive specifies how much information SLAPD should send to the system log (by way of `syslogd`). The loglevel directive accepts keywords (`any`, `none`, `trace`, and so on), integers (`0`, `128`, `32768`), and hexidecimal numbers (`0x2`, `0x80`, `0x100`).

Setting this to `none` will cause SLAPD to only log critical events. In order to turn *off* the logging altogether, use `0`. To turn *on* all the logging, which will generate massive amounts of logging for every request, use `any`. The SLAPD man page (`man slapd`) provides a complete list of all the supported log levels.

Module Directives

The last few directives in the *Basics* section are `modulepath` and `moduleload`. These are instructions for loading OpenLDAP modules.

A **module** is a special type of library that can be loaded when SLAPD starts up. Instead of compiling all of SLAPD's code into one large binary, the modules make it possible to create smaller library files for discrete functional units of LDAP code.

Typically, there are two different kinds of modules:

1. **Backends**: The OpenLDAP server can use different storage backends, including BDB, SQL database, flat files (in LDIF format), or even another LDAP directory server. Each of these backends can be compiled into its own module. Then, during configuration, we have the option of only loading the module (or modules) that we need.

2. **Overlays**: OpenLDAP includes a number of optional extensions, called overlays, which can modify behavior of the server (we will look at several overlays in the course of this book). These, too, are stored in modules.

Let's have a look at the directives we have used in our `slapd.conf` file:

- The `modulepath` directive provides the full path to the directory where the modules (the compiled libraries) are stored. By default, Ubuntu puts LDAP libraries in `/usr/lib/ldap`. If, for some reason, you have modules stored in multiple directories you can specify a list of paths, separated by colons:

  ```
  modulepath /usr/lib/ldap:/usr/local/lib/custom-ldap
  ```

- The `moduleload` directive instructs OpenLDAP to load a particular module. The directive takes either the file name of the module to be loaded (such as `back_hdb`) or a full path (beginning with `/`) to a module file. If just the name is specified, SLAPD will look in the directories specified in `modulepath`. If the entire path is specified, it will attempt to load from exactly that path (it will not use `modulepath` at all).

- `moduleload back_hdb` instructs SLAPD to load the module that provides services for storing the directory in the *Hierarchical Database* (HDB) backend. This is the database that we will configure in the *Database Configuration* section.

For now these are the only directives we need in the *Basics* section. There are other options though, and we will look at many of them in Chapters 4 and 5.

Database Configuration

The next section of our `slapd.conf` file is the database configuration section. This section handles the configuration of the database storage mechanisms. OpenLDAP is not limited to one database. More than one database can be used per server, where each database stores its own directory tree (or subtree). For example, a single OpenLDAP instance can serve a directory tree whose base is `o=My Company,c=US` from one database, and a directory tree whose root is `dc=example,dc=com` from a second database.

As we saw in Chapter 1, the base DN for a directory tree is made up of attribute name/attribute value pairs. For example, the DN `o=My Company, c=US` indicates that the organization name (o) is `My Company`, and its country of origin (c) is United States (whose two-letter ISO code is `US`). Likewise, the second DN is composed of attribute name/value pairs, this time representing domain components (dc) from the organization's registered domain name, here, the fictitious `Example.Com`.

We will look at this option in Chapter 5. In our simple `slapd.conf` file, we are defining only one database:

```
###########################
# Database Configuration #
###########################
database hdb
suffix "dc=example,dc=com"
rootdn "cn=Manager,dc=example,dc=com"
rootpw secret
directory /var/lib/ldap
# directory /usr/local/var/openldap-data
index objectClass,cn eq
```

The first directive in the database configuration section is the `database` directive. This specifies which database backend will be used. In this case we will be using the **Hierarchical Database (HDB)**, so we specify `hdb`.

HDB is the new generation storage mechanism for OpenLDAP. Like its predecessor, the BDB backend, HDB uses the Oracle Berkeley DB database for storage, but HDB stores entries hierarchically, a perfect fit for LDAP's tree strucutre. The old BDB backend is still supported, and you can use it by specificing `bdb` instead of `hdb` in the `database` directive.

The next directive, `suffix`, indicates which parts of the directory tree this database will hold. Basically, it indicates that this database's base will be the entry with the **Distinguished Name (DN)** specified in the `suffix` directive (`dc=example,dc=com`). We have discussed *Distinguished Names* in Chapter 1.

When the server receives a request for something in that tree (for example, `cn=Matt,dc=example,dc=com`), it will search in this database. The following figure gives a better idea:

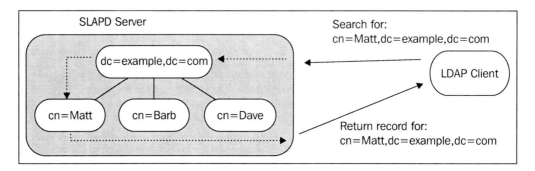

Here, the client is searching for a specific DN, `cn=Matt, dc=example, dc=com`. The SLAPD server contains a directory information tree whose base DN is `dc=example, dc=com`.

The DN `cn=Matt,dc=example,dc=com` is subordinate to `dc=example,dc=com`. It exists in the `dc=example,dc=com` tree. So, SLAPD searches the `dc=example,dc=com` database for a record whose DN is `cn=Matt,dc=example,dc=com`. Once the record is found, it is returned to the client.

What will happen if a client requests the record of `cn=Matt,dc=test,dc=net`? Since this DN does not contain a base DN handled by this server, the server will not search for the record. Depending on the configuration, it may either send an error back to the client or redirect the client to another server that might be able to handle such a request.

Likewise, if a client tries to *add* a record with a base DN other than the one specified in the suffix directive, the LDAP server will refuse to add the record to the directory information tree.

The `suffix` directive in `slapd.conf` specifies what the base DN will be for information stored or referenced in this database. This will determine, to a large degree, what records this database will contain, search for, or allow to be added.

 One database can have multiple trees (this is covered in Chapter 5).

The next two lines assign a record for the directory manager and give the manager entry a password. The `rootdn` directive specifies the DN that will be considered the administrator of this directory. By convention, the *root* DN is created by prepending `cn=Manager` to the *base* DN of the directory tree. Thus, our directory manager is `cn=Manager,dc=example,dc=com`. The next field, `rootpw`, is used to assign a password for the directory manager. Note that this is stored outside the directory rather than inside it. For example, the `userPassword` attribute of a record in the directory. This is to prevent the manager from being *locked out* of the directory.

The directory manager is a special user with special privileges. The manager's requests are not filtered through ACLs—the manager's access cannot be restricted. Furthermore, the manager has *write* access to all records in the directory under the specified suffix or suffixes. For that reason, the manager DN should be used for administrative tasks only and not for anything else.

Further, since the necessary fields for the manager are stored here in the `slapd.conf` file, there should *not* be a record in the directory with the manager's DN (this is recommended for best practices, though it is not explicitly prevented by SLAPD).

Since the manager's DN and password are stored in the `slapd.conf` file, and since the manager has access to everything in the directory, we should keep file system permissions on the `slapd.conf` file as restrictive as possible.

 Encrypting the Manager's Password
You can also give `rootpw` an encrypted password by using the `ldappasswd` utility, described in the next chapter.

The `directory` directive indicates which directory on the file system should hold the database files. In this case the database is stored at `/var/lib/ldap/`.

Finally, the `index` directive is composed of a list of attributes that should be indexed, followed by the type of matching that the index will be used for. Our example looked like this:

```
index objectClass,cn eq
```

This means that we are creating an index that will support equality (`eq`) matching on the attributes `objectClass` and `cn`. When the server gets a request for all the entries with `cn Rob` or `commonName Rob`, the server can greatly expedite service by accessing the index instead of searching the entire database. However, if the request was for `Rob*` (note the `*` wildcard character), then the server would not be looking for a CN that equals "Rob*", but for any CN that starts with "Rob". In this case, the index we created would not be used.

Multiple index directives can be used, and we could support faster CN searches for queries like `Rob*` by splitting the index directive into two different directives:

```
index objectClass eq
index cn eq,sub
```

In the given example, an equality (`eq`) index is maintained for `objectClass` attributes, while the `cn` attribute is indexed for equality matches (`eq`) and substring matches (`sub`).

Certain attributes do not support all index types. The `objectClass` attribute, for example, does not support substring (`sub`) index matching. When we will look at performance tuning in Chapter 5, we will see the indexing directive more carefully.

Once you have a database created, every time you modify the `index` directives in `slapd.conf`, you should rebuild the indexes with the `slapindex` command-line utility. Since we have not yet put any data in the database though, we don't need to run this command now.

Now we are ready to move on to the third and final section of our configuration file.

ACLs

The last section in the `slapd.conf` file is the ACL section. ACLs (Access Control Lists) determine which clients can access what data, and under what conditions. In Chapter 4, we will cover ACLs in much more detail. However, it is important to have some basic ACLs configured from the beginning, so we will briefly walk through two simple ACLs:

```
########
# ACLs #
########
access to attrs=userPassword
        by anonymous auth
        by self write
        by * none
```

```
access to *
        by self write
        by * none
```

ACLs are just fancy directives—directives with a complex syntax. They begin with the access directive, followed by a list of conditions. The conditions can span multiple lines as long as each continuation line begins with one or more white space characters (such as a tab or a space).

Line Continuations in slapd.conf file

Any directive, not just ACLs, can span multiple lines, as long as each continued line begins with a white space. For example, `moduleload back_hdb` can be written as:

```
moduleload
    back_hdb
```

Let's look at the first access control in detail:

```
access to attrs=userPassword
        by anonymous auth
        by self write
        by * none
```

The purpose of this access control is to keep a user's password protected. Specifically, it allows anonymous users to request that the server perform an authentication comparison (during the process of logging on) on a password. Additionally, it grants a user permission to change his or her own password. Finally, it denies everyone else any access to the password. That's what this rule is supposed to do. Now, how do we get that?

Each line of code having `by` should be indented:

`access to [resources]`

> `by [who] [type of access granted]`
>
> `by [who] [type of access granted]`
>
> `by [who] [type of access granted]`

Each `access` directive can have one `to` phrase, and any number of `by` phrases. Our first rule has three `by` phrases. Let's see these in more detail:

- In `access to attrs=userPassword`, `attrs` indicates that a list of one or more attributes will follow. In our case there is only one attribute: `userPassword`. The `userPassword` attribute is used to store the value of a password for an object in the directory.

 While not just any object in the directory can have a `userPassword`, there are many objects in the directory that are not users, but can have passwords. The most frequent use of the `userPassword` attribute is for records that describe users.

In this access control there is no explicit mention of particular parts of the directory to which this rule applies. Given this, the ACL will be enforced for *all* instances of `userPassword`. So, the rule specifies access to the `userPassword` attribute. The next three phrases will indicate who has access to `userPassword` attributes, and what kind of access they have.

- Next is `by anonymous auth`. This phrase grants an anonymous user (one who has not yet authenticated) permission to authenticate using a password. More accurately, it indicates that when a user submits a request for authentication, the directory server is allowed to perform an authentication operation (which amounts to comparing the submitted password with the value in the `userPassword` attribute for the corresponding user's entry).

- The last part of the `by` phrase specifies what sort of permissions are granted to the record. The permissions level can be granted in a few ways, which is discussed in detail in Chapter 4.

For the time being, though, we will look at four keywords that can be used in ACLs to grant common permission levels:

- `auth`: The server can perform an authentication operation using this resource.
- `read`: The client can have `auth` access and can also *read* this resource, but cannot make any changes.
- `write`: The client can have `auth` and `read` access to this resource and can also perform add, modify, and delete operations on whatever is specified by resource.
- `none`: The server should not give the client any access at all to this resource.

In Chapter 4, when we look at ACLs in depth, we will look at other keywords and explore creating finer-grained permissions levels, such as allowing write access without granting read access.

So, the second `by` phrase, `by self write`, means that once a DN (usually a user) has successfully connected and authenticated to the LDAP server, it can change the value of `userPassword`.

Finally, the last `by` phrase says `by * none`. The `*` is a wildcard that will apply to everyone. And `none`, as we came to know, denies any sort of access to the `userPassword` attribute. This rule says that everyone should be denied access to the password attribute.

This third `by` phrase provides a good illustration of how ACLs are applied. The ACL is evaluated in order. In the rules above, as soon as the server finds a rule that applies to the current DN, it will stop processing the ACL. Consider an example. When an anonymous user tries to authenticate (bind) with a DN and password, the server will check the ACLs to see if the DN has the right to request an authentication comparison using the `userPassword` attribute.

As SLAPD evaluates this ACL, it will see that the first `by` phrase applies; use that rule and skip the other two. But, on the other hand, if an authenticated user tries to read `userPassword` of another DN, the server will search `by` phrases until it finds one that matches. It will evaluate and skip the first two before applying the third, which denies that user the access to another record's `userPassword` attribute.

The Default by Phrase

When processing an ACL, SLAPD denies access by default. This means that every access directive ends with an implicit by phrase of by * none. So, to save space, we could have omitted the last phrase from both of our ACLs.

Now that we understand the first ACL, the second should be a breeze. Let's see the second one:

```
access to *
        by self write
        by * none
```

This last ACL becomes our default rule for the directory. It can be paraphrased this way: for any object and all its attributes (`to *`), if the currently connected DN is the DN of this object, it can write to the object (`by self write`). Otherwise, the currently connected DN has no access whatsoever (`by * none`). In short, it lets objects write to themselves, but denies everyone else all the permissions to the object.

Restricting the Manager

It should be noted that ACLs cannot be used to restrict the special directory manager account named in the `rootdn` directive.

Keep in mind that ACLs are processed sequentially. So this second rule will only apply if the earlier rule did not apply.

These access controls are very strict and will prevent directory users from getting much out of the directory. In Chapter 5 we will create some more rules which will make the directory more accessible, but for now these simple rules will suffice.

Verifying a Configuration File

We are now done working through the configuration file. The last thing to do before we start the server is to verify that the configuration file is valid.

OpenLDAP includes a tool for testing the configuration file to make sure that it is well-formed and that the directives are all used correctly. It also checks elements of the OpenLDAP environment to ensure that the requisite files are in the correct locations. The testing tool is called `slaptest` and it appears as:

```
$ sudo slaptest -v -f /etc/ldap/slapd.conf
```

Since the file system permissions on `slapd.conf` are very restrictive, we used `sudo` to execute the test as the root user. The `slaptest` command needs to know where the `slapd.conf` file is. This is specified with the `-f` parameter followed by the path to the configuration file. We also used the `-v` flag to require verbose output. Since nothing was wrong with `slapd.conf`, only one line was printed:

```
config file testing succeeded
```

But if anything is incorrect, `slaptest` will provide diagnostic information. Let's look at a misconfigured `slapd.conf` file:

```
# slapd.conf - Configuration file for LDAP SLAPD
##########
# Basics #
##########
include /etc/ldap/schema/core.schema
include /etc/ldap/schema/cosine.schema
include /etc/ldap/schema/inetorgperson.schema

pidfile /var/run/slapd/slapd.pid
argsfile /var/run/slapd/slapd.args
loglevel none
```

```
modulepath /usr/lib/ldap
# modulepath /usr/local/libexec/openldap
moduleload back_hdb

###########################
# Database Configuration #
###########################
database hdb
suffix "dc=example,dc=com"
rootdn "cn=Manager,dc=example,dc=com"
rootpw secret
directory /var/lib/ldap
# directory /usr/local/var/openldap-data
index objectClass sub,eq
index cn sub,eq

########
# ACLs #
########
access to attrs=userPassword
        by anonymous auth
        by self write
        by * none

access to *
        by self write
        by * none
```

This configuration file is a minor variation of the one we have been examining throughout this section. The problem is that the objectClass attribute cannot handle substring matches. The reason for this (explained in more detail in Chapter 6) is that the schema does not allow substring matching on the objectClass attribute.

Having made the above change, we run the slaptest command:

```
$ sudo slaptest -v -f slapd.conf
```

The following messages appear:

```
slapd.conf: line 48: substr index of attribute
                    "objectClass" disallowed
slaptest: bad configuration file!
```

As you can see this information is useful for quickly finding and fixing problems before attempting to start the server.

An Ubuntu Oversight

Due to a configuration oversight by Ubuntu packager maintainers, the `slaptest` program does not issue a warning if an unknown directive is found. As a result, a mistaken directive name may slip through the verification stage unnoticed. For example, misspelling `index` as `idnex` will not result in an error.

Testing slapd.conf with slapd

The slaptest command is actually nothing more than a symbolic link to slapd, the command used to start the server. While there are no distinct advantages to doing so, you can use the `slapd` program to test `slapd.conf`:

```
$ slapd -T dest -f /etc/ldap/slapd.conf
```

Once the configuration file passes muster with the `slaptest` program, we are ready to start our server.

At this point, we have walked through our basic `slapd.conf` configuration file. This configuration will get our directory up and running, and in later chapters of this book we will cover some more advanced settings that can be included here in the configuration file.

If you are interested in reading more about configuration options for `slapd.conf`, you may want to take a look at the manual (man) pages. The man pages for OpenLDAP provide a thorough (though sometimes tersely worded) reference. In particular, the `slapd.conf` page is very useful.

```
$ man slapd.conf
```

At the bottom of that page there is a list of other related manual pages, such as `slapd-hdb`, which lists directives specific to the HDB database.

Starting and Stopping the Server

At this point, we have configured our `slapd.conf` file. We are now ready to start our server. There are two different ways to run the SLAPD server: we can either use the init script provided with the distribution, or we can run the `slapd` command directly. Each way has its advantages, and we will look at both here.

Using the Init Script

The OpenLDAP packages that are installed with Ubuntu include a startup script that is located, along with other service startup scripts, in the /etc/init.d/ directory. The scripts in /etc/init.d/, usually referred to as the **init scripts**, are used to automatically *start* and *stop* services when the system run level changes (when the system boots, halts, or reboots), and by default, OpenLDAP should be configured to start when the server boots, and stop during halts and reboots.

The ldap init script provides a convenient way to start, stop, and restart the server. You can start it (if it is not already running) with the Ubuntu invoke-rc.d command:

```
$ sudo invoke-rc.d slapd start
```

You can use the same script to stop the server. Just change start to stop:

```
$ sudo invoke-rc.d slapd stop
```

Similarly, to restart, use the restart command instead of start or stop.

The init scripts set up default parameters and pass in many system options. Some of these are stored in a separate configuration file located at /etc/default/slapd. For example, by setting the SLAPD_USER and SLAPD_GROUP variables to a particular system user ID and group ID, you can run SLAPD as a user other than the default.

The OpenLDAP server must start as root, in order to bind to the correct TCP/IP port (389 or 636 by default). Then it will switch and use the user account and group specified in the file located at /etc/default/slapd.

> Ubuntu creates a special user and group, named openldap, for running SLAPD. Other distributions run SLAPD as root, which is not a good idea from a security point of view.

Other settings, such as logging settings, can also be made in this configuration file.

Running SLAPD Directly

Sometimes, it is useful to start SLAPD directly from the command line. This may make it easier to see error messages when starting of the server fails, or to test configurations before making any changes to the init script or its configuration files.

To start the SLAPD server directly, simply run the slapd command:

```
$ sudo slapd
```

This will start the SLAPD server in the background.

> If you compiled OpenLDAP from source, the `slapd` command will be at `/usr/local/libexec/`, which is not, by default, in `$PATH`. You will have to run the command using the full path: `/usr/local/libexec/slapd`.

The server will write its process ID to the location specified in the `pidfile` directive in `slapd.conf`. In our case, this is `/var/run/slapd/slapd.pid`. We can stop the server by using the standard `kill` command:

```
$ sudo kill `cat /var/run/slapd/slapd.pid`
```

This command first uses the `cat` program to print the contents of the file (which is simply the process ID of `slapd`). Note that the `cat` command is surrounded by backticks (`` ` ``), not single quotes (`'`). The backticks tell the shell to treat the statement as a command to be executed. The process ID is then passed to the `kill` command, which instructs the process to shut itself down.

In cases where the `slapd.pid` file is not available you might find it more expedient to kill the server with this command:

```
$ sudo kill `pgrep slapd`
```

Sometimes though, it is more useful to start the command in the foreground, and set debugging information to print out in the terminal window. This can be done quite easily as well:

```
$ sudo slapd -d config
```

In the command above we use the `-d` flag to print logging information to the shell's standard output. This means that `slapd` will print information to the terminal window. The `-d` flag takes one parameter — the debugging level. We have specified `config`, which instructs the server to print verbose logging information about the processing of the configuration file.

The output looks something like this:

```
@(#) $OpenLDAP: slapd 2.3.24 (Jun 16 2006 23:35:48) $
        mbutcher@bezer:/home/mbutcher/temp/openldap-2.3.24/servers/slapd
reading config file /etc/ldap/slapd.conf
line 6 (include /etc/ldap/schema/core.schema)
reading config file /etc/ldap/schema/core.schema
line 44 (rootdn "cn=Manager,dc=example,dc=com")
line 45 (rootpw ***)
```

```
line 47 (directory /var/lib/ldap)
line 48 (index objectClass eq)
index objectClass 0x0004
line 49 (index cn eq,sub,pres,approx)
index cn 0x071e
slapd starting
```

This can be one other useful way to ferret out configuration issues. The -d flag will take any of the debugging levels specified in the slapd.conf man page. I find acl useful for debugging access problems, and filter is often useful in figuring out trouble with searches.

When -d is specified the program will run in the foreground. To stop the server simply hit *CTRL+C*. This will stop the server and return you to a shell prompt.

Other useful command line parameters to use with slapd are -u and -g. Each takes one argument: -u takes a username and -g takes a groupname. These control the effective UID and GID (user ID and group ID) that SLAPD runs as. Once SLAPD has started and connected to the appropriate ports (which it must do as root), it will switch its UID and GID to the names specified in these parameters.

 To get a list of other command line flags that we can use with slapd, refer to the man page for slapd.

In the next section, we will be using some of the OpenLDAP clients to connect to our directory. This will require that the SLAPD server be running. You can verify that slapd is running by checking if /var/run/slapd/slapd.pid exists, or by running pgrep slapd, which will display the process ID of slapd if it's running. If no process ID number is returned, slapd is not running.

Configuring the LDAP Clients

In the last couple of sections we have focused exclusively on the SLAPD server. Now that the server is running we need to get the client configuration so that we can make test connections to the server.

Fortunately all of the OpenLDAP client programs share one common configuration file, ldap.conf, which is located in Ubuntu at /etc/ldap/ldap.conf (if you build from source, according to Appendix A, the default location for this file is /usr/local/etc/openldap/ldap.conf).

Other programs, such as those that use the OpenLDAP client libraries (like the PHP and Python LDAP APIs, may also use the `ldap.conf` file as a default location to retrieve basic configuration information.

Too Many ldap.conf Files

Occasionally, some Linux distributions will create two different `ldap.conf` files—one for OpenLDAP, and one for the PAM or NSS LDAP tools. This can lead to confusion about which `ldap.conf` file is used for which process. Ubuntu, however, gives the other packages distinctly named configuration files, like `/etc/pam_ldap.conf`.

A Basic ldap.conf File

The purpose of the `ldap.conf` file is two-fold:

1. It provided a place to define certain aspects of client behavior, such as how they treat SSL/TLS certificates or whether they follow alias entries.

2. It provides the OpenLDAP clients with useful defaults. By specifying some defaults, we can reduce the number of parameters we have to pass to the OpenLDAP clients when we run them from the command line.

An **alias** is an entry in the directory that points to some other entry. Conceptually, it is similar to a symbolic link in a UNIX/Linux file system, or to a shortcut in Microsoft Windows.

The `ldap.conf` file has three different kinds of directive:

- General settings, which specify things such as the default server and DN to use

- SASL-specific settings, which determine how the OpenLDAP clients will try to authenticate when using SASL (Simple Authentication and Security Layer) authentication mechanisms

- TLS-specific settings, which specify how OpenLDAP will handle connections that use SSL (Secure Sockets Layer) and TLS encryption

At this point we are only interested in the general settings. In later chapters, we will return to this file when configuring SSL/TLS and SASL.

Now, we need to look into a basic `ldap.conf` file. The `ldap.conf` file is located in the same directory as `slapd.conf`—`/etc/ldap/` (or `/usr/local/etc/openldap/` if you built from source). We will now insert the LDAP client settings into that basic `ldap.conf` file:

```
# LDAP Client Settings
URI   ldap://localhost
BASE   dc=example,dc=com
BINDDN   cn=Manager,dc=example,dc=com

SIZELIMIT   0
TIMELIMIT   0
```

Again, as with `slapd.conf`, lines that begin with a number sign (#) are treated as comments, and are ignored by the OpenLDAP client tools.

Next, we have directives:

- The URI directive indicates which server (or servers, as this directive can take multiple URIs, separated by spaces) is to be contacted if no server is explicitly specified by the client.

  Since the server is running on the same machine that we are going to be running client commands from, we should set the URI to `ldap://localhost`. This URI specifies that the default client connection should be made using the (unencrypted) LDAP protocol over the loopback interface (`127.0.0.1` or `localhost`). Since no port is specified it will use the default LDAP port, which is 389.

- The second directive is BASE. This tells the client programs where to start their search in the directory. It takes a full DN as a value. In this case we set it to the base DN of the server — to the DN of the root entry in our directory tree, so that all searches will start at the root.

  You may recall that when we were working on the database configuration section of `slapd.conf`, we set this same base DN, `dc=example,dc=com`, as the suffix for the database stored there. So, what we have done here is told the client to start at the same directory tree root that the server manages. This is generally the most convenient way to configure BASE in the `ldap.conf` file.

- The third directive, BINDDN, specifies the default DN that will be used when connecting to the server. In this file I have set it to the manager's DN, `cn=Manager,dc=example,dc=com`. While this will be very helpful when it comes to the examples in the next chapter it is not, in general, a good idea, and should never be set this way in a production environment. Usually the BINDDN default value should be set to a user that has limited privileges, or it should be omitted (in which case no default DN will be used).

Size and Time Limits

The next two directives, `SIZELIMIT` and `TIMELIMIT`, indicate the upper limits on the number of records returned (`SIZELIMIT`) and the amount of time the client will wait for the server to respond (`TIMELIMIT`). Here we have set both to 0, a special value for these directives that indicates that there should be no limit.

The way that size and time limits are handled can be a little confusing. On the client side there are two ways of specifying these limits: through the `ldap.conf` configuration file (as we are doing here) and through command-line parameters (as we will see in the next chapter).

However, the `SIZELIMIT` and `TIMELIMIT` directives above are not exactly defaults in the usual sense of the word. They are the absolute upper limit that the client can request. With command-line arguments the client can specify lower time and size limits, and those lower numbers will be used. But if the client attempts to specify larger size or time limits, they will be ignored, and the values of `SIZELIMIT` and `TIMELIMIT` will be used instead.

But the story doesn't end here. The SLAPD server can also define size and time limits (with the `limits`, `sizelimit` and `timelimit` directives in `slapd.conf`). If a client specifies a limit higher than the server's, the server will ignore the client's limit and use its own. We will look more at setting server limits in Chapter 5.

Now we have a functioning `ldap.conf` file that will alleviate the need to specify these parameters on the command line.

The last thing we need to do in this chapter is to use an OpenLDAP client to test out the SLAPD server.

Testing the Server

At this point, we have a SLAPD server configured and running, and we have an `ldap.conf` file that specifies many of the defaults for our tools. Now we are going to query the directory and fetch some information.

We haven't actually put any entries in our database, though. So what will we query? SLAPD does provide directory-based access to certain information, including currently-loaded schemas and subschemas, configuration information, and a special record called the **root DSE**. The root DSE (**DSA-Specific Entry**, where **DSA** stands for **Directory Service Agent**—the technical term for an LDAP server) is a special entry that provides information about the server itself. Like all other entries in an LDAP, the root DSE has a DN. Unlike all other entries, the root DSE's DN is an empty string.

Why use an empty string for a DN? The answer is simple: any client can connect to the server and find out about what sorts of operations the server supports, and all of this can be done without requiring the client to know anything about the directory structures hosted on the server. All it must do is perform a search with an empty DN.

 The LDAPv3 Directory Information Models specification (RFC 4512) states that a root DSE with an empty DN be provided by any standards-compliant LDAP server.

The root DSE contains information about what version of the LDAP protocol the server supports, what extensions to that protocol the server supports, and other useful information that helps clients fruitfully interact with the directory.

We will search for this entry using the `ldapsearch` command-line client.

Because of the restrictive way in which we set up our ACLs, we will have to authenticate to the directory in order to see the root DSE. And since we have only one defined user, the directory manager, we will log in as that user and perform a search for the root DSE:

```
$ ldapsearch -x -W -D 'cn=Manager,dc=example,dc=com' -b "" -s base
```

All of the above should go on one line at a shell prompt. In order to do the search, we must specify several different parameters:

- `-x`: This tells the server to use simple authentication (instead of the more complicated, but more secure, SASL authentication).
- `-W`: This tells the client to prompt us for an interactive password. The client will give the following prompt:

  ```
  Enter LDAP Password:
  ```

- `-D 'cn=Manager,dc=example,dc=com'`: This specifies the DN that we want to use to connect to the directory. In this case, we are using the directory manager account.
- `-b ""`: This sets the base DN for the search. In the `ldap.conf` file we set the default base to be `dc=example,dc=com`. But to get the root DSE, which is not under `dc=example,dc=com`, we need to specify an empty search base.
- `-s base`: This indicates that we want to search for just one (base) entry — the entry with the DN specified in the `-b` parameter (the empty DN of the root DSE).

When we run this search, this is the result returned from the server:

```
# extended LDIF
#
# LDAPv3
# base <> with scope baseObject
# filter: (objectclass=*)
# requesting: ALL
#
#
dn:
objectClass: top
objectClass: OpenLDAProotDSE

# search result
search: 2
result: 0 Success

# numResponses: 2
# numEntries: 1
```

At the top of the result is a summary of how the search was processed. The highlighted portion shows the root DSE entry. The server returned three attributes: the dn (which is empty) and two object class specifications.

The last section, beneath the highlighted section, displays a summary, including how many records were returned (two: the DSE entry and the summary) and the error code (0 for success).

This record is sparse, containing only a few attributes. And it doesn't give us much information about the directory's configuration or capabilities. But the root DSE contains much more information than appears here. How to we get at that information?

To get more extensive information out of the root DSE, we need to query for all of the **operational attributes** for the record.

Operational attributes, as explained in Chapter 1, are attributes that are intended for internal use. RFC 4512 states that many of the root DSE's attributes be treated as operational attributes.

Here's a modified version of the search that adds a filter for any object class '(objectclass=*)', and a request for all operational attributes (+). Since we are using the asterisk character (*) in the filter, the filter must be enclosed in single quotes to avoid shell expansion:

```
$ ldapsearch -x -W -D 'cn=Manager,dc=example,dc=com' -b "" -s base \
    '(objectclass=*)' +
```

The output of this command looks something like this:

```
Enter LDAP Password:
# extended LDIF
#
# LDAPv3
# base <> with scope baseObject
# filter: (objectclass=*)
# requesting: +
#
#
dn:
structuralObjectClass: OpenLDAProotDSE
configContext: cn=config
namingContexts: dc=example,dc=com
supportedControl: 1.3.6.1.4.1.4203.1.9.1.1
supportedControl: 2.16.840.1.113730.3.4.18
supportedControl: 2.16.840.1.113730.3.4.2
supportedControl: 1.3.6.1.4.1.4203.1.10.1
supportedControl: 1.2.840.113556.1.4.319
supportedControl: 1.2.826.0.1.334810.2.3
supportedControl: 1.2.826.0.1.3344810.2.3
supportedControl: 1.3.6.1.1.13.2
supportedControl: 1.3.6.1.1.13.1
supportedControl: 1.3.6.1.1.12
supportedExtension: 1.3.6.1.4.1.4203.1.11.1
supportedExtension: 1.3.6.1.4.1.4203.1.11.3
supportedFeatures: 1.3.6.1.1.14
supportedFeatures: 1.3.6.1.4.1.4203.1.5.1
supportedFeatures: 1.3.6.1.4.1.4203.1.5.2
supportedFeatures: 1.3.6.1.4.1.4203.1.5.3
supportedFeatures: 1.3.6.1.4.1.4203.1.5.4
supportedFeatures: 1.3.6.1.4.1.4203.1.5.5
supportedLDAPVersion: 3
supportedSASLMechanisms: NTLM
supportedSASLMechanisms: DIGEST-MD5
supportedSASLMechanisms: CRAM-MD5
entryDN:
subschemaSubentry: cn=Subschema

# search result
search: 2
result: 0 Success

# numResponses: 2
# numEntries: 1
```

Again the results above are for the same record—the root DSE record. Only now we get a much bigger record, containing all of the operational attributes for the record.

The information returned from the server this time includes lists of supported features, extensions, controls, and SASL mechanisms (most of which are not particularly human-friendly).

While many of the items in this record are not useful to us right now, some can be very useful in practice. For example, the supportedLDAPVersion attribute indicates what version of the LDAP protocol this server uses. The namingContexts attribute gives the base DN for each directory information tree hosted on this server. The supportedSASLMechanisms list tells us what sort of authentication routines can be performed when doing a SASL bind (which we will look at in detail in Chapter 4).

Some LDAP client programs will even query the root DSE and use this information to determine what kinds of operations the server will support, adjusting the client's own features to the level of service provided by the server.

What is most important about this exercise though, is that we have verified that we have successfully configured the SLAPD server, as well as the OpenLDAP clients. We have connected, authenticated (using a simple bind), and retrieved a record from the LDAP server.

Summary

The focus of this chapter has been on installing and configuring the OpenLDAP suite of tools. We installed OpenLDAP on an Ubuntu system, and then walked through the process of authoring a slapd.conf file. Once we had created and tested slapd.conf, we turned to the ldap.conf file, which contains settings and defaults used by the OpenLDAP clients. Finally, we used ldapsearch to request the root DSE record from the directory, verifying that we had both the client and the server configured.

In the next chapter, we will walk through the OpenLDAP utilities and client applications. In the process of doing this we will add some records to our directory.

3
Using OpenLDAP

Now that we have a basic OpenLDAP server installed, configured, and running, it is time to turn our attention to using OpenLDAP. In this chapter we will be looking at what the various applications in the **OpenLDAP suite** do. In the process, we will discuss LDAP operations, create our initial directory tree, and use the OpenLDAP clients and utilities to interact with the directory server. As we do this we will cover the following:

- The basic functional division of the OpenLDAP tools: daemons, clients, and utilities
- The basic directory server operations
- Building an initial directory tree in an LDIF file
- Loading the data into the directory
- Working with the directory records
- Searching the directory
- Setting passwords and authenticating against the directory

Along the way, we will also see many new LDAP terms and concepts.

A Brief Survey of the LDAP Suite

In the last chapter we saw that the OpenLDAP suite was composed of daemons, libraries, clients, and utilities.

In UNIX parlance, a daemon is a process that runs for long periods of time without user interaction. It is a process that runs in the background. A server is a type of daemon that answers requests from other applications (clients). There are two daemons in the OpenLDAP suite: the SLAPD daemon (server) and the SLURPD daemon. In the next section we will look at these two.

There are a host of utilities included with OpenLDAP too. Utilities are programs that assist in managing the directory but do not use the LDAP protocol. They do things like maintain indexes, dump the contents of the database, and assist with migrating records from one directory to another.

Clients, in contrast to utilities, are programs that connect to the directory server using the LDAP protocol and perform directory operations, such as searching for, adding, modifying, and deleting records from the directory.

We will look at all of the utilities and clients. But before we dive into that we will look at the daemons and some of the concepts involved in communication between LDAP clients and servers. This will give us the foundational knowledge for our work with the LDAP utilities and clients.

LDAP from the Server Side

OpenLDAP includes two daemons: **SLAPD** and **SLURPD**. SLAPD is the main server, and we will examine its operation throughout this book. SLURPD is a special-purpose daemon used for replicating directories. While it is still in use, it is now deprecated in favor of a more robust replication mechanism. We will cover it only briefly in this book.

SLAPD

The first, SLAPD, is the stand-alone LDAP daemon. It is the LDAP server. It listens for client requests and, when it receives a request, performs the requested operation and returns any necessary data. In the most common case a client will send a query message to the server. The SLAPD server will then look up the information and return the results. Let's consider an example (in conversational English):

Client: Log in as user Bob with the password Password

Server: Bob is now logged in

Client: Bob wants all of the usernames of users whose email addresses start with 'm'

Server: There are four users with email addresses that start with 'm'. The user IDs are: mattb, markd, melaniek, melindaq

Client: Log Bob off

Server: OK

This example is very simplistic (and omits lots of the details of an LDAP transaction), but it should give you the main idea of what SLAPD does.

The SLAPD program is called, appropriately enough, `slapd`. It is located at `/usr/sbin` (if you compiled from source, it is in `/usr/local/libexec`). In the previous chapter we configured SLAPD using the `/etc/ldap/slapd.conf` configuration file.

The SLAPD server handles all client interactions, including authentication, processing ACLs, performing searches, and handling changes, additions, and deletions of the data. It also manages the databases that store LDAP content. All of the clients that we look at in this chapter interact directly with SLAPD. The utilities provide maintenance services for SLAPD, though they rarely directly interact with the SLAPD server (they tend to operate on files that the directory uses).

Let's take a slightly more technical look at the simple LDAP exchange that we outlined here. We can break the exchange into two major parts: the authentication process (called **binding** in LDAP parlance) and the search process.

The Binding Operation

The first thing that must happen is the client must authenticate to the server. Keep in mind that in order to interact with an LDAP server the client must provide two pieces of information: a DN and a password.

Typically, there are two different ways by which a client can authenticate to a server: through a Simple Bind, and through an SASL Bind. It is possible to write custom methods of binding, too, but that's a significant undertaking. Let's look at the way clients connect to LDAP using the **Simple Bind** method.

Typically, to authenticate a user, SLAPD looks up the DN (and the DN's `userPassword` attribute) in the directory and verifies the following:

1. The supplied DN exists in the directory.
2. The DN is allowed to connect under the present conditions (such as from the originating IP address, or with the currently-implemented security features).
3. The password supplied matches the value of the DN's `userPassword` attribute.

In our example scenario the user Bob wants to bind to the directory. For Bob to bind according to the outlined steps, the client would have to provide Bob's full DN, which might be something like `cn=Bob,dc=example,dc=net`. But, not all clients know the full DN of the user. Most applications require only a username and password, not a full DN. To solve this problem, LDAP servers support the idea of the **Anonymous** user.

When the LDAP server receives a bind request with an empty DN and an empty password field, the server treats the user as Anonymous. The Anonymous user can be granted or denied access to information in the directory based on the ACLs specified for SLAPD. Generally, the task of the Anonymous user is to get Bob's DN out of the directory and request that Bob be authenticated.

How does this happen? The client first connects to the server as Anonymous, then searches the directory for Bob's entry with a filter of something like this: *entries whose CN is "Bob" and who have the objectclass "organizationalPerson"*.

 The actual LDAP filter for this request would look like this:
(&(cn=Bob)(objectClass=oraganizationalPerson))

Assuming that the filter is specific enough, and the directory actually has an entry for Bob, then the server would then send the client one DN: cn=Bob,dc=example, dc=net. The client would then re-bind, this time as cn=Bob,dc=example,dc=net (and with Bob's password), rather than as Anonymous.

In order for anonymous authentication to work, the ACLs will need to allow the Anonymous user to bind and attempt to perform authentication. The ACLs we added to slapd.conf in the previous chapter allowed the Anonymous user to request authentication services with the userPassword attribute.

In this chapter, we will use Simple Binding, though we will specify a full DN, rather than bind as Anonymous and search, and then rebind. Simple Bind sends the password from the client to the server. Without additional security (like SSL or TLS encryption), this makes the authentication process vulnerable to attacks. **SASL (Simple Authentication and Security Layer) Binding** provides another method of authenticating that relies on external security measures for added security. In Chapter 4, we will look at the authentication process in more detail, with particular emphasis on security.

The Search Operation

In our example scenario, after Bob authenticates to the server he searches for all the email addresses that begin with the letter *m*. Let's examine that process in a little more detail.

In order to search the directory we need to know the following things:

- **Base DN**: Where in the directory to start from
- **Scope**: How deep in the tree to look
- **Attributes**: What information we want retrieved
- **Filter**: What to look for

Let's look at what Bob wants to get out of the directory. Bob wants to get a list of all of the people in his organization, Example.Com, who have email addresses that begin with the letter *m*. From this information, we can construct a search.

First, Bob wants to know about everyone in the Example.Com organization. In the directory, this is everything under the Example.Com entry: `dc=example,dc=com`. Also, since we know that Bob wants all of the email addresses that begin with *m*, not just one layer down; we know that Bob wants to search the entire subtree under `dc=example,dc=com`. So we have:

- **Base DN**: `dc=example,dc=com`
- **Scope**: Entire subtree

Next, we want to know what attributes Bob wants the server to return. The DN will be automatically returned. Other than that, Bob is concerned only with the attribute that stores the email address. Email addresses are stored in the `mail` attribute. We could also grab any number of attributes, such as the user's name (`cn`) and telephone number (`telephoneNumber`). So we have:

- **Attributes**: `mail`, `cn`, `telephoneNumber`

Attribute Descriptions

The attribute referred to by `mail` also has a second name: `rfc822Mailbox`. These two names are called **attribute descriptions** because they both describe a common attribute. Each attribute has at least one attribute description, but it is legal to have multiple descriptions (such as `cn` and `commonName`, or `dc` and `domainComponent`). When you have an attribute with more than one description it doesn't matter which description you use. All should return the same results.

Finally, we need to create a filter from Bob's criteria. Bob wants all of the entries where the email address starts with the letter *m*.

Here is the search filter:

```
(mail=m*)
```

This simple filter is composed of four parts:

- First, the filter is enclosed in parentheses. Parentheses are used for grouping elements within the filter. For any filter, the entire filter should always be enclosed in parentheses.
- Second, the filter begins with an attribute description: `mail`.

- Third is the matching rule. There are four matching rules: equality (=), approximate match (~=), greater than or equal to (>=), and less than or equal to (<=). How these are used (and whether they can be used) is determined to a large degree by the directory schema, which we will discuss at length in Chapter 6. In this case the filter performs string matching.

- Finally, we have the assertion value — the string or pattern that we want results to match. In this case it is composed of the character m and the wildcard character (*). This indicates that the string must start with m, and can then have zero or more characters following it.

This type of search is called a **substring search**, because the filter provides only part of the string, and requests that the server respond with any entries that match the substring (according to the pattern supplied).

What if Bob also needed all of the users with email addresses that started with n? We could run two separate searches, or we could create a more elaborate filter:

```
(|(mail=m*)(mail=n*))
```

This filter is composed of two subfilters: (mail=m*) and (mail=n*). The first matches only mail addresses that start with *m*, while the second matches only addresses that start with *n*. These two subfilters are disjoined using the pipe (|) symbol. That means that an OR operation will be performed, and the filter will match a record if the record matches either (mail=m*) or (mail=n*).

The syntax may seem a little unusual at first, as the operator (the OR) comes before the two filters are listed.

 There are three logical operators that can be used in filters: AND (&), OR (|), and NOT (!).

Just to make things more interesting, let's say that Bob wants to restrict the list to only people whose offices have room numbers of 300 or above. We can simply add one more sub-filter to our list, and we will have the results that Bob is looking for:

```
(&(|(mail=m*)(mail=n*))(roomNumber>=300))
```

To visualize this a little better let's add some line breaks and spaces:

```
(&
  (|
    (mail = m*)
    (mail = n*)
  )
  (roomNumber >= 300)
)
```

Now it should be a little easier to see how this filter is interpreted. In the innermost level, mail addresses are considered matches if they start with *m* OR *n*. Now, these matches are only returned if they also have a room number greater than or equal to 300. They must match either `(mail=m*)` OR `(mail=n*)`, AND, in addition, must also have `(roomNumber >= 300)`.

Once Bob performs the search, with the base DN, scope, attributes, and filter, he will receive a response from the server that will contain a list of records that look something like this:

```
dn:cn=Matt B,dc=example,dc=com
mail: mattb@example.com
cn: Matt B
cn: Matthew B
telephoneNumber: +1 555 555 55555

dn: cn=Melanie K,dc=example,dc=com
mail: melaniek@example.com
cn: Melanie K
elephoneNumber: +1 555 555 4444
```

The search returns everything in appearing in the subtree below the DN `dc=example,dc=com` that matches our filter. The returned records only have the DN and the attributes that we specified: `mail`, `cn`, and `telephoneNumber`.

In our most complex filter, we used the `roomNumber` attribute. Why isn't it present in the records above? Even though it was used in the filter the attribute value would not be returned in the response unless we requested it.

Before going on, there is one last thing to mention about searching. During a search the entire request is checked against the list of access controls.

If an ACL specifies that Bob does not have access to the `telephoneNumber` attribute, then the search will return the same DNs but without the `telephoneNumber` attribute. Similarly, if an ACL denied Bob access to the records of certain people in the directory, then the server would send back the results for only those that Bob does have permission to see.

The server will not give Bob any indication that some information has been withheld because of an ACL.

More Operations: Additions, Modifications, and Deletions

In our illustration of Bob's search for email addresses we covered only binding and searching. Of course, LDAP supports adding, modifying, and deleting, as well. All three of these also require that the user first bind. And all three of these are also subject to ACL restrictions.

The Addition Operation

In an addition operation a new record is added to the server. In this case the client will have to provide a new (and unique) DN, and set of attribute/value pairs. The attribute/value pairs must include a list of object classes to which the entry belongs. For example, if the entry is going to be a new user with a user ID and an email account, then the modification would have to include at least three object class attribute/value pairs.

An entire record for a user to be added might look something like this:

```
dn: uid=bjensen,dc=exaple,dc=com
cn: Barbara Jensen
mail: bjensen@example.com
uid: bjensen
objectClass: person
objectClass: organizationalPerson
objectClass: inetOrgPerson
```

The Modification Operation

Modification acts on a particular record, specified by DN. Any number of changes can be done on a single record in one modification request.

For a particular record, a modification operation can add, replace, or remove attributes. And it can combine operations in the same request. That is, it can remove one attribute and replace another attribute in one request. Let's see these attributes:

- An **add** request takes an attribute name and one or more values. It will add those values to the existing set of values for that attribute. For example, consider a record like this:

  ```
  dn: cn=Matt,dc=example,dc=com
  cn: Matt
  telephoneNumber: 1 555 555 1234
  telephoneNumber: 1 555 555 4321
  objectClass: person
  ```

If we want to modify this record by adding `cn: Matthew`, the result will look like this:

```
dn: cn=Matt,dc=example,dc=com
cn: Matt
cn: Matthew
telephoneNumber: 1 555 555 1234
telephoneNumber: 1 555 555 4321
objectClass: person
```

Modification operations are processed in an "all or nothing" fashion. When multiple modifications are sent in one request, either they all succeed, or they all fail.

- A **replace** request also takes an attribute and one or more values. But the list of values replaces the existing values. For example, if Matt relocated and his telephone number changed, then replacing with the new attribute `telephoneNumber: 1 555 555 6543` would result in a record that looked like this:

```
dn: cn=Matt,dc=example,dc=com
cn: Matt
cn: Matthew
telephoneNumber: 1 555 555 6543
objectClass: person
```

The new number is added and the old numbers are removed.

- A **delete** request also takes an attribute and a list of values. It deletes only the values for an attribute that are specified in the list of values. For example, deletion of `cn: Matthew` would give us the following record:

```
dn: cn=Matt,dc=example,dc=com
cn: Matt
telephoneNumber: 1 555 555 6543
objectClass: person
```

Only the matching CN was removed. If, however, a delete request only specifies the attribute (with no values), then all instances of that attribute will be removed.

The Delete Operation

Finally, an entire LDAP record can be deleted. Like modifications, deletion operates on a particular record, the record's DN. During a delete operation, the entire record is removed from the directory — the DN and all attributes.

Only records that do not have children can be deleted from the directory. If an entry has children, the children must be removed from the directory (or relocated to another part of the tree) before the parent entry can be removed.

Infrequent Operations

There are a few operations that clients can call, but that tend to be used less than binding, searching, adding, modifying, and deleting. Three that we will look at just briefly are **ModifyDN, Compare,** and **Extended Operation**.

The ModifyDN Operation

ModifyDN is used in cases where the DN for a record must be changed. Generally, DNs should not be changed frequently as they are intended to be used as unique and stable locators within a directory tree. However, it is not difficult to envision cases where a DN needs to be changed. The following figure displays a (full) DN:

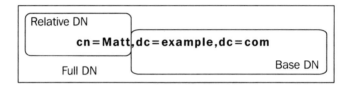

A (full) DN is composed of two parts:

- First, there is the part specific to the immediate record, called the **Relative DN** or the **RDN.** For example, in the DN cn=Matt,dc=example,dc=com, the RDN is the cn=Matt part.

- Second, there is the part that refers to the parent record of the DN. It is specific to this record. The dc=example,dc=com part in the same example points to the parent of this record.

Given the DN, we know how far down the directory tree this record is. It is one layer below the root of the tree—the base DN (dc=example,dc=com).

The ModifyDN operation provides a way to change just the RDN or the entire DN. Changing the latter equates to moving the record to another part of the directory tree.

The Compare Operation

A Compare operation takes a DN and an attribute value assertion (attribute = value), and checks to see if that attribute assertion is true or false. For example, if the client supplies the DN cn=Matt,dc=example,dc=com and the attribute value assertion cn=Matthew, then the server will return *true* if the record has an attribute cn with the value Matthew, or *false* otherwise. This operation can be faster (and also more secure) than fetching a record and doing the comparison on the client side.

In OpenLDAP ACLs, the auth permission setting (as well as the =x permission setting that we will look at in the next chapter) allows the Compare operation to be used, but does not allow the attribute value to be returned in a search. The read permission (=xw) allows both the Compare operation and the return of the attribute value in search results.

The Extended Operation

Finally, OpenLDAP implements the LDAP v.3 Extended Operation, which makes it possible for a server to implement custom operations.

The exact syntax of an Extended Operation will depend on the implementation of the extension. The supported Extended Operations are listed in the root DSE under the supportedExtension attribute. Take a look at the root DSE at the end of Chapter 2. In that record there are two extended operations:

- 1.3.6.1.4.1.4203.1.11.1: This **Modify Password extension** is defined in RFC 3062 (http://www.rfc-editor.org/rfc/rfc3062.txt). This extension provides an operation for updating a password in the directory.
- 1.3.6.1.4.1.4203.1.11.3: This **Who Am I? extension** is defined in RFC 4532 (http://www.rfc-editor.org/rfc/rfc4532.txt). This extension makes it possible for the currently active DN to find out about itself from the server.

Later in this chapter we will look at tools that use the Modify Password and the Who Am I? extensions.

SLAPD Summary

In this section we have looked at some of the operations that the SLAPD server makes available to the clients. We've looked at the most common operations (binding, searching, modifying, adding, and deleting). We've also looked at a few of the less-known operations like modifyDN, Compare, and Extended Operations as well.

By now you should have a good idea of what services the SLAPD server provides to clients. Clients can bind (or authenticate) to a SLAPD server and perform powerful searches of the directory. And through SLAPD the information in the directory tree can be maintained.

These concepts will be central to the rest of this chapter, and the rest of this book.

Next, we'll look at the SLURPD daemon, though we will not go into much detail.

SLURPD

SLAPD and SLURPD are the two daemons included in the OpenLDAP suite. Above, we looked at the SLAPD server. Now we will turn to the second daemon.

SLURPD, the Stand-alone LDAP Update Replication Daemon, is used less frequently than SLAPD, and is on its way to obsolescence. SLURPD provides one way of keeping multiple copies of an LDAP directory synchronized (see the discussion in Chapter 1). Basically it works by tracking the changes (additions, deletions, modifications) to a *master* SLAPD directory server. When a change is made to the master directory, SLURPD sends updates to all of the subordinate *slave* servers.

The SLURPD program, slurpd, is located at /usr/sbin (or /usr/local/libexec, if you compiled from source). In configurations where SLURPD is used, slurpd is typically started immediately after slapd. SLURPD does not have its own configuration file. It searches the slapd.conf file for configuration information.

In Chapter 7 we will look at the technology that will likely replace SLURPD: the LDAP Sync Replication capability that is built into recent (OpenLDAP 2.2 and later) versions of SLAPD.

Creating Directory Data

In the previous section we looked at the two LDAP daemons, SLAPD and SLURPD. But though we have a directory running already, we do not have any entries in our directory (other than the ones that are created by SLAPD, such as schema records and the root DSE).

In this section we will create a file for holding our LDAP data, and we will devise some directory entries to go in this file. In the next section we will load the data into the directory.

The LDIF File Format

Throughout this book we look at examples of LDAP records presented in plain text, with each line having an attribute description, followed by a colon and a value. The first line of the record is the DN, and usually the last lines of the record are the object class attributes:

```
dn: uid=bjensen,dc=exaple,dc=com
cn: Barbara Jensen
mail: bjensen@example.com
uid: bjensen
objectClass: person
objectClass: organizationalPerson
objectClass: inetOrgPerson
```

This format is the standard way of representing LDAP directory entries in a text file. It is an example of a record written in the **LDAP Data Interchange Format (LDIF)**, version 1.

> The LDIF file format was developed as part of the University of Michigan LDAP server project. In 2000, LDIF version 1 was standardized in RFC 2849. The standard is available online at http://www.rfc-editor.org/rfc/rfc2849.txt.

The LDIF standard defines a file format not only for representing the contents of a directory, but for representing certain LDAP operations, such as additions, changes, and deletions. In the section on the `ldapmodify` client, we will use LDIF to specify changes to records in the directory server, but right now we are interested in creating a file that represents the contents of our directory.

> LDIF is not the only directory file format. There is an XML-based directory markup language called **DSML (Directory Services Markup Language)**. While there is a standardized DSML version 1, the project seems to have lost momentum to the extent that the official website, dsml.org, is now gone. However, one Open Source DSML tools website hosts a mirror of the old dsml.org site: http://www.dsmltools.org/dsml.org/.
>
> The OpenLDAP suite does not directly support DSML.

Anatomy of an LDIF File

An LDIF file consists of a list of records, each of which represents an entry in the directory. Each entry must have a DN (since any LDAP entry requires a DN), and then one or more attributes or change records (`add`, `modify`, `delete`, `modrdn`, `moddn`). For now we will confine ourselves to attributes, and put off discussion of change records until we discuss `ldapmodify`.

Records are separated by empty lines, and each record must begin with a DN:

```
# First Document: "On Liberty" by J.S. Mill
dn: documentIdentifier=001,dc=example,dc=com
documentIdentifier: 001
documentTitle: On Liberty
documentAuthor: cn=John Stuart Mill,dc=example,dc=com
objectClass: document
objectClass: top

# Second Document: "Treatise on Human Nature" by David Hume
dn: documentIdentifier=002,dc=example,dc=com
documentIdentifier: 002
documentTitle: Treatise on Human Nature
documentAuthor: cn=David Hume,dc=example,dc=com
objectClass: document
objectClass: top
```

Lines that begin with a pound or number sign (#) are treated as comments, and ignored. Note that the pound sign must be the first character on the line, not preceded by any whitespace characters.

While it is customary for records to end with the `objectClass` attributes, this is done because it is considered easier to read. There is no requirement to do so. The order of attributes in an LDIF record is inconsequential.

An object class (which is defined in a schema definition) indicates what type or types of object the record represents. In the precvious example, the two records are both `documents`. The object class definition determines which attributes are required, and which are merely allowed. When authoring an LDIF file you will need to know which fields are required. The DN of any entry is, of course, required, as is the `objectclass` attribute. In the `top` object class, which represents the root of the schema hierarchy, there are no required fields other than `objectclass`. The `document` object class definition requires `documentIdentifier`, and allows eleven additional fields, including `documentTitle` (which takes a string value) and `documentAuthor` (which takes a DN value, pointing to another record in the directory).

The Document Object Class

LDAP directories can model a variety of different types of objects. The document object class, used in the previous example, represents documents (such as books, papers, and manuals) in the directory. The schema for the document object class and the related documentSeries object class is contained in cosine.schema and defined in section 3.2 of RFC 4524 (ftp://ftp.rfc-editor.org/in-notes/rfc4524.txt). Schemas will be discussed at length in Chapter 6.

Let's look at the list of attributes for the document and documentSeries object classes:

document	documentSeries
Required:	**Required:**
documentIdentifier	cn
Allowed:	**Allowed:**
documentTitle	description
documentAuthor	seeAlso
documentVersion	l
documentLocation	o
documentPublisher	ou
cn	telephoneNumber
description	
seeAlso	
l	
o	
ou	

Any attributes that are used in the DN but are not part of the directory's base DN must be present in the record. For example, consider the case where the base DN is dc=example,dc=com. An entry with the DN cn=Matt,dc=example, dc=com would have to have a cn attribute with the value Matt. In the previous examples, since documentIdentifier is used in the DN, there must be a matching documentIdentifier attribute in the record.

In fact, the document object class requires the documentIdentifier attribute so, in this case, even if the attribute was not used in the DN, any document record would still need a documentIdentifier.

Likewise, an entry with the DN cn=Matt,ou=Users,dc=example,dc=com would have to have the attributes cn:Matt and ou:Users.

Representing Attribute Values in LDIF

Not all attribute values are simple and short ASCII strings. LDIF provides facilities for encoding more complex types of data.

Sometimes attribute values won't fit on one line. If an attribute value is too long to fit on one line it can be continued on the next line, provided that the first character on the continued line is a whitespace character:

```
dn: documentIdentifier=003,dc=example,dc=com
documentIdentifier: 003
documentTitle: An essay on the nature and conduct of the passions
        and affections with illustrations on the moral sense.
documentAuthor: cn=Francis Hutchison,dc=example,dc=com
objectClass: document
objectClass: top
```

According to the RFC, an LDIF file can only contain characters in the ASCII character set. However, characters that are not in ASCII can be represented in LDIF using a base-64 encoded value. Entries whose value is base-64 encoded differ slightly. The attribute description is followed by two colons, instead of one:

```
dn: documentIdentifier=004,dc=example,dc=com
documentIdentifier: 004
documentTitle:: bW9uYWRvbG9neQ==
documentAuthor: cn=G. W. Leibniz,dc=example,dc=com
objectClass: document
objectClass: top
```

You should consider base-64 encoding under the following circumstances:

- When the attribute value contains binary data (such as a JPEG photo).
- When the character set is not ASCII. Generally, the directory data should be stored in UTF-8, but that means that in order to remain compliant to the LDIF standard, values should be base-64 encoded.
- When there are line breaks or other non-printing characters within the value. (Note that for such values to be accepted the schema must allow these characters or the directory server will not allow them to be uploaded even if they are encoded.)
- When the value begins with or ends with whitespace characters (that you want preserved), or begins with a colon (:) or a less-than sign (<).

Even DNs can be base-64 encoded, and you can use UTF-8 characters in a DN as long as the DN is base-64 encoded.

There are several UNIX/Linux utilities which can be used to base-64 encoded values. The most popular is the `uuencode` program that comes in the `sharutils` package. However, this program is not installed by default in Ubuntu. You can install it quickly from the command line with `apt-get`:

```
$ sudo apt-get install sharutils
```

Once `sharutils` is installed you can encode a value with `uuencode`:

```
$ echo -n " test" | uuencode -m name
begin-base64 644 name
IHRlc3Q=
====
```

In this example we are converting the string `" test"` (note the leading white space) into a base-64 encoded string. This is done with a couple of commands on the command line (using the Bash shell in this example).

The `uuencode` command is typically used to encode files for attachment to an email message, so we have to do a little work to get it to operate the way we want. First, we `echo` the string that we want to encode. The `echo` program, by default, adds a newline character onto the end of the string that it echoes. We use the `-n` flag to prevent it from adding the newline character.

The string `" test"` is echoed to the standard output (`/dev/stdout`), and then piped (`|`) into the `uuencode` command. The `-m` flag instructs `uuencode` to use base-64 encoding, and the `name` string is used by `uuencode` to generate a name for the attachment. While this is useful when using `uuencode` to generate email attachements, it serves no purpose for us. Since we are not attaching this file to anything it doesn't really matter what you put there; `foo` would work equally as well.

The `uuencode` program then prints three lines of output:

```
begin-base64 644 name
IHRlc3Q=
====
```

Only the second line of the code (highlighted one), the actual base-64 encoded value, matters to us. We can copy `IHRlc3Q=` and paste it into our LDIF file.

> Another popular tool for base-64 encoding is `mimencode`, provided by the `metamail` package. Both the Perl and Python scripting languages have base-64 encoding tools as well.

In some cases, inserting a lengthy attribute value (such as the entire base-64 encoded image file, or even a lengthy bit of text) into the LDIF file would make the file too large to efficiently edit with a text editor. Even a small image file would be hundreds of characters long when base-64 encoded. Instead of inserting the base-64 encoded string directly into the file you can use a special file reference, and the contents of the file will be retrieved and loaded into the directory when the LDIF file is imported.

```
dn: documentIdentifier=005,dc=example,dc=com
documentIdentifier: 005
documentTitle: Essays in Pragmatism
documentAuthor: cn=William James,dc=example,dc=com
description:< file:///home/mbutcher/long-description.txt
objectClass: document
objectClass: top
```

The highlighted line of code shows an example of inserting a reference to an external file.

There are two important features to note in this example:

- The left angle bracket (<) character is used to indicate that the file should be imported. This character evokes the UNIX/Linux shell, which uses the left angle bracket for the same purpose.

- The path to the file follows the standard `file://` URL scheme to represent the file path.

> Note that in the file scheme, you will usually need three slashes at the beginning (`file:///path/to/file`) to indicate that there is no host field. RFC 3986 (`ftp://ftp.rfc-editor.org/in-notes/rfc3986.txt`) defines the general structures of URIs and URLs. `file://` is one particular URL scheme, and is roughly defined in section 3.1 of RFC 1738 (`ftp://ftp.rfc-editor.org/in-notes/rfc1738.txt`).

In cases where you have attribute values in multiple languages you can store language information along with the attribute description:

```
dn: documentIdentifier=006,dc=example,dc=com
documentIdentifier: 006
documentTitle;lang-en: On Generation and Corruption
documentTitle;lang-la: De Generatione et Corruptione
documentAuthor: cn=Aristotle,dc=example,dc=com
objectClass: document
objectClass: top
```

The language information is stored in the directory, and clients will be able to use it to display the language appropriate to the locale.

This covers the basics of the LDIF file format, now we will move on and create an LDIF file to load into the directory.

Example.Com in LDIF

Now we are ready to model our directory tree in an LDIF file. The first thing to do is to decide on a directory structure. We are going to represent an organization in our directory tree. Of course the possibilities for the types of trees you can model are boundless, but we will stick to those most commonly used for LDAP directories.

There are two popular ways of defining the roots of an organizational directory tree:

1. The first is to create a root entry that indicates the official name of the organization and the geographic location (usually just the country) of the organization. Here are a few examples:

    ```
    o=Arius Ltd.,c=UK

    o=Acme GmBH,c=DE

    o=Example.Com,c=US
    ```

    In each of these three examples, o represents the organization name, and c is the two-character country code.

2. The second popular model is to use the organization's domain name. For example, if the company Airius has registered the `airus.co.uk` domain name, then the root DN would be composed of three **domain component** (dc) attributes:

    ```
    dc=airius,dc=co,dc=uk
    ```

    Likewise, the other two records could be re-written using their respective domain components:

    ```
    dc=acme,dc=de

    dc=example,dc=com
    ```

Using the organization/country configuration has its advantages. Corporations with multiple domains may find this form more appealing. But the second form, relying upon domain components instead, has become much more prevalent. In most circumstances, I prefer the domain component form because it is more closely related to the way much information is referenced on the Internet.

Of course, there is no hard and fast rule about how exactly the DN must be structured, and you may find other base DN structures more appealing.

Defining the Base DN Record

Now that we have chosen a base DN style, let's begin building a directory for Example.Com. LDIF files are read sequentially, record by record. So, the base DN must come first, since all other records will refer to it in their DNs. Likewise, as we build the directory information tree, we will need to make sure that the parent entries always appear in the file before their children.

Our base DN looks like this:

```
dn: dc=example,dc=com
description: Example.Com, your trusted non-existent corporation.
dc: example
o: Example.Com
objectClass: top
objectClass: dcObject
objectClass: organization
```

Let's start from the bottom and work backwards through the example. The record has three object classes: top, dcObject, and organization. As we have seen already, the top object class is the root of the hierarchy of object classes, and all records within the directory are in the top object class.

Here is the figure displaying the object classes:

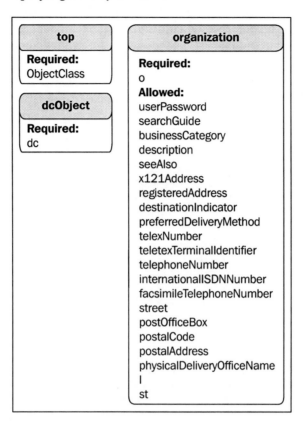

The dcObject object class simply describes domain components — pieces of a domain name. The domain www.packtpub.com, for example, has three domain components: www, packtpub, and com. Since we are using domain components in the DN, we need the dcObject class, which requires one attribute: dc.

You may notice that while in the DN there are two dc attributes (dc=example and dc=com), there is only one (dc:example) listed in the record. While it seems counter-intuitive at first glance, the reason is actually straightforward. The record is not describing the entire domain — just a single domain component (example). Like a DNS record, the parent component (com) refers to another entity somewhere else in a great big hierarchy.

So, each record that uses the dcObject object class can describe only one domain component, and hence have only one dc attribute in the record (though the DN may have multiple dc attributes, specifying in which part of the domain hierarchy this record resides).

But is the dc=com record supposed to be in our directory? Since the root of this directory (as specified in the slapd.conf file) is dc=example,dc=com, we would not expect to find the dc=com record within the database, as it is not under the dc=example,dc=com part of the tree (rather, dc=com is above, or superior to, this part of the tree).

Handling Requests for Records Outside the Directory Tree

What if a search request comes into our Example.Com directory for dc=com? Or what if we get a request for dc=otherExample,dc=com? These are records not expected to be in our directory. Using the referral directive in the slapd.conf file, you can direct requests of this sort to another server that might prove more authoritative on the matter. The syntax for the directive is referral <ldap URL>, for example: referral ldap://root.openldap.org.

Now we have specified what domain component our record describes. But we still need a little more. We can't just have a record with top and dcObject object classes for two reasons—one practical and the other technical.

Practically speaking, the record would not be particularly useful with just this sparse information, as it wouldn't really tell us about the base of the directory tree (other than that, it has a domain name).

Technically speaking, neither of the two object classes, top and dcObject, are sufficient for a complete record. The reason for this is that neither of these object classes are **structural object classes**, (top is abstract, and dcObject is auxiliary) and every record in the directory must have one object class that is considered the structural object class for that record. For a detailed explanation, as well as some useful information about structuring records, see Chapter 6.

What would make our base record more useful (and fulfill the record's requirement to have a structural object class)? The organization object class describes an organization, as the name suggests. It requires one field, o (or its synonym, organizationName), which is used to specify the (legal) name of the organization. Additionally the organization object class allows twenty-one optional fields that provide more detailed information about the organization, such as postalAddress, telephoneNumber, and location. In the previous example we used the description field, which is also among the twenty-one attributes allowed by the organization object class.

That is our base entry for our directory. It describes the record at the root of our directory information tree. Next we want to add some structure to our directory.

Structuring the Directory with Organizational Units

One of the strengths of LDAP's directory server model is its ability to represent data organized into hierarchies. In this section, we will use **Organizational Units (OUs)** to create a several subtrees beneath our dc=example,dc=com root.

Our Example.Com directory is intended primarily for holding user and account information. For that reason, we will want to use Organizational Units to create subtrees.

 If we were, for example, creating a directory of document records (as we did in the section entitled *The LDIF File Format*), instead of using OUs, we might instead use documentSeries records.

OpenLDAP does not provide a default OU subtree structure, so you will need to create your own. This can be done in many ways, but here we will see the two prominent theories of how OUs should be structured.

Theory 1: Directory as Organizational Chart

The first theory is that the directory should be structured to represent the organizational chart of the organization you are modeling. For example, if the organization has three main units—Accounting, Human Resources (HR), and Information Technology (IT)—then you should have three OUs. Here is a figure for the same:

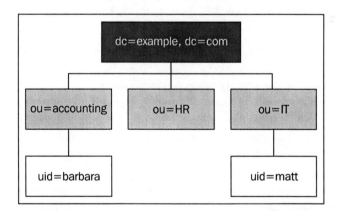

In the given screenshot, each OU represents a unit in the organizational chart. Employees who work in Accounting will have their user accounts in the directory subtree ou=Accounting,dc=example,dc=com, while employees in IT will have accounts in ou=IT,dc=example,dc=com.

This method has some obvious advantages. Knowledge of how the organization works will help you locate information in the directory. Conversely, the directory will serve as a tool for understanding how the organization is structured. Organizational relationships between people or records in the directory will be more easily ascertained. For example, a glance at the record (or just the DN) of `uid=Marvin,ou=Accounting,dc=example,dc=com`, and you will know that Marvin works in the same department as Barbara.

There are a few things to consider before structuring your directory this way though:

- First, while organizational structures change — sometimes too frequently — relocating DNs within the directory is not an easy task (and in some cases requires deleting a record from one part of the tree and creating a similar version in another part of the tree).

  If Barbara, the manager of Accounting, is transferred to Human Resources, her DN must change (to reflect the new OU). Some (older) backends do not allow DN changes, and so Barbara's Accounting record would need to be deleted, and then a new one created for her in the HR OU. Also, applications that stored the DN of the user would have to be reconfigured. Similarly, some employees may split their time between two departments. How would this case be handled?

- A second consideration, and one that is not at all obvious, has to do with the technical use of the LDAP directory. If user records are spread throughout the directory tree, then applications will need to be smart enough to search all over the tree for user records.

  This problem is usually solved by pre-authentication search techniques, such as binding as Anonymous or as a special authentication user, searching the directory for the account that will be used for authentication, and then binding as the correct account (if found). But not all clients (and not all directories, for that matter) allow pre-authentication searching. And pre-authentication searching can impose a bigger load on the server, whereas other techniques may be easier on the server.

- A third consideration has to do with what other sorts of information you want to store in your directory. If you are using the directory primarily as a tool for modeling the organizational chart, then this particular method of structuring the directory will be ideal for you. You can track employees, assets (fleet vehicles, computers, and so on), and other resources within the directory, and locate their position in the organization.

But if the main purpose of the directory is to create a directory of users of IT services, then this structure will be less than ideal, requiring applications to do much more work to locate users (and in some cases, requiring users to know more about their LDAP accounts).

Theory 2: Directory as IT Service

The second theory is that the directory should be structured to represent the way your system (networks, servers, user applications) will need to access the records. In this case the structure of the LDAP directory should be optimized for use by such IT services. While the organizational chart technique groups records by their relation to the organization, this method groups records into functional units, where a position in the directory is determined primarily by the tasks that applications and services will require the directory to perform.

One common way to structure the directory is to split it into a unit for users, a unit for groups, and a unit for system-level records that applications need, but users will not require access to. Let's see an example:

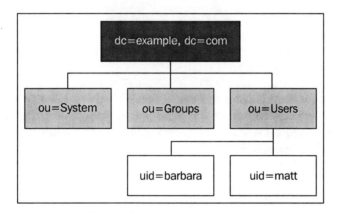

In this case, all of the user accounts are under a particular subtree of the directory: ou=Users,dc=example,dc=com. Applications need only search in one part of the directory to find user accounts, and when the organization changes, the structure of the directory need not also change.

 There is nothing magical about using organizational units (OUs) for partitioning the directory information tree. You can use other record types, and other attributes (such as cn—common name) to divide a directory into multiple branches. Using OUs is traditional, though perhaps not the most appropriate in cases where the directory information tree does not model the organizational chart.

This method, Also has some drawbacks. First, the directory structure does not, by design, provide any overt clues to the structure of the organization. Of course organizational information, such as department IDs, can be stored in individual records, and so can be retrieved that way.

More importantly though, if the directory supports a large number of users, the ou=Users branch is going to have a lot of records. This is not necessarily a performance problem, but it can make browsing the directory (as opposed to searching the directory) a tedious process.

In some cases, this problem is mitigated by adding additional subtrees under the user's branch. Sometimes this is done by creating a hybrid configuration where ou=User has subtrees that represent departments in the organization, such as ou=Accounting,ou=Users,dc=example,dc=com. Sometimes other classification systems, such as alphabetical schemes, are used to handle this situation: uid=matt,ou=m-p,ou=Users,dc=example,dc=com.

But for small and medium-sized ones, a user's branch typically does not have any additional subtrees, which eases the process of integrating with other applications.

LDAP also has object classes designed to describe groups of records in the directory. Usually, it does not make sense to store these in with the user accounts, so they can be moved to a separate branch.

Finally, the System branch is used to store records for things like system accounts, mail servers, web servers, and other miscellaneous applications often need (or perform best with) their own LDAP accounts. But if it can be helped, they shouldn't be grouped in with user accounts.

I've outlined two different ways of structuring the directory information tree—one mirroring the organization, and the other facilitating IT services. But these are only two ways of structuring the directory. You may find that other structures meet your needs better. However, for our purposes, we will use the IT services structure as we continue to build our LDIF file.

Expressing the OUs in LDIF

Now we are ready to write out our chosen OUs in LDIF. We will create three OUs—Users, Groups, and System—as follows:

```
# Subtree for users
dn: ou=Users,dc=example,dc=com
ou: Users
description: Example.Com Users
objectClass: organizationalUnit

# Subtree for groups
```

```
dn: ou=Groups,dc=example,dc=com
ou: Groups
description: Example.Com Groups
objectClass: organizationalUnit

# Subtree for system accounts
dn: ou=System,dc=example,dc=com
ou: System
description: Special accounts used by software applications.
objectClass: organizationalUnit
```

The three OUs have the same structure.

Each OU must have the organizationalUnit object class. This object class has one required attribute: ou. Here is a figure displaying the **organizationalUnit**:

```
┌─────────────────────────────────┐
│  ╭───────────────────────────╮  │
│  │   organizationalUnit      │  │
│  ╰───────────────────────────╯  │
│  Required:                      │
│  o                              │
│  Allowed:                       │
│  userPassword                   │
│  searchGuide                    │
│  businessCategory               │
│  description                    │
│  seeAlso                        │
│  x121Address                    │
│  registeredAddress              │
│  destinationIndicator           │
│  preferredDeliveryMethod        │
│  telexNumber                    │
│  teletexTerminalIdentifier      │
│  telephoneNumber                │
│  internationalISDNNumber        │
│  facsimileTelephoneNumber       │
│  street                         │
│  postOfficeBox                  │
│  postalCode                     │
│  postalAddress                  │
│  physicalDeliveryOfficeName     │
│  l                              │
│  st                             │
└─────────────────────────────────┘
```

 Note that the objectClass: top has been omitted from these records, as well as all of the following records in this chapter. All records are automatically assumed to be instances of the top object class, so it is not necessary to explicitly include the objectClass: top attribute.

The `description` attribute is optional and there are more than twenty additional (optional) attributes that can be added — most of which provide contact information of the organization unit, such as `telephoneNumber`, `postOfficeBox`, and `postalAddress`.

With our OUs in place we are ready to add a third tier to our directory tree. Before we start creating individual records let's get an overview of what this next tier will look like. Here is the directory tree structure with a group, a system account, and a pair of users:

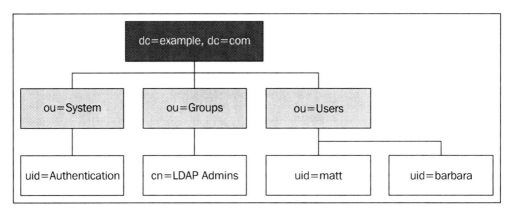

This is the directory information tree that we will create in the remainder of this section. Next, we will continue building an LDIF file first by adding the users, followed by a system record, and then a group.

Adding User Records

We will reserve the `Users` OU for records that describe people in the organization. In these accounts we want to store information about the user — things like first and last name, title, and department. Since the directory will also be a central resource for application information, we also want to store user ID, email address, and password.

A basic user record looks like this:

```
# Barbara Jensen:
dn: uid=barbara,ou=Users,dc=example,dc=com
ou: Users
uid: Barbara
sn: Jensen
cn: Barbara Jensen
givenName: Barbara
displayName: Barbara Jensen
mail: barbara@example.com
userPassword: secret
```

```
objectClass: person
objectClass: organizationalPerson
objectClass: inetOrgPerson
```

The user record for Barbara belongs to three object classes: `person`, `organizationalPerson`, and `inetOrgPerson`. All three of these are structural object classes, where `inetOrgPerson` is a child of the `organizationalPerson` class, which, in turn, is a child of the `person` object class. The attributes in Barbara's record are a mixture of the required and allowed attributes from the three object classes. The following figure displays the attributes in Barbara's record:

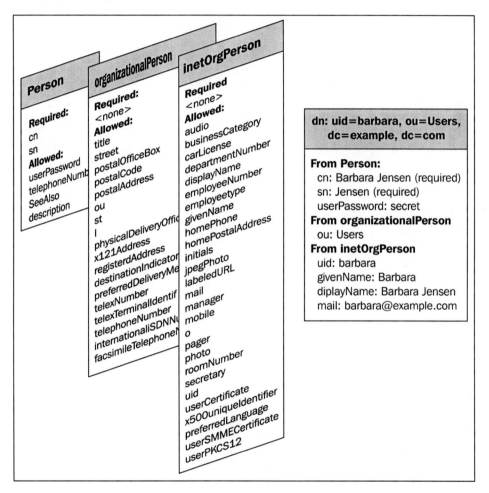

Since `inetOrgPerson` inherits from `organizationalPerson`, a record that has the `inetOrgPerson` object class also must have the `organizationalPerson` object class. And `organizationalPerson` inherits from the `person` object class, so `person`, is also required.

This means that all of the `inetOrgPerson` records will require `cn` (the user's full name) and `sn` (the user's surname) attributes, as all `inetOrgPerson` records are also person records. It also means that the record can have any combination of the forty-nine optional attributes defined between the three object classes.

Since `uid` and `ou` attributes were used in the DN, they are effectively required attributes as well. Furthermore, OpenLDAP will require that the record have a `uid` attribute and an `ou` attribute that have values that match the values in the DN—in other words, since the `ou` in the DN is Users, the `ou` attribute in the record must have the value Users. This behavior is dictated by the LDAP standard.

Different object classes, different schemas

While `person` and `organizationalPerson` are defined in the core schema (`core.schema`), `inetOrgPerson` is defined in its own schema (`inetOrgPerson.schema`), and is standardized on its own in RFC 2798 (`http://rfc-editor.org/rfc/rfc2798.txt`). The reason for this is largely historical: `person` and `organizationalPerson` were defined well before `inetOrgPerson` (and by different parties).

An `inetOrgPerson` record that utilizes more of the available attributes might look like this:

```
# Matt Butcher
dn: uid=matt,ou=Users,dc=example,dc=com
ou: Users
# Name info:
uid: Matt
cn: Matt Butcher
sn: Butcher
givenName: Matt
givenName: Matthew
displayName: Matt Butcher
# Work Info:
title: Systems Integrator
description: Systems Integration and IT for Example.Com
employeeType: Employee
departmentNumber: 001
employeeNumber: 001-08-98
mail: mbutcher@example.com
mail: matt@example.com
roomNumber: 301
telephoneNumber: +1 555 555 4321
```

```
mobile: +1 555 555 6789
st: Illinois
l: Chicago
street: 1234 Cicero Ave.
# Home Info:
homePhone: +1 555 555 9876
homePostalAddress: 1234 home street $ Chicago, IL $ 60699-1234
# Misc:
userPassword: secret
preferredLanguage: en-us,en-gb
objectClass: person
objectClass: organizationalPerson
objectClass: inetOrgPerson
```

In this example we are still using the same three object classes , but have selected many more of the optional attributes. One thing that may stand out in both Barbara's and Matt's records, is that there are an awful lot of attributes used simply for specifying the name of the person; cn, sn, givenName, and displayName are all fields related to the person's name. What's the point in having so many? There are two benefits achieved by providing diverse name fields:

- This reduces the amount of guess work that an application has to do when parsing names. Names can be ambiguous—for instance, John Stuart Mill's surname is Mill, while Mary Stuart Masterson's surname is Stuart Masterson. Explicitly specifying such things can reduce ambiguity.

- The different attributes allow additional information to be specified. Multiple cn and givenName values can specify different forms of a person's name, while displayName (which can only have one value, and cannot be used multiple times in the same record) ensures that the applications will consistently display the same name.

Common Names

The cn field is used by many different object classes in the directory, many of which do not describe persons. For this reason, a cn does not always contain the full name of a person. Groups, devices, and documents are amongst the things that may use the cn (or commonName) attribute.

In the previous examples the userPassword field, which contains the person's password, is in plain text. When this file is loaded into the directory, the value will be base-64 encoded, but it will not be *encrypted*. It is not at all secure to store clear-text passwords in the directory (and base-64 encoding does not improve the security of the password). Later in this section we will look at the ldappasswd tool, which encrypts passwords before storing them in the directory. Production directories should always store the userPassword value in encrypted form.

You may notice that in the homePostalAddress field, dollar signs ($) are used where one would normally expect to see line breaks. OpenLDAP does not automatically convert these to line breaks. But use of the dollar sign is an older way of representing line breaks without using base-64 encoding. Typically, it is only used in postal address related fields—and it is up to implementing applications to correctly interpret the dollar signs.

Both of these examples use the inetOrgPerson object class as their primary structural object class. This is because these records describe a person and use the uid attribute (and use it as part of the DN). Additionally, inetOrgPerson provides a number of attributes that are useful for modern information infrastructures; jpegPhoto, preferredLanguage, and displayName (amongst others) are all intended to be used primarily by modern computer agents rather than humans. As it is standardized and widely deployed (LDAP servers from Sun to Microsoft use it), it is the preferred object class for describing people within an organization.

Thus far we have created a base DN entry, some organizational units, and a few users. Now we will add a record describing a system account.

Adding System Records

Some of the entries in our tree—entries that we will need—do not describe users, and so do not belong in the Users organizational unit (OU). Instead, we will put such special records in the System OU. Likewise, the entities we are describing are not people, and so using the person, organizationalPerson, and inetOrgPerson object classes is not appropriate.

In this section we will create a new record for an account that will assist users in logging in. The function of the account will be described in detail in Chapter 4, but this account will need to be able to authenticate to the directory server and perform operations. But, again, this account is not for a specific person, and so it will not have personal data (like a surname or a given name).

Here's what our new system account, called authenticate, looks like:

```
# Special Account for Authentication:
dn: uid=authenticate,ou=System,dc=example,dc=com
uid: authenticate
ou: System
description: Special account for authenticating users
userPassword: secret
objectClass: account
objectClass: simpleSecurityObject
```

This record has two object classes: `account` and `simpleSecurityObject`. The first one, `account`, is the structural object class. An `account` object, which is defined in the Cosine schema (`cosine.schema`), describes an account used to access computers or networks. Let's have a look at the two object classes:

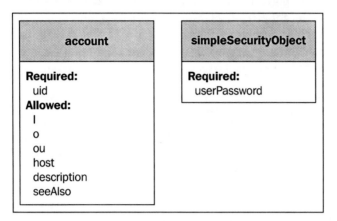

Our account, whose DN is `uid=authenticate,ou=System,dc=example,dc=com`, uses the `uid` attribute required by the `account` object class, as well as the `ou` and `description` fields from account. But the account object class does not have a field for storing a password. For that reason we need to add to the record the auxiliary object class `simpleSecurityObject`, which has one attribute: the required attribute `userPassword`.

> Auxiliary object classes can be combined with any other structural or auxiliary object classes. While using multiple structural object classes in one record requires that the object classes be related (for example as `organizationalPerson` is a child of `person`), auxiliary object classes do not need to be related to the object classes with which they are used. In this case `simpleSecurityObject` has no direct relation to account. See Chapter 6 for a more detailed explanation.

By adding the `simpleSecurityObject` auxiliary object class, we have now made it possible for our `account` record to have a password. Again, in our example, we have specified the password (`userPassword: secret`) in clear text. It is not safe to store unencrypted passwords in the directory. For information on encrypting LDAP passwords, see the section on `ldappasswd` later in this chapter.

Now we have created some records under two of our three organizational units: Users and System. Next, we will add a group under the Groups OU.

Adding Group Records

The last record we will add to our LDIF file is a record that describes a group of DNs. Groups provide a flexible method for collecting similar DNs by whatever criterion is needed. The DNs in a group do not have to be structurally similar—they can have completely different attributes and object classes, and can describe completely different things (such as a document and a person). Thus, it is up to the directory administrators and directory applications as to what sorts of DNs will be grouped into any particular group.

In our case, we are going to create a group to represent our directory administrators, and all of the DNs that belong to this group are DNs for users (in the Users OU, and with the inetOrgPerson structural object class).

```
# LDAP Admin Group:
dn: cn=LDAP Admins,ou=Groups,dc=example,dc=com
cn: LDAP Admins
ou: Groups
description: Users who are LDAP administrators
uniqueMember: uid=barbara,dc=example,dc=com
uniqueMember: uid=matt,dc=example,dc=com
objectClass: groupOfUniqueNames
```

Our group has the DN cn=LDAP Admins,ou=Groups,dc=example,dc=com. Note that we use the cn attribute, rather than uid, to identify the group. That is because the groupOfUniqueNames object class does not allow a uid attribute (and cn is required).

> Usually, you should use the groupOfNames object class rather than groupOfUniqueNames, because groupOfNames is the default grouping object class in OpenLDAP. We use a groupOfUniqueNames here to exhibit some of the features of LDAP group management in the later chapters.

A groupOfUniqueNames class is one of three grouping object classes defined in the core LDAP version 3 schema (core.schema). The other two are groupOfNames and organizationalRole.

These have been diplayed in the following figure:

groupOfUniqueNames	groupOfNames	organizationalRole
Required: uniqueMember cn **Allowed:** o ou owner description seeAlso businessCategory	**Required:** member cn **Allowed:** o ou owner description seeAlso businessCategory	**Required:** cn **Allowed:** roleOccupant ou st l street postOfficeBox postalCode postalAddress seeAlso description x121Address registeredAddress destinationalIndicator preferreDeliveryMethod physicalDeliveryOfficeName telexNumber teletexTerminalIdentifier telephoneNumber internationalISDNNumber facsimileTelephoneNumber

All three of these object classes are designed for collecting DNs. Each has an attribute that specifies the DN of a member of the group. In groupOfNames, the attribute is called, simply enough, member. The groupOfUniqueNames class, which does not differ in function from groupOfNames, uses uniqueMember as its membership attribute. The organizationalRole grouping class, which is intended to represent the group responsible for performing a particular role in the context of the organization, uses the roleOccupant attribute for membership.

In all three grouping object classes, the membership attribute (member, uniqueMember, or roleOccupant) can be specified multiple times, as we saw in the LDIF snippet for the LDAP Admins group.

What Kind of Group Should I Use?

How do you decide whether to use a `groupOfNames`, `groupOfUniqueNames`, or `organizationalRole`? By default, it is best to use `groupOfNames`, as it is treated as the default grouping object class by OpenLDAP. The `organizationalRole` object class is intended to be used as a way of defining what a person does within an organization. The `groupOfUniqueNames` object class was intended for a different use from `groupOfNames`, but implementation-wise, they function identically on OpenLDAP.

The `groupOfUniqueNames` and `groupOfNames` object classes both allow the `owner` attribute, which can also be used more than once (to, for example, model cases where a group has two owners). An `owner` attribute holds the DN of the record that is considered the owner of the group.

There is a fourth (but experimental) general purpose method for grouping in OpenLDAP, called **dynlist/dyngroup**. This uses a specific object class, the dynamic **groupOfURLs** grouping class, in conjunction with a special directory overlay. This method of grouping is expected to reach maturity in OpenLDAP 2.4.

In our example group, which is `groupOfUniqueNames`, we specified two `uniqueMember` attributes:

```
uniqueMember: uid=barbara,dc=example,dc=com
uniqueMember: uid=matt,dc=example,dc=com
```

Both of these DNs are members of the group. Note that SLAPD does not actively check to make sure that these DNs exist, nor does it automatically remove a DN from groups when the DN is removed from the directory.

Integrity Checking

SLAPD can be configured to do integrity checking on records using the RefInt (Referential Integrity) overlay discussed in Chapter 5. This overlay can be used to make sure that group member DNs stay synchronized with the entries in the directory information tree.

Thus, directory administrators and directory applications must be careful to perform additional verification and cleanup when working with groups. When a DN is deleted from the directory, a directory-wide search for attributes that take DN values should be performed to make sure that attributes such as `member` and `roleOccupant` (and, for that matter, `seeAlso`) do not point to the newly-deleted DN.

The Complete LDIF File

Finally, we have finished building our LDIF file. We will save it in a file named `basics.ldif`, since it contains the basic elements of our directory. Here is what it looks like:

```
# This is the root of the directory tree
dn: dc=example,dc=com
description: Example.Com, your trusted non-existent corporation.
dc: example
o: Example.Com
objectClass: top
objectClass: dcObject
objectClass: organization

# Subtree for users
dn: ou=Users,dc=example,dc=com
ou: Users
description: Example.Com Users
objectClass: organizationalUnit

# Subtree for groups
dn: ou=Groups,dc=example,dc=com
ou: Groups
description: Example.Com Groups
objectClass: organizationalUnit

# Subtree for system accounts
dn: ou=System,dc=example,dc=com
ou: System
description: Special accounts used by software applications.
objectClass: organizationalUnit

##
## USERS
##

# Matt Butcher
dn: uid=matt,ou=Users,dc=example,dc=com
ou: Users
# Name info:
uid: matt
cn: Matt Butcher
sn: Butcher
givenName: Matt
givenName: Matthew
displayName: Matt Butcher
# Work Info:
```

```
title: Systems Integrator
description: Systems Integration and IT for Example.Com
employeeType: Employee
departmentNumber: 001
employeeNumber: 001-08-98
mail: mbutcher@example.com
mail: matt@example.com
roomNumber: 301
telephoneNumber: +1 555 555 4321
mobile: +1 555 555 6789
st: Illinois
l: Chicago
street: 1234 Cicero Ave.
# Home Info:
homePhone: +1 555 555 9876
homePostalAddress: 1234 home street $ Chicago, IL $ 60699-1234
# Misc:
userPassword: secret
preferredLanguage: en-us,en-gb
# Object Classes:
objectClass: person
objectClass: organizationalPerson
objectClass: inetOrgPerson

# Barbara Jensen:
dn: uid=barbara,ou=Users,dc=example,dc=com
ou: Users
uid: barbara
sn: Jensen
cn: Barbara Jensen
givenName: Barbara
displayName: Barbara Jensen
mail: barbara@example.com
userPassword: secret
objectClass: person
objectClass: organizationalPerson
objectClass: inetOrgPerson

# LDAP Admin Group:
dn: cn=LDAP Admins,ou=Groups,dc=example,dc=com
cn: LDAP Admins
ou: Groups
description: Users who are LDAP administrators
uniqueMember: uid=barbara,dc=example,dc=com
uniqueMember: uid=matt,dc=example,dc=com
```

```
objectClass: groupOfUniqueNames

# Special Account for Authentication:
dn: uid=authenticate,ou=System,dc=example,dc=com
uid: authenticate
ou: System
description: Special account for authenticating users
userPassword: secret
objectClass: account
objectClass: simpleSecurityObject
```

In the next section, we will look at the OpenLDAP utilities, and we will use these utilities to load our LDIF file into the directory.

Using the Utilities to Prepare the Directory

So far in this chapter we have looked at the server operations, and created an LDIF file representing our initial directory information tree. In the remainder of this chapter we are going to look at two groups of tools. In this part we are going to look at the OpenLDAP utilities. In the next part we will look at the OpenLDAP clients.

Unlike the OpenLDAP clients, the utilities do not use the LDAP protocol to connect to a server and perform directory operations. Instead they work on a lower level, interacting directly with OpenLDAP directories and data files. The OpenLDAP suite includes eight utilities that perform administrative tasks. We will look at these tools as we go through the process of creating, loading, and verifying directory data.

The aim of this section is to explain the basic use of these utilities. Each utility has a handful of command-line flags that can be used to further modify the behavior of the utility. We will see some of the more useful flags, but if you want detailed information, you should consult the excellent OpenLDAP man pages.

In recent versions of OpenLDAP the utilities do not actually exist as stand-alone programs. Instead, they are all compiled into the slapd program, and symbolic links are created to point from the utility name to the slapd program. Using the ls command, we can look at the utilities to see how this is done:

```
$ ls -og /usr/local/sbin
```

This is what we get:

```
total 0
lrwxrwxrwx 1 16 2006-08-17 11:37 slapacl -> ../libexec/slapd
lrwxrwxrwx 1 16 2006-08-17 11:37 slapadd -> ../libexec/slapd
```

```
lrwxrwxrwx 1 16 2006-08-17 11:37 slapauth -> ../libexec/slapd
lrwxrwxrwx 1 16 2006-08-17 11:37 slapcat -> ../libexec/slapd
lrwxrwxrwx 1 16 2006-08-17 11:37 slapdn -> ../libexec/slapd
lrwxrwxrwx 1 16 2006-08-17 11:37 slapindex -> ../libexec/slapd
lrwxrwxrwx 1 16 2006-08-17 11:37 slappasswd -> ../libexec/slapd
lrwxrwxrwx 1 16 2006-08-17 11:37 slaptest -> ../libexec/slapd
```

All eight of the utilities are just symbolic links to the slapd program. When slapd gets executed, it checks to see what program name was used when it was executed, and then it acts like that program. For example, when slapd is called as slapadd, it acts as a program for loading data into the directory. If it is called as slaptest, it acts as a program for verifying the format of and directives in the configuration file.

As we proceed through the description of the utilities we will cover them as if they were separate programs because that is how they are treated.

Since we created an LDIF file in the last part, we will begin this section by looking at the tool that loads the LDIF file into the directory backend.

slapadd

The slapadd program is used to load directory data, formated as LDIF files, directly into OpenLDAP. It is executed from within an operating system shell (for example a command prompt or shell script).

The slapadd program does not use the LDAP protocol to connect to a running server. Instead, it works directly with the OpenLDAP backend. For that reason, when you run slapadd you must first shut down the directory server. Otherwise, you may end up with conflicts between the slapd server process and the slapadd process as they both try to exclusively manage the same databases.

When Should slapadd be Used?

There are many tools for loading records into the directory, including the OpenLDAP client ldapadd (which connects to the server over the LDAP protocol and performs one or more add operations). So, how do we figure out which program to use under any particular set of circumstances?

Well, slapadd is intended to be used to load large amounts of directory data, generally for the purpose of creating a new directory, or restoring a directory from a backup. Because it requires that the directory be taken offline, this utility is not generally a good candidate for performing routine updates. The ldapadd program (discussed in the *Clients* section later in this chapter) is a much better candidate for that sort of operation.

What Does slapadd Do?

The `slapadd` utility reads the `slapd.conf` file (and any included files), loads the appropriate backend databases, and then reads LDIF data (usually from a file). As it reads the data, it verifies that all of the records are correctly constructed (that the DNs are in a tree that the server manages, that the records use the right attributes for their object classes, that all required fields are there, that the record is formatted correctly, and so on), and then it loads the records into the appropriate backend.

Since `slapadd` does not connect over the LDAP protocol, it does not require any authentication to the directory. It does, however, require write access to the directory database files. So `slapadd` is usually run from the shell of either the user that runs the directory (often `ldap` or `slapd`) or from the root account.

Loading the LDIF File

In the previous part of this chapter we created an LDIF file containing a handful of records for our directory tree. Now we will load this LDIF file into our directory. This will take four steps:

- Stop the `slapd` server
- Test the LDIF file with `slapadd`
- Load the directory with `slapadd`
- Restart the `slapd` server

Stopping the Server

We covered the process of starting and stopping the server at the end of Chapter 2. To summarize, though, we can stop a version installed from the Ubuntu package using the `invoke-rc.d` command:

```
$ sudo invoke-rc.d slapd stop
```

With the version compiled from source (see Appendix A), this can be done by finding the `slapd` process ID and killing the process (or using the `killall` program):

```
$ sudo kill `pgrep slapd`
```

Next, we need to make sure that the LDIF file we created in the last part is correctly formatted.

Running ldapadd in Test Mode

Running in test mode before doing the actual load can greatly reduce the amount of time it takes to load a new LDIF file because it will help you catch LDIF errors before things get written to the directory. Normally `slapadd` adds records one at a time as it reads them. So if there are three records in a file, the first record will be added to the directory before the second or third records are read. If there is an error in a record later in the file, then the directory will be partially loaded, and you will either have to creatively alter the LDIF file or destroy the database and start again.

Using test mode, we can make sure that the LDIF file does not have any errors before we start loading records into the directory. This should just eliminate cases where an LDIF file is only partially imported because of bad records.

We can use the `slapadd` program to do this before we try to load the data into the directory:

```
$ sudo slapadd -v -u -c -f /etc/ldap/slapd.conf -l /tmp/basics.ldif
```

This command uses five flags:

- `-v` flag: This puts the program into "verbose" mode, where it will print out extra information about what is happening (and, if the process fails, what led to the failure). Usually it is a good idea to run `slapadd` in verbose mode, especially when loading an untested LDIF file.

- `-u` flag: This tells `slapadd` to run in test (or *dry-run*) mode. When this is enabled, `slapadd` will evaluate the file as if it were going to load the file into the directory, but it won't actually put any records in the directory.

- `-c` flag: This tells `slapadd` to keep processing the file even if it hits a bad record. Using this flag, we can run through the file once and get a list of all of the records that are not correctly formatted.

- `-f` flag: This flag, which takes as an argument the path to the server's configuration file, specifies which configuration file should be used. In most cases you can omit this, and `slapadd` will just look in the default place (usually `/etc/ldap/slapd.conf`).

- `-l` flag: This points to the LDIF file we want to load. In this case we are loading the `basics.ldif` file, which is located in the system's `/tmp` directory.

In cases where there is an error in the LDIF file, `slapadd` will print out some helpful information. For example, if we try to load an obviously broken file that looks like this:

```
# This is the root of the directory tree
dn: dc=example,dc=com
description: Example.Com, your trusted non-existent corporation.
dc: example
o: Example.Com
objectClass: top
objectClass: dcObject
```

```
objectClass: organization
```

Broken

```
# Subtree for users
dn: ou=Users,dc=example,dc=com
ou: Users
```
ferble: glarp
```
description: Example.Com Users
objectClass: organizationalUnit
```

In this file the broken lines are highlighted. When we run `slapadd`, we will get an error:

```
added: "dc=example,dc=com"
str2entry: entry -1 has no dn
slapadd: could not parse entry (line=11)
<= str2entry: str2ad(ferble): attribute type undefined
slapadd: could not parse entry (line=18)
```

Here, `slapadd` tested our first record, `dc=example,dc=com`, without problems, but then encountered a line that did not begin with a DN (on line 11). It skipped that record. On line 18 it encountered another error: the `ferble` attribute is not defined by any of the object classes in the record.

When run successfully against the LDIF file we created earlier in this chapter, the output looks like this:

```
$ sudo slapadd -v -u -c -f /etc/ldap/slapd.conf -l basics.ldif
added: "dc=example,dc=com"
added: "ou=Users,dc=example,dc=com"
added: "ou=Groups,dc=example,dc=com"
added: "ou=System,dc=example,dc=com"
added: "uid=matt,ou=Users,dc=example,dc=com"
added: "uid=barbara,ou=Users,dc=example,dc=com"
added: "cn=LDAP Admins,ou=Groups,dc=example,dc=com"
added: "uid=authenticate,ou=System,dc=example,dc=com"
```

No errors. We are ready to proceed to the third step: importing the records into the directory.

Importing the Records Using slapadd

To do the actual import of the records into the directory, we use the `slapadd` command with a subset of the flags used in the previous section. We omit the -u flag (for testing) and the -c flag (so that it doesn't continue if it encounters a bad record).

Using the -q flag

To load the directory faster, you can add the -q flag, which turns off some of the time-consuming checks slapadd performs on the data. But before using this flag, make sure you test the LDIF data first (using the method just described). Otherwise you might end up with an unusable directory.

Now, the command looks like this:

```
$ sudo slapadd -v -f /etc/ldap/slapd.conf -l basics.ldif
```

And, this is what we get as output:

```
added: "dc=example,dc=com" (00000001)
added: "ou=Users,dc=example,dc=com" (00000002)
added: "ou=Groups,dc=example,dc=com" (00000003)
added: "ou=System,dc=example,dc=com" (00000004)
added: "uid=matt,ou=Users,dc=example,dc=com" (00000005)
added: "uid=barbara,ou=Users,dc=example,dc=com" (00000006)
added: "cn=LDAP Admins,ou=Groups,dc=example,dc=com" (00000007)
added: "uid=authenticate,ou=System,dc=example,dc=com" (00000008)
```

Note that the output is just slightly different this time; at the end of each line, there is an ID number enclosed in parentheses. This ID number makes up part of the record's entryCSN attribute, which is used internally to monitor the record.

As with many LDAP servers, OpenLDAP attaches special **operational attributes** to records. In these attributes, OpenLDAP stores directory-centric information about the record. We will talk about these more when we discuss the slapcat utility.

We have just populated our directory with the eight records we created earlier in the chapter. We are now ready to start the directory.

Restarting the Directory

In Chapter 2 we discussed starting and stopping the directory. This can be done with the init script:

```
$ sudo invoke-rc.d slapd start
```

Or, if you installed according to Appendix A, slapd can be run directly:

```
$ sudo /usr/local/libexec/slapd
```

If Something Went Wrong...

It sometimes happens that midway through a `slapadd`, the program encounters an error — either in the LDIF file itself, or from some external consideration — and aborts the directory import part way through. In these cases you may need to start over. But merely re-running the `slapadd` operation will give errors like this (the error may vary depending on the backend you are using):

```
$ sudo slapadd -v -f /usr/local/etc/openldap/slapd.conf -l
    basics.ldif
=> hdb_tool_entry_put: id2entry_add failed: DB_KEYEXIST: Key/data
    pair already exists (-30996)
=> hdb_tool_entry_put: txn_aborted! DB_KEYEXIST: Key/data pair
    already exists (-30996)
slapadd: could not add entry dn="dc=example,dc=com" (line=9):
    txn_aborted! DB_KEYEXIST: Key/data pair already exists (-30996)
```

What is going on here?

What has happened is that some of the entries from the `basics.ldif` file have already been imported into the directory, but perhaps not all of them. There are various ways to attempt to work around this. You can try to prune the LDIF file down to just the records that haven't been added already. You can try to run the `slapadd` program in continuation mode (with the `-c` flag) and hope that all of the remaining records are added correctly.

But you may find that the best way of dealing with these cases is to simply destroy and rebuild the directory. While this sounds like a rather extreme measure, it has one distinct advantage over other methods: it avoids the problem of inconsistent records that can be caused with failed `slapadd` commands. Thus, it is often the best way of recovering from failed directory imports.

> Errors in the index files can also be induced by `slapadd` failures. If you decide not to destroy and recreate your directory after a failed `slapadd`, make sure you run the `slapindex` utility (covered later in this chapter) after loading new records to the directory.

Destroying and Recreating the Directory Files

In most of the OpenLDAP backends that can be loaded with `slapadd`, the backend stores data somewhere on the file system or in a relational database. After a failed `slapadd` you may find that the best way to recover is to destroy all of the data in the underlying backend, and then start over.

Currently, we are using the hdb backend (see Chapter 2). The method used here will apply equally well to other BerkeleyDB backends (bdb and ldbm in bdb mode), and can be easily adapted to cover the (deprecated) ldbm with gdbm backend.

For other sorts of backends, such as those that use relational databases like PostgreSQL, or custom backends like back-perl, you will need to examine the documentation on those backends to determine the best way of clearing the records from the directory.

For the hdb and bdb backends, the directory data files are stored on the file system. In Ubuntu, these are located at /var/lib/ldap. If you followed the directions in Appendix A, the database files are located at /usr/local/var/openldap-data/.

Here's what the contents of the /var/lib/ldap directory look like:

```
alock      __db.002    __db.005    dn2id.bdb    objectClass.bdb
cn.bdb     __db.003    DB_CONFIG   id2entry.bdb
__db.001   __db.004    DB_CONFIG.example    log.0000000001
```

Here you can see all of the directory database files (which start with __db.), the directory index files (which end with .bdb), and the BerkeleyDB transaction logs (which begin with log.). There are a few other files in this directory, such as alock and DB_CONFIG, that we don't need to delete. To delete the files, we use rm with a list of expressions that match only the files we want to delete:

```
$ sudo rm __db.* *.bdb log.*
```

This removes just the files we don't want. Now the directory should contain only a couple of files:

```
alock      DB_CONFIG    DB_CONFIG.example
```

That's all it takes to destroy the database. Now we can re-create the directory by loading the (corrected, if necessary) LDIF file with the slapadd command:

```
$ sudo slapadd -v -l basics.ldif
```

And this message is returned:

```
added: "dc=example,dc=com" (00000001)
added: "ou=Users,dc=example,dc=com" (00000002)
added: "ou=Groups,dc=example,dc=com" (00000003)
added: "ou=System,dc=example,dc=com" (00000004)
added: "uid=matt,ou=Users,dc=example,dc=com" (00000005)
added: "uid=barbara,ou=Users,dc=example,dc=com" (00000006)
added: "cn=LDAP Admins,ou=Groups,dc=example,dc=com" (00000007)
added: "uid=authenticate,ou=System,dc=example,dc=com" (00000008)
```

That is all there is to destroying and recreating a directory.

slapindex

The next utility that we will examine is `slapindex`. This utility manages the index files for OpenLDAP backends that use indexes (such as `hdb`, `bdb`, and the deprecated `ldbm`).

OpenLDAP maintains a set of index files to expedite searching for records. These are stored outside of the main directory database, and as records are added, modified, and removed from the directory, the `slapd` server modifies the index files accordingly.

But in certain circumstances, the `slapd` server may not have sufficient information to know about changes it needs to make to the index files and, in those cases, the indexes will need to be rebuilt manually.

 Like `slapadd`, `slapindex` should not be run while the server is running. Before running `slapindex`, you should stop `slapd`.

There are three common cases that require use of the `slapindex` command:

1. When a utility, usually `slapadd`, is used to add records to an *existing* database.
2. When the indexing directives in `slapd.conf` are changed, or new indexes are added (see Chapter 2 and the *Performance Tuning* section of Chapter 5).
3. On other (rare) occasions, external conditions or failed `slapadd` commands may get the directory database and the directory indexes out of sync. The main symptom of this synchronization error is that searches using `ldapsearch` will fail to return records that are known to be in the directory.

In these three cases, `slapindex` should be run:

```
$ sudo slapindex -q -f /etc/ldap/slapd.conf
```

This will rebuild all of the indexes for the first database defined in `slapd.conf` (we only have one database defined).

The `-q` flag instructs slapindex to perform some additional checking operations, which will greatly expedite the process of re-indexing. Skipping such checks is generally safe with the `slapindex` utility, though it should only be done with great care when using `slapadd`.

The `-f` flag, which takes the path to a configuration file, specifies the `slapd` configuration file. If this flag is omitted (as we have done), `slapindex` will look in the default location for the `slapd.conf` file.

If you want to monitor the progress of slapindex, you can use the -v flag to turn on verbose output.

slapcat

The slapcat program dumps the entire contents of a directory into an LDIF file. It is a convenient tool for creating a backup of the directory, and can also be useful for examining the data is in the directory.

Of course, there is a similar client application, ldapsearch, which can also dump the entire contents of the directory. How do you know when to use each? Since ldapsearch uses the LDAP protocol to contact the server, bind, and then run LDAP search operations, it incurs more overhead. slapcat, on the other hand, works directly with the backend. ldapsearch is limited by time and size limits, set both in the client configuration file, ldap.conf, and in the server's configuration in slapd.conf (see Chapter 2). The ldapsearch command is also limited by ACLs, while no ACLs are applied to slapcat.

Clearly then, for operations such as backing up the directory, slapcat ought to be used rather than ldapsearch.

As of version 2.3 of OpenLDAP, if you are using the hdb or bdb backends, you can safely run slapcat while slapd is running; there is no need to shutdown the directory server in order to make a backup copy.

The man page for slapcat in OpenLDAP incorrectly indicates that it is unsafe to run slapcat while the directory server is running. This is simply an artifact of the earlier versions of OpenLDAP (2.2 and earlier), in which slapcat could not be run while slapd was running. Note that it is still unsafe to run slapcat against an ldbm backend while slapd is running.

When we covered slapadd earlier in this chapter, we used that utility to load records in basics.ldif into the directory. Now we can use slapcat to view those records.

```
$ sudo slapcat -l basics-out.ldif
```

The -l flag, which takes a path for an argument, indicates what file the output should be written to. In this case it is writing to the file basics-out.ldif. If -l is omitted, then the LDIF data will be sent to standard output, which will usually be printed straight to your screen.

As with the other utilities, the -f flag can be used to specify the path to the SLAPD configuration file. The -a flag, which takes an LDAP filter, can be used to specify a pattern that records must match before they are dumped to output. You can use this flag to dump just a subtree. For example, we could dump only records in the Users OU with this command:

```
$ sudo slapcat -a "(entryDN:dnSubtreeMatch:=ou=Users,
                    dc=example,dc=com)"
```

This would return complete records for only the following three DNs:

- ou=Users,dc=example,dc=com

- uid=matt,ou=Users,dc=example,dc=com

- uid=barbara,ou=Users,dc=example,dc=com

Operational Attributes

Let's take a closer look at the output for just the record of the base DN:

```
$ sudo slapcat -a "(dc=example)"
dn: dc=example,dc=com
description: Example.Com, your trusted non-existent corporation.
dc: example
o: Example.Com
objectClass: top
objectClass: dcObject
objectClass: organization
structuralObjectClass: organization
entryUUID: b1a00a7c-c587-102a-9eb2-412127118751
creatorsName: cn=Manager,dc=example,dc=com
modifiersName: cn=Manager,dc=example,dc=com
createTimestamp: 20060821173908Z
modifyTimestamp: 20060821173908Z
entryCSN: 20060821173908Z#000000#00#000000
```

The highlighted attributes should look unfamiliar, as they did not exist in the original LDIF file that we created. These are internal **operational attributes** that OpenLDAP automatically maintains.

Different operational attributes play different roles in OpenLDAP, and these attributes may be useful for directory managers and LDAP-aware applications.

For example, the `creatorsName`, `modifiersName`, `createTimestamp`, and `modifyTimestamp` fields often come in useful. OpenLDAP automatically retains the following record-level information:

1. When and by whom each record was created.
2. When and by whom each record was last modified.

The `entryUUID` attribute provides a **Universally Unique Identifier (UUID)** for a record, which serves as an identifier that is more stable than DN (which can change), and is supposed to be, according to the specification in RFC 4122 (`http://rfc-editor.org/rfc/rfc4122.txt`), "an identifier unique across both space and time, with respect to the space of all UUIDs." See the `entryUUID` RFC at `http://rfc-editor.org/rfc/rfc4530.txt`.

The `entryCSN` (**Change Sequence Number**) attribute is used by the SyncRepl replication provider to determine what records need to be synchronized between LDAP servers. We will see this in more detail in Chapter 7.

Finally, the attribute `structuralObjectClass` is added. This attribute specifies which of the object classes is to be treated as the structural object class. Recall that when we created our records for Matt and Barbara, each record had three object classes: `person`, `organizationalPerson`, and `inetOrgPerson`. All three are structural object classes, and all three are related (`inetOrgPerson` is a child of `organizationalPerson`, which in turn is a child of `person`). But each record can have only one structural object class. As I noted above, the one farthest down the tree becomes the structural object class, and the others are treated, essentially, as abstract object classes. We can see this if we use `slapcat` to dump Barbara's record:

```
$ sudo slapcat -a '(uid=barbara)'
dn: uid=barbara,ou=Users,dc=example,dc=com
ou: Users
uid: barbara
sn: Jensen
cn: Barbara Jensen
givenName: Barbara
displayName: Barbara Jensen
mail: barbara@example.com
userPassword:: e1BMQUlOfXNlY3JldA==
objectClass: person
objectClass: organizationalPerson
objectClass: inetOrgPerson
structuralObjectClass: inetOrgPerson
entryUUID: b1ae9916-c587-102a-9eb7-412127118751
creatorsName: cn=Manager,dc=example,dc=com
```

```
modifiersName: cn=Manager,dc=example,dc=com
createTimestamp: 20060821173908Z
modifyTimestamp: 20060821173908Z
entryCSN: 20060821173908Z#000005#00#000000
```

Note that the `structuralObjectClass` attribute has the value `inetOrgPerson`.

At this point we've examined the `slapcat` tool, as well as the `slapindex` and `slapadd` tools. These three are the most often used utilities. But there are a few others that can come in handy in certain circumstances. So next, we will look at `slapacl`.

slapacl

Writing ACLs can be frustrating and difficult to test. In order to ease the process of testing the efficacy of ACLs in the `slapd.conf` file, the OpenLDAP suite includes a tool for testing ACLs directly. We will make greater use of this tool when we test ACLs in Chapter 4, but we will see an introduction to the utility here.

In Chapter 2, we added the following ACL to `slapd.conf`:

```
access to attrs=userPassword
        by anonymous auth
        by self write
        by * none
```

This ACL specifies that for any given record in the directory, if it has `userPassword`, the following rules should be applied to requests for access to that attribute:

- The `anonymous` user should be able to authenticate using `userPassword`.
- It should allow a DN the permissions to modify (and read) its own password.
- It should deny all other DNs all access to this record's `userPassword`.

That means that `uid=matt,ou=Users,dc=example,dc=com` should not be able to write a new `userPassword` value for `uid=barbara,ou=Users,dc=example,dc=com`. We can use the `slapacl` utility to test this:

```
$ sudo slapacl -v -D "uid=matt,ou=Users,dc=example,dc=com" -b
    "uid=barbara,ou=Users,dc=example,dc=com" "userPassword/write"
```

This command might look daunting at first, but it is actually very simple. Let's look at the arguments in sequence:

- The `-v` flag tuns on verbose output.
- The `-D` flag is used to tell `slapacl` which DN is trying to access the directory. In this case, we said: `-D "uid=matt,ou=Users,dc=example,dc=com"`. That is, `slapacl` is testing to see if the DN for Matt can get access.

- The -b flag indicates which record we want the given DN to try to access. In this case it is Barbara's DN, since we want to test if Matt can write Barbara's password: -b "uid=barbara,ou=Users,dc=example,dc=com".

- Finally, the last argument specifies what attribute we want to access, and what sort of privilege we are requesting. In this case, we want the userPassword attribute, and we want to see if Matt has write access to it ("userPassword/write").

So, in the end, we are testing to see if Matt's DN can write a new userPassword for Barbara's record. Here is the result of the slapacl command:

```
authcDN: "uid=matt,ou=users,dc=example,dc=com"
write access to userPassword: DENIED
```

That's the result we would expect. Because of this ACL, Matt cannot write to Barbara's userPassword attribute.

slapauth

The slapauth tool is used to test SASL authentication to the directory. When an application attempts to bind using SASL, instead of specifying a complete DN (like uid=matt,ou=Users,dc=example,dc=com), the application passes in a user ID (u: matt) along with a few other bits of information, such as a realm identifier and an authentication mechanism.

We will cover SASL authentication in Chapter 4. If you do not already have experience with SASL you may want to read on, and come back to this section after reading Chapter 4.

OpenLDAP can then take that information and use a regular expression to guess what DN that user belongs to. But it can be difficult to figure out what the regular expressions will look like. The slapauth tool is useful in testing what one particular SASL request will look like when OpenLDAP receives it.

For example, we could add the following SASL configuration directives to our slapd.conf file:

```
authz-policy from
authz-regexp
  "^uid=([^,]+).*,cn=auth$"
  "uid=$1,ou=Users,dc=example,dc=com"
```

The regular expression in `authz-regexp` should convert from a SASL authzID format to an LDAP DN:

```
$ sudo slapauth -U "matt" -X "u: matt"
ID: <matt>
authcDN: <uid=matt,ou=users,dc=example,dc=com>
authzDN: <uid=matt,ou=users,dc=example,dc=com>
authorization OK
```

The first parameter, `-U matt`, sends a test request with the SASL authcID of `matt`. The `-X "u: matt"` parameter sends a test request with the authzID `u: matt`. These should then output a correctly formatted DN, according the the regular expression in `authz-regexp`.

We will use `slapauth` more in Chapter 4 when we set up SASL authentication.

slapdn

The **slapdn** tool is used to test whether a given DN is valid for this directory server. Specifically, it tests a DN against the defined schemas to make sure that the DN is valid.

Here are a few examples of `slapdn` in action:

```
$ sudo slapdn 'cn=Foo,dc=example,dc=com'
DN: <cn=Foo,dc=example,dc=com> check succeeded
normalized: <cn=foo,dc=example,dc=com>
pretty: <cn=Foo,dc=example,dc=com>

$ sudo slapdn 'ou=New Unit,dc=example,dc=com'
DN: <ou=New Unit,dc=example,dc=com> check succeeded
normalized: <ou=new unit,dc=example,dc=com>
pretty: <ou=New Unit,dc=example,dc=com>
```

In these two examples, the DNs checked out. `slapdn` tested the DNs, and then printed out the normalized version (all lowercase, extra spaces removed) and the pretty (originally formated) version.

Here's an example of a failure:

```
$ sudo slapdn 'fakeAttr=test,dc=example,dc=com'
DN: <fakeAttr=test,dc=example,dc=com> check failed 21
    (Invalid syntax)
```

In this case no schema was found that had the attribute `fakeAttr`. Here's another failed case:

```
$ sudo slapdn 'documentSeries=Series 18,dc=example,dc=com'
DN: <documentSeries=Series 18,dc=example,dc=com> check failed 21
    (Invalid syntax)
```

While `documentSeries` is defined in a schema it is an object class, not an attribute, and object class names cannot be used in constructing DNs.

The usefulness of the `slapdn` program is limited to only rare cases where you need to test a DN against a directory without being able to look at the `slapd.conf` file to find out what schemas are loaded (or, alternately, search the schemas using the `ldapsearch` program).

slappasswd

The `slappasswd` utility is a tool for encrypting passwords according to schemes supported by OpenLDAP, such as the one described in RFC 2307 (`http://rfc-editor.org/rfc/rfc2307.txt`).

Storing and Using Passwords in OpenLDAP

When we created our basic LDIF file, we used the `userPassword` attribute for storing passwords. For example, our authentication account record looked like this:

```
# Special Account for Authentication:
dn: uid=authenticate,ou=System,dc=example,dc=com
uid: authenticate
ou: System
description: Special account for authenticating users
userPassword: secret
objectClass: account
objectClass: simpleSecurityObject
```

The `userPassword` field has the password in plain text. When the value is loaded into the directory `userPassword` is encoded with base-64, and looks like this:

```
userPassword:: c2VjcmV0
```

But this is not encrypted—just encoded in an easily reversible way. While it might prevent the directory administrator from accidentally seeing the user's password, base-64 encoding will do nothing to prevent an attacker from figuring out the password.

Using the Python scripting language, you can easily encode and decode strings with the built-in `base64.b64encode()` and `base64.b64decode()` functions.

But OpenLDAP does not require you to store passwords in unencrypted text. In fact, it is best if you do not. OpenLDAP supports a number of one-way hashing algorithms that can be used to store the passwords in a way in which they cannot be decrypted.

The `slappasswd` program provides the tools to create a hashed value of a password. That hashed value can then be used in the `userPassword` field of an LDIF file.

OpenLDAP supports five different password hashing schemes: Crypt (`CRYPT`), Message Digest 5 (`MD5`), salted MD5 (`SMD5`), Secure Hashing Algorithm, the SHA-1 version (`SHA`), and Salted SHA (`SSHA`). By default, OpenLDAP uses the most secure of the available hashing algorithms: `SSHA`.

Passwords are stored in the `userPassword` field in a format according to section 5.3 of RFC 2307 (`http://rfc-editor.org/rfc/rfc2307.txt`). An encrypted password looks like this:

```
{SSHA}71xEB2E59cuoPEQLErY44bYMHwCCgbtR
```

At the beginning of the password, the section in curly braces (`{}`) indicates which of the five password schemes was used. In this case it is the default SSHA algorithm. The remainder of the field is the digested hash of the password.

While the hashed password cannot be decrypted, when a user tries to bind to the server, OpenLDAP takes the password the user supplies and encrypts it using the same algorithm as the value (and same salt) of the value of `userPassword`. If the two hashed passwords match, then OpenLDAP logs the user on. If the two do not match, OpenLDAP responds with an error message indicating that authentication failed.

Generating a Password with slappasswd

Armed with this basic understanding of how passwords are used and stored, we can now look at the `slappasswd` program. This program can be used to encrypt a password and format it for insertion into an LDIF file. The command can be called with no arguments:

```
$ slappasswd
New password:
Re-enter new password:
{SSHA}71xEB2E59cuoPEQLErY44bYMHwCCgbtR
```

In this case, since no parameters were specified on the command line, `slappasswd` prompts for a password, and then prompts for verification of the password. Then, it prints out the encrypted value of the password. We can use this value in an LDIF record:

```
dn: uid=nicholas,ou=Users,dc=example,dc=com
cn: Nicholas Malebranche
sn: Malebranche
uid: nicholas
ou: Users
userPassword: {SSHA}71xEB2E59cuoPEQLErY44bYMHwCCgbtR
objectClass: person
objectClass: organizationalPerson
objectClass: inetOrgPerson
```

In some cases, typing and retyping passwords may be too tedious, and a faster method of encrypting a number of passwords is preferred. You can either use the -T flag to point to a file containing a list of clear-text passwords to be hashed, or you can specify the password on the command line with the -s flag:

```
$ for i in  foo bar baz ; do slappasswd -s $i; done
{SSHA}p3zm8Sq/jgAMxYkniwnu+ym954qjIRiG
{SSHA}Fklv7m0n0wIw8sLQOe2IxDRsexZegzUT
{SSHA}FOLOLnR0fgmw7jP8p1WRQEJXoX3fJsyG
```

In this shell command, each of the three clear-text passwords, `foo`, `bar`, and `baz`, are encrypted by `slappasswd`.

> On a multi-user system, other users may have access to your command history, and thus would be able to see these passwords in cleartext. Caution should be used when specifying passwords (or other sensitive information) on the command line.

By using the -h flag, you can specify which hashing algorithm `slappasswd` should use:

```
$ slappasswd -h {MD5} -s test
{MD5}CY9rzUYh03PK3k6DJie09g==
$ slappasswd -h {SMD5} -s test
{SMD5}vWw5aAcoIbJ1PS9BMnp/KF5XS5g=
$ slappasswd -h {SHA} -s test
{SHA}qUqP5cyxm6YcTAhz05Hph5gvu9M=
```

In the above commands, the same password, `test`, is encrypted using three different hashing schemes.

Next we will turn to the last OpenLDAP utility — `slaptest`.

slaptest

The `slaptest` utility is used for checking the format and directives used in the `slapd.conf` file (and any files included by `slapd.conf`).

Running `slaptest` is simple:

```
$ slaptest -v -f /etc/ldap/slapd.conf
```

The `-v` flag turns on verbose output, and the `-f` flag, which takes one argument, specifies which configuration file to check. If `-f` is omitted, then the default `slapd.conf` file (usually `/etc/ldap/slapd.conf`) is checked.

As noted in the previous chapter, the version of `slaptest` provided by Ubuntu Linux does not print warnings if a directive in `slapd` is unknown. This is non-standard behavior. Most of the time OpenLDAP is compiled with such warnings enabled.

If the configuration file is correctly formatted and the directives are all valid and operational, then `slaptest` will print out a basic success message:

```
config file testing succeeded
```

If anything goes wrong however, `slaptest` will print out diagnostic information. For example, if I add an include directive to `slapd.conf` that points to a file that does not exist, `slaptest` will print an error:

```
$ sudo slaptest
could not stat config file "/non/existent/file": No such file or
    directory (2)
slaptest: bad configuration file!
```

This output should be helpful for tracking down the problem in the configuration files. In this case it was caused by a line that looks like this:

```
include /non/existent/file
```

This is the last of the OpenLDAP utilities. Now we will turn to the client applications that are included with the OpenLDAP suite.

Performing Directory Operations Using the Clients

There are a host of OpenLDAP clients, all stored at /usr/bin (or /usr/local/bin if you compiled according to Appendix A). The OpenLDAP clients communicate over the LDAP protocol. They are all standards-compliant, and follow the LDAPv3 protocol (which was last updated in June 2006).

While some of the clients provide the basic standardized LDAP operations, such as search, add, and delete, others implement one or more of the LDAP extensions. But since the suite of tools does follow the standards, these tools should work against any standards-compliant LDAP directory server.

In this part of the chapter we will take a brief look at each of the OpenLDAP clients and see how they can be used to interact with an LDAP server. We do not have the space to cover all of the details of each client, so we will focus on the most useful and common features of each client. The OpenLDAP man pages (which are installed with OpenLDAP) are detailed and informative, and they provide a good source of further information for these clients.

 Most of the utilities in the last part required that the SLAPD server must not not be running. All of the tools in this section, however, connect to a SLAPD server. So make sure your server is running before trying the examples in this part.

Common Command-Line Flags

All of the OpenLDAP clients are command-line applications that use UNIX-style flags to pass parameters to the program. For the sake of continuity common flags (like -D, -b, and -H) are used consistently across all of the clients.

In Chapter 2 we configured our directory server to handle basic directory operations. However, we did not configure it to use SASL authentication (which is covered in Chapter 4). To authenticate to the server we will be using what is called **simple binding**. In simple binding the client authenticates by sending a full DN and password to the server.

The clients require different command-line flags depending on whether they do a simple bind or a **SASL bind**. Now we will see those necessary for simple binding. Those flags needed for SASL binding are covered in Chapter 4.

Common Flags

There are command-line flags for the simple binding process. Some of the common flags are as follows:

- -D: The -D flag is used to specify the full DN of the user who will bind to the directory server (this is used for simple binding).

- -W, -w, -y: Each of these flags indicates a different source for the password. Let's see them one by one:
    - ◦ The -W flag indicates that the user should be interactively prompted to enter a password.
    - ◦ The -w flag takes the password string for a value. We can use it to specify the password on the command line.
    - ◦ The -y flag takes a file name as an argument. It will use the contents of the file as a password. These flags are mutually exclusive—you can only use one of these per command.

> The -y flag uses the entire contents of a file for the password. This means that if there is a line break in the file, it will be treated like part of the password. To create a password file, you can use the echo command with the -n flag: $ echo -n "secret" > my_pw.

- -x: The -x flag specifies that the client will use a simple bind. If this is not specified, the client will try a SASL bind.

- -H, -h: These two flags provide different ways of specifying which host to connect to. -H takes an LDAP URL (-H 'ldap://example.com:389'). -h simply takes the host name (-h example.com), and can be used with -p to specify a port. Unless you do not have a choice, use -H. The -h flag is provided only for backward compatibility, and may disappear in future versions.

- -Z: This flag is used to indicate that the client should issue a **Start TLS** command to the server, so that traffic is encrypted according to the TLS standard. But if TLS negotiation fails, the client will still continue to operate. Using two Z's (-ZZ) will make it mandatory that the traffic be encrypted. If negotiation fails, then the client will disconnect. TLS is covered in more detail in the next chapter.

- -b: This is used to specify a base DN (-b 'dc=example,dc=com').

- -f: The -f flag takes a filename as a parameter. The client will then read the contents of the file and build requests based on the contents of the file.

- -v: This flag will turn on verbose output. It is useful when troubleshooting.

These are the common flags used by the clients in the OpenLDAP suite. But these represent only a subset of the flags used by each client, as each client implements the flags needed to accomplish its task.

Setting Defaults in ldap.conf

In Chapter 2, in the section entitled *Configuring the LDAP Clients*, we looked at the ldap.conf file. In that file, we set some useful defaults. In particular we set these three:

```
URI ldap://localhost
BASE dc=example,dc=com
BINDDN cn=Manager,dc=example,dc=com
```

If you omit host settings (-H, -h), then the value of URI will be used. If the client needs a base DN, and none is set with the -b flag, then the value of BASE is used. Likewise, if the client uses simple binding (with -x), and doesn't specify a DN with -D, then the value of BINDDN will be used.

Since we have an ldap.conf file created already, many of the examples will omit the -H and -b flags.

While ldap.conf is shared by all clients, you can create a user-specific LDAP configuration file in your home directory. The LDAP clients will look for user-specific configuration files named ldaprc and .ldaprc in your home directory ($HOME).

Now we are ready to look at the client commands.

ldapsearch

The first client we will look at is also the most often used tool: ldapsearch. As the name suggests, this is a tool for searching the directory information tree.

The ldapsearch client connects to the server, authenticates a user, and then (as that user) runs one or more **search operations**, returning the results in LDIF format. When it is done performing searches, it closes the connection and exits. Since ldapsearch is a network client it can be used to search both local directories or a remote directory server.

A Simple Search

Let's take a look at a simple search command. In this command we will log in as the directory manager and request the record for the entry with the user ID *barbara*:

```
$ ldapsearch -x -W -D 'cn=Manager,dc=example,dc=com' -b \
  'ou=Users,dc=example,dc=com' '(uid=barbara)'
```

Here is the result:

```
Enter LDAP Password:
# extended LDIF
#
# LDAPv3
# base <ou=Users,dc=example,dc=com> with scope subtree
# filter: (uid=barbara)
# requesting: ALL
#

# barbara, Users, example.com
dn: uid=barbara,ou=Users,dc=example,dc=com
ou: Users
uid: barbara
sn: Jensen
cn: Barbara Jensen
givenName: Barbara
displayName: Barbara Jensen
mail: barbara@example.com
userPassword:: c2VjcmV0
objectClass: person
objectClass: organizationalPerson
objectClass: inetOrgPerson

# search result
search: 2
result: 0 Success

# numResponses: 2
# numEntries: 1
```

In this example we ran the ldapsearch command with four flags: -x, -W, -D, and -b. For a description of these flags see the *Common Command-Line Flags* section. In a nutshell though, -x, -W, and -D are all parameters used for authenticating to the directory. They instruct the client to bind to the directory with simple authentication (-x) as the DN specified by -D (the directory manager in this case), then prompt the user to enter a password interactively (-W).

The -b flag sets the base DN for the search. This is set to ou=Users,dc=example, dc=com. Given this, ldapsearch will start searching in the Users OU.

If we had omitted the -b flag, the value of BASE in `ldap.conf` would have been used, which would have set the base DN to `dc=example,dc=com`.

After all of the command-line flags and their arguments, we specified an LDAP filter:

```
(uid=barbara)
```

This is the filter that the server will use for searching. We covered search filters in more detail earlier in this chapter, in the section entitled *The Search Operation*. In this case though, the search filter is straightforward: it matches only records that have the attribute named `uid` with the attribute value of `barbara`.

 Many attributes have more than one name (these are properly called **attribute descriptions**). For example, the attribute that labels user IDs has the attribute descriptions `uid` and `userID`. In the case above, a search for `(uid=barbara)` will also match directory entries with and attribute of the form `userID: barbara`.

When this command is run, it will first prompt the user to enter a password (because of the `-W` flag), and then connect to the server and attempt to bind as the specified DN (`cn=Manager,dc=example,dc=com`). Then, if the bind is successful, it will request all records that match the filter, `(uid=barbara)`. As the example illustrates, the server will return the entire record of the user, or as much of it as the ACLs allow, in the case of a non-manager user.

The results are returned in LDIF format, with comments sprinkled throughout. The first set of comments provides basic information about the search:

```
# extended LDIF
#
# LDAPv3
# base <ou=Users,dc=example,dc=com> with scope subtree
# filter: (userID=barbara)
# requesting: ALL
#
```

The first line indicates that this record is in extended LDIF format. This is LDIF version 1.0, plus some comments. Beneath that, we get a summary of the search, including the following:

- Version of LDAP used (v3)
- What the base DN is (`ou=Users,dc=example,dc=com`).

- What type of search will be performed. In this case, it is a **subtree search**, which means the server will look in all records beneath the base DN.
- What the operating search filter is (`(userid=barbara)`).
- What attributes the client wants returned. `ALL` indicates that the client wants all available attributes returned.

The central part of the file contains the full record for Barbara. Beneath the record is a brief summary of the results:

```
search: 2
result: 0 Success

# numResponses: 2
# numEntries: 1
```

The first line, `search`, indicates that we performed two search operations (one for binding and one to execute the filtered search).

The second, `result`, inidcates the result code that the server sent back. `0 Success` indicates that our search ran without encountering any errors.

The extended (and thus commented) results add some additional information. `numResponses` indicates that the server sent two responses back to the client (one for the bind, one for the search). And `numEntries` indicates how many entries were returned by the search. In this case there was only one — Barbara's record.

Restricting Returned Fields

Sometimes we don't want to get a DN's entire record back. Instead, we just want a couple of attributes. This can be accomplished by specifying a list of attributes at the end of the command:

```
$ ldapsearch -x -w secret -D 'cn=Manager,dc=example,dc=com' -b \
        'ou=Users,dc=example,dc=com' -LLL '(userID=matt)' mail cn
```

Here is the result:

```
dn: uid=matt,ou=Users,dc=example,dc=com
cn: Matt Butcher
mail: mbutcher@example.com
mail: matt@example.com
```

Note that in this example we used the `-w secret` flag to specify the password on the command line. We also used the `-LLL` flag to suppress all of the extraneous comments printed in the LDIF output.

Specifying the password on the command line can be a security risk. Other users on the system may be able to access this information through command-line histories (like the Bash shell's history feature) and operating system constructs (like the /proc file system in Linux).

In addition to the filter, (userID=matt), I also added a list of attributes that I wanted returned: cn and mail. The returned record contained four lines: the dn, the two mail attributes, and the cn attribute. The DN is always returned.

Requesting Operational Attributes

You may have noticed that the record returned for Barbara by ldapsearch is quite a bit different than the record returned by slapcat.

We covered slapcat in the part of this chapter entitled *Using the Utilities to Prepare the Directory*.

Let's compare the two. First, here's the ldapsearch output:

```
$ ldapsearch -x -w secret -D 'cn=Manager,dc=example,dc=com' -b
'ou=Users,dc=example,dc=com' -LLL '(userID=barbara)'
dn: uid=barbara,ou=Users,dc=example,dc=com
ou: Users
uid: barbara
sn: Jensen
cn: Barbara Jensen
givenName: Barbara
displayName: Barbara Jensen
mail: barbara@example.com
userPassword:: c2VjcmV0
objectClass: person
objectClass: organizationalPerson
objectClass: inetOrgPerson
```

Now, here's the slapcat output:

```
$ sudo slapcat -a '(uid=barbara)'
dn: uid=barbara,ou=Users,dc=example,dc=com
ou: Users
uid: barbara
sn: Jensen
cn: Barbara Jensen
givenName: Barbara
```

```
displayName: Barbara Jensen
mail: barbara@example.com
userPassword:: c2VjcmV0
objectClass: person
objectClass: organizationalPerson
objectClass: inetOrgPerson
structuralObjectClass: inetOrgPerson
entryUUID: bec561c4-c5b0-102a-81c0-81bc30f92d57
creatorsName: cn=Manager,dc=example,dc=com
modifiersName: cn=Manager,dc=example,dc=com
createTimestamp: 20060821223300Z
modifyTimestamp: 20060821223300Z
entryCSN: 20060821223300Z#000005#00#000000
```

The output of `slapcat` has a host of additional attributes—namely the special operational attributes that the directory maintains internally. We can retrieve the operational attributes with `ldapsearch` either by specifying them by name along with the list of desired attributes, or by using the special plus sign (+) attribute list specifier at the end of the `ldapsearch` command:

```
$ ldapsearch -x -w secret -D 'cn=Manager,dc=example,dc=com' -b
    'ou=Users,dc=example,dc=com' -LLL '(userID=barbara)' +
```

And, this is what we get:

```
dn: uid=barbara,ou=Users,dc=example,dc=com
structuralObjectClass: inetOrgPerson
entryUUID: bec561c4-c5b0-102a-81c0-81bc30f92d57
creatorsName: cn=Manager,dc=example,dc=com
modifiersName: cn=Manager,dc=example,dc=com
createTimestamp: 20060821223300Z
modifyTimestamp: 20060821223300Z
entryCSN: 20060821223300Z#000005#00#000000
entryDN: uid=barbara,ou=Users,dc=example,dc=com
subschemaSubentry: cn=Subschema
hasSubordinates: FALSE
```

Specifying the + list does not return all attributes—only the operational attributes. To get all of the regular attributes and all of the operational attributes, you will need both the + specifier and the * (asterisk) specifier. The * specifier indicates that we want all of the standard attributes. This is the output:

```
$ ldapsearch -x -w secret -D 'cn=Manager,dc=example,dc=com' -b
    'ou=Users,dc=example,dc=com' -LLL '(userID=barbara)' '*' +
dn: uid=barbara,ou=Users,dc=example,dc=com
ou: Users
```

```
uid: barbara
sn: Jensen
cn: Barbara Jensen
givenName: Barbara
displayName: Barbara Jensen
mail: barbara@example.com
userPassword:: c2VjcmV0
objectClass: person
objectClass: organizationalPerson
objectClass: inetOrgPerson
structuralObjectClass: inetOrgPerson
entryUUID: bec561c4-c5b0-102a-81c0-81bc30f92d57
creatorsName: cn=Manager,dc=example,dc=com
modifiersName: cn=Manager,dc=example,dc=com
createTimestamp: 20060821223300Z
modifyTimestamp: 20060821223300Z
entryCSN: 20060821223300Z#000005#00#000000
entryDN: uid=barbara,ou=Users,dc=example,dc=com
subschemaSubentry: cn=Subschema
hasSubordinates: FALSE
```

Now we have the complete list of attributes. Using this combination of arguments, we can generate LDIF files suitable for making backups (assuming the ACLs are not preventing access to something). While `slapcat` will outperform `ldapsearch` for this task, the fact that `ldapsearch` can run remotely over the network is attractive in many cases.

> Note that in the given record, `ldapsearch` has returned three operational attributes that do not show up with `slapcat`: `entryDN`, `subschemaSubentry`, and `hasSubordinates`. These values are generated dynamically at runtime and do not exist in the LDAP backend. For that reason they are not exported with `slapcat`. Since they are generated dynamically, they are not useful values to back up.

It is also possible to run multiple queries in sequence using `ldapsearch`. This is done by using an external file to store filter information for multiple searches.

Searching Using a File

The `ldapsearch` client can use a file to build and execute multiple queries. Let's say we have a plain text list of user IDs, and we want to get the last name for each user ID. The file, `userIDs.txt`, looks like this:

```
matt
barbara
```

We can use `ldapsearch` to dynamically build a filter and run a search for each user's surname. To do this, we use the `-f` flag, and point to the `userIDs.txt` file, and then we build a special filter. Here is the command line to be executed:

```
$ ldapsearch -x -D 'cn=Manager,dc=example,dc=com' -b \
    'ou=Users,dc=example,dc=com' -w secret -f userIDs.txt '(uid=%s)' sn
```

Most of this should look familiar, by now. But notice the filter: `'(uid=%s)'`. This filter uses the special `%s` placeholder to indicate where the values from the file ought to be placed. As `ldapsearch` runs, it will read through the `userIDs.txt` file line by line, and with each line, it will execute a search, substituting the value of the line for `%s` in the filter. The results look like this:

```
# extended LDIF
#
# LDAPv3
# base <ou=Users,dc=example,dc=com> with scope subtree
# filter pattern: (uid=%s)
# requesting: sn
#

#
# filter: (uid=matt)
#
# matt, Users, example.com
dn: uid=matt,ou=Users,dc=example,dc=com
sn: Butcher

# search result
search: 2
result: 0 Success

# numResponses: 2
# numEntries: 1

#
# filter: (uid=barbara)
#
# barbara, Users, example.com
dn: uid=barbara,ou=Users,dc=example,dc=com
sn: Jensen

# search result
search: 3
result: 0 Success

# numResponses: 2
# numEntries: 1
```

In this example the ldapsearch client actually ran two different search operations. It first expanded (uid=%s) to (uid=matt) and ran a search; then, it expanded (uid=%s) to (uid=barbara), and ran another search. In each case, it returned only the dn (which is always returned for a match) and the requested sn attribute.

You can also create filters in a file, and have multiple search filters run. For example, we could create a file named filters.txt with the following lines:

```
&(ou=System)(objectClass=account)
&(uid=b*)(ou=Users)
```

Since each line will be inserted into a filter, we do not need the outer set of parentheses. Now we can use these lines to dynamically build filters with ldapsearch:

```
$ ldapsearch -x -D 'cn=Manager,dc=example,dc=com' -b \
    'dc=example,dc=com' -w secret -f filters.txt '(%s)' cn description
```

We will get this output:

```
# extended LDIF
#
# LDAPv3
# base <dc=example,dc=com> with scope subtree
# filter pattern: (%s)
# requesting: cn description
#

#
# filter: (&(ou=System)(objectClass=account))
#
# authenticate, System, example.com
dn: uid=authenticate,ou=System,dc=example,dc=com
description: Special account for authenticating users

# search result
search: 2
result: 0 Success

# numResponses: 2
# numEntries: 1

#
# filter: (&(uid=b*)(ou=Users))
#
# barbara, Users, example.com
dn: uid=barbara,ou=Users,dc=example,dc=com
cn: Barbara Jensen
```

```
# search result
search: 3
result: 0 Success

# numResponses: 2
# numEntries: 1
```

In this case the filter (%s) was expanded in the first case to (&(ou=System)(objectC lass=account)), and in the second case to (&(uid=b*)(ou=Users)).

Using techniques like this it becomes possible to execute a number of complex searches with one command.

We will continue using the ldapsearch client throughout this book. Now that we have a basic idea as to how it works, we will move on to the next client in the OpenLDAP suite.

ldapadd

This is a command-line program used for adding new entries to an LDAP directory. The ldapadd command is not actually a stand-alone client. It is just a link to the ldapmodify program. When ldapmodify sees that it has been called as ldapadd, it will assume that it should request that the server perform an **add operation**, instead of requesting a modify operation.

In the most simple case, ldapadd can be used to enter a new record from the command line:

```
$ ldapadd -x -W -D 'cn=Manager,dc=example,dc=com'
Enter LDAP Password:
```

Once we have been successfully authenticated, the cursor will move to the next line and wait for the input. We can directly enter a record. As soon as we hit *Enter* twice (creating a blank line, which indicates the end of a record), ldapadd will send the record to the server:

```
dn: uid=adam,ou=Users,dc=example,dc=com
cn: Adam Smith
sn: Smith
uid: adam
ou: Users
objectClass: person
objectClass: organizationalPerson
objectClass: inetOrgPerson

adding new entry "uid=adam,ou=Users,dc=example,dc=com"
```

The highlighted portion is the text that we entered. It specifies one entire record (a record for a user named Adam Smith).

After we pressed the return key twice, inserting a blank line, the record was sent to the server. The client indicated that it was adding the record: `adding new entry "u id=adam,ou=Users,dc=example,dc=com"`. No error message followed. This means that the add was successful.

Once a record is added the cursor will move to a blank line, waiting for the `dn` attribute of the next record.

```
dn: cn=Foo,dc=example,dc=com
farble: gork
objectClass: account

adding new entry "cn=Foo,dc=example,dc=com"
ldap_add: Undefined attribute type (17)
        additional info: farble: attribute type undefined
```

In this example the record that we entered (again, highlighted) contained an undefined attribute, and the server balked with the same error message. In cases where the server sends an error message, the `ldapadd` client prints the error message and exits. To re-enter the record you will have to re-run `ldapadd`.

But as long as new records are valid and the server does not report an error, `ldapadd` will continue prompting (or rather listening) for new records. When finished, use the *CTRL-C* key combination to exit the program.

Adding Records from a File

While typing a record directly into the client may be useful on occasion, in most cases it is far more convenient (and less error prone) to create the records in a plain text file, and then load them all at once with the `ldapadd` program.

As usual, the records in the text file should be formated in LDIF. Here, for example, are the contents of the file `user_records.ldif`:

```
dn: uid=david,ou=Users,dc=example,dc=com
cn: David Hume
sn: Hume
uid: david
ou: Users
objectClass: person
objectClass: organizationalPerson
objectClass: inetOrgPerson

dn: uid=immanuel,ou=Users,dc=example,dc=com
```

```
cn: Immanuel Kant
sn: Kant
uid: immanuel
ou: Users
objectClass: person
objectClass: organizationalPerson
objectClass: inetOrgPerson
```

We can add all of the records in a file:

```
$ ldapadd -x -w secret -D 'cn=Manager,dc=example,dc=com' -f \
    user_records.ldif
adding new entry "uid=david,ou=Users,dc=example,dc=com"

adding new entry "uid=immanuel,ou=Users,dc=example,dc=com"
```

Just as when we added records interactively, here the absence of an error message indicates that the record was successfully added.

Next we will look at modifying records that already exist in the directory.

ldapmodify

The `ldapmodify` program is used to modify an existing entry. It can add, change, and delete the attributes of a entries in the directory. It can also be used to add new entries (together with attributes for the entry).

Like `ldapadd`, `ldapmodify` can be run interactively. It can be used to add, modify, and remove records.

Adding a Record with ldapmodify

The syntax for adding a record is almost identical in `ldapmodify` to that of `ldapadd`:

```
$ ldapmodify -w secret -x -D 'cn=Manager,dc=example,dc=com'
```

Here is the result:

```
dn: uid=nicholas,ou=Users,dc=example,dc=com
changetype: add
cn: Nicholas Malebranche
sn: Malebranche
uid: nicholas
ou: Users
objectClass: person
objectClass: organizationalPerson
objectClass: inetOrgPerson

adding new entry "uid=nicholas,ou=Users,dc=example,dc=com"
```

The only difference is the addition of the `changetype` instruction after the `dn`. This tells `ldapmodify` what sort of LDAP operation should be performed on this record.

 The `changetype` instruction is not an attribute, though it looks like one. It is not part of the record, but rather an instruction (in LDIF format) to tell the server what operation it should use.

There are four possible values for `changetype`:

- `add`
- `modify`
- `modrdn`
- `delete`

Each of these corresponds to an LDAP operation. The `add` change-type is used to add a new record (essentially performing the same add operation as `ldapadd`). The `modify` change-type takes an existing record and modifies it in some way (for example, by adding, replacing, or removing attributes). The `modrdn` change-type changes the relative DN (or RDN) of a record. The `delete` change-type deletes the entire record from the directory server.

Modifying Existing Records

Usually it is easier to add records with `ldapadd`. Where the `ldapmodify` client really shines is in its ability to modify existing records, adding, removing, or replacing attributes within a record.

Let's add a `givenName` field to one of the records we added in the last section:

```
$ ldapmodify -x -W -D 'cn=Manager,dc=example,dc=com'
```

This gives the following output:

```
Enter LDAP Password:
dn: uid=david,ou=Users,dc=example,dc=com
changetype: modify
add: givenName
givenName: David

modifying entry "uid=david,ou=Users,dc=example,dc=com"
```

Just as with `ldapadd`, once the authentication phase has been done, `ldapmodify` waits for a DN to be given. After the `dn` attribute is specified, the `changetype` should follow.

When using a `modify` change-type, as we do here, we must also specify exactly what attributes we are going to change, and how we will change them. The modify change-type is the only type that requires this further specification. Here is the figure displaying the several change-types:

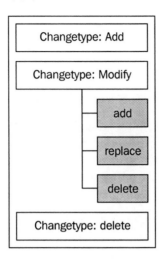

In this case, we want to add a new attribute to the the `uid=david, ou=Users, dc=example, dc=com` record. And the attribute we want to add is `givenName`. So, the line that specifies that we will add a `givenName` attribute reads `add: givenName`.

Next, we want to specify the attribute and attribute value:

```
givenName: David
```

Then, by hitting *Enter* twice, we indicate that the record is complete. Just as with `ldapadd`, `ldapmodify` indicates which record it is modifying. If the server does not return an error, `ldapmodify` will wait for another modify record.

The `add` modification type is one of three that `ldapmodify` supports. Operations can only be specified if the change-type is set to modify. The three modification types are:

- `add`: Adds new attributes to an existing record
- `replace`: Replaces existing attribute values with new attribute values
- `delete`: Removes attributes from the record

More than one of these operations can be done in a single transaction:

```
$ ldapmodify -w secret -x -D 'cn=Manager,dc=example,dc=com'
dn: uid=immanuel,ou=Users,dc=example,dc=com
changetype: modify
add: givenName
givenName: Manny
-

replace: cn
cn: Manny Kant

modifying entry "uid=immanuel,ou=Users,dc=example,dc=com"
```

In this example we first add `givenName`, and then replace the existing `cn` value with a new one. Between the two modification requests we use a dash (-) to indicate that we are still working on the same record. Remember, a blank line indicates that we are done with the record. Now, if we look up the record with `ldapsearch`, it looks like this:

```
$ ldapsearch -x -w secret -D 'cn=Manager,dc=example,dc=com' -LLL \
    '(uid=immanuel)'
dn: uid=immanuel,ou=Users,dc=example,dc=com
sn: Kant
uid: immanuel
ou: Users
objectClass: person
objectClass: organizationalPerson
objectClass: inetOrgPerson
givenName: Manny
cn: Manny Kant
```

The `cn` has been replaced, and the `givenName` attribute has been added.

If the modification is adding several attributes, rather than splitting the additions up using dashes, you can group them together:

```
dn: uid=nicholas,ou=Users,dc=example,dc=com
changetype: modify
add: description title
description: This is a test
title: Cartesian philosopher
```

Note that, in this case, the `add` line has two attribute names (`description` and `title`), followed by both attributes. And just as with `ldapadd`, we can put these change records into a plain text file, and then use the `-f` flag, which takes the path to a file, to have `ldapmodify` read the commands from the file instead of from the interactive prompt:

```
$ ldapmodify -x -w secret -D 'cn=Manager,dc=example,dc=com' -f \
    change-nicholas.ldif
modifying entry "uid=nicholas,ou=Users,dc=example,dc=com"
```

Using the `modify` change-type we can delete an attribute:

```
dn: uid=nicholas,ou=Users,dc=example,dc=com
changetype: modify
delete: title
```

Deleting an attribute from the record has the result of deleting all of the attribute values from the record. For example, if Nicholas had two titles specified, the above would remove them both.

To delete just one specific attribute, the request must also name the attribute value to be deleted:

```
dn: uid=nicholas,ou=Users,dc=example,dc=com
changetype: modify
delete: title
title: Cartesian philosopher
```

That will delete any `title` attribute values that contain the exact string "Cartesian philosopher", leaving any other attribute values intact.

Modifying the Relative DN

The third change type is for modifying relative DNs—the portion of the DN that identifies the current record (see the discussion at the beginning of this chapter).

For example, we can change the RDN portion of the DN for our user `uid=immanuel,ou=Users,dc=example,dc=com`:

```
$ ldapmodify -w secret -x -D 'cn=Manager,dc=example,dc=com'
dn: uid=immanuel,ou=Users,dc=example,dc=com
changetype: modrdn
newrdn: uid=manny
deleteoldrdn: 0

modifying rdn of entry "uid=immanuel,ou=Users,dc=example,dc=com"
rename completed
```

In this example, we use the `modrdn` change-type to instruct SLAPD to change the RDN portion of the user's DN. The `newrdn` instruction supplies the new RDN portion, and the `deleteoldrdn` instruction determines whether the old attribute value (`uid=immanuel`) will be deleted or retained. Setting `0` indicates that the old attribute value should not be deleted, while `1` will result in the old attribute value's removal.

Now, if we search for that user, we can observe the modification:

```
$ ldapsearch -x -W -D 'cn=manager,dc=example,dc=com' -LL \
    '(sn=kant)' uid
Enter LDAP Password:
version: 1

dn: uid=manny,ou=Users,dc=example,dc=com
uid: immanuel
uid: manny
```

In some cases we don't want the old RDN attribute value to be kept. In such cases, setting the `deleteoldrdn` value to 1 will remove the old RDN attribute values:

```
$ ldapmodify -w secret -x -D 'cn=Manager,dc=example,dc=com'
dn: uid=manny,ou=Users,dc=example,dc=com
changetype: modrdn
newrdn: uid=immanuel
deleteoldrdn: 1

modifying rdn of entry "uid=manny,ou=Users,dc=example,dc=com"
rename completed
```

This changes the RDN back to `uid=immanuel`, and since `deleteoldrdn` is set to 1, the old UID value (`manny`) should be deleted. We can verify this with `ldapsearch`:

```
$ ldapsearch -x -W -D 'cn=manager,dc=example,dc=com' -LL \
    '(sn=kant)' uid
Enter LDAP Password:
version: 1

dn: uid=immanuel,ou=Users,dc=example,dc=com
uid: immanuel
```

Note that, in addition to the changed DN, the old `uid` attribute value (`manny`) is no longer present in the record. It has been replaced.

We will take another look at modifying relative DNs when we examine the `ldapmodrdn` client.

Moving a Record with modrdn

The `modrdn` change-type can be used for more than just changing the RDN. It can be used for changing a record's superior entry, essentially relocating a record within the directory information tree.

For this operation to work however, the backend database type must support this sort of modification. Currently, the only storage database that supports this is HDB. In Chapter 2, we set up `slapd.conf` to store the `dc=example,dc=com` tree in an HDB backend.

Now, we can issue a compound ModRDN operation, in which we change the record's RDN, and move the record to a different OU:

```
$ ldapmodify -w secret -x -D 'cn=Manager,dc=example,dc=com'
dn: uid=manny,ou=users,dc=example,dc=com
changetype: modrdn
newrdn: uid=immanuel
deleteoldrdn: 1
newsuperior: ou=system,dc=example,dc=com
```

In this example, we change the user's UID from manny back to immanuel. Since deleteoldrdn is 1, the old RDN (uid=manny) will be removed from the record.

The newsuperior instruction tells SLAPD what the new base portion of the DN ought to be. This will effectively move the record from the ou=users branch to the ou=system branch of our directory information tree.

 Unlike modifying a user's RDN, changing a record's superior will not modify any of the fields in the record. Thus, our record above would still have the ou=Users attribute.

Again, we can use ldapsearch to see the newly modified record:

```
$ ldapsearch -x -W -D 'cn=manager,dc=example,dc=com' -LL
    '(sn=kant)' uid
```

And, we get:

```
Enter LDAP Password:
version: 1
dn: uid=immanuel,ou=system,dc=example,dc=com
uid: immanuel
```

Notice that not only has the uid changed, but also the ou in the DN.

In order to use the newsuperior instruction, you must first specify a modrdn. Thus, if we wanted to move the record for this user back to the users OU, we would still have to specify the user's new RDN.

So how do you move a record without changing the RDN?

Since the modrdn change-type does not require that the new RDN be different from the old one, a record can be moved with modrdn simply by setting the newrdn to be the same as the old RDN:

```
$ ldapmodify -w secret -x -D 'cn=Manager,dc=example,dc=com'
dn: uid=immanuel,ou=system,dc=example,dc=com
```

```
changetype: modrdn
newrdn: uid=immanuel
deleteoldrdn: 1
newsuperior: ou=users,dc=example,dc=com

modifying rdn of entry "uid=immanuel,ou=system,dc=example,dc=com"
rename completed
```

In this case, `newrdn: uid=immanuel` does not actually change the RDN of the user. But this is necessary in order to change the superior.

The `newsuperior` instruction indicates that the record should be moved (back) to the `ou=users,dc=example,dc=com` tree. One last `ldapsearch` of this record shows us the results of that change:

```
$ ldapsearch -x -W -D 'cn=manager,dc=example,dc=com' -LL
    '(sn=kant)' uid
Enter LDAP Password:
version: 1

dn: uid=immanuel,ou=users,dc=example,dc=com
uid: immanuel
```

Once again, the record is back in the `Users` OU.

Deleting Entire Records

Finally, using the `delete` change-type, we can delete an entire record with `ldapmodify`:

```
$ ldapmodify -w secret -x -D 'cn=Manager,dc=example,dc=com'

dn: uid=nicholas,ou=Users,dc=example,dc=com
changetype: delete

deleting entry "uid=nicholas,ou=Users,dc=example,dc=com"
```

When deleting a record all we need to specify are the DN and the change-type.

Essentially, using the delete change-type performs the same task as is done using the `ldapdelete` client.

ldapdelete

The `ldapdelete` tool is used to delete one or more records from the directory. It performs the same operation as the `delete` change-type used in `ldapmodify`.

If you want to delete a record with `ldapdelete`, you must know its DN. This tool will not search for, say, all records that have a specified address, and then delete them all.

The syntax of the `ldapdelete` command is simple:

```
$ ldapdelete -x -w secret -D 'cn=Manager,dc=example,dc=com' \
    'uid=nicholas,ou=Users,dc=example,dc=com'
```

After the usual flags (-x, -w, -D), `ldapdelete` takes the DN that is to be deleted (this is the DN for `uid=nicholas` on the second line of the command). Upon execution it will request that the server delete the record. Assuming that the record exists and the user is allowed (by the server's ACLs) to delete the record, then the record will be removed from the directory.

ldapcompare

This tool is used to ask the server whether a particular entry (identified by a DN) has a particular attribute that matches the attribute specified. If the entry does have a matching attribute, then `ldapcompare` returns TRUE. Otherwise, it returns FALSE.

Here is a pair of examples:

```
$ ldapcompare -x -w secret -D 'cn=Manager,dc=example,dc=com' \
    'uid=david,ou=Users,dc=example,dc=com' 'givenName:David'
TRUE
$ ldapcompare -x -w secret -D 'cn=Manager,dc=example,dc=com' \
    'uid=david,ou=Users,dc=example,dc=com' 'cn:Dave Hume'
FALSE
```

In the first example `ldapcompare` requested that the server examine the record for `uid=david,ou=Users,dc=example,dc=com` to see if it had the attribute `givenName` with the value `David`. The record did have an attribute `givenName: David`, and so the return value is TRUE.

The second example performed a similar compare on the same record; it looked for the attribute `cn` with the value `Dave Hume`. While the record does have a `cn` attribute, the value of that attribute is `David Hume`, not `Dave Hume`. So the server returned FALSE.

Base-64 Encoding with ldapcompare

In cases where the value to compare is not an ASCII string, you should base-64 encode the value and use the double colon syntax (: :) that we used in our LDIF files. Example: `givenName::RGF2aWQ=`

An LDAP compare operation is often much faster than a search operation. In cases where the same task can be accomplished with `ldapsearch` and `ldapcompare`, it is often more efficient to use `ldapcompare`.

ldapmodrdn

The `ldapmodrdn` client is used to change the Relative DN (RDN) portion of a DN. This client requests a ModifyDN operation. `ldapmodrdn` takes the full DN of an existing record, and the relative DN that should replace the existing RDN for the record:

```
$ ldapmodrdn -x -w secret -D 'cn=Manager,dc=example,dc=com'
    'uid=immanuel,ou=Users,dc=example,dc=com' 'uid=manny'
```

This example requests that the RDN for `uid=immanual,ou=Users,dc=example,dc=com` be changed from `uid=immanuel` to `uid=manny`.

Now let's take a look at the record after the change. We will search by the `sn` field:

```
$ ldapsearch -x -w secret -D 'cn=Manager,dc=example,dc=com' -LLL \
    '(sn=Kant)' uid

dn: uid=manny,ou=Users,dc=example,dc=com
uid: immanuel
uid: manny
```

Here, the filter is looking for records with the surname `Kant` and requesting that only the `uid` attribute be returned. Recall that we did not ever add a `uid` attribute with the value `manny`—we only had `uid: immanuel`.

But looking at the results, we can see that not only has the DN been modified, but a new user ID attribute has been added for us. In some cases it is fine that the modification of the RDN results in adding (rather than replacing) an attribute value. But in other cases this is inconvenient or even illegal (because of the schema).

For example, we might have a record in the directory that describes a subtree of records that have to do with the company website. Such a record might look like this:

```
dn: dc=www,dc=example,dc=com
dc: www
```

```
ou: Website
objectClass: organizationalUnit
objectClass: dcObject
```

Now, say we wanted to change the RDN to point not to www, but to web. Using ldapmodrdn the way we did earlier would generate an error:

```
$ ldapmodrdn -x -w secret -D 'cn=Manager,dc=example,dc=com' \
    'dc=www,dc=example,dc=com' 'dc=web'
Rename Result: Constraint violation (19)
Additional info: attribute 'dc' cannot have multiple values
```

The reason for this error is that the schema definition for dc specifies that there can be only one dc attribute value per record.

 The dc (or domainComponent) attribute is defined in core.schema.

The solution to this problem is to use the -r flag for ldapmodrdn.

```
$ ldapmodrdn -x -w secret -D 'cn=Manager,dc=example,dc=com' -r
    'dc=www,dc=example,dc=com' 'dc=web'
```

The -r flag causes ldapmodrdn to replace, rather than add, the existing attribute value. Now the resulting record looks like this:

```
dn: dc=web,dc=example,dc=com
ou: Website
objectClass: organizationalUnit
objectClass: dcObject
dc: web
```

There is only one dc attribute listed, and it has the newly set value, web.

Modifying the Superior DN with ldapmodrdn

Just as we saw earlier with the modrdn change-type for ldapmodify, we can change the superior DN (the base portion of a record's DN) with ldapmodrdn.

The Right Backend

Not all backends support this type of renaming. Currently, the HDB backend is the only storage backend to support changing the superior reference in a DN. Other non-storage backends (like ldap) may pass on these operations to the underlying storage mechanism, which in turn may or may not support this degree of renaming.

Also, as with the `modrdn` change type, `ldapmodrdn` must specify a replacement RDN even if that RDN is the same as the current one. In other words, an RDN is required, even if the RDN is not a new RDN. We will see an example of this below.

The `-s` flag for `ldapmodrdn` specifies the new superior DN. Thus, to move the entry `uid=barbara,ou=users,dc=example,dc=com` to the `ou=system` branch of the directory, we can use a command like this:

```
ldapmodrdn -x -w secret -D 'cn=Manager,dc=example,dc=com' \
    -s "ou=system,dc=example,dc=com" -r \
        "uid=barbara,ou=users,dc=example,dc=com" "uid=barbara"
```

This is a long command, and it is thus broken up into three lines:

- The first line contains the flags that handle binding to the directory, and these should be familiar by now.

- The second line begins with the `-s` flag, which takes a DN for a parameter. This is the flag that specifies what the new superior DN will be. In this case, it is `ou=system,dc=example,dc=com`.

  The `-r` flag, as we have seen before, instructs SLAPD to replace the old RDN with the new one.

- On the third line is the DN for the entry we want to modify, `uid=barbar, ou=users,dc=example,dc=com`, and the new RDN. Since we want to keep the same RDN (but move the record to a new subtree), we set this last value to `uid=barbara`, which is the RDN that the existing record has.

After we run this command we can see the results with `ldapsearch`:

```
$ ldapsearch -x -W -D 'cn=manager,dc=example,dc=com' -LL
    '(uid=barbara)' uid ou
Enter LDAP Password:
version: 1

dn: uid=barbara,ou=system,dc=example,dc=com
ou: Users
uid: barbara
```

The base portion of Barbara's new record is now `ou=system,dc=example,dc=com`.

Just as with the `modrdn` changetype for `ldapmodify`, changing a superior entry will not change any attributes in the record. Thus, even though this record is now in the sytem OU, it still has the attribute `ou: Users`.

It is possible to construct Relative DNs that have more than one attribute value. For example, I can use a combination of uid and l (for location) in the RDN portion:

```
dn: uid=matt+l=Chicago,ou=Users,dc=example,dc=com
```

In such cases, the plus sign (+) is used to indicate that both the attribute are to be considered part of the RDN.

ldapmodrdn is smart enough to handle these cases. It will add (or replace) all of the attributes used in the RDN.

In the case where the -r flag is specified, there are some things to be aware of. First, ldapmodrdn will replace all of the fields used in the new RDN. Second, if there is a value in the initial RDN that is removed from the RDN, then the attribute value will be removed from the record as well. For example, here is our starting record:

```
dn: cn=Matt Butcher+l=Chicago,dc=example,dc=com
cn: Matt Butcher
sn: Butcher
l: Chicago
objectClass: person
objectClass: organizationalPerson
```

Notice that the DN uses both the cn and the l attributes, both of which are present in the body of the record. Now, if we use ldapmodrdn with the -r flag and replace cn=Matt Butcher+l=Chicago with cn=Matt Butcher, the l: Chicago attribute will be removed from the record:

```
dn: cn=Matt Butcher,dc=example,dc=com
sn: Butcher
objectClass: person
objectClass: organizationalPerson
cn: Matt Butcher
```

So, when using ldapmodrdn with multi-attribute RDNs, be judicious when using the -r flag.

ldappasswd

In the utilities section we looked at encrypting passwords with slappasswd. That tool was used to generate encrypted values for inclusion in LDIF files. The ldappasswd client, in contrast, connects to the server and changes a password value in the directory. If needed it can be used to automatically generate a password, as well.

Unlike `ldapadd` and `ldapmodify`, which use the LDAP v.3 standard Add and Modify operations, the `ldappasswd` client uses an extension operation—the **LDAP Password Modify Extended Operation** as defined in RFC 3062 (`http://rfc-editor.org/rfc/rfc3062.txt`).

> When loading passwords from an LDIF file, or from `ldapadd` or `ldapmodify`, if you send the server a cleartext password, the password will be stored in the directory in an unencrypted string. This is not safe. You should either use `slappasswd` to generate an encrypted password for inclusion in an LDIF, or you should use `ldappasswd` to set the password.

As long as the ACLs permit, a user can change her or his password with the `ldappasswd` client:

```
$ ldappasswd -x -W -S -D 'uid=matt,ou=Users,dc=example,dc=com'
New password:
Re-enter new password:
Enter LDAP Password:

Result: Success (0)
```

The `-S` flag is the only new flag used here. It indicates that `ldappasswd` should prompt the user to enter (and re-enter) a new password. The `-W` flag, as you may recall, prompts the user to enter a current password interactively.

The order in which the user enters the passwords differs from the norm. The user is prompted to first enter and re-enter a new password, and then to enter the current password.

It is also possible for an administrator (or one with write permissions to the `userPassword` attribute of a given record) to change a password for another user:

```
$ ldappasswd -x -w secret -D 'cn=Manager,dc=example,dc=com' -s secret \
'uid=barbara,ou=Users,dc=example,dc=com'

Result: Success (0)
```

In this case the directory manager is changing the value of the `userPassword` attribute for `uid=barbara,ou=Users,dc=example,dc=com`. Rather than using `-S` and entering the password at an interactive prompt, the password has been specified on the command line: `-s secret`.

The password, when changed through `ldappasswd`, is automatically encrypted by the server before it is stored in the record:

```
# barbara, Users, example.com
dn: uid=barbara,ou=Users,dc=example,dc=com
userPassword:: e1NTSEF9UzFTUnQ1bkkvcHZGOGt3UklVU3J3TkRHZHFSS3hOQ1Y=
```

If we decode the `userPassword` value, it reads: `{SSHA}S1SRt5nI/pvF8kwRIUSrwNDGdqRKxNCV`. The password is stored in an irreversible SSHA hash.

> **Setting the Default Encryption Scheme**
>
> You can specify which encryption scheme the server should choose when encrypting passwords. To specify the algorithm, use the `password-hash` directive in `slapd.conf`. Example: `password-hash {SMD5}`

Finally, `ldappasswd` can request that the server generate a strong password for that DN. If no flag is set that indicates, the source of the password (for example `-s`, `-S`, or `-T`), then `ldappasswd` requests that one be generated. Here is the request:

```
$ ldappasswd -x -w secret -D 'cn=Manager,dc=example,dc=com'  \
    'uid=barbara,ou=Users,dc=example,dc=com'
New password: dS9R4Kvc
Result: Success (0)
```

The server responded to this request with a generated password, `New password: dS9R4Kvc`, which has already been encrypted and stored in the `userPassword` attribute on the server.

ldapwhoami

The last client in the OpenLDAP suite is `ldapwhoami`. This client provides a client implementation of the **"Who am I?" Extended Operation**. This operation provides information about the DN who is currently bound to the directory.

The `ldapwhoami` command simply requires enough information to authenticate to the directory server:

```
$ ldapwhoami -x -w secret -D 'cn=Manager,dc=example,dc=com'
dn:cn=Manager,dc=example,dc=com
Result: Success (0)
```

As you can see from this example, all this client does is reply with the DN of the user we connected with. This tool comes in useful when debugging SASL authentication, which does not require a DN to connect. We will look at SASL configuration in the next chapter.

Summary

In this chapter we have taken a closer look at the tools in the OpenLDAP suite. We began by looking at the SLAPD and SLURPD servers. In particular, we looked at the major LDAP operations, such as bind, search, add, modify, and delete.

Next we created a basic directory information tree in an LDIF file. In doing this, we familiarized ourselves with LDIF – the text format for representing LDAP directory data.

From there we looked at the utilities and clients in the OpenLDAP suite. Along the way, we loaded our directory information tree from LDIF into the directory, and then added to and modified that data.

At this point you should be comfortable working with the tools included in OpenLDAP. In the next chapter we are going to return to the SLAPD server and take a close look at LDAP security.

4
Securing OpenLDAP

In Chapter 2 we installed OpenLDAP and created a basic configuration file for the SLAPD server. Then, in the last chapter, we turned our attention to LDAP operations and LDAP clients. Now we will return to the SLAPD server, but with a specific focus: **security**. We will take a look at three major security considerations with OpenLDAP: securing connections between the server and client connections, authenticating users of the directory, and specifying what data particular users can access (and in what capacity they can access it). We will look at these security considerations on a practical level and, in doing so, we will cover the following:

- Configuring SSL and TLS to protect network data
- Using simple binding to authenticate DNS (Domain Name System) for using the directory
- Using SASL to provide more robust authentication services
- Integrating SASL and client SSL/TLS certificates for authentication
- Configuring Access Control Lists (ACLs) to establish rules about what data users can access

LDAP Security: The Three Aspects

As we have seen already, the directory contains sensitive information. One example of such sensitive information is the userPassword attribute. But other information that may be considered sensitive, such as personal information or confidential information about the organization, may exist in the directory. Such information needs to be protected.

We might ask what is meant by *protection* in this case. For it is certainly not the case that we want to prevent *all* clients from seeing *everything*. What we want rather, is to allow people to get at specific pieces of the directory information. But, on the other hand, there are cases where we want to deny certain users the ability to get at certain pieces of directory information. So protecting our data becomes a matter of providing information in some cases, while denying it in other cases.

While it is possible to draw finer-grained distinctions, here we are going to consider three broad aspects of security where we want to make sure that we are protecting the directory and its information. These three aspects are as follows:

- **Connection Security**: This is the process of protecting directory information (and client information) as it is passed between a client and the directory server. We will talk about this in the context of network security with SSL and TLS.

- **Authentication**: This is the process of ensuring that the user who tries to access the information in the directory is who he/she/it claims to be. In this chapter we will look at two types of authentication: simple and SASL Binding. SASL stands for **Simple Authentication and Security Layer**.

- **Authorization**: This is the process of ensuring that an identified or authenticated user is allowed to access pieces of information within the directory. OpenLDAP ACLs are used to specify rules for authorization.

In this chapter we will look at each of these three aspects of security. By combining all three we will be able to provide suitably fine-grained protection for our directory information.

Securing Network-Based Directory Connections with SSL/TLS

The first element of security that we will examine is network security. Most clients connect to OpenLDAP over a network interface, and client requests, as well as the server's responses, are transferred over a network.

The LDAP protocol, by default, sends and receives messages in clear text. In this case no attempt is made to obscure the data as it is being transmitted across the network. Sending in clear text has a few advantages:

- It is easier to configure and maintain.

- LDAP services can function faster. The process of encrypting and decrypting messages can be processor-intensive, and eliminating that processing can serve to speed things up.

But these advantages come at the cost of security. Other devices on the network may be able to intercept these unencrypted transmissions and read their contents and in doing so, they may obtain sensitive information. On a small Local Area Network (LAN) the risks may be smaller (though still present). On a large scale network, such as the Internet, the dangers are much greater.

In this section we will walk through the process of configuring **Secure Sockets Layer (SSL)** and **Transport Layer Security (TLS)** encryption to protect data as it is transmitted over a network. SSL and TLS are very similar, to the point where the terms are often used (acceptably) as synonyms. TLS though, is a refinement of SSL, and has been implemented in ways that are more flexible than the typical SSL implementation. The StartTLS method of securing a connection is an example.

The Basics of SSL and TLS

OpenLDAP provides two methods for encrypting network traffic. The first is to have OpenLDAP listen on a special port for requests (port 636, the LDAPS port, is used by default). Transmissions on this port will automatically be encrypted. This method is older, introduced as an addition to LDAP v2, but it is no longer the preferred method.

The second method, which is part of the LDAP v3 standard, is to allow clients connecting over the standard port (usually port 389) to request to switch from clear text transmissions to encrypted transmissions. I will cover both configurations here.

Secure Sockets Layer (SSL) is a security process, originally developed by Netscape Communications for their web browser, designed to provide a safe way of exchanging trusted information between a server and any client on the network. There are two major features of the SSL process: establishing authenticity and conducting securely encrypted transactions.

As SSL developed and evolved it was handed over to a standard body, the **Internet Engineering Task Force (IETF)**, for standardization and continued development. IETF renamed it **Transport Layer Security (TLS)** and released version 1.0 (as RFC 2246). SSL 3.0 and TLS 1.0 do not have any notable differences, and most servers that support one also support the other. Because of their similarity and shared heritage, I refer to them jointly as SSL/TLS.

Authenticity

Proving authenticity and providing encryption are the two major features of SSL/TLS. In regards to the first, SSL/TLS provides a way to establish the authenticity of the server (and, if desired, the client too). What this means is that SSL/TLS makes it possible for the client to be reasonably sure that the server belongs to whom it claims to belong.

Consider the case of online banking. If I use my browser to log on to my bank's website and conduct a few transactions, I want to be sure that the website I am connected to really is my bank's website, and not some other website masquerading as my bank. SSL/TLS provides tools to establish the authenticity of the server using **X.509 certificates**. An X.509 certificate has three important pieces of information:

- Information about the individual or organization that owns the certificate
- A public encryption key (which we will discuss in the next section)
- The **digital signature** of a certificate authority (CA)

A certificate is designed as a sort of assurance that a server is associated with a particular individual or organization. When I contact a server that I believe to be my bank's, I want some assurance that it is, in fact, my bank's server. So one piece of information contained in the certificate is information about who owns the certificate. We can inspect this information ourselves, but since the certificate has a digital signature, it is also possible for software to computationally verify this — in a way much more reliable than reading the certificate and simply trusting that the certificate is accurate.

The digital signature is an encrypted bit of information. It is encrypted with a special "private" key that is owned by a Certificate Authority. The CA can then issue a public key that client software can use to verify that the certificate was in fact signed by the CA. The CA then, plays a very important role in establishing trust. We will discuss public and private keys in the *Encryption* section.

Certificate Authorities are responsible for issuing certificates. Ideally, a CA is a trusted source that can verify the authenticity of the certificate, and provide assurance that the certificate is really owned by the organization or individual that claims to own it.

There are a number of commercial CAs that provide certificate generation services for a price. To obtain a certificate through these services, an organization or individual must provide a certain amount of information that can be used to verify that the person or organization signing up for the certificate is legitimate. Once investigation of this material has been done, and the person or organization has paid the requisite fee, the CA issues a digitally-signed certificate.

The certificates of large CAs are included by default in most SSL-aware applications, such as popular web browsers (like Mozilla Firefox) and SSL libraries (like OpenSSL). These certificates include the public keys necessary for verifying digital signatures. Thus, when a client gets an X.509 certificate that is signed by one of these CAs, it has all of the tools it needs to verify the certificate's authenticity.

But it is possible, and often useful, for an organization or individual to simply create a locally used CA, and then use that CA to generate certificates for in-house applications. This is what we will do when we create a certificate for OpenLDAP.

Of course, certificates generated this way may not be considered reliable to users outside of your organization, but hosting an individual or organization-wide CA can be an effective way to add security to your own network, without having to purchase certificates from a commercial vendor.

 Not all CAs use the same form of authoritative signing (and not all CAs charge for certificates). Some CAs, such as Cacert.org, use what is called a **web of trust** technique for establishing authenticity. In the web of trust the authenticity of a certificate is established by peers who can play the role of assuring that the certificate is owned by the person or organization that it claims to be owned by. For more information visit `http://www.cacert.org/`.

We have discussed the first role of SSL/TLS, establishing authenticity. Next we will turn to the second role of SSL/TLS; providing encryption services.

Encryption

SSL/TLS provides the features required for sending encrypted messages back and forth between the client and the server. In a nutshell the process goes like this: the server sends the client its certificate, and inside the certificate (among other things) is the server's **public key**. The public key is the first half of a pair of keys. A public key can be used for encrypting a message, but not decrypting it. A second key, the **private key**, is then used for decrypting a message. The server keeps its private key to itself, but gives out its public key to any client that requests it. Clients can then send messages to the server that only the server can decrypt and interpret.

Depending on the configuration the client also sends the server its public key, which the server can use to send messages that only the client can decrypt. At this point, each can transmit encrypted messages to the other.

But there is a drawback to using public/private keys: they are slow and resource-intensive. Rather than trading all information through these public/private key combos, the client and server then negotiate a set of temporary symmetric encryption keys (which use the same key to encrypt and decrypt messages) that they will both use for the duration of the session. All traffic between the two clients is encrypted using these keys. Once the session is complete, both the client and server discard the temporary keys.

For a more detailed introduction to SSL and TLS, as well as pointers to further sources of information, see the Wikipedia entry for Transport Layer Security: `http://en.wikipedia.org/wiki/Transport_Layer_Security`.

StartTLS

As it is typically implemented, SSL requires that the server listen for encrypted traffic on a port separate from the one it uses for unencrypted traffic. All traffic that comes over the SSL port is assumed to be SSL-encrypted traffic. This means that every server that needs to provide both cleartext and encrypted services must listen on at least two different ports.

The multi-port requirement seemed to some to be unnecessary, inelegant, and wasteful. There is no reason why the client should not be able to request on a cleartext (non-SSL) connection that further communication between the client and server be encrypted. The client and server could then perform all of the SSL/TLS negotiation over the same connection, and not have to switch to another SSL/TLS-only port. This suggestion was standardized in RFC2487 as **StartTLS**.

Which to Pick: StartTLS or LDAPS?

The standardized way of implementing SSL/TLS in LDAP v.3 is to use the StartTLS method. This method should be implemented whenever possible. However, external considerations (such as network firewalling or clients without StartTLS support) may require that you use LDAPS and a dedicated SSL/TLS-protected port. LDAPS support is now listed as deprecated, though it is not yet slated for removal from OpenLDAP. Both options can be used on the same server.

In a StartTLS-supporting server, if the client sends the server the command `STARTTLS` then the server will begin the TLS encryption process. Assuming the TLS negotiation is successful, the client and server will then continue their transactions using encrypted traffic.

StartTLS has the obvious advantage of requiring only one listening port per server. And, it makes it possible for clients and servers to communicate in cleartext for unimportant data, and then switch over to TLS when security becomes important. Since encryption is resource intensive, requiring extra processing power to encrypt and decrypt messages, streamlining services the StartTLS way can improve performance and free up resources for other tasks.

There is a drawback for StartTLS though. Since both encrypted and cleartext traffic are sent over the same port, the method of simply blocking a port to prevent insecure data transmissions (by using a firewall for instance) is not effective with StartTLS. Security measures must be capable of inspecting transmissions at the protocol level.

In order to improve security services in such cases, OpenLDAP provides methods of testing the **security strength factor (SSF)** of a connection to see if it is encrypted (and if so, if the encryption scheme is strong enough). We will look at SSF in more detail later in this chapter in the section on *Using Security Strength Factors*.

At this point, you should have a fairly good idea of how SSL and TLS function. Now we will move on to more practical matters. We will create our own CA, and our own certificate, and then configure OpenLDAP to support SSL/TLS and StartTLS.

Creating an SSL/TLS CA

In order to create a Certificate Authority and generate certificates, you will need to have OpenSSL installed. Since many Ubuntu packages, including the OpenLDAP packages, require OpenSSL, it should be installed already.

If you build from source, as detailed in Appendix A, you may also enable support for SSL/TLS using the OpenSSL libraries.

> If you have a certificate already, you can skip this section and move to the *Configuring StartTLS* section. OpenLDAP uses certificates in the PEM format.

The first thing we will need to do is create our new CA.

While it is possible to manually configure your CA using the `openssl` command line tool, it is much simpler to use the `CA.pl` Perl script that is included with OpenSSL. This script streamlines many of the configuration options for OpenSSL, and the first thing that we will use it for is creating the environment for our new CA.

> Ubuntu maintains documentation on creating a new Certificate Authority the "long way" (creating all of the files by hand). This documentation is detailed and well worth reading. While I will follow the conventions established there, I will be using the `CA.pl` script to do most of the heavy lifting (`https://help.ubuntu.com/community/OpenSSL`).

You can put the CA environment anywhere on your system. Some prefer to keep CA files with the rest of the SSL configuration at /etc/ssl/. Others prefer keeping the certificate authority in a user directory so that it does not get overwritten during system upgrades (an unlikely, but possible, event). In keeping with the Ubuntu suggestion to keep CA info in a user's home directory, I will just put mine in my home directory, /home/mbutcher/:

```
$ cd ~
$ /usr/lib/ssl/misc/CA.pl -newca
```

Note that the CA.pl script is not in $PATH, so you will need to type in the entire path to the script.

Finding CA.pl

Different operating system distributions will put CA.pl in different places. If running which CA.pl does not return any results, you may want to consult the man pages for SSL (man config or man CA.pl), or use the find or slocate utilities to find the CA.pl file.

The argument -newca instructs CA.pl to set up a new certificate authority environment. This will generate a directory structure along with a number of files.

The first thing that CA.pl will do is prompt you to enter a CA file:

```
$ /usr/lib/ssl/misc/CA.pl -newca
CA certificate filename (or enter to create)
```

Hit *Enter* to create a new CA certificate. CA.pl will then generate a new key and then prompt you for a password:

```
CA certificate filename (or enter to create)

Making CA certificate
Generating a 1024 bit RSA private key
....++++++
................................++++++
unable to write 'random state'
writing new private key to './demoCA/private/cakey.pem'
Enter PEM pass phrase:
Verifying - Enter PEM pass phrase:
-----
```

Once you have entered and re-entered your password, `CA.pl` will collect some information from you about your organization:

```
You are about to be asked to enter information that will be
    incorporated into your certificate request.
What you are about to enter is what is called a Distinguished Name or
    a DN.
There are quite a few fields but you can leave some blank
For some fields there will be a default value,
If you enter '.', the field will be left blank.
-----
Country Name (2 letter code) [AU]:US
State or Province Name (full name) [Some-State]:Illinois
Locality Name (eg, city) []:Chicago
Organization Name (eg, company) [Internet Widgits]:Example.Com
Organizational Unit Name (eg, section) []:
Common Name (eg, YOUR name) []:Matt Butcher
Email Address []:matt@example.com

Please enter the following 'extra' attributes
    to be sent with your certificate request
A challenge password []:mypassword
An optional company name []:Example.Com
```

`CA.pl` walks you through the process of creating a main certificate. The highlighted lines in the code listing are those where you will have to provide information at an interactive prompt. After setting the country, state, and city name for my locale, we set the **Organization Name** to **Example.Com**. While we left the **Organizational Unit** field blank, you can use that to further specify what part of the organization this CA is a member of.

 You should consider using the same fields in your certificate that you used for your root DN when you set up your directory information tree in the previous two chapters.

Usually the **Common Name** and **Email Address** fields should contain information about the organization. Sometimes **Common Name** is used for the server name (as will be the case when we create our certificate). Sometimes, it is used for contact information. In the case that follows, we used my name and email. If the CA is to be the "official" CA for your organization, you should set this to the official contact person for certificate inquiries.

Next, CA.pl will begin the process of generating a certificate request for the CA certificate. In other words, CA.pl will create a new certificate that will be the CA's own certificate. The first step in doing this is to create a certificate request. We will need to set a challenging password for the certificate request. We can also set a company name too. With the above information, CA.pl will continue the process of generating a new certificate:

```
Using configuration from /usr/lib/ssl/openssl.cnf
Enter pass phrase for ./demoCA/private/cakey.pem:
Check that the request matches the signature
Signature ok
Certificate Details:
        Serial Number:
          bf:2f:58:47:b1:6d:31:4d
        Validity
          Not Before: Oct 10 21:34:28 2006 GMT
          Not After : Oct  9 21:34:28 2009 GMT
        Subject:
          countryName               = US
          stateOrProvinceName       = Illinois
          organizationName          = Example.Com
          commonName                = Matt Butcher
          emailAddress              = matt@example.com
        X509v3 extensions:
          X509v3 Basic Constraints:
              CA:FALSE
            Netscape Comment:
              OpenSSL Generated Certificate
          X509v3 Subject Key Identifier:
07:92:9B:35:CB:B7:EE:92:A8:33:61:B0:DC:F7:88:E9:4F:06:9F:7F
          X509v3 Authority Key Identifier:
keyid:07:92:9B:35:CB:B7:EE:92:A8:33:61:B0:DC:F7:88:E9:4F:06:9F:7F

Certificate is to be certified until
    Oct 9 21:34:28 2009 GMT (1095 days)

Write out database with 1 new entries
Data Base Updated
```

We will be prompted to enter a pass phrase. This is the pass phrase we created first (when prompted to **Enter PEM pass phrase**). If we enter the pass phrase correctly, CA.pl will generate our new certificate and display its contents on the screen.

We have now created a Certificate Authority. Now we are ready to start generating a certificate to be used by SLAPD.

Due to a bug in some versions of CA.pl, you may have to cd into the ./demoCA directory (the directory that CA.pl -newca created) and add a symbolic link to itself: ln -s ./demoCA. This is because CA.pl occasionally expects to find files in the current directory (./), which it assumes to be demoCA/, and sometimes it expects to find files in ./demoCA (which, of course, is equivalent to demoCA/demoCA/). You can also fix this simply by editing the dir= line under [CA_default] in the /etc/ssl/openssl.cnf file, and setting it to an absolute path.

Creating a Certificate

Creating a certificate is a two-step process:

1. We need to generate the Certificate Request.
2. We need to sign the request with the CA's signature.

Let's see these steps in detail.

Creating a New Certificate Request

The first step in creating a valid SSL certificate is to create a Certificate Request. In the process, we will specify what information we want to show up on the certificate.

There are a few ways to generate Certificate Requests. For example, you can use the openssl command line tool and specifying a number of command line parameters. But, following our previous example, we will use CA.pl and let the application prompt us for information as is necessary.

To generate a new request we will run CA.pl -newreq. In the next example the highlighted lines are lines that require us to enter information:

```
$ /usr/lib/ssl/misc/CA.pl -newreq
Generating a 1024 bit RSA private key
.....++++++
....................++++++
unable to write 'random state'
writing new private key to 'newkey.pem'
Enter PEM pass phrase:
Verifying - Enter PEM pass phrase:
-----
You are about to be asked to enter information that will be
    incorporated into your certificate request.
What you are about to enter is what is called a Distinguished Name or
    a DN.
There are quite a few fields but you can leave some blank
```

```
For some fields there will be a default value,
If you enter '.', the field will be left blank.
-----
Country Name (2 letter code) [AU]:US
State or Province Name (full name) [Some-State]:Illinois
Locality Name (eg, city) []:Chicago
Organization Name (eg, company) [Internet Widgits]:Example.Com
Organizational Unit Name (eg, section) []:
Common Name (eg, YOUR name) []:example.com
Email Address []:matt@example.com

Please enter the following 'extra' attributes
to be sent with your certificate request
A challenge password []:
An optional company name []:
Request is in newreq.pem, private key is in newkey.pem
```

This should look familiar. It is similar in most respects to the process of generating a Certificate Authority.

First, we will be prompted to enter a pass phrase. We will use this pass phrase in a few moments.

Next, we will be asked to supply information about the organization that this certificate will represent. As before the fields are Country Name, State/Province Name, Locality, Organization Name, Organizational Unit, Common Name (of the contact person), and the Email for the contact person. Again, as before, we entered the information for Example.Com.

This time, however, we set the Common Name field to be the domain name of the server that the certificate is for—example.com. It is very important that you use the correct domain name for the server. During the certificate negotiation process clients will check the Common Name field to see if it matches the domain name of the server. If the names do not match the user may get an error message, or the client application may simply terminate the connection.

The extra *password* and *optional company name* are sometimes used in the certificate request process. Since we are doing the requesting and the signing ourselves we don't need to complete either of these fields.

Now we should have two files in the CA directory:

- One called newreq.pem, which contains a base-64 encoded representation of our certificate request
- One called newkey.pem, which contains the base-64 encoded private key

We are now ready to move on to the second step.

Signing the Certificate Request

The Certificate Request has all of the information required for a certificate, but it
still lacks the digital signature of the CA. The next step, then, will be to use the
CA we created previously to sign this new certificate. To do this, we will run
CA.pl -signreq:

```
$ /usr/lib/ssl/misc/CA.pl -signreq
Using configuration from /usr/lib/ssl/openssl.cnf
Enter pass phrase for ./demoCA/private/cakey.pem:
Check that the request matches the signature
Signature ok
Certificate Details:
        Serial Number:
            ba:49:df:f5:8e:7e:77:c2
        Validity
            Not Before: Oct 12 21:23:49 2006 GMT
            Not After : Oct 12 21:23:49 2007 GMT
        Subject:
            countryName               = US
            stateOrProvinceName       = Illinois
            localityName              = Chicago
            organizationName          = Example.Com
            commonName                = example.com
            emailAddress              = matt@example.com
        X509v3 extensions:
            X509v3 Basic Constraints:
                CA:FALSE
            Netscape Comment:
                OpenSSL Generated Certificate
            X509v3 Subject Key Identifier:
47:DD:90:8F:79:90:2E:C0:CC:B3:95:62:35:C4:D8:6C:5D:A2:EE:88
            X509v3 Authority Key Identifier:
                keyid:6B:FB:66:33:5D:DB:CC:40:42:D7:71:F7:F0:
D0:7C:94:3E:8F:CD:58

Certificate is to be certified until
    Oct 12 21:23:49 2007 GMT (365 days)
Sign the certificate? [y/n]:y

1 out of 1 certificate requests certified, commit? [y/n]y
Write out database with 1 new entries
Data Base Updated
Signed certificate is in newcert.pem
```

The `CA.pl -signcert` command looks for `newreq.pem` and then begins the signing process. First, we need to enter the pass phrase for the CA. If that is correct, then `CA.pl` will display the certificate in `newreq.pem` and ask if we want to sign it. Finally, it will ask us to commit these changes.

Once the changes are committed a new file will be created, named `newcert.pem`.

There are two important files that we now have:

- `newkey.pem`, which contains the private key
- `newcert.pem`, which contains the signed certificate.

We've just got a few loose ends to tie up, and then we can move on to configuring SLAPD to use SSL/TLS.

Configuring and Installing the Certificates

We have only three more steps to do, here. The first one has to do with the pass phrase we set on our certificate.

Remove the Pass Phrase from the Key

Be very careful here! When generating our certificate request, we set a pass phrase on the certificate. This encrypted the `newkey.pem` file with a pass phrase.

If you use a key file that is encrypted with a pass phrase, then every time you use this certificate, you will have to enter a password. This means, in our case, that every time we start OpenLDAP, we will have to enter a pass phrase. Unless we have stringent security requirements (and are willing to put up with the hassle of typing the pass phrase every time we start or restart the server), we probably do not want the key file to be encrypted.

So, we will need to create an unencrypted version of the key file using the `openssl` command:

```
$ openssl rsa < newkey.pem > clearkey.pem
```

This is what we get:

```
Enter pass phrase:
writing RSA key
```

In this example the command `openssl rsa` executes the OpenSSL RSA tool, which will decrypt the key. Using `< newkey.pem`, we sent the file contents of `newkey.pem` into `openssl` to be decrypted. Then, using `> clearkey.pem` we directed `openssl` to write the cleartext key file to the `clearkey.pem` file. In order to complete this operation, `openssl` prompts for the pass phrase. Now `clearkey.pem` has the unencrypted private key for our certificate.

The `clearkey.pem` file now contains an unencrypted private key. This file should be protected from misuse. You should set strict permissions on this file so that other users of the system cannot access it.

The openssl Program

The `openssl` program performs dozens of SSL-related functions, from generating certificates to emulating a network-based SSL client. Its syntax is notoriously difficult though. That is why we have been using the `CA.pl` wrapper script to perform common tasks. But some tasks can only be done with the `openssl` command. Should you need them though, `openssl` has excellent man pages: `man openssl`.

Relocate the Certificates

The second task is to move our new certificate and key to a useful location on the server, and give the PEM files useful names as well. If this certificate is to be used by lots of different services, it might make sense to locate it in the shared directory. But for our cases we will only be using the SSL certificate for LDAP, so we can put the files in `/etc/ldap/` (or `/usr/local/etc/openldap/` if you built from source).

The two files with which we are concerned are `newcert.pem` and `clearkey.pem`. We need to rename and move those two keys:

```
$ sudo mv cacert.pem /etc/ldap/example.com.cert.pem
$ sudo mv clearkey.pem /etc/ldap/example.com.key.pem
```

Now, we need to set permissions and ownership on the certificate files. Since we did not add a pass phrase to the key, we should also make sure that only the OpenLDAP user can read the key file:

```
$ sudo chown root:root /etc/ldap/example.com.*.pem
$ sudo chmod 400 /etc/ldap/example.com.key.pem
```

The first line changes the owner and group of the two PEM files to the `root` user and the `root` group. The second line sets the mode so that only the owner can read the file, and no one else has any access.

If you are running OpenLDAP as a user other than root (and it is a good idea to do so), then the files should be owned by that user instead of root; for example `chown oenldap example.com.*.pem`.

Install the CA Certificate

The third task is to install the CA's public certificate so that other applications on the system can use that certificate to verify the authenticity of the certificate we just generated. First, we need to copy the CA certificate to the local certificate database for Ubuntu. In the process we will give it a user-friendly name:

```
$ sudo cp cacert.pem /usr/share/ca-certificates/Example.Com-CA.crt
```

Then, edit the `/etc/ca-certificates.conf` file, and add `Example.Com.crt` at the end of the file.

Finally, run `update-ca-certificates`:

```
$ sudo update-ca-certificates
Updating certificates in /etc/ssl/certs....done.
```

The CA certificate has now been installed. The `/etc/ssl/certs` directory is now the authoritative source for CA certificates.

> UNIX and Linux systems other than Ubuntu and Debian may not have the `update-ca-certificates` script. Consult the system documentation to find out how to update the certificate database on such systems.

Optional: Clean Up

If you want, you can do a little clean-up in the CA directory. Delete the encrypted key file and the certificate request file, both of which are in the `demoCA/` directory:

```
$ rm newkey.pem newreq.pem
```

Also, make sure `clearkey.pem` is no longer present in the `demoCA/` directory.

Now we are ready to configure OpenLDAP to use our new certificates. First, we will configure StartTLS support, which is the easiest, then we will configure SSL/TLS support on the LDAPS port, port 636.

Configuring StartTLS

In the previous sections we created our new certificate and key, and placed the two files in the `/etc/ldap` directory. In this section we will set up StartTLS (which we introduced earlier in this chapter in the StartTLS section). Setting up StartTLS requires only a few extra lines in the `slapd.conf` file.

Again, StartTLS is the standard way (according to RFC 4511) of providing SSL/TLS security to OpenLDAP. For security reasons support for StartTLS should be provided whenever practical.

In the `slapd.conf` file, just before the `BDB Database Configuration` section, insert the SSL/TLS options:

```
##########
# SSL/TLS #
##########
TLSCACertificatePath     /etc/ssl/certs/
TLSCertificateFile       /etc/ldap/example.com.cert.pem
TLSCertificateKeyFile    /etc/ldap/example.com.key.pem
```

Basically, there are only three directives we need to specify to get StartTLS working:

- The first directive, `TLSCACertificatePath`, tells SLAPD where to find all of the CA certificates that it will need for verifying certificates. The definitive location is, as we saw before, the `/etc/ssl/certs/` directory.

- The second directive, `TLSCertificateFile`, specifies the location of the signed certificate.

- The third directive, `TLSCertificateKeyFile`, specifies the location of the corresponding key file, which has the private encryption key for the certificate.

> There are a handful of other TLS-specific directives that allow you to provide detailed constraints on TLS connections (such as which suites of ciphers can be used, and whether the client needs to provide a certificate to the server). Complete documentation on these can be found in the TLS section of the `slapd.conf` man page: `man slapd.conf`.

That's all we need to get SLAPD to perform StartTLS. Restart SLAPD so that the changes take effect.

Configuring Client TLS

We do need to add a directive or two to `ldap.conf` — the configuration file that the OpenLDAP clients use. As with SLAPD, we need to direct the clients to the correct location of the new CA certificate so that they can verify the server certificate.

At the bottom of the `ldap.conf` file we can add the appropriate directive:

```
TLS_CACERTDIR /etc/ssl/certs
```

Clients will use this directive to locate the CA certificates for checking digital signatures on the certificates they get from servers. If you know that you are only going to use certificates signed by a specific CA, you can use the `TLS_CACERT` directive to point to a specific CA certificate file, instead of a directory containing one or more certificates.

By default, OpenLDAP clients always perform a check on the digital signatures. If a server sends a certificate that was signed by a CA other than those at /etc/ssl/certs/ (or whatever directory TLS_CACERTDIR points to), then the client will close the connection and print an error message to the screen.

Sometimes though, the correct CA certificate is not available, and it is worthwhile to get the encryption support of TLS even if it is not possible to verify the identity of the server.

In such cases you may find it necessary to change the way OpenLDAP clients perform identification checks. For example, it might be desirable to try to verify the certificate, but to continue with the connection even if there is no appropriate CA locally. To accomplish this, use the following directive in slapd.conf:

```
TLS_REQCERT allow
```

In this case, if there is no CA certificate or if the certificate sent cannot be verified, the session will continue, rather than exiting with an error message. TLS_REQCERT has a few different levels of checking, ranging from strict (always verify) to never (do not even bother trying to verify certificates).

At this point, we can use ldapsearch to test a connection. To instruct a client to use StartTLS, we need to use the -z flag. But if just -z is specified, if the client fails TLS negotiation with the server, it will continue with the transaction in clear text. In other words, with -z, TLS is preferred, but not required. To make TLS required, we will add an extra z to the flag, making it -ZZ:

```
$ ldapsearch -LLL -x -W -D 'cn=Manager,dc=example,dc=com' -H \
            ldap://example.com -ZZ '(uid=manny)'
```

This should prompt for a password and then return one result:

```
Enter LDAP Password:
dn: uid=manny,ou=Users,dc=example,dc=com
sn: Kant
uid: immanuel
uid: manny
ou: Users
objectClass: person
objectClass: organizationalPerson
objectClass: inetOrgPerson
givenName: Manny
cn: Manny Kant
```

If the result comes back like this, then TLS was successfully configured. But TLS can be difficult to get configured because it is strict by design. Small errors in configuration (like using a domain name that differs from the one in the CN field of the certificate) can prevent TLS from working. Consider this example:

```
$ ldapsearch -LL -x -W -D 'cn=Manager,dc=example,dc=com' -H \
    ldap://localhost -ZZ '(uid=manny)'

ldap_start_tls: Connect error (-11)
    additional info: TLS: hostname does not match CN in peer
    certificate
```

In this case, the host name specified on the command line (`localhost`) differed from the one in the CN field of the certificate (`example.com`). Even though, in this case, the two domain names are hosted on the same system, TLS will not accept the mismatch.

Other common errors in TLS are:

- Reversing the values of the `TLSCertificateFile` and the `TLSCertificateKeyFile` directives
- Forgetting to install the CA certificate (which results in an error indicating that the server certificate cannot be verified)
- Forgetting to set the client CA path correctly in `ldap.conf`
- Setting the read/write permissions (or the ownership) on the key file (or the certificate file) in such a way that the SLAPD server cannot read it

While OpenLDAP can be forgiving in many areas, TLS configuration is not one of them. It pays to take extra care when configuring TLS and SSL.

Configuring LDAPS

Now that we have configured TLS, we need to take only a few additional steps to enable SSL/TLS on its own port. The traditional port for running dedicated TLS/SSL-protected LDAP traffic is port 636, the LDAPS port.

Most of the time it is better to use StartTLS. However, network considerations (like clients that do not support StartTLS or policies dictating mandatory blocking on ports that allow non-encrypted text) might warrant using LDAPS.

Keep in mind that LDAPS and StartTLS can both be used for the same server. SLAPD can accept LDAPS traffic on a dedicated port, and continue to provide the StartTLS feature on an LDAP port.

Like the StartTLS configuration, this configuration requires that the slapd.conf file have the TLSCertificateFile, TLSCertificateKeyFile, and TLSCACertificateDir directives set.

Getting SLAPD to listen on this port requires passing an additional parameter when starting slapd. In Ubuntu, as with other Debian-based distributions, configuration parameters can be set in the /etc/defaults/slapd file. In that file we just need to set SLAPD_SERVICES. When the start script is executed, SLAPD will start all of the services listed here.

```
SLAPD_SERVICES="ldap:/// ldaps:///"
```

The given code tells SLAPD to listen on all available IP addresses on both the default LDAP (port 389) and the default LDAPS (port 636). If we wanted SLAPD to only listen on one address for LDAP traffic, but all addresses for LDAPS traffic, we could replace the above with:

```
SLAPD_SERVICES="ldap://127.0.0.1/ ldaps:///"
```

Here, the ldap://127.0.0.1/ tells SLAPD to only listen on the loopback address for LDAP traffic, while ldaps:/// indicates that SLAPD should listen for LDAPS traffic on all of the IP addresses configured for this host. You will need to restart SLAPD in order for these changes to take effect.

Similarly, if you built from source and want to start slapd directly, the -h command line flag lets you specify which services to start:

```
/usr/local/libexec/slapd -h "ldap:/// ldaps:///"
```

That is all there is to configuring LDAPS. We can now test it with ldapsearch:

```
ldapsearch -LL -x -W -D 'cn=Manager,dc=example,dc=com' -H \
    ldaps://example.com '(uid=manny)'
```

There are two crucial differences between this ldapsearch and the ones we used when testing StartTLS:

- The protocol for the URL specified after the -H flag is ldaps:// rather than ldap://.

- There is no -Z or -ZZ flag here. Those flags tell the client to send the StartTLS command, and SSL/TLS over a dedicated port do not recognize the StartTLS command.

If you get an error doing the given search, but StartTLS is working properly, the first place to look is at the firewall settings. Typically, firewalls allow traffic on port 389, but block 636. It is also useful to make sure that the server is actually listening on port 636. You can check this from a shell prompt using `netstat -tcp -l`, which will print out a list of what ports are being used. If LDAPS (636) does not show up, then check `/etc/defaults/slapd` again to make sure that the `SLAPD_SERVICES` directive is set correctly.

Debugging with the OpenSSL Client

In some cases it is useful to be able to connect to SLAPD over LDAPS and watch the certificate processing. The `openssl` program can do this with its built-in `s_client` client application:

```
$ openssl s_client -connect example.com:636
```

The `-connect` parameter takes a host name followed by a colon and a port number. When this command is run, `openssl` will connect to a remote server using SSL, and perform the certificate negotiation. The entire negotiation process is written to the screen. If certificate negotiation succeeds, then `openssl` leaves the connection open, and you can type in raw protocol commands at the command line. To exit, just hit *CTRL+C*.

Now we have both StartTLS and TLS/SSL working. We have one more short item to cover in this section, and then we will move on to authentication.

Using Security Strength Factors

There are advantages to running StartTLS. It is simpler to configure, it is easier (in many respects) to debug, and complex transactions can switch back and forth from cleartext to encryption as needed.

But there is one clear drawback: we can use a standard firewall to block non-encrypted traffic when all clear text goes over one port and all encrypted traffic goes over another. But when both go over the same port, many firewalls can't do much to verify that the traffic is secure.

But OpenLDAP does provide some tools for implementing this sort of security in SLAPD, instead of in a firewall.

OpenLDAP can examine the integrity and encryption state of a connection and, based on those features, assign a **Security Strength Factor (SSF)** to that connection. An SSF is a numeric representation of the strength of the protective measures used.

Most of the SSF numbers simply reflect the key length of the encryption cipher. For example, since the maximum key length for **DES** is 56, when a connection is protected using DES, the SSF is 56. **Triple-DES (3DES)**, which is the cipher used by default in Ubuntu's OpenSSL configuration, has a key length of 112. Hence, its SSF is also 112. The **AES** cipher, which is strong and can be computed quickly, can use different key sizes. AES-128 uses a 128-bit key, while AES-256 uses a 256-bit key. In the case of AES then, the SSF will reflect the key size.

There are two special SSF numbers: 0 and 1. An SSF of 0 indicates (as might be expected) that no security measures have been implemented. An SSF of 1 indicates that only integrity checking on the connection is being done.

OpenLDAP can use SSF information to determine whether a client is allowed to connect to the directory. SSF information can also be used in ACLs and in SASL configuration, effectively allowing complex rules to be built as to what conditions a client connection must satisfy before getting access to perform certain operations on the directory.

We will look at SASL authentication and ACLs later in this chapter, but right now we will look at using SSFs in the `security` directive in `slapd.conf` as a way of specifying how secure a connection must be in order to access the database.

The security Directive

The `security` directive can be used in two different contexts in `slapd.conf`. If it is put near the top of the file, before any backend databases are defined, then it is placed in the *global* context and will apply to all connections. On the other hand, if the security directive is placed within a backend definition, then it will only be applied to that particular database. For example, consider a case where there are two backends:

```
include /etc/ldap/schema/core.schema

modulepath /usr/local/libexec/openldap
moduleload back_hdb
# Other configuration directives ...

# DB 1:
database hdb
suffix "ou=Users,dc=example,dc=com"
# More directives for DB 1...
# DB 2:
database bdb
suffix "ou=System,dc=example,dc=com"
# More directives for DB 2...
```

This partial example of a `slapd.conf` file defines two directory backends. Now, if the `security` directive is used before the first database is defined (namely before the line that says `database hdb`), then it will be applied globally to all connections.

But if we wanted to allow non-encrypted connections to DB 2, but allow only well-encrypted connections to DB 1 (which houses all of our user entries), we could use separate `security` directives:

```
include /etc/ldap/schema/core.schema

modulepath /usr/local/libexec/openldap
moduleload back_hdb
loglevel stats
# Other configuration directives ...

# DB 1:
database hdb
suffix "ou=Users,dc=example,dc=com"
security ssf=112
# More directives for DB 1...

# DB 2:
database bdb
suffix "ou=System,dc=example,dc=com"
security ssf=0
# More directives for DB 2...
```

Note the addition of the two highlighted lines—two separate `security` directives, one for each database backend.

Now, restarting the directory (note that the `loglevel` is set to `stats`), we can test out the security parameters with `ldapsearch`. First, we will try to search the `Users` OU with a non-TLS connection:

```
$ ldapsearch -x -W -D 'uid=matt,ou=Users,dc=example,dc=com' -b \
            'ou=Users,dc=example,dc=com' '(uid=david)' uid
```

In the log we see entries like this:

```
conn=0 fd=12 ACCEPT from IP=127.0.0.1:48758 (IP=0.0.0.0:389)
conn=0 op=0 BIND dn="uid=matt,ou=Users,dc=example,dc=com" method=128
conn=0 op=0 RESULT tag=97 err=13 text=confidentiality required
conn=0 fd=12 closed (connection lost)
connection_read(12): no connection!
```

The third line indicates that the server returned error number 13: `confidentiality required`. This is because we did not do anything to protect the connection. Using simple authentication (which is not encrypted) and failing to use TLS/SSL resulted in the client connection having an effective SSF of 0.

Next, let's do the same search with TLS turned on:

```
$ ldapsearch -x -W -D 'uid=matt,ou=Users,dc=example,dc=com' -b \
            'ou=Users,dc=example,dc=com' -Z '(uid=david)' uid
```

Note that in this example, the `-Z` flag is included to send the StartTLS command. Now, the server log says:

```
conn=1 fd=12 ACCEPT from IP=127.0.0.1:44684 (IP=0.0.0.0:389)
conn=1 op=0 STARTTLS
conn=1 op=0 RESULT oid= err=0 text=
conn=1 fd=12 TLS established tls_ssf=256 ssf=256
conn=1 op=1 BIND dn="uid=matt,ou=Users,dc=example,dc=com" method=128
conn=1 op=1 BIND dn="uid=matt,ou=Users,dc=example,dc=com" mech=SIMPLE
ssf=0
conn=1 op=1 RESULT tag=97 err=0 text=
```

There are a few things to note about this result. On the second line, OpenLDAP reports that it is doing StartTLS. Two lines later it reports: `TLS established tls_ssf=256 ssf=256`. This line indicates that the TLS connection has an SSF of 256 (since the connection is using AES-256), and that the total SSF of the connection is 256.

If you look a few lines lower, on the second line that begins BIND, you will notice that there another SSF is reported: `ssf=0`. Why?

OpenLDAP measures SSF on various aspects of the connection. First, as we can see above, it checks the SSF of the network connection. TLS/SSL connections are assigned an SSF based on their cipher strength.

But during the bind phase when the client authenticates to the directory, OpenLDAP also measures the SSF of the authentication mechanism. The simple (`mech=SIMPLE`) authentication mechanism does not encrypt the password, and so it is always given an SSF of 0.

The total SSF for the connection, however, remains at 256, with the TLS SSF being 256 and the SASL SSF at 0.

A Fine-Grained security Directive

The `security` directive that we have looked at so far is basic. It simply requires that the overall SSF be 112 (3DES encryption) or greater, but we can make it more specific.

For example, we can simply require that any TLS connection have at least a 128 bit key:

```
security tls=128
```

This will require that all incoming connections use TLS with a strong (128 bit or greater) cipher.

> In some cases it is desirable to define which TLS/SSL ciphers or cipher families will be used. This cannot be done with the `security` directive. Instead, you will need to use the `TLSCipherSuite` directive, which will allow you to give a detailed specification for which ciphers are acceptable for TLS/SSL connections.

Or, if we only wanted to define a strong SSF for connections that try to perform a simple bind (as opposed to an SASL bind), then we can specify an SSF just for simple binding:

```
security simple_bind=128
```

This will require that some strong TLS cipher be used to protect the authentication information.

> If you plan to allow simple binding, and you are running on a non-secure network, you are strongly advised to configure TLS/SSL and require TLS encryption during the bind operation using the `security` directive.

You can also use the `update_ssf` keyword in the `security` directive to set the SSF necessary for updating operations. Thus you could specify that only low-grade encryption is needed for reading the directory, but high-grade encryption must be used for performing updates to directory information:

```
security ssf=56 update_ssf=256
```

In the coming section, we will look at SASL configuration. You can use the `security` directive to set SSF for SASL binding as well using the `sasl=` and `update_sasl=` phrases.

Finally, in rare cases where OpenLDAP is listening on a local socket (that is, `ldapi://`), you can use `security transport=112` (or whatever cipher strength you desire) to ensure that traffic coming over that socket is encrypted.

At this point, we have completed our examination of SSL and TLS. Next, we will move on to the second of our three aspects of security: authentication.

Authenticating Users to the Directory

As we have seen earlier in the book, OpenLDAP supports two different methods of binding (or authenticating) to the directory. The first is to use simple binding. The second is to use SASL binding. In this part we will look at each of these two methods of authentication.

It is not necessary to choose one or the other. OpenLDAP can be configured to do both, at which point it is up to the client as to which method will be used. Simple binding is easier to configure (there is very little configuration that must be done). But SASL is more secure and more flexible, though these benefits come at the cost of added complexity.

The basics of the bind operation and the authentication process are covered early in Chapter 3. While we will review some of that materials here, you may find it useful to glance back at that section.

Simple Binding

The first form of authentication we will look at is simple binding. It is simple not necessarily from the user's perspective, but it is definitely easier to configure, and the process of binding is easier on the server, too, since less processing is needed.

To perform a simple bind the server requires two pieces of information: a DN and a password. If both the DN and the password fields are empty then the server attempts to bind as the Anonymous user.

During a simple bind the client connects to the server and sends the DN and password information to the server, without adding any additional security. The password, for example, is not specially encrypted.

If the client is communicating over TLS/SSL, then the whole transaction will be encrypted, and so the password will be safe. If the client is not using TLS/SSL then the password will be sent over the network in cleartext. This, of course, is a security issue, and should be avoided (perhaps by using the `security` directive discussed in the previous section, or by using an SASL bind instead of a simple bind).

There are two common ways in which client applications attempt to perform a simple bind. The first is sometimes called **Fast Bind**. In a Fast Bind, the client supplies a full DN (uid=matt,ou=users,dc=example,dc=com) and also a password (myPassword). It is faster than the common alternative (binding as anonymous and searching for the desired DN).

> **Cyrus SASLAuthd**, which provides SASL authentication services to other applications, is the application in which the term "Fast Bind" was first used. SASLAuthd is a useful tool for providing SASL authentication services. We will look at it again in the next section. Nowhere in the OpenLDAP documentation, is the term "Fast Bind" used.

The directory first performs, as the anonymous user, an **auth** access on the userPassword attribute of the DN that the client supplies. In an auth access the server compares the value of the supplied password to the value of the userPassword stored in the directory. If the userPassword value is hashed (with, for example, SSHA or SMD5), then SLAPD hashes the password that the user supplies, and then compares the hashes. If the values match, OpenLDAP binds the user and allows it to perform other LDAP operations.

> The OpenLDAP command-line clients, when used with the -x option, perform simple binding. The clients require that you specify the entire user DN and a password, and they then perform a Fast Bind.

That's a Fast Bind. But there is a second common method of doing a simple bind—a method designed to eliminate the requirement that the user know an entire DN.

In this second method (which is not, incidentally, called a "slow bind"), the client application requires that the user only know some particular unique identifier— usually the value of uid or cn. The client application then binds to the server as anonymous (or another pre-configured user) and performs a search for a DN that contains the matching attribute value. If it finds one (and only one) matching DN, then it re-binds, using the retrieved DN and the user-supplied password.

Usually, client applications that use simple bind will need a base DN. The second method of performing a simple bind requires one additional piece of information not required in a Fast Bind: a search filter. The filter is usually something like (&(uid=?)(objectclass=inetOrgPerson)), where the question mark (?) is replaced by the user-supplied value.

Using an Authentication User for Simple Binding

While it is more convenient for the user when only a user ID or a CN is required, the second method we have seen may raise an additional concern: the Anonymous user, in order to perform the search, must have *read* access to all user records in the directory. This means that anyone can connect to the directory (remember, Anonymous has no password) and perform searches.

In many cases this isn't a problem. Allowing someone to see a list of all the users in the directory may not be a security concern at all. But in other cases, such access would not be acceptable.

One way to work around this problem is to use a different user (rather than Anonymous) to perform the search for the user's DN. In the last chapter, we created just such an account. Here is the LDIF record we used:

```
# Special Account for Authentication:
dn: uid=authenticate,ou=System,dc=example,dc=com
uid: authenticate
ou: System
description: Special account for authenticating users
userPassword: secret
objectClass: account
objectClass: simpleSecurityObject
```

The purpose of this account is to log into the server and perform searches for DNs. In other words, it conducts the same job as the Anonymous user, but it adds a little more security, since clients that use the `uid=authenticate` account will have to have the appropriate password, too.

To make this clear let's look at the case where a client, configured to use the Authenticate account, binds a user that identifies himself as `matt` with the password `myPassword`.

Here's a step-by-step breakdown of what happens when doing a bind operation this way:

1. Client connects to the server and starts a bind operation with the DN `uid=autenticate,ou=system,dc=example,dc=com` and the password `secret`.

2. The server, as Anonymous, compares the Authenticate password, `secret`, with the value of the `userPassword` attribute for the `uid=autenticate,ou=system,dc=example,dc=com` record.

3. If the above succeeds, then the client (now logged in as the Authenticate user) performs a search with the filter: `(&(uid=matt)(objectclass=inetOrgPerson))`. Since `uid` is unique, the search should return either 0 or 1 record.

4. If one matching DN is found (in our case, it would be `uid=matt,ou=user, dc=example,dc=com`), then the client tries to re-bind as this DN, and using the password the user initially supplies to the client (`myPassword`).

5. The server, as Anonymous, compares the user-supplied password, `myPassword`, with the value of the `userPassword` attribute of `uid=matt, ou=user,dc=example,dc=com`.

6. If the password comparison succeeds then the client application can continue performing LDAP operations as `uid=matt,ou=user,dc=example,dc=com`.

The process is lengthy and it requires that the client application be configured with bind DN and password information for the Authenticate user, but it adds an additional layer of security to an Anonymous bind and search.

In this section, we have looked at three different ways of performing a simple bind. Each of these methods is useful in particular circumstances, and when used in conjunction with SSL/TLS, simple binding does not pose a significant security threat when the password is transmitted across the network.

Simple Binding Directives in slapd.conf

There are only a few directives in `slapd.conf` that have any bearing on simple binding. Simple binding is allowed by default. To prevent SLAPD from accepting simple bind operations, you can use the `require SASL` directive which will require that all bind operations are SASL bind operations. Additionally, the `security` directive provides the `simple_bind=` SSF check, which can be used to require a minimum SSF for simple bind operations. This is covered in more detail in the section entitled *The security Directive*.

Later in this book we will examine several third party applications that use simple binding when connecting to the directory.

But there are times when it is desirable to have an even more secure authentication process, or when the bind-search-rebind method of simple binding is too much for the client to do. In such cases using SASL binding may be even better.

SASL Binding

SASL provides a second method of authenticating to the OpenLDAP directory. SASL works by supplanting the simple bind method outlined above with a more robust authentication process.

The SASL standard is defined in RFC 2222
(`http://www.rfc-editor.org/rfc/rfc2222.txt`).

SASL supports a number of different kinds of underlying authentication
mechanisms, ranging from login/password combinations to more complex
configurations like **One-Time Passwords (OTP)** and even **Kerberos**
ticket-based authentication.

While SASL provides dozens of different configuration options, we will cover only
one. We will configure SASL for doing **DIGEST-MD5** authentication. It is slightly
more difficult to set up than some SASL mechanisms, but does not require the
detailed configuration involved in **GSSAPI** or Kerberos.

Later in this chapter, we will integrate our SASL work with our SSL/TLS work, and
use the **SASL EXTERNAL mechanism** for authenticating to the directory with client
SSL certificates.

 The Cyrus SASL documentation (at `/usr/share/doc/libsasl2`
or available online at `http://asg.web.cmu.edu/sasl/`) provides
information on implementing other mechanisms.

In DIGEST-MD5 authentication, the user's password will be encrypted by the SASL
client, sent across the network in its encrypted form only, then decrypted by the
server and compared to a cleartext version of the password.

The advantage to using DIGEST-MD5 is that the password is protected when
transmitted over the network. The disadvantage, however, is that the passwords
must be stored on the server in cleartext.

Contrast this with the way simple bind works. In a simple bind the password
itself is not encrypted when crossing the network, but the copy of the password
stored in the database is stored in an encrypted format (unless you configure
OpenLDAP otherwise).

Keep in mind that when SSL/TLS is used, all data transmitted over the connection is
encrypted, including passwords.

Configuring SASL is more complex than configuring simple bind operations. There
are two parts to configuring SASL support:

- Configuration of Cyrus SASL
- Configuration of OpenLDAP

Configuring Cyrus SASL

When we installed OpenLDAP in Chapter 2, one of the packages we installed was Cyrus SASL (the library was named `libsasl2`). We will also need the SASL command-line tools, which are included in the `sasl2-bin` package:

```
$ sudo apt-get install sasl2-bin
```

Included in this package are the `saslpasswd2` program and the SASL testing client and server applications.

Now we are ready to start configuring.

The SASL Configuration File

The SASL library can be used by numerous applications, and each application can have its own SASL configuration file. SASL configuration files are stored in the `/usr/lib/sasl2` directory. In that directory, we will create a configuration file for OpenLDAP. The file, `slapd.conf`, looks like this:

```
# SASL Configuration
pwcheck_method: auxprop
sasldb_path: /etc/sasldb2
```

 Do not confuse this `slapd.conf`, located at `/usr/lib/sasl2` with the main `slapd.conf` file at `/etc/ldap/`. These are two different files.

As usual, lines that begin with the pound sign (#) are comments. The second line determines how SASL will try to check passwords. For example, SASL comes with a stand-alone server, **saslauthd**, which will handle password checking. In our case though, we want to use the `auxprop` plugin, which does the password checking itself, rather than querying the `saslauthd` server.

The last line tells SASL where the password database (which stores a cleartext version of all of the passwords) is located. The standard location for this database is `/etc/sasldb2`.

Setting a User Password

As we get started, we will store the SASL password in the `/etc/sasldb2` database. To add a password to the database we use the `saslpasswd2` program:

```
$ sudo saslpasswd2 -c -u example.com matt
```

Note that we have to run the above using `sudo` because the password file is owned by root. Both `sudo` and `saslpasswd2` will prompt you to enter a password.

The `-c` argument for `saslpasswd2` indicates that we want the user ID to be created if it does not already exist. `-u example.com` sets the **SASL realm**. SASL uses realms as a way to partition the authentication name space. Client applications typically provide SASL with three pieces of information: the username, the password, and the realm. By default, clients will send their domain name as the realm.

Using realms, it is possible to give the same user name different passwords for different applications or application contexts. For example, `matt` in realm `example.com` can have one password, while `matt` in realm `testing.example.com` can have a different password.

For our purposes we need only one realm, and we will name it `example.com`. When the given command is run it will prompt for a password for user `matt`, and then prompt for a password confirmation. If the passwords match, it will store the password in clear text in the SASL password database.

Now we are ready to configure OpenLDAP.

Configuring SLAPD for SASL Support

The OpenLDAP side of SASL configuration is done in the `slapd.conf` file for the server, and the `ldap.conf` file for the client. In this section, we will focus on the SLAPD server.

When OpenLDAP receives a SASL authentication request it receives four pieces of information from the client. The four fields of information it gets are:

- Username: This field contains the ID that the user supplied when authenticating.
- Realm: This field contains the SASL realm in which the user is authenticated.
- SASL Mechanism: This field indicates which authentication system (mechanism) was used. Given our SASL configuration, this should be DIGEST-MD5.
- Authentication Information: This field is always set to `auth` to indicate that the user needs authentication.

All of this information is compacted into one DN-like string that looks like this:

```
uid=matt,cn=example.com,cn=DIGEST-MD5,cn=auth
```

The order of the fields above is the same as the order of the bulleted list: User-name, realm, SASL mechanism, and authentication information. Note however, that the realm is not required and might not always be present. If SASL does not use any realm information, the realm field will be omitted.

Of course, we do not have any records in our LDAP with DNs like the SASL string above. So, in order to correlate the authenticated SASL user with a user in the LDAP, we need to set up some method of converting the above DN-like string into a DN that is structured like the DNs in the directory. So we want to make the given string into something like this:

```
uid=matt,ou=Users,dc=example,dc=com
```

There are two ways of doing this mapping. We can either configure a simple string replacement rule to convert the SASL information string to a DN like the last one, or we could perform a search of the directory for an entry with a uid that is matt, and then, if a match is found, use that matching entry's DN.

Each of these two methods has its advantages and disadvantages. Using string replacement is faster, but it is less flexible, and it may not be sufficient for complex directory information trees. Using string replacement it may be necessary to use several authz-regexp directives in a row, each one with a different regular expression and replacement string.

Searching for the user on the other hand, can be much more flexible in a directory with lots of subtrees. But it will incur the overhead of doing an additional search of the LDAP tree, and it may require tweaking ACLs to allow pre-authentication searches.

Both methods use the same directive in slapd.conf: the authz-regexp directive. Let's look at an example of each method, beginning with the string replacement method.

Using a Replacement String in authz-regexp

The authz-regexp directive takes two parameters: a regular expression for getting information out of the SASL DN-like string, and a replacement function (which is different depending on whether we do string replacement or a search).

For our regular expression we want to take the username from the SASL information and map it to the uid field in a DN. We don't really need any of the information in the other three SASL fields, so our regular expression is fairly simple:

```
"^uid=([^,]+).*,cn=auth$"
```

This rule starts at the beginning of the line (^) and looks for an entry that starts with uid=. The next part, ([^,]+), stores characters after uid= and before a comma (,) in a special variable called $1. The rule reads "match as many characters as possible (but at least one character) that are not commas and store them in the first variable ($1)."

After that, the rule (using .* to match anything) skips over the realm (if there is one) and the mechanism, and then looks for a match at the end of the line: cn=auth$ (where the dollar sign ($) indicates a line ending).

Once the regular expression is run we should have a variable, $1, which contains the user's name. Now we can use that value in a replacement rule, setting the uid value to the value of $1. The entire authz-regexp line looks like this:

```
authz-regexp "^uid=([^,]+).*,cn=auth$"
                "uid=$1,ou=Users,dc=example,dc=com"
```

After the authz-regexp directive, I have inserted the regular expression we just looked at. After the regular expression comes the replacement rule, which instructs SLAPD to insert the value of $1 in the uid field of this template DN.

The authz-regexp directive can go anywhere in the slapd.conf file before the first database directive.

Since authz-regexp is the only necessary directive for configuring SASL, we can now test SLAPD from the command line, without making any additional changes to slapd.conf:

```
$ ldapsearch -LLL -U matt@example.com -v '(uid=matt)' uid
ldap_initialize( <DEFAULT> )
SASL/DIGEST-MD5 authentication started
Please enter your password:
SASL username: matt@example.com
SASL SSF: 128
SASL installing layers
filter: (uid=matt)
requesting: uid
dn: uid=matt,ou=Users,dc=example,dc=com
uid: matt
```

Previously, we have used the -x flag, combined with -W and -D, to do a simple bind with a full DN and a password.

With SASL however, we don't need the full DN. All we need is a shortened connection string. So, instead of using the -x, -W, and -D flags, we just use -U matt@example.com. The -U flag takes a SASL username and (optionally) a realm. The realm is appended to the username, separated by the *at* sign (@). So, in the given example, we are connecting with username matt and realm example.com.

Next, ldapsearch prompts for a password (see the highlighted line in the example). This is not our LDAP password, but our SASL password—the one in the account we created when we ran saslpasswd2.

To review, what is happening in the previous command is this:

- The client is connecting to SLAPD requesting an SASL bind.
- SLAPD uses the SASL subsystem (which checks the `/usr/lib/sasl/slapd.conf` file for settings) to tell the client how to authenticate. In this case, it tells the client to use DIGEST-MD5.
- The client sends the authentication information to SLAPD.
- SLAPD performs the translation specified in `authz-regexp`.
- SLAPD then checks the client's response (using the SASL subsystem) against the information in `/etc/sasldb2`.
- When the client authentication succeeds, OpenLDAP runs the search and returns the results to the client.

Now we are ready to look at using `authz-regexp` to search the directory with a specific filter.

Using a Search Filter in authz-regexp

In this case, we want to search the directory for an entry that matches the username (`uid`) received during the SASL bind. Recall that the SASL authentication information comes in a string that looks like this:

```
uid=matt,cn=example.com,cn=DIGEST-MD5,cn=auth
```

In the last case, we mapped the given directly on to a DN of the form:

```
uid=<username>,ou=users,dc=example,dc=com.
```

But what do we do if we don't know, for example, if the user `matt` is in the Users OU or the System OU? A simple mapping function will not work. We need to search the directory. We will do this by changing the last argument in our `authz-regexp` directive.

Our new `authz-regexp` directive looks like this:

```
authz-regexp "^uid=([^,]+).*,cn=auth$"
             "ldap:///dc=example,dc=com??sub?(uid=$1)"
```

This regular expression is the same as the one in the previous example. But the second argument to `authz-regexp` is an LDAP URL.

 For an overview of writing and using LDAP URLs see **Appendix B**.

This LDAP URL instructs SLAPD to search in the base dc=example,dc=com (using a subtree (sub) search) for an entry whose uid equals the value of $1, which gets replaced by the value retrieved from the regular expression in the first argument to authz-regexp. If the user matt attempts to authenticate, for example, the URL will look like this:

```
ldap:///dc=example,dc=com??sub?(uid=matt)
```

When SLAPD performs that search against our directory information tree, it will get a single record back—the record with the DN uid=matt,ou=Users,dc=example, dc=com.

Here's an example using ldapsearch. It is the same example used in the previous section, and it should have the same results even though we are using the LDAP search method:

```
$ ldapsearch -LLL -U matt@example.com -v '(uid=matt)' uid
ldap_initialize( <DEFAULT> )
SASL/DIGEST-MD5 authentication started
Please enter your password:
SASL username: matt@example.com
SASL SSF: 128
SASL installing layers
filter: (uid=matt)
requesting: uid
dn: uid=matt,ou=Users,dc=example,dc=com
uid: matt
```

A Note on ACLs and Search Filters

When SLAPD reads the search filter, it performs a search of the directory. But the search is done as the Anonymous user. What this means is that we will need to make sure that the Anonymous user will need to have the requisite permissions to search the directory using the filter.

Given our last example, the Anonymous user will need to be able to search the dc=example,dc=com subtree for uid values. The ACLs that we created in Chapter 2 do not grant the Anonymous user any such permission. We will need to add one rule to our ACLs in order to allow the search to operate successfully:

```
access to attrs=uid
        by anonymous read
        by users read
```

This rule, which should appear at the top of the list of ACLs, grants read access to the uid attribute to anonymous and to any authenticated users on the system. The important part, in this example, is that Anonymous gets read access.

Keep in mind that by adding this rule, we are making it possible for unauthenticated users to see what user IDs exist in the database. Depending on the nature of your directory data, this may be a security issue. If this is a problem you can either use the string replacement method (remember, you can use several `authz-regexp` expressions in a row to handle more complex pattern matching), or you can try to reduce exposure to the `uid` field by building more restrictive ACLs

Later in this chapter, we will take a more detailed look at ACLs.

Failure of Mapping

In some cases the mapping done by `authz-regexp` will fail. That is, SLAPD will search the directory (using the search filter) and not find any matches. The user, however, is authenticated, and SLAPD will not fail to bind.

Instead, what will happen is that the user will bind as the SASL DN. Thus, the effective DN may be something like:

```
uid=matt,cn=example.com,cn=digest-md5,cn=auth
```

It makes no difference that there is no actual record in the directory with that username. The client will still be able to access the directory.

But this DN is also subject to ACLs, so you can write access controls targeted at users who have authenticated through SASL but who do not have a DN corresponding to a record in the directory.

Removing the Need to Specify the Realm

In our configuration all of the users are in the same realm, `example.com`. Rather than typing that the username and the realm be typed in every time, we can configure a default realm in `slapd.conf` by adding the following directive:

```
sasl-realm   example.com
```

If we restart the server with this new modification, we can now run an `ldapsearch` without having to specify the realm:

```
$ ldapsearch -LLL -U matt -v '(uid=matt)' uid
ldap_initialize( <DEFAULT> )
SASL/DIGEST-MD5 authentication started
Please enter your password:
SASL username: matt
SASL SSF: 128
SASL installing layers
filter: (uid=matt)
requesting: uid
dn: uid=matt,ou=Users,dc=example,dc=com
uid: matt
```

This time, passing -U matt was sufficient for authentication. SLAPD automatically inserted the default realm into the SASL information.

Debugging the SASL Configuration

Getting the correct SASL configuration can be frustrating. One way of improving your ability to debug is to configure logging in such a way that you can see what is going on during a SASL transaction. The `trace` debugging level (1) can be used to watch what is happening in SASL. You can either set the debug level in `slapd.conf` to trace (or just the digit 1), or you can run `slapd` in the foreground on the command line:

```
$ sudo slapd -d trace
# some of the voluminous output removed...
slap_sasl_getdn: u:id converted to uid=matt,cn=DIGEST-MD5,cn=auth
>>> dnNormalize: <uid=matt,cn=DIGEST-MD5,cn=auth>
<<< dnNormalize: <uid=matt,cn=digest-md5,cn=auth>
==>slap_sasl2dn: converting SASL name uid=matt,cn=digest-md5,cn=auth
                to a DN
slap_authz_regexp: converting SASL name
                uid=matt,cn=digest-md5,cn=auth
slap_authz_regexp: converted SASL name to
                uid=matt,ou=Users,dc=example,dc=com
slap_parseURI: parsing uid=matt,ou=Users,dc=example,dc=com
ldap_url_parse_ext(uid=matt,ou=Users,dc=example,dc=com)
>>> dnNormalize: <uid=matt,ou=Users,dc=example,dc=com>
<<< dnNormalize: <uid=matt,ou=users,dc=example,dc=com>
<==slap_sasl2dn: Converted SASL name to
                uid=matt,ou=users,dc=example,dc=com
slap_sasl_getdn: dn:id converted to

                uid=matt,ou=users,dc=example,dc=com
```

Following this log, we can see the initial SASL string, `uid=matt,cn=DIGEST-MD5,cn=auth`, and watch as it is normalized, run through the regular expression, and converted to `uid=matt,ou=users,dc=example,dc=com`.

The `ldapwhoami` client and the `slapauth` utility are also useful when attempting to debug SASL. An example of using `ldapwhoami` to evaluate the results of `authz-regexp` is given in the next section.

Using Client SSL/TLS Certificates to Authenticate

SASL and SSL/TLS can be used in combination to perform **SASL EXTERNAL authentication**. In SASL EXTERNAL authentication the SASL module relies upon an external source, in this case a client's X.509 certificate, as a source of identity.

Using this configuration a client with an appropriately signed certificate can bind to SLAPD without having to enter a username and password, but in a way that is still secure.

How does this work? Just as it is possible to issue a server a certificate for SSL/TLS communication, it is also possible to issue one to a user or client. We have discussed already how a certificate provides, in a secure way, identity information about a server. A client certificate can serve the same purpose.

Authentication, using SASL EXTERNAL works like this:

- The client and server communicate with SSL/TLS protection, either using LDAPS or using StartTLS
- When the server sends its certificate, it requests that the client also provide a certificate
- The client sends its own certificate, which includes the following
    - Identity information
    - A public key
    - The signature of a certificate authority that the server will recognize
- The server, after verifying the certificate, passes the identity information on to SLAPD through the SASL subsystem
- SLAPD then uses that information to bind

Since the certificate sent by the client contains all of the information needed to verify the client's identity, no login/password combination is needed.

Configuring the SASL EXTERNAL mechanism requires the following steps:

1. Create a new client certificate
2. Configure the client to send the certificate
3. Configure SLAPD to correctly handle client certificates
4. Configure SLAPD to correctly translate the identity information provided in the client certificate

Creating a New Client Certificate

Creating a new client certificate is not significantly different from creating a server certificate. We will use the same certificate authority that we created earlier in this chapter.

First, we need to create a new certificate request:

```
$ /usr/lib/ssl/misc/CA.pl -newreq
Generating a 1024 bit RSA private key
...........++++++
..++++++
unable to write 'random state'
writing new private key to 'newkey.pem'
Enter PEM pass phrase:
Verifying - Enter PEM pass phrase:
-----
You are about to be asked to enter information that will be
    incorporated into your certificate request.
What you are about to enter is what is called a Distinguished
    Name or a DN.
There are quite a few fields but you can leave some blank
For some fields there will be a default value,
If you enter '.', the field will be left blank.
-----
Country Name (2 letter code) [AU]:US
State or Province Name (full name) [Some-State]:Illinois
Locality Name (eg, city) []:Chicago
Organization Name (eg, company)
    [Internet Widgits Pty Ltd]:Example.Com
Organizational Unit Name (eg, section) []:
Common Name (eg, YOUR name) []:matt
Email Address []:matt@example.com

Please enter the following 'extra' attributes
    to be sent with your certificate request
A challenge password []:
An optional company name []:
Request is in newreq.pem, private key is in newkey.pem
```

This process is just like the one before, though the fields are completed specifically for the user who is represented by this certificate. For example, if we were generating this certificate for Barbara, we would complete the **Common Name** and **Email Address** fields with her information.

What should go in the Common Name field?

Earlier we used the CN field to store a domain name. What should go in an individual's CN field? One option is to use the user's full name. A more pragmatic option is to use an identifier that is used in the user's LDAP DN (such as the value of the user's `uid` attribute). This makes mapping from a certificate to an LDAP record easier.

Now, we have the new request (`newreq.pem`) and key (`newkey.pem`). The next thing to do is sign the certificate with our CA's digital signature:

```
$ /usr/lib/ssl/misc/CA.pl -signreq
Using configuration from /usr/lib/ssl/openssl.cnf
Enter pass phrase for ./demoCA/private/cakey.pem:
Check that the request matches the signature
Signature ok
Certificate Details:
    Serial Number:
       ba:49:df:f5:8e:7e:77:c6
    Validity
      Not Before: Jul  4 03:28:28 2007 GMT
      Not After : Jul  3 03:28:28 2008 GMT
    Subject:
      countryName               = US
      stateOrProvinceName       = Illinois
      localityName              = Chicago
      organizationName          = Example.Com
      commonName                = matt
      emailAddress              = matt@example.com
    X509v3 extensions:
      X509v3 Basic Constraints:
        CA:FALSE
      Netscape Comment:
        OpenSSL Generated Certificate
      X509v3 Subject Key Identifier:
9A:97:8F:8C:95:1F:E0:6E:50:BD:DF:F4:C5:71:68:92:3F:A0:30:DD
      X509v3 Authority Key Identifier:
keyid:6B:FB:66:33:5D:DB:32:40:42:D7:71:F7:F0:D0:7C:94:3E:8F:CD:58

Certificate is to be certified until
    Jul 3 03:28:28 2008 GMT (365 days)
Sign the certificate? [y/n]:y

1 out of 1 certificate requests certified, commit? [y/n]y
```

```
Write out database with 1 new entries
Data Base Updated
unable to write 'random state'
Signed certificate is in newcert.pem
```

Now, we have the signed certificate stored in the file `newcert.pem`.

The next thing to do is to move these files to a location that will be convenient for the user. In this case, we will make a new directory in the user's home directory and move the files into that directory:

```
$ sudo mkdir /home/mbutcher/certs

$ sudo mv new*.pem /home/mbutcher/certs

$ sudo chown -R mbutcher:mbutcher /home/mbutcher/certs
```

In these three lines, we make a new directory for the certs. In this case, the new `certs/` directory is in the user's home directory.

Then we move the newly-created certificate files into the new directory. We could rename these files but for now the generic name will suffice.

Finally, we need to make sure that the user has access to his or her certificates. This is done with the `chown` command.

The certificates are ready to use.

Configuring the Client

The next thing we need to do is configure the client to use the certificate and key. This is done by creating `.ldaprc` file in the user's home directory.

A **.ldaprc file** is a "personal" version of an `ldap.conf` file. It supports all of the directives normally included in `ldap.conf`, plus a couple of special directives, like the `TLS_CERT` and `TLS_KEY` directives.

Since I am the user `mbutcher`, I will create this file in my own home directory:

```
$ cd /home/mbutcher
$ touch .ldaprc
```

Now we can edit the `.ldaprc` file. This file needs to indicate that the client is using the SASL EXTERNAL mechanism. Also, it must contain directives about the certificate and key files that we want to use. Additionally, it is not a bad idea to specify the location of the CA certificates (or even to the specific certificate for the CA that signed the server's certificate), though this is usually done at a global level with the `ldap.conf` file.

The `.ldaprc` file then, looks like this:

```
SASL_MECH EXTERNAL
TLS_CERT /home/mbutcher/certs/newcert.pem
TLS_KEY /home/mbutcher/certs/newkey.pem
TLS_CACERT /etc/ssl/certs/Example.Com-CA.pem
```

The first directive, `SASL_MECH`, indicates what SASL mechanism the client is using. In our case the client is using the `EXTERNAL` SASL mechanism.

The `TLS_CERT` directive points to the location of the client's signed X.509 certificate, and the `TLS_KEY` directive indicates the location of the client's private key file.

The `TLS_CACERT` directive points to the specific certificate used for signing the server's certificate. This will be used by the client libraries to verify the identity of the server during SSL/TLS negotiation.

At this point the client is ready. Now we need to configure SLAPD.

Configuring the Server

SLAPD needs to do a few things in order to make the SASL EXTERNAL mechanism work:

- It must request a certificate from the client (otherwise the client will not present one)

- It needs to translate the identity information given in the client certificate into a DN that is meaningful in our environment

To set the server to request a client certificate is a matter of adding one directive. In the global section of the `slapd.conf` file, before any database directive is specified, the `TLSVerifyClient` directive should be added:

```
TLSCACertificateFile     /etc/ssl/certs/Example.Com-CA.pem
TLSCertificateFile       /etc/ldap/example.com.cert.pem
TLSCertificateKeyFile    /etc/ldap/example.com.key.pem
TLSVerifyClient          try
```

Only the highlighted line is new. The other lines we added earlier in the chapter.

`TLSVerifyClient` determines whether SLAPD will take steps to request and verify client certificates. There are four possible values:

- `never`: Never request a client certificate. This is the *default*. If no certificate is requested the client will not provide one. Hence SASL EXTERNAL authentication cannot be used when the `TLSVerifyClient` is set to `never`.

- `allow`: This will cause SLAPD to request a certificate from the client but if the client does not provide one, or if the provided one is not good (for example if the signature cannot be verified), the session will continue.

- `try`: In this case SLAPD will request a certificate from the client. If the client does not provide a certificate the session will continue. However, if the client provides a certificate that is bad, the session will terminate.

- `demand`: This will cause SLAPD to require a certificate from the client. If the client does not provide one, or if the provided one is not good, the session will terminate.

In the last example we set `TLSVerifyClient` to `try`. This simply means that if the client submits a certificate, it must be a valid certificate (with a known CA signature) before SLAPD will allow the connection. But it will also allow clients to connect without supplying a certificate (though such clients will not be able to use SASL EXTERNAL authentication).

If we wanted to force clients to provide a certificate then we would use the `demand` keyword instead of `try`.

At this point, we have SSL/TLS configured correctly. Now, we need to add one additional step: we need to map the identity provided by the certificate (which happens to be a DN) onto a DN for a directory user.

 Translating the certificate DN into another DN is not strictly necessary. A user can bind using a certificate DN even if it is not in the directory. ACLs can be written to target such DNs too.

The DN in the client certificate we create looks like this:

```
dn:email=matt@example.com,cn=matt,o=example.com,l=chicago,\
    st=illinois,c=us
```

Note that this is one long line.

The DN contains the information we entered when running `CA.pl -newreq`. What we want to do is translate this DN into the DN of the corresponding LDAP record: `uid=matt,ou=users,dc=example,dc=com`.

How is this translation done? Using the `authz-regexp` directive that we examined earlier in the section on SASL authentication.

There are two fields in the certificate's identity string that are particularly helpful in identifying the user: email and cn. Thus, a simple regular expression can capture these two fields:

```
^email=([^,]+),cn=([^,]+).*,c=us$
```

This will assign the email address to $1, and the CN to $2.

From here we could either specify an LDAP URL with a filter for looking up DNs by email address, or we could substitute the CN for the UID field used in the LDAP DN (since the CN maps cleanly onto UID).

We will use this second method, and create authz-regexp that looks like this:

```
authz-regexp "^email=([^,]+),cn=([^,]+).*,c=us$"
             "uid=$2,ou=Users,dc=example,dc=com"
```

This directive maps the CN value of the certificate DN to the UID attribute in the LDAP authorization DN. Thus, when a client connects with a certificate with the DN dn:email=matt@example.com,cn=matt,o=example.com,l=chicago, st=illinois,c=us, SLAPD will translate that into the DN uid=matt,ou=users, dc=example,dc=com.

Now we are ready to test things out.

Testing with ldapwhoami

The ideal client for testing this process is ldapwhoami. This will allow us to connect and bind with SASL EXTERNAL. In addition it will indicate whether or not authz-regexp mapped the certificate DN to our LDAP DN.

After restarting SLAPD to load the changes, we can test the server:

```
$ ldapwhoami -ZZ -H 'ldap://example.com'
Enter PEM pass phrase:
SASL/EXTERNAL authentication started
SASL username: emailAddress=matt@example.com,CN=Matt, \
               O=Example.Com,L=Chicago,ST=Illinois,C=US
SASL SSF: 0
dn:uid=matt,ou=users,dc=example,dc=com
Result: Success (0)
```

First, let's take a closer look at the command entered:

```
ldapwhoami -ZZ -H 'ldap://example.com'
```

The -zz flag requires that StartTLS negotiation be done successfully. Using only one z will attempt StartTLS, but not close the connect if the negotiations fail. Using -zz is always a good idea when attempting authentication with the SASL EXTERNAL mechanism.

Next, the -H 'ldap://example.com' parameter provides the URL of the SLAPD server. Remember that for StartTLS negotiation to work, here, the domain in the LDAP URL must match the domain in the server's certificate.

What happens when this command is executed? First, the user is prompted for a pass phrase:

```
Enter PEM pass phrase:
```

This prompt is actually generated by the SSL/TLS subsystem (OpenSSL). Recall that the key that we generated is protected by a pass phrase. In order to read the key file, the OpenSSL subsystem requires the pass phrase.

But didn't I say that the SASL EXTERNAL method can obviate the need for entering a password? Yes, it can—but to do so, we would need to remove the passphrase from the key as we did when generating the server certificate:

```
openssl rsa < newkey.pem > clearkey.pem
```

Then the TLS_KEY directive in .ldaprc would need to be adjusted to point to the clearkey.pem file.

Removing the pass phrase may be desirable in some circumstances, and undesirable in others. Keep in mind that removing the pass phrase from the key will make it easier for the certificate to be hijacked by someone else. A key without a pass phrase should be carefully protected by permissions and other means.

Once the user's pass phrase has been entered, SASL authentication begins:

```
SASL/EXTERNAL authentication started
SASL username: emailAddress=matt@example.com,CN=Matt, \
               O=Example.Com,L=Chicago,ST=Illinois,C=US
SASL SSF: 0
```

As can be seen here, the SASL EXTERNAL mechanism is used, and the SASL username is set to emailAddress=matt@example.com,CN=Matt, O=Example.Com,L=Chicago,ST=Illinois,C=US. Finally, the SASL security strength factor is set to 0 because no SASL security mechanism has been used. Instead, the security mechanisms are *external* to SASL. Since we are using SSL/TLS with an AES-256 encyrpted certificate, the overall SSF will still be 256.

One important detail to note is that SLAPD will normalize the DN. In normalized form the DN will look like this:

```
email=matt@example.com,cn=matt,o=example.com,l=chicago,st=illinois,\
   c=us
```

The `emailAddress` attribute has been converted to `email`, and all uppercase strings have been converted to lowercase. The `authz-regexp` that we looked at above operates on this normalized version of the DN.

Finally, the last few lines of output are the results of the LDAP Who Am I? operation:

```
dn:uid=matt,ou=users,dc=example,dc=com
Result: Success (0)
```

According to SLAPD, the client is currently performing directory operations with an effective DN of `uid=matt,ou=users,dc=example,dc=com`. This means that our mapping was successful.

What would the output look like if the `authz-regexp` mapping was not successful? It would look something like this:

```
$ ldapwhoami -ZZ -H 'ldap://example.com'
Enter PEM pass phrase:
SASL/EXTERNAL authentication started
SASL username:
emailAddress=matt@example.com,CN=Matt,O=Example.Com,L=Chicago,
   ST=Illinois,C=US
SASL SSF: 0
dn:email=matt@example.com,cn=matt,o=example.com,l=chicago,
   st=illinois,c=us
Result: Success (0)
```

The highlighted portion shows the result of the Who Am I? operation. The DN returned is simply the normalized form of the certificate DN—not the desired LDAP DN.

Going Further with SASL

SASL is a flexible tool for handling authentication. Here we have looked at only two SASL mechanisms: DIGEST-MD5 and EXTERNAL. But there are many other possibilities. It can be used in conjunction with robust network authentication systems like Kerberos. It can take advantage of secure One Time Password systems, like Opiekeys. And it can be used as an interface to more standard password storage systems, like PAM (Pluggable Authentication Modules).

While such configurations are outside of the scope of this book, there are many resources available. The SASL documentation (installed locally on Ubuntu in `/usr/local/doc/libsasl/index.html`), and the OpenLDAP Administrator's Guide (`http://openldap.org`), both provide more information about different SASL configurations.

Now we will move on from authentication to authorization, and turn our attention to ACLs.

Controlling Authorization with ACLs

We've looked at connection security and authentication. Now we are ready to look at the last aspect of security: authorization. What we are specifically interested in is controlling access to information in our directory tree. Who should be able to access a record? Under what conditions? And how much of that record should they be able to see? These are the sorts of questions that we will address in this section.

The Basics of ACLs

The primary way that OpenLDAP controls access to directory data is through Access Control Lists (ACLs). When the SLAPD server processes a request from a client, it evaluates whether the client has permissions to access the information it has requested. To do this evaluation SLAPD sequentially evaluates each of the ACLs in the configuration files, applying the appropriate rules to the incoming request.

 Previously in this chapter, we have looked at *authentication* using simple and SASL binding. ACLs provide *authorization* services, which determine what information a given DN has access to.

ACLs were introduced in Chapter 2 in the section entitled *ACLs*. This section will develop the basic examples discussed there.

An ACL is just a fancy configuration directive (the `access` directive) for SLAPD. Like certain other directives, the `access` directive can be used multiple times. There are two different places in the SLAPD configuration where ACLs can be placed. Firstly, they can be placed in the global configuration outside of a database section (that is, near the top of the configuration file). Rules that are placed at this level will apply globally to all backends. In the next chapter we will look at the case where a single directory has multiple backends.

Secondly, ACLs may be placed within a backend section (somewhere beneath a `database` directive). In this case, the ACLs will only be used when handling requests for information within database. In Chapter 2, we put our ACLs within the backend section, and we did not create any global `access` directives.

How does all of this work out in practice? When are global rules used, and when are backend-specific rules used? If a backend has no specific ACLs, then the global rules will apply. If a backend does have ACLs, then the global rules will only be applied if none of the backend-specific rules apply. If the request is for a record which is not stored in any backend, such as the Root DSE or the `cn=subschema` entry, then only the global rules will be applied.

Within their context ACLs are evaluated top-down, from the first directive in the configuration file to the last. So, when backend-specific rules are tested, SLAPD begins testing with the first rule on the list and continues sequentially until either a stopping rule matches or SLAPD reaches the end of the list.

In Chapter 2 we put the ACLs directly in the `slapd.conf` configuration file. In this section we will put them in their own file and use the `include` directive in `slapd.conf` to direct SLAPD to load the ACL file. This will allow us to separate the potentially lengthy ACLs from the rest of the configuration file.

Let's take a quick look at the format of an ACL, and then we will move on to some examples which will help clarify the intricacies of the ACL method.

An access directive looks like this:

```
access to [resources]
        by [who] [type of access granted] [control]
        by [who] [type of access granted] [control]
    # More 'by' clauses, if necessary....
```

An `access` directive can have one `to` phrase, and any number of `by` phrases. We will take a look at the `access to` phrase first, then the `by` phrase.

Access to [resources]

In the `access to` part, an ACL specifies what is to be restricted in the directory tree by this rule. In the given rule we used [resources] as a placeholder for this section. An ACL can restrict by DN, by attribute, by filter, or by a combination of these. We will first look at restricting by DN.

Access using DN

To restrict access to a particular DN, we would use something like this:

```
access to dn="uid=matt,ou=Users,dc=example,dc=com"
        by * none
```

 The by * none phrase simply rejects access to anyone. We will cover this and other rules when we discuss the by phrase later in this chapter.

The rule would restrict access to that specific DN. Any time a request is received that needs access to the DN uid=matt,ou=Users,dc=example,dc=com, SLAPD would evaluate this rule to determine whether that request is authorized to access this record.

Restricting access to a specific DN can be useful at times, but there are several other supported options to the DN access specifier that come in useful for more general rule-making.

It is possible to restrict access to subtrees of a DN, or even by DN patterns. For example, if we wanted to write a rule that restricted access to entries beneath the Users OU, we could use an access clause like this:

```
access to dn.subtree="ou=Users,dc=example,dc=com"
        by * none
```

In this example the rule restricts access to the OU and any records subordinate to it. This is accomplished by using dn.subtree (or the synonym dn.sub). In our directory information tree there are a number of user records in the Users OU subtree. These records are children of the Users OU. The DN uid=matt,ou=Users, dc=example,dc=com, for example, is in the subtree, and an attempt to access the record would trigger this rule.

Along with dn.subtree, there are three other keywords for adding structural restrictions to the DN access specifier:

- dn.base: Restrict access to this particular DN. This is the default, and dn.exact and dn.baselevel are synonyms of dn.base.

- dn.one: Restrict access to any entries immediately below this DN. dn.onelevel is a synonym.

- dn.children: Restrict access to the children (subordinate) entries of this DN. This is similar to subtree, except that the given DN itself is not restricted by the rule.

The dn clause accepts one other modifier that can be used to do sophisticated pattern matching: dn.regex. The dn.regex access specifier can process POSIX extended regular expressions. Here is an example of a simple regular expression in dn.regex:

```
access to dn.regex="uid=[^,]+,ou=Users,dc=example,dc=com"
        by * none
```

This example would restrict access to any DN with the pattern uid=SOMETHING, ou=Users,dc=example,dc=com, where SOMETHING can be any string that is at least one character long and has no commas (,) in it. Regular expressions are a powerful tool for writing ACLs. We will discuss them more in the section *Getting More from Regular Expressions* after we look at the by phrase.

Access using attrs

In addition to restricting access to records by DN, we can also restrict access to one or more attributes within records. This is done using the attrs access specifier.

In the examples we've seen, when we restricted access we were restricting access at a record level. The attrs restriction works at a finer-grained level: it restricts access to particular attributes within records.

For example, consider a case where we want to limit access to the homePhone attribute of all records in our directory information tree. This can be done with the following access phrase:

```
access to attrs=homePhone
        by * none
```

The attrs specifier takes a list of one or more attributes. In the given example, we just restricted access to the homePhone attribute. If we wanted to block access to homePostalAddress as well, we could modify the attrs list accordingly:

```
access to attrs=homePhone,homePostalAddress
        by * none
```

Let's say that we wanted to restrict access to all of the attributes in the organizationalPerson object class. One way of doing this would be to create one long list: attrs=title,x121Address,registeredAddress, destinationIndicator,.... But such a method would be time-consuming, difficult to read, and clumsy.

Instead, there is a convenient shorthand notation for this:

```
access to attrs=@organizationalPerson
        by * none
```

This notation should be used carefully, however. This code does not just restrict access to the attributes explicitly defined in `organizationalPerson`, but also all of the attributes already defined in the `person` object class. Why? Because the `organizationalPerson` object class is a subclass of `person`. Therefore, all of the attributes of `person` are attributes of `organizationalPerson`.

Sometimes it useful to restrict access to all attributes *not* required or allowed by a particular object class. For example, consider the case where the only attributes we want to restrict are those that are not specified in the `organizationalPerson` object class. We can do that by replacing the *at* sign (@) with an exclamation point (!):

```
access to attrs=!organizationalPerson
        by * none
```

This will restrict access to any attributes unless they are allowed or required by the `organizationalPerson` object class.

There are two special names that can be specified in the attributes list but that do not actually match an attribute. These two names are `entry` and `children`. So we have two cases:

- If `attrs=entry` is specified, then the record itself is restricted.
- If `attrs=children`, then the records that are children of this record are restricted.

These two key words are not particularly useful in cases where only an `attrs` specifier is used, but they can be much more useful when `attrs` and `dn` specifiers are used in conjunction.

Sometimes it is useful to restrict by the value of an attribute (rather than by an attribute name). For example, we may want to restrict access to any `givenName` attribute that has the value `Matt`. This sort of thing can be accomplished using the `val` (value) specifier:

```
access to attrs=givenName val="Matt"
        by * none
```

Like the `dn` specifier, the `val` specifier has `regex`, `subtree`, `base`, `one`, `exact`, and `children` styles.

 When using the `val` specifier you can have no more than one attribute in the `attrs` list. The `val` specifier will not work on object class lists either.

With `val.regex` you can use regular expressions for matching. We can modify the last example to restrict access to any `givenName` that starts with the letter M:

```
access to attrs=givenName val.regex="M.*"
        by * none
```

In cases where the attribute value is a DN (like the `member` attribute for a `groupOfNames` object), the `regex`, `subtree`, `base`, `one`, and `children` styles can be used to restrict access based on the DN in the attribute value.

```
access to attrs=member val.children="ou=Users,dc=example,dc=com"
        by * none
```

> **Specifying an Alternate Matching Rule**
>
> By default, the `val` comparison uses the equality matching rule. You can select a different matching rule however, by inserting a slash (/) after `val`, and then entering the name or OID of the matching rule:`access to attrs=givenName val/caseIgnoreMatch="matt"`.

Access using Filters

One of the lesser used but surprisingly powerful features of the `access` phrase is support for LDAP search filters as a means of restricting access to records. We looked at the LDAP filter syntax at the beginning of Chapter 3 when we discussed the search operation. Here we will use filters to restrict access to parts of a record.

Filters provide a way to support value matching for entire records (instead of just attribute values, as is done with `attrs`). For example, using filters we can restrict access to all records that contain the object class `simpleSecurityObject`:

```
access to filter="(objectClass=simpleSecurityObject)"
        by * none
```

This will restrict access to any record in the directory information tree that has the object class `simpleSecurityObject`. Any legal LDAP filter can be used in a filter specifier. For example, we could restrict access to all records that have the given name Matt, the given name Barbara, or the surname Kant:

```
access to
    filter="(|(|(givenName=Matt)(givenName=Barbara))(sn=Kant))"
        by * none
```

This code uses the "or" (disjunction) operator to indicate that if the request needs access to records that have given names with the values of Matt or Barbara, or if the request needs access to a record with the surname Kant, this rule should be applied.

Combining Access Specifiers

We have looked at three different access specifiers: `dn`, `attrs`, and `filter`. And in the previous sections we have used each. Now we will combine them to create even more specific access rules.

The order of combination is as follows:

`access to` [*dn*] [*filter*] [*attrs*] [*val*]

The `dn` and `filter` specifiers come first, as they both deal with records as a whole. Then `attrs` (and `val`), which function at the attribute level, come next. Let's say that we want to restrict access to records in the Users OU just in the cases where the record has an `employeeNumber` attribute. To do this we can use a combination of a DN specifier and a filter:

```
access to dn.subtree="ou=Users,dc=example,dc=com"
    filter="(employeeNumber=*)"
        by * none
```

This ACL will only restrict access when the request is for records in the `ou=Users, dc=example,dc=com` subtree and the `employeeNumber` field exists and has some value.

In a similar fashion, we can limit access to attributes for records in a certain subtree. For example, consider the case where we want to restrict access to the `description` attribute, but only for records that are in the the System OU. We can do this by combining the DN and attribute specifiers:

```
access to dn.subtree="ou=System,dc=example,dc=com"
    attrs=description
        by * none
```

By this rule, a client could access the record with DN `uid=authenticate, ou=System,dc=example,dc=com`, but it would not be able to access the `description` attribute of that record.

By carefully combining these access specifiers it is possible to articulate exact access restrictions. We will see some more in action as we continue on to the `by` phrase.

By [who] [type of access granted] [control]

The `by` phrase contains three parts:

- The **who field** indicates what entities are allowed to access the resource identified in the access phrase

- The **access field** (type of access granted) indicates what can be done with the resource

- The third optional part, which is usually left off, is the **control field**

To get the gist of this distinction, consider the by phrase that we have been working with in the previous sections: by * none. In this by phrase, the who field is * (an asterisk character), and the access field is none. The control field is omitted in this example.

The * is the universal wildcard. It matches any entity, including anonymous and all DNs. The none access type indicates that no permissions at all should be granted to the entity identified in the who specifier. In other words, by * none means that no access should be granted to anyone.

> The directory manager (cn=Manager,dc=example,dc=com), specified in the slapd.conf file with the rootdn directive, is an exception. It cannot be restricted by any access control. Thus, by * none does not apply to the manager.

We will explore the who field in detail, but before getting to that, let's examine the access field.

The Access Field

There are six distinct privileges that a client can have, in regards to an entry or attribute. There is also a seventh privilege specifier that equates to the removal of all privileges:

1. w: Writes access to a record or attribute.

2. r: Reads access to a record or attribute.

3. s: Searches access to a record or attribute.

4. c: Accesses to run a comparison operation on a record or attribute.

5. x: Accesses to perform a server-side authentication operation on a record or attribute.

6. d: Accesses to information about whether or not a record or attribute exists ('d' stands for 'disclose').

7. 0: Does not allow access to the record or attribute. This is equivalent to -wrscxd.

These seven privileges can be specified in a by clause. To set one or more of these access privileges, use the = (equals) sign.

For example, to allow the server to compare a record's `givenName` field to a `givenName` specified by a client, we could use the following ACL:

```
access to attrs=givenName
     by * =c
```

This will allow any client to attempt a compare operation. But that is the only operation it will allow. By this rule, no one can read from or write to this attribute. How does this work out in practice? When we use the `ldapsearch` client to attempt to read the value of the `givenName` attribute, we do not get any information about the `givenName`:

```
$ ldapsearch -LLL -U matt "(uid=matt)" givenName
SASL/DIGEST-MD5 authentication started
Please enter your password:
SASL username: matt
SASL SSF: 128
SASL installing layers
dn: uid=matt,ou=Users,dc=example,dc=com
```

The only thing the server returns for our query is the DN of the record that matches the filter. No `givenName` attribute is returned.

However, if we use the `ldapcompare` client, we can ask the server to tell us whether or not the DN has a `givenName` field with the value 'Matt':

```
$ ldapcompare -U matt uid=matt,ou=Users,dc=example,dc=com \
    "givenName: Matt"
SASL/DIGEST-MD5 authentication started
Please enter your password:
SASL username: matt
SASL SSF: 128
SASL installing layers
TRUE
```

The `ldapcompare` client sends a DN and an attribute/value pair to the server, and asks the server to compare the supplied attribute value with the server's copy of the attribute value for the record with the given DN.

Here the `ldapcompare` client will request that the SLAPD server look up the record for `uid=matt,ou=Users,dc=example,dc=com` and check to see if the `givenName` attribute has the value 'Matt'. The server will answer TRUE, FALSE, or (if there is an error) UNDEFINED.

In this case, the server responded TRUE. This indicates that the server performed the comparison, and the values matched. The combination of the ldapsearch and ldapcompare examples should illustrate how the ACL worked: while the server-side compare operation is permitted, the client does not have access to read the attribute value.

Multiple access privileges can be granted in one by phrase. To modify in order to allow reading (r), comparing (c), and disclosing (d) on the givenName attribute, we can use the following ACL:

```
access to attrs=givenName
        by * =rcd
```

Now, both the ldapsearch and ldapcompare commands that we ran should succeed.

There are cases where permissions are inherited from other ACLs (we will look at some later). In such cases, we can selectively add or remove specific permissions by using + (plus sign) to add and – (minus sign) to remove.

For example, if we know that all the users already have compare (c) and disclose (d) on all the attributes, but we want to add *read* privileges just for the givenName attribute, we can use the following ACL:

```
access to attrs=givenName
        by * +r
```

 An access control that grants compare and disclose, and then continues processing might look something like this: access to attrs=givenName, sn by * =cd break. This uses the break control to instruct SLAPD to continue processing ACLs. If this rule appeared in the SLAPD configuration above the rule access to attrs=giveName by * +r, then a request to the givenName attribute would have the effective permissions =rcd.

Likewise, if we needed to remove the compare operation just for the givenName attribute, we could use a by clause like by * -c.

The 0 access privilege removes all privileges. It cannot be used with the + or – operators, it can only be used with the = operator. The following ACL removes all privileges for all users to the givenName attribute:

```
access to attrs=givenName
        by * =0
```

This is the same as the by clause: by * -wrscdx.

These access controls are good for fine-grained control, but sometimes it is nice to have shortcuts. OpenLDAP has seven shortcuts that handle common configurations of access controls:

Keyword	Privileges
none	0
disclose	d
auth	xd
compare	cxd
search	scxd
read	rscxd
write	wrscxd

The none keyword we have seen before and it is the same as =0. Looking at the other keywords and their associated privilege, a pattern emerges: each keyword adds one new privilege, to the privileges of the previous keyword. Thus, auth has the =d privilege from disclose, plus the x privilege, and compare has =xd from auth and adds the c privilege. The write keyword at the bottom has all privileges.

Because this general accumulation of privileges captures the usual use cases while remaining more readable, keywords are used more frequently than privilege strings. In most of our examples from here on, we will use the keyword unless there is a specific reason to use the privilege string instead.

Of the seven keywords, disclose, auth, compare, search, read, and write can be prefixed with one of two prefixes: self and realself. The self prefix indicates that if the value in question refers to the user's DN, then the user may have certain privileges. Thus selfwrite indicates that the user has =wrscxd permissions if and only if the value of the attribute in question is the user's DN.

The realself prefix is similar, but it carries the additional stipulation that the DN not be proxied. These prefixes are particularly useful when dealing with groups and other membership-based records.

For example, the following ACL allows a user write access to the uniqueMember attribute only if the uniqueMember attribute contains that user's DN: access to attrs=uniqueMember by users selfwrite.

Now that we have covered the access field we will move on to the who field.

The who Field

We have always used * in the who field. However, the who field is the richest of the ACL fields, providing twenty-three distinct forms, most of which can be used in combinations. In order to efficiently cover ground, we will cover the major forms on their own, and then group similar forms together and treat them as units.

The five most frequently used forms are *, anonymous, self, users, and dn.

The * and anonymous Specifiers

The * specifier, as we have already seen, is a global match. It matches any client, including the anonymous user.

The anonymous specifier matches only clients that bind to the directory as the Anonymous user (see Chapter 3 for details on the Anonymous user). This refers, then, to clients that have not authenticated to the directory. Since the process of authentication requires that the client connect Anonymously, and then attempt to bind as a DN with a specific password, the anonymous user almost always needs permissions to perform an auth operation, in which the client sends the DN and password to the directory and asks the directory to verify that the information is correct. For that reason, you will likely need an ACL that looks like this:

```
access to attrs=userPassword
        by anonymous auth
```

This grants the Anonymous user the ability to do an auth operation. Note that every ACL ends with an implicit phrase: by * none. In other words, if permissions are not explicitly specified none are granted.

Note that the ACL above does not allow users to modify their own passwords. That's where the self specifier comes in.

The self Specifier

The self specifier is used to specify access controls for a DN on its own record. Thus, we can use the self specifier to allow a user to modify her or his own userPassword value:

```
access to attrs=userPassword
        by anonymous auth
        by self write
```

If we log in as uid=matt,ou=Users,dc=example,dc=com and try to modify the userPassword value of our own record (dn: uid=matt,ou=Users,dc=example,dc =com), SLAPD will allow us to change the password. But it will not (according to the rule above) allow us to modify anyone else's userPassword value.

The `self` specifier can be further modified with a `level` style. The `level` style indicates whether (and how many) parent records or child records are to be treated as if they were part of `self`. The `level` style takes an integer index. Positive integers refer to parents, while negative integers refer to children.

Thus `access to ou by self.level{1} write` indicates that the current DN has write permissions to the `ou` of its parent. Likewise, `access to ou by self.level{-1} write` indicates that the current DN has write permission to the `ou` of any of its immediate children.

The users Specifier

The `users` specifier refers to any authenticated client. The anonymous user is not included in `users` because it represents a client that has not authenticated.

This specifier comes in very handy when you need to allow anyone who has authenticated access to some resources. For example, in an enterprise directory we would likely want to allow all users the ability to see each other's names, telephone numbers, and email addresses:

```
access to attrs=sn,givenName,displayName,telephoneNumber,mail
        by self write
        by users read
```

The dn Specifier

The `dn` specifier performs similarly in the `by` phrase to the role it plays in the `access to` phrase. It specifies one or more DNs. The `dn` has the `regex`, `base`, `one`, `subtree`, and `children` modifiers, all of which perform the same way here as they did in the `access to` phrase. Here's an example using a few different DN patterns:

```
access to dn.subtree="ou=System,dc=example,dc=com" attrs=description
        by dn="uid=barbara,ou=Users,dc=example,dc=com" write
        by dn.children="ou=System,dc=example,dc=com" read
        by dn.regex="uid=[^,]+,ou=Users,dc=example,dc=com" read
```

This rule restricts access to the description attributes of anything in the System OU subtree. The user `uid=barbara,ou=Users,dc=example,dc=com` has write permissions to the description, while any child users of the System OU have *read* permissions. Users with DNs of the form `uid=SOMETHING,ou=Users,dc=example,dc=com` also have *read* access to the description.

In addition to the regular DN modifiers, a `dn` in the `by` clause can also have a `level` modifier. Level allows the ACL author to specify exactly how many levels down a `by` phrase should go. Recall that the `dn.one` specifier indicates that any record directly below the specified DN is to be granted the specified permissions. For example `by dn.one="ou=Users,dc=example,dc=com" read` grants any direct descendant of the Users OU read permissions. So `uid=matt,ou=Users,dc=example,dc=com` would be granted read access, but `uid=jake,ou=Temp,ou=Users,dc=example,dc=com` would not be granted such access because he is two levels down. The `dn.level` specifier lets us arbitrarily specify how many levels to descend. For example, `by dn.level{2}` `="ou=Users,dc=example,dc=com" read` would allow both `matt` and `jake` read access.

> **Proxy Authentication and Real DNs**
>
> If SLAPD is set up to allow Proxy Authentication, in which case one DN is used for authentication, and then another DN is used for performing other directory operations, it is sometimes useful to write ACLs based on the DN used for authentication (the real DN). The `realdn` specifier can be used for this. It functions just like the `dn` specifier, except that it operates on the real DN. Also, `realanonymous`, `realusers`, `realdnattr`, and `realself` can be used to restrict based on the real DN. See the `slapd.access` man page for more: `man slapd.access`.

Groups and Members

Sometimes it is useful to grant group members the access to an object. For example, if you have an Administrators group, you may wish to grant any member of that group write access to all of the records in the System OU.

One might expect that the way to set permissions for group members is simply to use the group as the value of a `dn` specifier in an ACL. However, that is not the case since the `dn` specifier refers to the group record as a whole, and has nothing at all to do with the members of the group, each of which has its own record elsewhere in the directory.

Instead, what we need is a way to search the member attributes of a particular group record, and then grant access to the DNs listed in the record. The group specifier provides exactly this sort of capability.

Group evaluation can be done with the `group` specifier. In its simplest form it is used like this:

```
access to dn.subtree="ou=System,dc=example,dc=com"
        by group="cn=Admins,ou=Groups,dc=example,dc=com" write
        by users read
```

This ACL will grant members of the `cn=Admins,ou=Groups,dc=example,dc=com` group write access to anything in the System OU, while giving all other users read-only permissions.

Order Matters

ACL by phrase are evaluated sequentially, and by default SLAPD will stop processing by phrases when it hits a match. In other words, if the by phrases in the above rule were reversed, members of LDAP Admins would never be given write permission because they would always match the by `users read` phrase. Evaluation of the ACL would stop before group membership was checked.

But the ACL above will only work on groups whose object class is `groupOfNames`, and whose membership attribute is `member`. This is because groupOfNames is the default grouping object class, and member is the default membership attribute.

When we created our LDAP Admins group in Chapter 3, it was not `groupOfNames`, nor did it use the `member` attribute for membership. Our record looked like this:

```
dn: cn=LDAP Admins,ou=Groups,dc=example,dc=com
cn: LDAP Admins
ou: Groups
description: Users who are LDAP administrators
uniqueMember: uid=barbara,ou=Users,dc=example,dc=com
uniqueMember: uid=matt,ou=Users,dc=example,dc=com
objectClass: groupOfUniqueNames
```

We used the `groupOfUniqueNames` object class and the `uniqueMember` membership attribute. In order to get the ACL to match these constraints we will need to specify the object class and membership attribute in the `group` specifier:

```
access to dn.subtree="ou=System,dc=example,dc=com"
        by group/groupOfUniqueNames/uniqueMember=
            "cn=LDAP Admins,ou=Groups,dc=example,dc=com" write
        by users read
```

Note the change in the highlighted line. Using slashes (/) we have specified first the object class then the membership attribute that should be used to determine who what entries represent members. When this `by` phrase is evaluated, SLAPD will find the DN `cn=LDAP Admins,ou=Groups,dc=example,dc=com`, check to see if it has object class `groupOfUniqueMembers`, and then grant write permissions to a DN if it is specified in a uniqueMember attribute.

Using this expanded notation, you can use other membership-based records as groups. For example, you can use the `organizationalRole` object class with the `roleOccupant` membership attribute.

Like many other specifiers, the group specifier also supports regular expressions with the `regex` style. Thus, we could create a rule that would allow members of any group in OU Groups write access to the System OU by expanding our last example:

```
access to dn.subtree="ou=System,dc=example,dc=com"
        by group/groupOfUniqueNames/uniqueMember.regex=
           "cn=[^,]+,ou=Groups,dc=example,dc=com" write
        by users read
```

The second and third lines should be combined into one long line in `slapd.conf`. The regular expression in the group specifier would match any DN with a CN component at the beginning. For all such entries, if the object class is `groupOfUniqueMembers`, then the SLAPD will grant membership to a user who is a `uniqueMember` of one of those groups.

Member-Based Record Access

What if a group member needs to modify the record of the group to whom she or he belongs? One way to allow this is with the `dnattr` specifier. The `dnattr` specifier grants access to a record only if the client's DN appears in a certain attribute of the record. For example, the following example allows a group member (`uniqueMember`) of a group (which is a `groupOfUniqueNames` object) access to the group record:

```
access to dn.exact="cn=LDAP Admins,ou=Groups,dc=example,dc=com"
        by dnattr=uniqueMember write
        by users read
```

The second line specifies that if the client's DN is in the list of values for the `uniqueMember` attribute, then that client should be given write access to the entire group record. Other users, according to the third line, will have read access.

Network, Connections, and Security

SLAPD can use information about the client's connection (including network and security information) in access control lists. This feature provides an additional layer of network security that complements SSL/TLS and SASL.

The following are network or connection level specifiers:

- `peername`: This is used to specify a range of IP addresses (for `ldap://` and `ldaps://`).

- `sockname`: This is used to specify a socket file for an LDAPI listener (`ldapi://`).

- `domain`: This is used to specify a domain name for `ldap://` and `ldaps://` listeners.

- `sockurl`: This is used to specify a socket file in URL format (`ldapi://var/run/ldapi`) for an LDAPI listener.

- `ssf`: The overall security strength factor (SSF) of the connection.

- `transport_ssf`: The SSF for the underlying transport layer of the network.

- `tls_ssf`: The SSF for the SSL/TLS connection. This works with SSL/TLS connections on LDAPS listeners and Start TLS on LDAP listeners.

- `sasl_ssf`: The SSF of the SASL connection.

The SSF specifiers (`ssf`, `transport_ssf`, `tls_ssf`, and `sasl_ssf`) perform the same checks as the SSF parameters to the SLAPD `security` directive (discussed in the first part of this chapter). In this case, however, SSFs may be used to selectively restrict (or grant) access to portions of the directory information tree. SSF specifiers require an integer value for the level of security desired. For example, using `ssf=256` will require that the overall SSF of a connection be 256. But `tls_ssf=56` will require that the SSF of the TLS/SSL layer be at least 56, regardless of what the SSF of the SASL configuration is. For more information on SSFs, see the section earlier in this chapter entitled *Using Security Strength Factors*.

For example, the following ACL will only grant *write* access to the specified DN when the client has connected with a strong SASL cipher:

```
access to dn.subtree="ou=users,dc=example,dc=com"
        by self sasl_ssf=128 write
        by users read
```

This rule allows users to modify their own records only if they have authenticated with SASL using a security mechanism with a strength of 128 (DIGEST-MD5) or more. All other users would only get read access.

Combining Specifiers in a by Phrase

As the rule above illustrates, multiple specifiers can be used in a single by phrase. When this happens all specifiers must be matched before the indicated rights will be granted (or denied).

The `peername` specifier is used for setting restrictions based on information about the IP connection. It can be used to complement other components in network security, like SSL/TLS. The `peername` specifier can take an IP address or a range of IP addresses (using subnet masks) and can also specify a source port.

The following rule grants write access to local connections, read access to connections on the local LAN (address from 10.40.0.0 through 10.40.0.255), and denies access to all other clients. Remember, every rule ends with an implicit `by * none`.

```
access to *
        by peername.ip=127.0.0.1 write
        by peername.ip=10.40.0.0%255.255.255.0 read
```

Note that the `peername` specifier requires the ip style for specifying an IP address. It also supports the `regex` style (`access to * by peername.regex="^IP=10\.40\.0\.[0-9]+:[0-9]+$" write`) and the `path` specifier to replicate the behavior of `sockname`.

> **Regular Expressions for IP Addresses**
>
> For an IP address, the format of the string used in regular expression evaluation is this: `IP=<address>:<port>`. If you are creating a precise regular expression make sure to deal with the `IP=` prefix and the port information. A regular expression like this will fail: `peername.regex="^10.40.12[0-9]$"`. Why? Because it is missing the `IP=` and port information.

A more useful version of the rule above would deny access to anything in the directory if it was not in the particular ranges, but would leave further access controls to rules appearing later in the ACL list. This can be done using the special `break` control described in the next section. We could also added SSF information, so connections coming over non-local connections must also use strong SSL/TLS encryption. Here is the rule:

```
access to *
        by peername.ip=127.0.0.1 break
        by peername.ip=10.40.0.0%255.255.255.0 tls_ssf=128 break
```

The above rule might appear difficult to read, but here is what it does:

- If the connection is local (coming over 127.0.0.1 or `localhost`), then SLAPD allows further processing of the ACL list (that's what `break` does). Whether or not the user then gets access to resources is dependent on other rules.

- If the connection comes from an address on the LAN and it is using strong SSL/TLS encryption, then SLAPD will continue processing the ACL list.

- Under any other connecting circumstances the connection is rejected. For example, if a connection comes from the LAN but does not use sufficiently strong SSL/TLS, the connection will be closed. This behavior is caused by the implicit `by * none` phrase.

For more on the `break` control, see the section called *The Control Field*.

Sometimes it is more useful to be able to specify which domain names (rather than which IP addresses) should be granted access. This can be done with the `domain` specifier:

```
access to *
        by domain.exact="main.example.com" write
        by domain.sub="example.com" read
```

In the example above, the second line provides write access to any client connection coming from the domain name `main.example.com`. The third line grants read access to the domain `example.com`, and any subdomain of `example.com`. So, if a server with the domain name `test2.example.com` made a request, it would be granted access under the third rule. However, `testexample.com` would not match because it is not a subdomain of `example.com` — it is a different domain altogether.

When SLAPD encounters a domain specifier in an ACL, it takes the IP address of the client connection and does a reverse DNS lookup to get the host name. In light of this there are two things to keep in mind when using the domain specifier.

First, the name returned by a reverse DNS lookup may not be what you expect based on a forward DNS lookup. For example, doing a DNS lookup on `ldap.example.com` returns the address 10.40.0.23. However, doing a reverse DNS lookup on 10.40.0.23 returns `mercury.example.com`. Why?

It is because `ldap.example.com` is in DNS parlance, a **CNAME record**, and `mercury.example.com` is an **A record**. Practically speaking, what this means is that `ldap.example.com` is an alias to the server's real (**canonical**) name, which is `mercury.example.com`. The practical consequence is this: when you write an ACL using the `domain` specifier, make sure you use the A record domain name, not the CNAME record name. Otherwise, SLAPD will apply the rule to the wrong domain name.

Looking up DNS Information

There are many tools for looking up DNS information. Most Linux distributions, including Ubuntu Linux, provide the `host` and `dig` commands for command-line DNS lookups. The `host` command gives brief sentence-like information like this: `ldap.example.com is an alias for mercury.example.com`. The `dig` command, in contrast, gives detailed technical information.

The second thing to keep in mind when considering the domain specifier is that it is less reliable than using IP address information. DNS addresses can be spoofed, which means another server on the network can claim to be `ldap.example.com` and send traffic that looks, to SLAPD, like it is coming from the real `ldap.example.com`.

One way to diminish the risk of this is to use client-side SSL/TLS certificates and configure SLAPD to require that the client send a signed certificate to authenticate before it can perform any other directory operations. Unfortunately, client-side certificates cannot be selectively required through ACLs. Instead you will have to use the directive `TLSVerifyClient demand` in the `slapd.conf` file.

The `sockname` and `sockurl` specifiers are used for servers that run with UNIX local socket Inter Process Communication (IPC) instead of network sockets. These directives can be used to restrict local connections that use the IPC layer instead of connecting through the IP network.

 It is uncommon to run LDAPI. Generally it is used only in situations where IP network connections cannot or should not be used. In typical cases, local clients connect to SLAPD over LDAP, using the URL `ldap://localhost/` rather than using LDAPI.

For example, we could use the following ACL to allow only local (LDAPI) connections to write to the record, while users who connected through a different mechanism could only read the record:

```
access to dn.exact="uid=matt,ou=Users,dc=example,dc=com"
        by sockurl="ldapi://var/run/ldapi" write
        by users read
```

The second line indicates that only LDAPI connections that connect through a particular LDAPI socket file should gain write access to the DN. All other clients (`users`) will get read permissions.

Advanced Step: Using the set Specifier

In addition to the syntax we have examined just now, there is an experimental type of `by` phrase—the **set** syntax. The `set` syntax can be used to create a compact and powerful set of conditions for access. Since it allows Boolean operators, and has a method for accessing attribute values, a single rule in the `set` syntax can accomplish what would otherwise take tremendously complex ACLs.

The basic idea behind the `set` syntax is this. By using a rule composed of conditions joined by operators, SLAPD creates a set of objects which have access to the record in question. If the result of an evaluation of a `set` specifier is a set that contains one or more members, then the `by` phrase is considered a match and permissions are applied. If, on the other hand, the set is empty, then SLAPD will continue evaluating the `by` phrases for that rule to see if it can find another match.

> The `set` specifier uses operations of the sort used in set theory. When using the set specifier you may find it helpful to think in terms of set theory, with sets (lists of items) and set operations, such as union (&) and intersection (|).

Here is a simple ACL using a `set` specifier to replicate the behavior of the `group` specifier. It provides write access to records in the System OU only to clients in the LDAP Admins group. All others get read access only:

```
access to dn.subtree="ou=System,dc=example,dc=com"
        by set="[cn=ldap admins,ou=groups,dc=example,dc=com]/
            uniqueMember & user" write
        by users none
```

The second line, highlighted above, contains the `set` specifier, which contains a `set` statement. The text in the square brackets specifies a DN, which is the DN of the LDAP Admins group. To access the values of the `uniqueMember` attribute we append `/uniqueMember` to the DN. When SLAPD expands this, it will contain the set of all `uniqueMembers` in the LDAP `Admins group`. In set-theoretic notation (which is not used by OpenLDAP, but which is helpful to understand what is happening), the set of group members would look like this:

```
{ uid=matt,ou=users,dc=example,dc=com ;
    uid=barbara,ou=users,dc=example,dc=com }
```

There are two members (the two `uniqueMembers`) for the LDAP Admins group.

The & (ampersand) operator performs a union operation on two sets. The **user keyword** expands to the set that contains one member: the DN of the current client. So, if I perform a search, binding as `uid=matt,ou=users,dc=example,dc=com`, then the user set will contain one record:

```
{ uid=matt,ou=users,dc=example,dc=com }
```

When the & operator is applied, it will generate the intersection of the two sets. That is, the resulting set will contain only members that are in both of the original sets. Since only the record for UID `matt` is in both, the resulting set will contain just the DN for `matt`:

```
{ uid=matt,ou=users,dc=example,dc=com }
```

The resulting set is not empty so it is considered a match. The result of the set evaluation, then, is that the `uid=matt,ou=users,dc=example,dc=com` will be granted access based on the `set` specifier.

 Sets are case-sensitive, and always use the normalized DN form. What this means is that the DNs in sets should always be lowercase.

Consider a case though, when the user is not a member of the LDAP Admins group. If `uid=david,ou=users,dc=example,dc=com` binds, can he perform read and write operations? When the set specifier is run, the first of the two sets (group membership) will evaluate to the same thing it did above:

```
{ uid=matt,ou=users,dc=example,dc=com ;
    uid=barbara,ou=users,dc=example,dc=com }
```

But the user keyword will expand to this:

```
{ uid=david,ou=users,dc=example,dc=com }
```

There are no items in the intersection of these two sets, so the resulting set, after the & operator is applied, is an empty set:

```
{ }
```

There are no matches, so this `by` phrase fails to apply. The last line in our ACL (by `users none`) will then apply, and the `uid=david` will be given no access permissions.

Let's look at another example. We will use the set specifier to implement a rule where, when a client DN tries to access a record DN, it is given write access only if the two DNs are the same, or else it is given read access if they are in the same OU. Otherwise, the client DN is denied access to the record DN. Here's the ACL:

```
access to dn.subtree="dc=example,dc=com"
        by set="this & user" write
        by set="this/ou & user/ou" read
```

The first line indicates that this rule will apply to the record `dc=example,dc=com` and everything under it.

The second line takes the intersection of the sets generated by two keywords: `this` and `user`. The `this` keyword expands to the set containing the DN of the requested record. The `user` keyword, as we saw, expands to the DN of the client.

So, if the client `uid=david,ou=users,dc=example,dc=com` requests access to its own record, the resulting set operation will be as follows:

```
{ uid=david,ou=users,dc=exampls,dc=com } &
    { uid=david,ou=users,dc=example,dc=com }
```

Since both sets contain the same member, the resulting set (the intersection of the two) is { `uid=david,ou=users,dc=example,dc=com` }. The end set is not empty, so the user will be granted write access.

Now let's look at the third line of the given ACL. This rule will return a non-empty set whenever the requested DN and the client DN both have the same value for the `ou` attribute. If `uid=david,ou=users,dc=example,dc=com` requests the record for `uid=matt,ou=users,dc=example,dc=com`, then SLAPD will check the values of their respective OU attributes.

The set identified by `this/ou` will be expanded to contain the values of all of the OU attributes in the requested record (the record for `uid=matt,ou=users,dc=example,dc=com`). This set is:

```
{ 'Users' }
```

Note that in this case the value is not a DN, but a string. Sets can perform matching operations on strings as well as DNs.

The set identified by `user/ou` will be expanded to contain the values of all of the OU attributes in the client's record. The record for `uid=david,ou=users,dc=example,dc=com` contains one value for the `ou` attribute, and the resulting set will contain that one attribute value:

```
{ 'Users' }
```

SLAPD will compute the intersection of { `'Users'` } & { `'Users'` }, which is { `'Users'` }. Since the set is not empty, `uid=david,ou=users,dc=example,dc=com` will be granted access to read the record of `uid=matt,ou=users,dc=example,dc=com`.

The `set` specifier provides one way of granting access to a record *only* in the case that a record contains a certain attribute. If we only want to grant write access to records with the title attribute, we can use the following rule:

```
access to dn.child="ou=Users,dc=example,dc=com"
        by set="this/title" write
```

In this ACL, if the requested record has a single `title` attribute, then the result of the evaluation of the above rule will be a set containing one element. However, if the record attribute has no title attribute, then the resulting set will be empty, and write access will not be granted.

In our directory the record of `uid=matt,ou=users,dc=example,dc=com` has the following title attribute:

```
title: Systems Integrator
```

But the record `uid=barbara,ou=users,dc=example,dc=com` does not have a title attribute at all. So if the record for `uid=matt` was requested, then the resulting set, based on the above ACL, would be:

```
{ 'Systems Integrator' }
```

So if an authenticated user attempted to access the record for `uid=matt`, SLAPD would grant access. In contrast, the set for `uid=barbara` would be { }, the empty set. So a user trying to access the record having `uid=barbara` would be denied access.

Using a similar set specifier, we could grant access to a record depending not only on the existence of an attribute, but on its value too:

```
access to dn.child="ou=Users,dc=example,dc=com"
        by set="this/objectclass & [person]" write
```

According to the above rule, write access will be granted for anything in the Users OU only if the entry has an `objectclass` attribute with the value `person`. Note that in this case the square brackets are used to define a string literal.

If a client were to access the record `uid=barbara,ou=users,dc=example,dc=com`, the first part of our `set` statement would evaluate to the following set:

```
{ 'person' ; 'organizationalPerson' ; 'inetOrgPerson' }
```

Those are the three object classes for the `uid=barbara` record. The other part, `[person]`, would be expanded to this set:

```
{ 'person' }
```

When the union is computed, the result would be the set { `'person'` } and so write access would be granted.

These are just a few of the basic operations that can be done with the `set` specifier. Unfortunately, `set` is not documented in the `slapd.access` man page. However, there is a lengthy and informative article on using set in the OpenLDAP official FAQ-O-Matic: `http://www.openldap.org/faq/data/cache/1133.html`.

The control Field

The last field in the `by` phrase is the control field. There are only three possible values for the control field: `stop`, `break`, and `continue`. If no control field is specified, `stop` is assumed. For example, `by * none` is the same as `by * none stop`.

The first value, `stop`, indicates that if that particular by clause matches, no further checking of ACLs for matching should occur. Consider the following (admittedly contrived) case:

```
access to attr=employeeNumber, employeeType, departmentNumber
        by users=cd
        by dn="uid=matt,ou=Users,dc=example,dc=com" +r
access to attr=employeeNumber
        by users +w
```

If I bind as `uid=matt,ou=Users,dc=example,dc=com` and try to modify my `employeeNumber`, will I be allowed to? No, I will not.

The reason I will not be able to modify the record is because I will only have the permissions granted by the first by phrase: `by users =cd` (remember, `by users =cd` is the same as `by users=cd stop`). As soon as SLAPD sees that I match the first `by` phrase of the first ACL, it will stop testing ACLs. Thus it will never reach the rule that grants my DN `+r` access, nor will it reach the rule that grants all users `+w` to the `employeeNumber` attribute.

This is an example of the `stop` control, which is used implicitly by all three rules.

Now, if I wanted to make sure that after the first `by` phrase SLAPD continues to evaluate phrases within the ACL, I could re-write the ACLs using the `continue` control:

```
access to attr=employeeNumber, employeeType, departmentNumber
        by users-=cd continue
        by dn="uid=matt,ou=Users,dc=example,dc=com" +r
access to attr=employeeNumber
        by users +w
```

After running the same test on these rules, the DN `uid=matt,ou=Users,dc=example,dc=com` would have the permissions `=cdr`.

The `continue` control instructs SLAPD to continue processing all of the `by` phrases in the *current ACL*. Once it is done evaluating that ACL though, it will not continue to look for matches in other ACLs.

In order to tell SLAPD to look at different rules for matches, we would have to use the break control. When SLAPD encounters an applicable clause that ends with a break control, it stops processing the current ACL but continues looking at other ACLs to see if they apply.

Thus, to get write permissions with our ACL we would want the following ACLs:

```
access to attr=employeeNumber, employeeType, departmentNumber
        by users=cd continue
        by dn="uid=matt,ou=Users,dc=example,dc=com" +r break

access to attr=employeeNumber
        by users +w stop
```

Now what will happen when the user with UID matt attempts accesses an employeeNumber?

First, the by phrase of the first ACL will be evaluated, and matt will be granted =cd. Because of the continue control, SLAPD will then examine the second by clause, which will also match for the user matt. Thus, matt will have =rcd when the processing of the first ACL completes.

Due to the break control the second ACL will also be evaluated, and matt will be granted +w as well, bringing his final permissions up to =wrcd.

Using the continue and break controls is one way to incrementally handle permissions. In complex configurations, judicious use of continue and break can make maintaining ACLs much easier, and can reduce the total number of ACLs.

Getting More from Regular Expressions

In the previous sections we have looked at using regular expressions in both the access to phrase and the by phrase. But we can use both in conjunction. We can store information about the matches identified in the access to phrase, and use that information later in the by phrases.

To temporarily store matching information in an access to phrase we can surround the regular expression with parentheses. Here's an example:

```
access to dn.regex="ou=([^,]+),dc=example,dc=com"
        by dn.children,expand="ou=$1,dc=example,dc=com" read
```

This ACL grants a client the DN access to read a record DN only if both the client DN and the record DN are in the same part of the directory tree (that is, if both are in the same OU).

In the first line of the given ACL we used parentheses to capture the match from the regular expression [^,]+, which will be the value of the ou= component of the DN. Again, [^,]+ says "match all charcters that are not ','."

In the second line we used the dn.children specifier but supplemented it with an extra keyword: expand. The expand keyword tells SLAPD to substitute matches from the access to clause into this phrase.

Because of the expand keyword, the variable $1 is substituted with the value of the match in the first line. Everything captured between '(' and ')' in the regular expression will be stored in $1.

Variable names are assigned in order. The first set of parenthesis in the regular access to phrase gets stored in $1. If a second set of parenthesis existed, the matching information inside of those would be stored in $2 and so on for each additional set of parenthesis.

For example, we might want an ACL like this:

```
access to dn.regex="uid=([^,]+),ou=([^,]+),dc=example,dc=com"
        by dn.children,expand="uid=$1,ou=$2,dc=example,dc=com" write
```

This rule would grant a client DN access to read and write any entries subordinate to its own record but deny other uses the ability to even read those entries.

 Address books are sometimes implemented in OpenLDAP by storing a user's addresses as subordinate entries to the user's own entry in the directory. There is an example of this in the OpenLDAP FAQ-O-Matic: http://www.openldap.org/faq/data/cache/1005.html

Notice that the first line stores two variables. The UID goes in $1 and the OU goes in $2. These are expanded in the second line.

It is also possible to use matches from the access to phrase in regular expressions in the by phrase:

```
access to dn.regex="uid=[^,]+,ou=([^,]+),dc=example,dc=com"
        by dn.regex="uid=[^,]+,ou=$1,dc=example,dc=com" write
```

In the first line only the results of the second regular expression are captured and stored in a variable. The second line also contains a regular expression, and it makes use of the $1 variable to retrieve the value of the OU from the first line. Note that dn.children,expand was replaced with dn.regex. The expand keyword need not be added for regular expressions.

The rule grants write access to a client DN for any user record that is in the same OU of that directory tree.

We have looked at some simple, though useful, regular expressions in these ACLs. But much more complex regular expressions can be composed, making ACLs even more powerful. As you compose more advanced regular expressions you may find some other sources of information helpful. Along with the `slapd.access` man page, the POSIX extended regular expressions man page (`man regex`) may turn out to be useful as well.

Debugging ACLs

Debugging ACLs can be frustrating. They are complex, security sensitive, and require detailed testing. But there are three tools that make the debugging and testing process easier.

The first is just the `ldapsearch` command-line client. It can be used to carefully craft filters designed to test the processing of ACLs. The `ldapcompare` tool also comes in handy when you need to test comparison operations.

But it is also useful to make the most of LDAP's logging directives. The `trace` and `acl` debugging levels each provide detailed information about ACL processing. The `acl` level, for example, records each ACL evaluation. This can be very useful in determining what rules are run and when. We find the `trace` debugging level to be useful as well, as it provides information about how each evaluation was performed, including how regular expressions were expanded.

> **Running SLAPD in the Foreground**
>
> Sometimes it is easier to test ACLs by running SLAPD in the foreground, instead of as a daemon process, and printing debugging and logging information to standard out. For example, we can print ACL and trace debugging out this way: `slapd -d "acl,trace"`. Note that you will want to run this command as the appropriate user (such as `openldap`). To terminate the process use the *Ctrl-C* keyboard combination.

Finally, the `slapacl` command line utility provides a detail-oriented tool for evaluating ACLs directly. Since it does not connect to the SLAPD server over the LDAP protocol it allows more direct testing of just the ACLs.

For example, we can check whether or not a particular SASL user, `matt`, can access the record `cn=LDAP Admins,ou=Groups,dc=example,dc=com` and *read* the value of the `description` attribute:

```
$ slapacl -U matt -b "cn=LDAP Admins,ou=Groups,dc=example,dc=com" \
    "description/read"
```

The -U matt param specifies the SASL user name. The -b "cn=LDAP Admins, ou=Groups, dc=example, dc=com" param indicates which record we want to test against, and the last field, "description/read" indicates the attribute and the access level. This will simply return ALLOWED if the ACLs allow read access, or DENIED otherwise.

Likewise, we can test other LDAP operations. For example, we can test whether a user has permissions to compare:

```
$ slapacl -U matt -b "uid=matt,ou=Users,dc=example,dc=com"
    "uid/compare"
authcDN: "uid=matt,ou=users,dc=example,dc=com"
compare access to uid: ALLOWED
```

In this example we have included the response. The first response line indicates how the SASL DN was resolved, and the second line indicates that compare access on uid was allowed.

The slapacl program essentially runs its own SLAPD and as such, it can be set to print complete processing logs to the screen. For example, to turn on trace debugging we can just add the -d trace param to the given command:

```
$ slapacl -U matt -b "uid=matt,ou=Users,dc=example,dc=com" -d trace
    "uid/compare"
slapacl init: initiated tool.
slap_sasl_init: initialized!
hdb_back_initialize: initialize HDB backend
hdb_back_initialize: Sleepycat Software: Berkeley DB 4.3.29:
    (September  6, 2005)
bdb_db_init: Initializing HDB database
>>> dnPrettyNormal: <dc=example,dc=com>
# LOTS of lines deleted...
<<< dnPrettyNormal: <uid=matt,ou=Users,dc=example,dc=com>,
    <uid=matt,ou=users,dc=example,dc=com>
entry_decode: ""
<= entry_decode()
compare access to uid: ALLOWED
slapacl shutdown: initiated
====> bdb_cache_release_all
slapacl destroy: freeing system resources.
```

As you can see slapacl provides detailed evaluation information in this case.

Using the LDAP command-line clients, detailed logging, and the slapacl command, debugging and testing ACLs can be done effectively.

A Practical Example

In this part of the chapter, we have taken a low-level look at ACLs in OpenLDAP. We have covered many of the details of the ACL system. Now it is time to implement what we have covered so far to create a generic set of ACLs for our directory information tree.

In Chapter 2 we created a bare-bones set of ACLs in our `slapd.conf` file. Here's what we created then:

```
########
# ACLs #
########
access to attrs=userPassword
        by anonymous auth
        by self write
        by * none

access to *
        by self write
        by * none
```

Now, we will create a new, more practical list of ACLs.

The first thing we will do is move the ACLs out of `slapd.conf` and into a separate file: `acl.conf`. This will keep the lengthy list of ACLs separate from the rest of our configuration. To do this we will replace the ACLs above with an `include` directive:

```
########
# ACLs #
########
include /etc/ldap/acl.conf
```

When SLAPD is started it will include the contents of `/etc/ldap/acl.conf` at the location where the `include` statement appears. Recall that ACLs are backend-specific. Each different database can have its own ACLs (and multiple databases can be defined in the same `slapd.conf` file). So it is important to put the `include` directive after the database `directive` in `slapd.conf`.

Now we will begin editing the `acl.conf` file. The rules that we will write will be simple, and designed for a directory where most of the directory users are allowed to view most of the information in the directory. A higher-security directory may have a far more complex list of ACLs.

Since ACLs are evaluated in order from top to bottom we want to carefully craft our rules so that important restrictions are implemented right away.

If there are network-based access rules they should usually appear at the top of the ACL list so that they are evaluated first. For example, if we want to restrict access to the entire database if the host is not in our LAN, we would use the following rule:

```
access to *
        by peername.ip=127.0.0.1 none break
        by peername.ip=10.40.0.0%255.255.255.0 none break
```

By this rule only access from the localhost (127.0.0.1) and from inside of our 10.40.0.0 subnet will be allowed to access the directory. Since the break control is specified, later rules may modify the none permission, granting clients more permissions. All other connections will be closed immediately.

Next, we want to grant members of the LDAP Admins group write access to everything in the dc=example,dc=com tree:

```
access to dn.subtree="dc=example,dc=com"
        by group/groupOfUniqueNames/uniqueMember=
            "cn=LDAP Admins,ou=Groups,dc=example,dc=com" write
        by * none break
```

This immediately grants write access to the members of the LDAP Admins group. For all other clients though, SLAPD will continue processing.

 No ACLs need to be written for the directory manager, the DN specified in the slapd.conf directive rootdn. This DN always has full access to the directory information tree, and ACLs will have no effect on this user.

Next, we want to make sure that the userPassword field is available to the anonymous user for authentication purposes. We also want to allow users to be able to modify their own passwords, but otherwise we want userPassword unavailable for reading and writing by others. Note that by the previous rule the LDAP Admins will also be able to modify passwords for users.

```
access to attrs=userPassword
        by anonymous auth
        by self write
```

In some cases, other users may need auth access to the password as well, in which case you may need to add by users auth to the given list.

We also need to grant access to the uid attribute if we are using the ldap:// URL form for SASL binding in the authz-regexp directive. This is because the filter in the LDAP URL is run as anonymous (see the discussion in the *Configuring SLAPD for SASL Support Subsection*).

Additionally, we don't want to let users try to modify their own `uid`, since `uid` is used in the DN:

```
access to attrs=uid
        by anonymous read
        by users read
```

Now Anonymous and all authenticated users will be able to access the `uid` attribute of any record in the directory to which they have access.

There are also a few other attributes we don't want users to be able to modify — even in their own records.

We don't want users to try to modify their OU attributes, since OU attributes are also used in DNs. We also don't want them to be able to modify their `employeeNumber` or their `employeeType`:

```
access to attrs=ou,employeeNumber,employeeType by users read
```

We have a special account, `uid=Authenticate,ou=System,dc=example,dc=com`, which will be used on occasion to help with bind requests. This user should not have access to anything else other than what we specified:

```
access to *
        by dn.exact="uid=Authenticate,ou=System,dc=example,dc=com"
            none
        by users none break
```

Again, the last line instructs SLAPD to continue processing ACLs for users who aren't having the authentication account. This line will also stop the anonymous user from browsing the rest of the tree since the implicit rule at the end, `by * none`, will catch the anonymous user.

> The `uid=Authenitcate` user was already granted, in an earlier rule, access to the `uid` attribute, which is the attribute that this account will use to search for user information needed to bind.

Let's say that we don't want regular users (DNs in the Users OU) to be able to access records in the System OU of our directory (which is typically used for system accounts). We can implement this with the following rule:

```
access to dn.subtree="ou=System,dc=example,dc=com"
        by dn.subtree="ou=Users,dc=example,dc=com" none
        by users read
```

This denies access to users in the Users OU, but allows other users (like System accounts) access to these records.

We also want to give every user the ability to read and write records below its own, but restrict others from accessing those records. This makes it possible for users to store their own information (like address books) inside of the directory:

```
access to dn.regex="^.*,uid=([^,]+),ou=Users,dc=example,dc=com$"
        by dn.exact,expand="uid=$1,ou=Users,dc=example,dc=com write
```

Finally, the last rule we want is a default rule. This rule should answer the question, "What do we want to happen when no other rules are matched?" We want users to be able to modify their own records and see the records of others:

```
access to *
        by self write
        by users read
```

Now our list of ACLs is complete. Altogether, this is what they look like:

```
##################################################
# ACLs
# These are ACLs for the first database section
# of the slapd.conf file found in this directory
##################################################
##
## Restrict by IP address:
access to *
        by peername.ip=127.0.0.1 none break
        by peername.ip=10.40.0.0%255.255.255.0 none break

## Give Admins immediate write access:
access to dn.subtree="dc=example,dc=com"
        by group/groupOfUniqueNames/uniqueMember="cn=LDAP
            Admins,ou=Groups,dc=example,dc=com" write
        by * none break

## Grant access to passwords for auth, but allow users to change
## their own.
access to attrs=userPassword
        by anonymous auth
        by self write

## This rule is needed by authz-regexp
## (Note: Since uid is used in DN, user cannot change its own uid.)
access to attrs=uid
        by anonymous read
        by users read
```

```
## Don't let anyone modify OUs, employee num or employee type.
access to attrs=ou,employeeNumber,employeeType by users read

## Stop authentication account from reading anything else. This also
## stops anonymous.
access to *
        by dn.exact="uid=Authenticate,ou=System,dc=example,dc=com"
            none
        by users none break

## Prevent DNs in ou=Users from seeing system accounts
access to dn.subtree="ou=System,dc=example,dc=com"
        by dn.subtree="ou=Users,dc=example,dc=com" none
        by users read

## Allow user to add subentries beneath its own record.
access to dn.regex="^.*,uid=([^,]+),ou=Users,dc=example,dc=com$"
        by dn.exact,expand="uid=$1,ou=Users,dc=example,dc=com" write

## The default rule: Allow DNs to modify their own records. Give
## read access to everyone else.
access to *
        by self write
        by users read
```

While they certainly won't meet all needs, these rules provide a good starting point for balancing security and usability of the directory. Furthermore, they set the stage for some of the things we will be doing later in this book.

In later chapters of this book, the mentioned ACLs will be revisited and fine-tuned to allow additional features, like directory replication.

Summary

The focus of this chapter has been OpenLDAP security, and we have covered a lot of ground. We began with connection-level security, where we configured SSL/TLS encryption for our directory server. We used StartTLS over the standard LDAP port, and also configured the older (LDAP v2) LDAPS protocol on port 636. Next, we looked at the process of authenticating to the LDAP. In that part we covered both simple binding and SASL binding. Finally, we took a detailed look at access control lists (ACLs), finishing the chapter with a basic set of ACLs.

In the next chapter we will look at advanced configuration of OpenLDAP's SLAPD server. We will configure our server to host multiple backend databases and we will use directory overlays to add powerful additional features to our SLAPD server.

5
Advanced Configuration

In the last chapter, we looked at securing our OpenLDAP server with SSL/TLS, simple and SASL authentication, and ACL-based authorization rules. All of these measures were implemented through configuration files for SLAPD. In this chapter, we will look at some other advanced features of SLAPD, including:

- Configuring multiple database backends
- Tuning directory performance
- Working with directory overlays
- Adding integrity checks
- Adding uniqueness constraints

Multiple Database Backends

As we have worked on OpenLDAP so far we have been using only one directory tree (dc=example,dc=com) and one backend database (an HDB database configured in slapd.conf). This works well for most of the small directory servers. It is simple to configure and all of the data is stored in the same place.

But there are a number of more complex-use cases where it makes sense to have one directory server that handles multiple directory trees, where each tree is stored in its own backend database. Here are some situations in which this sort of configuration might make sense:

- One directory server hosts the directory information trees for multiple organizations
- One large directory server is broken up into multiple smaller trees and subtrees for performance and replication reasons
- Two or more previously existing directory information trees are being gradually consolidated (as in the case of a corporate merger)

Of course, there are other scenarios that might require an LDAP server with multiple backends. These are just a few examples of common situations.

How does a SLAPD with multiple backends works? Let's examine a simple example. Say we have two directory information trees, the dc=example,dc=com tree that we have used in previous chapters, and dc=demo,dc=net.

We want to host both of these on the same SLAPD server. But we don't want the data for dc=example,dc=com to be stored in the same database files as dc=demo,dc=net (that could present problems later on if we ever had to split up the databases). And, of course, we don't want searches for records in one directory tree to return entries from the other.

Configuring a new database is primarily a matter of defining the new database in slapd.conf. After that is done we just need to create some data and load it into the new database.

The slapd.conf File

We created the slapd.conf file in Chapter 2. In previous chapters we have modified small sections of slapd.conf, but now we are going to step back and take a look at the overall structure of the slapd.conf file.

As mentioned in Chapter 2, the slapd.conf file can be broken into component pieces. Initially we created three sections, which we called *Basics*, *Database*, and *ACLs*. In the last chapter we looked extensively at ACLs, as well as the security directives which (for the most part) are defined in the first, *Basics* section. Let's see how the structure of our slapd.conf file looks:

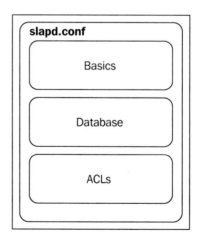

Now it is time to refine the model a little bit. The *Basics* section contains global configuration parameters. That is, the parameters defined there are effective for the entire SLAPD server, regardless of how many database backends it has.

The *Database* section contains directives that pertain to a specific database backend, where each backend often hosts only one directory information tree. Parameters in this section define which backend (such as BDB, HDB, LDIF, SQL) is used, what the specific parameters and overlays are for that backend, which DN will be the manager for that database, and so on. There can be multiple *Database* sections in one `slapd.conf` file. In fact, configuring multiple database sections is how we accomplish hosting multiple database backends on one SLAPD server.

Finally, the *ACL* section is really a subsection of the *Database* section (though, as we saw in the last chapter, ACLs can be used at the global level, as well). Each database can have its own set of access controls. So a more accurate picture of the `slapd.conf` file would look more like this:

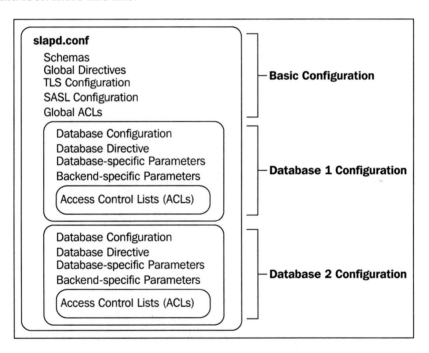

This figure is more representative of how the `slapd.conf` file is composed. The previous example shows two separate databases (though the number of databases is certainly not limited to two), each of which has its own directives, and its own ACLs.

While global ACLs are mentioned in the *Basic Configuration* section, they are not visually separated into their own section in part because their role there is not as significant as the use of ACLs in the context of a backend. Global ACLs should be used primarily to protect the root DSE, `cn=Config`, and `cn=Subschema` portions of the tree (see Appendix C), but not much more. Most ACLs should be placed in the appropriate *Database Configuration* section.

Now we are ready to turn to the configuration file itself and see how the previous diagram is put into practice.

A basic multiple database setup can be done easily by adding just over a dozen lines to our `slapd.conf` file. We will begin with the existing backend configuration that we created in Chapter 2 and add a new database backend beneath it:

```
##############################
# BDB Database Configuration #
##############################
# Database 1: Example.Com

database        hdb
suffix          "dc=example,dc=com" "o=My Company,c=US"
rootdn          "cn=Manager,dc=example,dc=com"
rootpw          secret
directory       /var/lib/ldap
#directory       /usr/local/var/openldap-data
index   objectClass     eq
index   cn      eq,sub,pres,approx
index   uid     eq,sub,pres

########
# ACLs #
########
include /etc/ldap/acl.conf

#############################
# Database 2:  Demo.Net

database        hdb
suffix          "dc=demo,dc=net"
rootdn          "cn=Manager,dc=demo,dc=net"
rootpw          secret
directory       /var/lib/ldap/demo.net
#directory       /usr/local/var/openldap-data/demo.net
index   objectClass     eq
index   cn      eq,sub,pres,approx
index   uid     eq,sub,pres

########
# ACLs #
########
```

```
access to attrs=userPassword
        by anonymous auth
        by self write
access to dn.sub="dc=demo,dc=net" by users read
```

We have just configured two databases:

- The `Example.Com` directory is handled by the first database
- The `Demo.Net` directory is handled by the second database

There are a few important things to note about this configuration:

- Each directory has a separate manager account. This is useful when each directory is managed by a different individual or group.
- The directory for the second database is different than that of the first. Remember that the directory is the location where the database files are stored. Each backend must have its own storage directory.
- As we discussed earlier, each database section can (and should) have its own ACLs and a different set of ACLs can be specified for each database defined in `slapd.conf`. The ACLs in the previous example are minimal.

Creating and Importing a Second Directory

Before we can import data, we need to create the location where the data will be stored. In the `slapd.conf` file fragment, the `directory` directive points to `/var/lib/ldap/demo.net`. However, this directory does not yet exist. We need to create it:

```
$ sudo mkdir /var/lib/ldap/demo.net
```

> If SLAPD is run as a user other than `root`, make sure to change the ownership on the `demo.net/` directory. The SLAPD user ought to own the directory. For example, if the user `ldap` runs `slapd`, do this:
>
> ```
> chown ldap /var/lib/ldap/demo.net
> ```

Next, we need to create an LDIF file that contains the basic records for our new directory. In Chapter 3, we created an LDIF file with the main tree structures for the `dc=example,dc=com` directory information tree. Here we will create just a minimal directory structure in a file called `demo.net.ldif`:

```
# This is the root of the directory tree
dn: dc=demo,dc=net
description: Demo.Net
dc: demo
```

```
o: Demo.Net
objectClass: top
objectClass: dcObject
objectClass: organization
# Subtree for users
dn: ou=Users,dc=demo,dc=net
ou: Users
description: Demo.Net Users
objectClass: organizationalUnit

# George Berkeley
dn: uid=george,ou=Users,dc=demo,dc=net
ou: Users
uid: george
sn: Berkeley
cn: George Berkeley
givenName: George
displayName: George Berkeley
mail: george@demo.net
objectClass: person
objectClass: organizationalPerson
objectClass: inetOrgPerson
```

This file creates the top-level entry—a single subtree branch (for users) and a single user.

Now that we have an LDIF file, we can import it with `slapadd`. If you have not already done so, stop SLAPD while running `slapadd`. We run the following command to import:

```
$ sudo slapadd -b 'dc=demo,dc=net' -l demo.net.ldif
```

By default, `slapadd` tries to import the data into the first directory specified in `slapd.conf`. However, in our case we want the data to be stored in the second directory. Thus, in the previous example, we used the `-b` flag to specify the base DN of the second directory. Instead of doing `-b 'dc=demo,dc=net'`, we could have done `-n 2`, which instructs `slapadd` to put the records in database two.

Now we have a second database with a handful of entries. We can start up the server and test it with `ldapsearch`:

```
$ ldapsearch -LLL -x -W -D 'cn=Manager,dc=demo,dc=net' -b \
             'dc=demo,dc=net' '(objectclass=*)' description
```

This is what we will get:

```
Enter LDAP Password:

dn: dc=demo,dc=net
```

```
description: Demo.Net
dn: ou=Users,dc=demo,dc=net
description: Demo.Net Users

dn: uid=george,ou=Users,dc=demo,dc=net
```

Binding to the `dc=demo,dc=net` directory tree as the manager of that directory, we can verify that the three records we added exist. Note that only the description attribute is to be returned. That is why only `dn` and `description` are displayed.

No ACLs are in place in the `demo.net` portion of `slapd.conf` that would prevent users of the `example.com` database from seeing information in the `demo.net` directory. For example, the user `uid=matt,ou=users,dc=example,dc=com` can retrieve information from the `demo.net` directory:

```
$ ldapsearch -LLL -U matt -b 'dc=demo,dc=net' '(uid=george)' mail
```

This is the output:

```
SASL/DIGEST-MD5 authentication started
Please enter your password:
SASL username: matt
SASL SSF: 128
SASL installing layers

dn: uid=george,ou=Users,dc=demo,dc=net
mail: george@demo.net
```

If we want to prevent this behavior, we can do so with ACLs. For example, we could replace the rule that reads `access to dn.sub="dc=demo,dc=net" by users read` to a rule that restricts reading to entries within the `dc=demo,dc=net` tree:

```
access to dn.sub="dc=demo,dc=net"
        by dn.sub="dc=demo,dc=net" read
```

This would deny entries outside of the `dc=demo,dc=net` tree from accessing these records. A similar rule would have to be added to the ACLs in the `dc=example,dc=com` section to block access from users in the `dc=demo,dc=net` tree.

Now we have a directory with two different databases. In later parts of this book, we will examine other aspects of using multiple databases. For example, later in this chapter we will look at using the `glue` overlay to connect two databases together in one search. In Chapter 7 we will look at doing replication with multiple databases. But next we will look at some performance tuning options for SLAPD.

Performance Tuning

In Chapter 2 we created a basic `slapd.conf` file. Our focus there, though, was on getting a basic server running. In the last chapter, we took a close look at the directives that had to do with security. While creating a second database backend just now, we took a higher-level look at the `slapd.conf` file.

In this part, we will continue working on `slapd.conf`, but here we will focus on parameters that help you tailor the server to the performance needs of your organization. Later in this part we will look at the `DB_CONFIG` file that the Berkeley DB backends (BDB and HDB) use. The optimizations made in that file can lead to significant performance improvements in OpenLDAP.

Terminology: Databases and Backends

The distinction between databases and backends is a fine-grained one, and often the terms are used interchangeably. Here is the difference.

- A **database** is a location (a file, a relational database, a network resource) where a directory information tree is stored.

- A **backend** is a particular mechanism that is used to store databases (or, in some cases, to direct SLAPD to a remote database). Backends are coded as modules, which means they can be loaded dynamically at startup.

Performance Directives

We have already created a `slapd.conf` file that SLAPD uses for managing the directory server. We will continue building on this configuration file as we look at the next batch of directives.

We will break the directives into two different classes:

- Those that are global, and should be placed in the basic configuration section at the top of the `slapd.conf` file

- Those that apply only to individual database backends

Of those that apply to database backends, some are available to all backend types (such as BDB, SQL, Shell, LDIF, and so on), and there are some that apply only to a specific backend type. Since we are using an HDB backend (the default), we will focus on directives that can be used by that backend.

Global Directives

The global directives must be placed at the top part of the `slapd.conf` file, before any database sections are defined. These directives apply to the entire SLAPD server, not just a particular directory information tree within that server.

The first three directives we will see are used to optimize the interaction between the client and the LDAP server. These directives are the `timelimit`, `sizelimit`, and `idletimeout` directives. After that, we will look at the `threads` directive, which is used to tune SLAPD's threading.

 Fine-grained limits on size and time can be set per-database using the `limit` directive, discussed later in this section. For example, this directive can be used to set time and size limits based per user or group.

Time Limits

The `timelimit` directive is used to specify the maximum amount of time SLAPD will work on a particular operation before stopping the operation and returning a message to the client.

Some operations, like searching a large directory for an attribute that is not indexed, can take a long time. Other times, clients connecting over slow network links and requesting large amounts of data can also take up significant time. Such lengthy searches can slow the entire server down, and on a busy server it can also prevent other clients from connecting and getting timely responses. And, of course, not all client applications deal well with lengthy waiting periods.

In order to avoid these problems, there is a `timelimit` directive, which gives you the ability to set the maximum amount of time the server will wait for an operation to complete before ending the operation and returning a message to the client.

The default time limit is 3600 seconds. In this example, we will lower it to only five minutes:

```
timelimit 300
```

Remember, this directive is a *global* directive, and must be placed in the configuration file before any `database` directives.

Sometimes it is useful to eliminate all time limits. This does have the disadvantage of allowing a connection to occupy resources for an unspecified amount of time and, if too many connections did this, the result would be lengthy delays (and perhaps, in extreme cases, denial of service) for clients. But, in controlled environments, this might be a risk that can be taken. To turn off time limits use the keyword `unlimited`:

```
timelimit unlimited
```

With this setting the server will not return a message to the client until the operation is complete.

These examples represent the basic use of time limits, but sometimes a more sophisticated time limit configuration is desirable. The OpenLDAP developers created a more advanced form of the `timelimit` directive to handle such complex time limit settings. In this form, the `timelimit` directive can set two different sorts of time limits:

- **Soft limit**: The soft limit is the default time limit that the server uses if the client does not include a desired time limit in its request.

- **Hard limit**: The hard limit is the absolute longest time that the server will spend processing a request.

Understanding this difference will help to know how the client and the server handle timing issues.

When a client connects to the directory and performs a search, it might send its own time limit request, which instructs the server to take no longer than that amount of time to do the search. For example, if a client sends a time limit of 30 seconds, it will expect the server to take no longer than 30 seconds to respond. If the server's hard time limit is higher than the time limit sent by the client, then the server will set the limit for that request to the client's requested time limit. However, if the server's hard limit is lower than the client's then it will use its own hard limit for that request.

So, if the server's hard time limit is 60 seconds, and the client requests a 30 second time limit, the server will use the 30 second limit. If, however, the server's hard time limit is 10 seconds and the client requests a 30 second limit, the server will use its hard 10-second limit, since it is lower.

Setting the Client Time Limit

For OpenLDAP clients like `ldapsearch`, you can set the client time limit by editing `ldap.conf` (or your `.ldaprc` file) and adding the `TIMELIMIT` directive. In the `ldap.conf` file, `TIMELIMIT` takes only one parameter: time limit in seconds. For example, to set the time limit to 30 seconds: `TIMELIMIT 30`.

Where does the soft limit come in? The client does not always supply a time limit and, in these cases, you may want to set a limit that is lower than the hard limit. That is, if the default hard limit is an hour, that may be a perfectly legitimate limit to set as a maximum limit, but a default of a minute or two is a better limit for those clients that don't need the longer limit.

 If you set a soft limit higher than the hard limit, the hard limit will be used.

Now we can look at the expanded form of the `timelimit` directive to see an example of setting the hard and soft limits. Typically, both are set in the same command (though you can set one without setting the other):

```
timelimit time.soft=30 time.hard=300
```

In this example the soft time limit is 30 seconds, while the hard time limit is 300 seconds. This allows clients that request longer limits to get longer processing time, while setting a lower default for clients that do not provide time limits when making requests.

What does the client get if the time limit is reached? The server will return as much of the processing as it could complete, but it will also include a warning that the time limit was exceeded.

Note that on a busy server a request may get queued, but not actually be executed until a thread becomes available to do the processing. In such cases, the time that the request waits for a thread is not counted against the time limit. The timer for the time limit begins when the worker thread begins processing the request, not when the server receives the request.

 The backend-specific limits directive discussed later in this chapter provides fine-grained time and size-limit support. For example, you can set time limits on particular users or group members.

Idle Timeouts

Along with limiting the amount of time SLAPD spends processing a request you can also limit how long SLAPD should allow a client to remain connected, but idle. A connection is idle if it is connected to SLAPD but is not performing any operations. For example, a client may connect to SLAPD, perform a bind, and then keep the connection open, perhaps waiting for input from a user.

In many cases, there is no harm in allowing clients to remain connected, but idle. Idle clients do not require attention by one of the server's threads, so they do not use up valuable resources. Because of this, the default behavior of the server is to simply allow idle connections to remain connected indefinitely.

But on occasion (sometimes because of limitations in another part of the system), it is desirable to prevent clients from connecting and remaining idle. Use the `idletimeout` directive to set a timeout. Like the simple form of `timelimit`, `idletimeout` takes just one argument, the number of seconds a connection can be idle before SLAPD closes the connection:

```
idletimeout 3600
```

Size Limits

Along with setting limits on the amount of time that an operation can take, it is also possible to set limits on the number of records a search operation can return. Clients can easily perform broad searches that will return many records. Without a size limit in place a search with the filter (`objectclass=*`) would, if not restricted by ACLs, return every record in the search base. And if such a search was performed on a database that held millions of records, SLAPD would send all of those records back to the client.

In most cases it makes sense to set an upper limit on the number of records that can be returned in any one search. By default, SLAPD will only return the first 500 records. But that number can be changed with the `sizelimit` directive.

In its simple form the `sizelimit` directive takes only one parameter, the maximum number of records to return:

```
sizelimit 1000
```

As with `timelimit` though, there is an expanded form of the `sizelimit` directive, and like `timelimit`, `sizelimit` has both soft and hard limits. The expanded `sizelimit` directive also has a third property that can be set, and this property is called `unchecked`.

Hard and soft limits function similarly in `sizelimit` as they do in `timelimit`. The hard limit determines the maximum number of search results that will be returned in any search. Just as is the case with time limits, clients can also send information telling the server the maximum number of entries the client wants back. If no such information is set the value of the soft limit will be used.

If the server finds more records than the `sizelimit` allows, it will return the maximum number of records as well as an error message: `Size limit exceeded`.

The unchecked condition is a little bit more complex. In cases where a search requests matches for an attribute that is not indexed, SLAPD may find a large number of records that it needs to test to see if they match the client's filter. Sometimes the number of candidate records is quite large. The unchecked property can be used to set a limit on the maximum number of records that can be selected as candidates for matching. This can prevent poorly-tuned databases from consuming lots of time and resources searching through huge potential records for those that match.

 Indexing attributes that are commonly searched is the best way to avoid this situation. Indexing is discussed later in this chapter.

If a client's request produces more candidates than allowed by the unchecked property, the server will return an error (Administrative limit exceeded) and will not do the search at all.

The unchecked property will keep the server from spending too much time on such tasks, but at the expense of the client's ability to run queries against the database. Perfectly legitimate searches can be blocked this way. For that reason, the unchecked property should be used with care. The default is to not limit the number of candidates. This is equivalent to specifying size.unchecked=unlimited.

Here's an example of setting all three in one directive:

```
sizelimit size.soft=500 size.hard=1000 size.unchecked=2000
```

In this example, the soft size limit is set to 500, while the hard limit is set to 1000, and the maximum number of unchecked records to be analyzed is 2000. Note that the unchecked size limit should, as a matter of practice, be set to a value larger than the hard limit.

Threads

The last few directives have dealt with setting limits on the server's performing requested operations. These can prove valuable ways of preventing resources from being wasted or misused. Now however, I want to turn to a directive that governs the server's ability to handle requests.

SLAPD is a multi-threaded application. Unlike other servers, SLAPD does not start subprocesses to handle searching. Instead, the SLAPD server is a single process that has many different threads executing concurrently within that processes.

Each thread can perform its own task. So, if a server has sixteen threads (the default for OpenLDAP's SLAPD server), then it can perform sixteen different tasks at the same time. Roughly speaking, threads perform operations. A single client can make a single connection, and then request several different operations, each of which may be done by a different thread (although no more than half of the total threads will be dedicated to a single client).

Sixteen threads, the default, is excessive. Recent performance testing has shown that running a busy server at eight threads performs better than running sixteen, even at high loads. Why? The answer, in a nutshell, is that more threads introduce more competition for the same resources. SLAPD is efficient enough that delegating work to a smaller thread pool is typically faster than using a large thread pool, and incurring thread scheduling overhead.

Lowering the thread count has additional benefits. It is estimated that each thread costs at least 13MB (and perhaps quite a bit more, depending on the configuration of SLAPD and the hardware on the machine). Enterprise LDAP directories can certainly handle this sort of overhead, but on a host that runs LDAP along with many other services, reducing the number of threads might boost the server's performance in other areas, and still perform at the same speeds (or better) as it would when running sixteen threads.

 In future versions of OpenLDAP, the default thread count will very likely be reduced from sixteen to eight.

The `threads` directive is used to set the maximum number of threads that SLAPD will create. It takes an integer:

```
threads 8
```

In typical OpenLDAP configurations, this setting is optimal, though small servers with little traffic may benefit by dropping the thread pool to as low as four.

Proxies and Threads

If you are running busy SLAPD proxy server (with a `proxy` or `ldap` backend, covered in Chapter 7) that queries remote directory servers, you may benefit by having much larger thread pools. Since the worker thread is occupied until the remote LDAP server responds, a thread can remain occupied for long periods of time. In order to keep clients from being denied service you may want to add threads.

Note that the lowest number of threads allowed is 2. This is the minimum number of threads OpenLDAP needs to provide basic service.

Directives in the Database Section

Some directives go in the database section instead of the main portion of the configuration file. And of these, some database directives are specific to the particular backend being used. Along with the backend-neutral directives, we will see a few directives that can be used in BDB/HDB backends.

Limits

We looked at the `sizelimit` and `timelimit` directives, both of which are used in the global section. But in the Database section, there is another directive used for setting limits, and this directive provides finer-grained control over who is limited. You can, for example, set lower or higher limits for individual DNs, subtrees, or for members of a group. The directive for doing these things is the `limit` directive.

A `limit` directive is similar to an ACL. It has three parts: the directive itself, the who-phrase, and one or more limit-phrases. Here's an example:

```
limits users size=20
```

This directive sets a limit for all authenticated users (using the `users` keyword). Only twenty records will be returned before SLAPD will return the message:
`Size limit exceeded.`

The `limit` directive supports two limit-phrases: `size` and `time`. As with the `sizelimit` directive discussed above, `size` can use the `soft`, `hard`, and `unchecked` styles. Similarly, `time` can use the `soft` and `hard` styles. Since more than one limit-phrase can be used, we can create a more robust set of limits. Here's an example limiting the anonymous user to only short result sets, and only if the operation can be done quickly:

```
limits anonymous
   size.soft=5 size.hard=15 size.unchecked=100
   time.soft=5 time.hard=30
```

This sets all three size limits, as well as both time limits, for the anonymous user. This would keep the anonymous user from running lengthy searches.

As we have seen, the `anonymous` and `users` keywords can be used in the who-phrase. But just as in ACLs, the `dn` specifier, along with its modifiers (`exact`, `base`, `onelevel`, `subtree`, `children`, and `regex`) can also be used.

The dn field and its modifiers were covered in detail in the section on *Access Control Lists* in the previous chapter.

Using the dn field we can create limits for particular DNs, DN patterns, or subtrees. For example, we can set a size limit for a particular user:

```
limits dn="uid=matt,ou=Users,dc=example,dc=com" size=50
```

This will set the size limit to 50 for this particular user only. If this is the only limits statement, then SLAPD will apply the size limit set in sizelimit to all other DNs.

Similarly, we can set a size limit for all DNs in a subtree with a directive like this:

```
limits dn.sub="ou=Users,dc=example,dc=com" size=50
```

The above limit will apply to uid=matt,ou=Users,dc=example,dc=com as well as all other users in that same branch of the directory information tree.

Finally, limits can also be set by group. In this case the limits will apply to any member of the group. As with ACLs, the limits directive's who-phrase uses the group field to indicate that SLAPD should base restrictions on group membership:

```
limits group="cn=Admins,ou=Groups,dc=example,dc=com" size=unlimited
```

This directive sets the limit for members of the Admins group to unlimited, which means that no limiting will be enforced on these group members.

Just as with ACLs, only records with the object class groupOfNames are automatically considered to be groups. But other object classes function as groups, as well. For example, in Chapter 3 we created a group with the object class groupOfUniqueNames. That group's DN was cn=LDAP Admins, ou=Groups, dc=example,dc=com.

In order to use that record as a group we need to specify more information in the limits clause:

```
limits group/groupOfUniqueNames/uniqueMember="
            cn=LDAPAdmins,ou=Groups,dc=example,dc=com" size=unlimited
```

When putting a directive, such as the given one into a slapd.conf file note that the entire group field (from group to the end of the DN) must be on one line.

This limits directive will allow search results of unlimited size for members of the group cn=LDAP Admins, ou=Groups,dc=example,dc=com. The group type explicitly indicates the object class of the record (groupOfUniqueNames) and the field that is to be treated as the membership field for that group (uniqueMember). Thus, when

SLAPD checks limits, it will look at the LDAP Admins record, check to see if it has the groupOfUniqueNames object class, and then evaluate whether the user who connected is listed in one of the uniqueMember values in the record. If so, then that user's size limit will be set to unlimited.

Read-only and Restrict Directives

One way to improve performance on a busy server is to limit what clients can do on the server. For example, if the information in a directory is static (that is, no users ought to be able to change data), then it may be best to put the directory server into a read-only mode. Or perhaps limiting just specific operations (such as adding new records or deleting records) is sufficient.

There are two directives that can be placed in the slapd.conf file for achieving these results: readonly and restrict.

The readonly directive is simple. It is either on or off. By default it is off, so the directory allows writing operations (add, modify, delete, and so on). Here's how it is used to configure SLAPD as a read-only directory server:

```
readonly on
```

When this directive is set, a client that attempts to modify information in the directory information tree will get an error message from the server:

```
ldap_modify: Server is unwilling to perform (53)
additional info: operation restricted
```

> Not even the manager can perform modifications to the directory when readonly is turned on.

Binding, searching, and other operations that do not involve changing directory information can continue to function as normal though.

> Extended operations, such as the **Password Modify extended operation**, are not affected by the readonly directive. For that reason the ldappasswd client, for example, will still change a password in the directory even if readonly is turned on.
>
> To prevent this, use the restrict operation to restrict one or all extensions. The Password Modify extended operation is defined in RFC 3062 (http://www.ietf.org/rfc/rfc3062.txt).

Sometimes setting the server to read-only mode is too stringent. It may be desirable to just prevent certain operations. This can be accomplished with the `restrict` directive.

The `restrict` directive takes a list of one or more LDAP operations that should be disallowed. These are the operations that `restrict` understands:

- `add`
- `bind`
- `compare`
- `delete`
- `modify`
- `rename`
- `read` (a special pseudonym that prevents all reading operations like search, compare, and bind)
- `search`
- `write` (a special pseudonym that prevents all writing operations and is equivalent to setting `readonly on`)

In addition to these nine, there is one special type for handling extension: `extended=<OID>`. In the extended type, `<OID>` should be replaced with the Object Identifier (OID) for the extended operation that you want to restrict.

For example, we can prevent users from adding, renaming, and deleting entire entries with the following directive:

```
restrict add delete rename
```

This will prevent a user from adding new entries, renaming existing entries (that is, changing the DN), or deleting entries. With the above configuration in the database section of `slapd.conf`, we cannot add or remove entries with the command-line tools:

```
$ ldapadd -U matt -f john_locke.ldif
```

Here is what we get:

```
SASL/DIGEST-MD5 authentication started
Please enter your password:
SASL username: matt
SASL SSF: 128
SASL installing layers
```

```
adding new entry "cn=John Locke, ou=users,dc=example,dc=com"
ldap_add: Server is unwilling to perform (53)
        additional info: operation restricted

$ ldapdelete -U matt "uid=manny,ou=users,dc=example,dc=com"
SASL/DIGEST-MD5 authentication started
Please enter your password:
SASL username: matt
SASL SSF: 128
SASL installing layers
ldap_delete: Server is unwilling to perform (53)
        additional info: operation restricted
```

Notice that in both cases the server responded: `Server unwilling to perform`. However, modifying an attribute in the record is still allowed, as are searching, comparing, and binding.

As we noted before, extended operations can be restricted using the `extended` type with the `restrict` directive. Unlike the other types though, `extended` takes a value—we can specify which extended operation we want to restrict. Unfortunately, the value must be in the unfriendly OID format. To find out the correct OID you can either check your server's Root DSE entry (see Appendix C), or you can read the RFC for the desired extended operation.

Once you have the OID number it is easy to set a restriction. For example, to prevent clients from performing the *Password Modify* extended operation use the following:

```
restrict extended=1.3.6.1.4.1.4203.1.11.1
```

Attempting to use the `ldappasswd` client to modify a password will result in an error:

```
$ ldappasswd -x -W -D 'cn=Manager,dc=example,dc=com' -S
    'uid=barbara,ou=users,dc=example,dc=com'
```

Here is the error:

```
New password:
Re-enter new password:
Enter LDAP Password:
Result: Server is unwilling to perform (53)
Additional info: extended operation restricted
```

The `restrict` directive provides a convenient way of limiting what operations clients can perform.

Index (BDB/HDB Backends Only)

If you are running a SLAPD server with the BDB or HDB backends (the most commonly-used backends), then the `index` directive is the single most important performance-related directive.

The `index` directive, which is specified in the database section for each BDB or HDB database, indicates which fields SLAPD should build and maintain an index for. An index is a separate database file that is optimized for speedy access during LDAP read operations.

When a client uses a search filter with an attribute that is not indexed, SLAPD searches through every record in the directory for the desired attribute, then checks the value of that attribute against the attribute value or filter supplied by the client.

If the attribute is indexed on the other hand, the SLAPD server simply searches the appropriate attribute index for the value, and quickly returns a list of matching records.

An index search is much faster than a full directory search and, the larger the directory, the more noticeable the difference.

The task of determining which attributes must be indexed is left up to you, and the attributes that you ought to index should be determined by which object classes are used in your directory information tree, and which reading operations (searches, binds, compares) are run against your directory server. Directories primarily oriented around information about people (using `person`, `organizationalPerson`, and `inetOrgPerson` object classes) should probably have indexes for commonly used attributes such as `cn`, `sn`, and `uid`.

When we created our basic `slapd.conf` file in Chapter 2, we configured the following indexes:

```
index   objectClass   eq
index   cn   eq,sub,pres,approx
index   uid   eq,sub,pres
```

There are three indexes specified above: one for `objectClass`, one for `cn`, and one for `uid`.

The first line creates an index for the `objectClass` attribute. The index is optimized for equality (`eq`) matches (that is, searches like `objectclass=person`, but not searches such as `objectclass=*son`). This index should always be included, as the vast majority of reading operations will use the `objectClass` attribute.

The second line is the index for the cn attribute. Along with configuring this index to efficiently handle equality (eq) matches, it is also configured to efficiently perform substring (sub) and approximation (approx) matches, as well as doing quick tests to see if the attribute is present (pres). Here is a brief explanation of each of the index optimization types:

- approx: This optimizes searches for approximation matching. If a search operation is made request approximate matches (cn~=mat), this index may be used to speed up the approximation matching.

- eq: This optimizes for equality matching. Filters that request an exact match, such as (uid=matt) or (objectclass=person) make use of the eq optimization. It is very important that the objectclass attribute have an index optimized for equality. When using directory replication or other overlays, you may also need to index other frequently used attributes.

- sub: This optimizes substring matching. A substring search occurs when a search request sends a part of a string and asks that attribute value that contains that part be returned. For example, the filter (uid=*ar*) should match any UIDs that contain the string ar. Users mark and karen would both match this filter.

- subinitial: This is a special type of sub optimization that optimizes matching the first part of the string only. It is good for handling filters like (uid=mar*), but not filters like (uid=*ark).

- subfinal: This is also a special type of sub optimization. This one optimizes matching the last part of the string, and performs well for filters like (uid=*ark).

- pres: The pres type optimizes the index for cases where a search merely needs to see if an attribute is present.

Not all attributes though, support all of the index options. For example, the objectclass attribute does not support approx, sub, or any of the sub variants, and does not benefit from having a pres index.

Indexes and Schemas

An object class' schema defines what matching rules an attribute supports, and the type of matching rule determines whether or not it can support a particular type of index. See Chapter 6.

In general, adding indexes for commonly-used attributes is a good thing. It speeds up searching and other reading operations, and since the majority of LDAP operations are reading operations, this can be a boon to performance.

But maintaining indexes does slow down writing operations that involve indexed attributes, since those attributes have to be maintained not only in the main database, but also in the index database files. Also, each index requires additional cache space for efficiently searching, which means adding more indexes will consume more memory. For those reasons, it is best to index only the attributes that are frequently used in searching operations, rather than indexing everything.

When an `index` directive is added or modified though, SLAPD does not automatically re-index all of the entries in the directory. You will need to do it by hand. For example, after looking at common searches on our system, we determine that it would be good to add indexes for the `sn` and `member` attributes. Other applications often run searches to find out what groups particular DNs are members of, and an index of this attribute would expedite those searches.

To service these needs we will add the following new `index` directives:

```
index sn eq,sub,approx
index member eq
```

But once we have added these to `slapd.conf`, we will need to stop SLAPD and run the `slapindex` program to rebuild the index files:

```
$ sudo slapindex -q
```

This will rebuild all of the indexes. The `-q` (quick) flag will greatly speed up the process, as it skips performing consistency checks of the database.

Avoid Rebuilding Indexes

A `slapindex` procedure will rebuild all indexes. When adding an index to a large directory, you may want to avoid rebuilding all of the other indexes. One way to do this is to comment out the existing indexes in `slapd.conf` (leaving only the new index lines uncommented), run `slapdindex`, and then remove the comments from the existing indexes. The next version of OpenLDAP will support a more convenient way of adding indexes.

The `slapindex` program will print error messages if any of the optimizing types are not allowed for an attribute (like if one tries to add substring indexing to `objectclass`). But when it runs successfully, it will quietly exit without printing any messages.

Once `slapindex` is finished, SLAPD can be restarted.

Controlling the Cache (BDB/HDB Only)

With BDB and HDB backends, SLAPD stores frequently-accessed records in a cache so that it doesn't have to read directory information from disk with every request. By default, SLAPD retains one-thousand records in the cache. But busy directory servers with a few thousand entries or more will benefit from having a larger cache. This can be done with the `cachesize` directive:

```
cachesize 2000
```

The above directive doubles the default cache size, instructing SLAPD to keep 2000 records in memory.

What happens when the cache is full? By default, SLAPD simply drops the last item in the cache (leaving a cache of 2000 with 1999 full slots). On a busy server, emptying just one cache entry at a time can have slight negative impacts on performance, since it is possible that if a number of searches are executed in rapid succession, each one missing a cache hit, the last entry of the cache would be freed up and filled with every request. This scenario is more likely to happen with the cache is disproportionately small, when compared to the number of entries in the database.

The `cachefree` directive can be used to instruct SLAPD to drop more than one item from the cache when it fills:

```
cachefree 5
```

This example instructs SLAPD to drop the last five entries in the cache.

Ideally, the cache size should remain as close to the actual number of entries in the database as memory constraints will permit. At least, though, the cache should be large enough that frequently requested records can remain in memory. For example, if your directory server functions as an address book, then the cache should be large enough that the user records, as well as their ancestor records, can all be kept in cache at the same time.

 These caching directives are not the only ones of importance for SLAPD. See also the `set_cachesize` directive in the `DB_CONFIG` file section.

The third cache directive is `idlcachesize`. The `idlcachesize` directive is used for caching the results of frequently performed searches, and a large cache here will make searches of often used searches much faster. With the HDB database, it is suggested that this be *three times* the `cachesize` value:

```
cachesize 2000
idlcachesize 6000
```

We have now finished taking a look at the `slapd.conf` configuration options. Now we will turn to another configuration file that can be used to tailor the performance of SLAPD.

Reducing Disk I/O Latency (BDB/HDB Only)

When LDAP operations write new data to the directory and SLAPD is using the BDB or HDB backends the data is stored in memory first, and then flushed to the database files stored in the operating system.

On a very busy directory server (or a server with really slow disk I/O), it is sometimes desirable to trade off data security for speed. There are two directives in particular that instruct SLAPD to make this trade off:

- The first, and the less risky of the two, is the `dirtyread` directive which takes no parameters.

  Consider the case where one client performs a write operation to modify a record, and then another client performs a read operation on that same record before SLAPD has written the first client's changes to disk. Should the server return the unmodified data stored on disk, or the modified data that has not yet been committed? Usually it does the first, sending the *clean*, but soon-to-be out-of-date record to the client.

  The term "dirty read" describes the second case, where the server sends the client information that has not been committed. While returning this data may be faster, it might possibly be inaccurate; the server may reject or abort the modification request of the first client even after having sent the modified data to the second client.

  The `dirtyread` directive only increases the risks that a client may get inaccurate data.

- The second directive, `dbnosync`, carries a higher risk.

  Normally, when an operation changes directory information, the changes are written to disk as soon as possible. Data stored in memory is flushed to the files in the Berkeley DB subsystem. But performing disk I/O can slow the server. One way to speed this up is to instruct SLAPD to delay writing the information to the log file on the disk, and this is done with the `dbnosync` directive.

  The risk in running with `dbnosync` though, is that in the event that the server should die without a clean shutdown, modifications made to the directory, but not yet written to disk, will be lost. However, there is no greater risk of corrupting the database — the database will still be recoverable, though the most recent changes may be lost.

You can reduce (though not eliminate) the risks of running with `dbnosync` by also using the `checkpoint` directive. Setting a checkpoint causes SLAPD to periodically write data to the disk. The `checkpoint` directive takes two parameters: a maximum size (in kilobytes), and a time limit (in minutes). SLAPD will checkpoint the database anytime the amount of data written is greater than the maximum size or after the specified interval of time has passed. Here is an example of the `checkpoint` directive:

```
checkpoint 1024 30
```

This instructs SLAPD to checkpoint the database (flushing any new data from memory to the file system) whenever more than one megabyte of data has been written to the database and every 30 minutes.

Due to the increased risks with these directives, it is generally better to try other means of improving performance (such as altering the cache or tuning the `DB_CONFIG` file) before implementing these directives.

The DB_CONFIG File

The `DB_CONFIG` file is technically not an OpenLDAP configuration file at all. It is a Berkeley DB configuration file, and is specific to the BDB and HDB backends only. It provides a series of settings for the Berkeley database engine.

> Berkeley DB is an Open Source embedded database, now maintained by Oracle. Because it is robust and reliable, actively maintained, and widely support, it is a popular product in both open source and proprietary applications. For more information about Berkeley DB, see Oracle's website: `http://www.oracle.com/database/berkeley-db/index.html`

Since the entire directory information tree, as well as the indexes, for a BDB/HDB backend is stored in a Berkeley DB database, a properly configured `DB_CONFIG` file is the most important facet of directory performance.

When experimenting with the `DB_CONFIG` file and trying out new configurations, it is best to use a non-production server, and to use `slapcat` to make a full backup of the directory data before you make any changes.

The `DB_CONFIG` file is not stored with the OpenLDAP configuration files. Instead, it is stored alongside the database files at `/var/lib/ldap` (or `/usr/local/var/openldap-data`). Unlike the other configuration files, it is read only when the database is created or recovered. As of OpenLDAP 2.3, if SLAPD detects changes in

`DB_CONFIG` when it is starting up, it will attempt to perform a database recovery in order to incorporate the changes, and you may see an entry like this in your log file:

```
bdb_db_open: DB_CONFIG for suffix dc=example,dc=com has changed
Performing database recovery to activate new settings
```

Likewise, when you create a new directory, the Berkeley DB subsystem will read the `DB_CONFIG` file and create the databases according to the directives therein.

> Make sure your database has a `DB_CONFIG` file. If your database directory does not have a `DB_CONFIG` file present, you will be using the factory defaults for Berkeley DB, which are very conservative. On anything but a small (<100 entries) directory server, the defaults will be insufficient, and result in poor performance.

OpenLDAP distributions include a default `DB_CONFIG` file tuned for general use. It should be located at `/var/lib/ldap` already (though it is sometimes labeled `DB_CONFIG.example`, in which case you will need to rename it to just `DB_CONFIG`). In Ubuntu Linux, an Ubuntu-customized `DB_CONFIG` file is located at `/usr/share/doc/slapd/examples/DB_CONFIG`. We will start by using the version included with the OpenLDAP source distribution (which is configured for enterprise use). The default version looks something like this:

```
# one 0.25 GB cache
set_cachesize 0 268435456 1
# Data Directory
#set_data_dir db

# Transaction Log settings
set_lg_regionmax 262144
set_lg_bsize 2097152
#set_lg_dir logs
```

We have removed some of the comments from the header and footer of the file, but preserved all of the settings.

For standard usage on a medium-sized directory, these settings are good. If your directory is performing sufficiently fast and your system is not strapped for resources, you need not feel compelled to change the default settings.

The `DB_CONFIG` file contains directives that directly pertain to the performance of the underlying Berkeley DB files. We will go through these six settings in order. The most important directive is the first.

At the end of this section we will also look at three additional directives used for tuning Berkeley DB lock handling.

 Some of the directives we examined earlier are synonyms for DB_CONFIG directives. For example, dbnosync does the same thing as the DB_CONFIG directive set_flags DB_TXN_NOSYNC.

Setting the Cache Size

The BDB/HDB backend attempts to keep as much of the directory as possible in memory in the form of a cache. This keeps directory reading quick since SLAPD does not have to read information from the disk.

While it might not be possible (on a system with other services, a good economic trade-off) to keep the entire directory in the cache, the server will run faster if at least the most frequently used entries are kept in the cache.

The set_cachesize directive determines how much memory SLAPD will allocate for a directory cache. The directive takes three arguments:

- The number of gigabytes of space to allocate for the cache
- The number of bytes of space to allocate for the cache
- The number of segments to use for the the cache

The first and second are added together and should not, when combined, be larger than 4 GB. The third determines how many data segments the Berkeley DB backend will break the cache into. The values 1 and 0 both result in a single cache segment (which is usually desired).

In the default OpenLDAP DB_CONFIG file, the set_cachesize directive looks like this:

```
set_cachesize 0 268435456 1
```

The total size of the cache is 256 megabytes (268435456/1024/1024), and the entire cache is stored in one segment. For our tiny directory, this is far more than we need. It is a safe setting, though the full 256 megabytes will not be allocated.

A good rule of thumb for estimating the minimum amount of cache you will need in a small or medium-sized directory is to allocate two megabytes of cache for every 100 megabytes of LDIF data, plus one megabyte of cache per index. Larger directories will definitely benefit though, from carefully-tuned caches. For a finer-grained calculation, see the OpenLDAP FAQ-O-Matic entry on setting cache sizes: http://www.openldap.org/faq/data/cache/1075.html.

Configuring the Data Directory

The set_data_dir directive takes one parameter, which is the path to the directory that contains the database files. In the previous example this directive is commented out. Since the DB_CONFIG file is stored in the same directory as the BDB files themselves you should not need to set this directive. It only needs to be set when the DB_CONFIG file is loaded from a location outside of the database directory.

Optimizing BDB/HDB Transaction Logging

The last three directives relate to transaction logging. As modifications are made to the Berkeley DB, the complete details of the transaction are written to log files, named log.XXXXXXXXXX, where the ten X's are replaced by digits from 0-9. The first log file is log.0000000001, and once it grows too large, a new log file is created by incrementing the number: log.0000000002.

The log files comprise a record of all that has happened in a database. In fact, they are so complete that they can be used to rebuild a corrupt database. The log file format is not plain text, and cannot be read using the usual tools (like cat, more, or less). To read it you will need to use the db_printlog command (or dbX.Y_printlog, where X.Y is replaced by the major and minor version numbers of the database, such as db4.2_printlog). This will display a record for each transaction made to the databases.

Recovering a Corrupt BDB/HDB Database

The log files written by the Berkeley DB subsystem can be used to recover a corrupt database. The Berkeley DB distribution includes a tool called db_recover (or dbX.Y_recover, where X.Y is the major and minor version number, such as db4.3_recover). The db_recover tool uses the log files to fix corrupted databases. For more information view the man page for db_recover.

At startup SLAPD automatically performs a recovery on the BDB directory to ensure that the database is in a stable state. It is only in rare cases that a system administrator will have to manually work with the log files.

Since these transaction log files play such an important role in the safety of SLAPD's data, it is good to ensure that the environment is properly tuned.

The set_lg_regionmax directive controls the amount of memory allocated to storing the names of Berkeley DB files. It takes one argument: the amount of space to be allocated (in bytes). The file above allocates 256 KB for storing names, and this should be fine for almost all applications. Only in rare cases where there are many index files would it be necessary to raise this limit (I have never yet encountered such a situation).

The next directive, `set_lg_bsize`, is used to allocate the amount of memory used to buffer data before it is written to the transaction log. It too takes one argument: the amount of space (in bytes) to be used for a buffer. The setting in our file allocates two megabytes of space. When a modification is made to the BDB/HDB database, information about the modification is not written to the log until the transaction is complete. Until it is written it is temporarily stored in an in-memory buffer, whose size is no bigger than the value of `set_lg_bsize`.

Since most LDAP data is relatively short, two megabytes is usually sufficient. But if your particular directory frequently stores large chunks of data (such as image files), you may consider increasing the buffer size for the transaction log to accommodate the largest chunks of data. For example, if the directory stores images as large as ten megabytes, `set_lg_bsize` should be set at `10485760` (which is 10 * 1024 *1024).

Howard Chu, one of the OpenLDAP developers, points out that when increasing the `set_lg_bsize` flag to a value this large, you will also have to raise the maximum size limit for the log file using the `set_lg_max` flag. The maximum size for the log file must be *at least* four times the value of `set_lg_bsize`.

```
set_lg_max 41943040
```

Finally, the last directive, `set_lg_dir`, points to the log file for BDB. By default, these log files are stored in the same directory as the rest of the database files (`/var/lib/ldap/` or `/usr/local/var/openldap-data/` if you compiled from source). However, since logs are crucial in recovery of the database, it is not a bad idea to store the log files in a different location than the databases. For example, you might want to store the logs on a different hard disk than the database files. To do so, uncomment the `set_lg_dir` directive and set it to the absolute path of the desired destination directory:

```
set_lg_dir /usr/local/var/ldap/
```

This directive will instruct the Berkeley DB subsystem to write the log files to `/usr/local/var/ldap` instead of the same directory that the BDB files are located.

 Regularly backing up the Berkeley DB files (including the log files) is a good idea. A more portable way of backing up the data is to dump a copy of the directory using the `slapcat` tool. This will export the database into LDIF format, which can be easily imported into a SLAPD server, regardless of the backend format.

Tuning Lock Files

There are three additional parameters that should be included in the `DB_CONFIG` file. These are the three directives that tune the locking mechanisms in Berkeley DB.

Certain operations on the database will require that the data be locked to prevent the introduction of data inconsistency. For example, it is not good to allow two different threads to modify the same record at the same time. Berkeley DB uses a locking mechanism to prevent this from happening.

There are three directives that are used to tune the locking subsystem. These are:

- `set_lk_max_objects`: The maximum number of objects that can be locked at a given time
- `set_lk_max_locks`: The maximum number of locks that can be requested at a time
- `set_lk_max_lockers`: The maximum number of simultaneous lock requests

In the default Ubuntu `DB_CONFIG` file these are all set to 5000, but lower values (between 1500 and 3000) may be more desirable:

```
# Number of objects that can be locked at the same time.
set_lk_max_objects      5000
# Number of locks (both requested and granted)
set_lk_max_locks        5000
# Number of lockers
set_lk_max_lockers  5000
```

Setting these values at a sufficiently high value will prevent the database from running out of locks, and thus denying database access.

> To see if your Berkeley DB lock settings are adequate, you can use the following command, which prints detailed information about locks and lockers:
>
> **db4.2_stat -c**

More about Berkeley DB

The directives we have covered in this section are those that get the most attention for OpenLDAP. However, there are other directives, and judicious use of such settings can also improve the performance and reliability of the BDB and HDB backends.

Some information about these parameters can be found in OpenLDAP's FAQ-O-Matic (`http://www.openldap.org/faq/data/cache/1072.html`). For a thorough understanding, though the best resource is the *Berkeley DB Reference Guide*. The newest version can be found here: `http://www.oracle.com/technology/documentation/berkeley-db/db/ref/toc.html`

At this point we have looked at the `slapd.conf` and `DB_CONFIG` files, examining some of the ways that these files can be modified to improve the performance of SLAPD. Next, we will turn to a different topic: extending the functionality of SLAPD using directory overlays.

Directory Overlays

As the OpenLDAP project has grown, more and more features have been added. Initially, these features were added directly to the SLAPD server's code base. But as features were rolled into OpenLDAP, both the code and the configuration became increasingly complex.

To address this problem, OpenLDAP developers introduced a new concept in OpenLDAP 2.2 that made it easier to introduce new features while reducing the complexity of the underlying code. The developers introduced a modular system called **overlays**. An overlay is a chunk of code that can modify the behavior of the SLAPD.

When SLAPD receives a request for a database configured to use an overlay, the overlay is given an opportunity to perform processing on the request before any information is retrieved from the underlying database. As a result overlays can be used to perform additional processing of requests.

How is an overlay added to the directory server? It is through special directives in the `slapd.conf` file. The `overlay` directive is placed in the database configuration section, though an overlay sometimes intercepts operations that are not backend-specific.

More than one overlay can be used in a database. When overlays are used this way, they are said to be **stacked**. As we will see later in this chapter the order of overlay directives is very important because SLAPD sequentially goes through the overlay stack, calling the overlays one at a time.

A Brief Tour of the Official Overlays

In OpenLDAP 2.3 there are sixteen *official* overlays included with the OpenLDAP distribution, and a handful of contributed and unofficial overlays. Almost all of the official overlays are described in the man pages. Here we have a brief description of each of the sixteen; we will also see a few useful overlays in more detail. In the later chapters we will also make use of overlays.

The *official* overlays are as follows:

1. `accesslog`: The access logging overlay is used to record information about directory access and utilization. Rather than recording the data in the file system, information is stored as records inside a special log directory. Logs can then be retrieved through LDAP clients, or by using a tool such as `slapcat` to dump the logs into a flat (LDIF) file. We will implement this overlay in the next chapter, and use it again in Chapter 7 to improve replication.

2. `auditlog`: The audit logging overlay records information on changes to the directory. Unlike the more powerful access logging overlay, audit log stores information in a file in the file system.

3. `chain`: In complex directory environments, one directory may have information that another directory does not have. That second directory may be configured to *refer* clients of the first directory. Typically, a referral involves sending the client information about redirecting its query, and then the client is left to chase the referral. The chain overlay handles referral chasing on the server side; the server will follow the referral itself and return the complete information to the client.

4. `denyop`: The deny operation overlay performs the same sort of function as the restrict directive discussed earlier in this chapter. It disallows clients from performing certain LDAP operations. In the next section we will use this overlay.

5. `dyngroup`: The `dyngroup` overlays provide ways of creating dynamic groups based on specific attributes in an object. This provides a powerful method of grouping records.

6. `dynlist`: It is similar to the `dyngroup` overlay.

7. `glue`: The glue overlay, which is built-in and loaded by default, makes it possible to link two databases together so they appear as if they were one large directory information tree. For example, if one database contains `dc=example,dc=com`, and a second database holds `ou=Users,dc=example,dc=com`, the glue overlay makes it possible for searches of `dc=example,dc=com` to return entries from the `ou=Users,dc=example,dc=com` database. The `subordinate` directive must be used in the database section of `slapd.conf` to indicate which databases should be glued.

8. `lastmod`: The last modification overlay creates a special record in the directory information tree that contains information about what the most recently modified record is and when it was modified.

9. `pcache`: The proxy cache overlay caches the results of an LDAP search. This overlay is mainly used with the `ldap` backend. With this combination, SLAPD can be configured to use another LDAP server as its backend, but speed up client requests by keeping a cached copy of the data in a special database.

10. `ppolicy`: The password policy overlay allows you to enforce certain restrictions, such as password expiration dates and password length. The password policy overlay is described in the next chapter.

11. `refint`: The referential integrity overlay is used to keep directory entries consistent when records are deleted or DNs are modified. For example, if a DN is deleted from the directory and the `refint` overlay is used, SLAPD will search the directory for other references to this DN (such as group memberships) and remove those references as well. We will look at this later in the chapter.

12. `retcode`: This overlay is designed to help LDAP client implementors test how their code responds to abnormal server responses.

13. `rwm`: The rewriting and mapping overlay provides a facility for taking a client request and re-writing or mapping parts of the request to other values. This can be used in conjunction with a proxying LDAP server to re-write attribute names and DNs.

14. `syncprov`: The synchronization provider overlay is used by SLAPD servers that act as providers from which other SLAPD servers replicate data. We will discuss this more in Chapter 7.

15. `translucent`: The `translucent` overlay is similar to the proxy overlay. When a client requests a record, it retrieves the record from a remote server. But, it can do more — it can store a local copy of the record that can override portions of the remote record.

16. `unique`: The `unique` overlay enforces attribute uniqueness. It is used to ensure that, for specified attributes, a given attribute value exists in only one record in the directory. This is useful to keep multiple users from having the same email address (`mail`) or user ID (`uid`) attribute values.

Each of the overlays documented here (except for `denyop`) has a corresponding man page that can be accessed using the command `man slapo-<name of overlay>`, where `<name of overlay>` is replaced with the abbreviated name of the overlay. For example, to get the man page for the `translucent` overlay, run the command: `man slapo-translucent`.

In the remainder of this chapter we will cover a few simple overlays in detail. In the next few chapters we will cover several sophisticated overlays, using them to address common directory server needs.

Configuring an Overlay: denyop

Since we have covered the basic concepts behind the `denyop` overlay when we looked at the `restrict` directive, and since `denyop` is simple to implement, we will look at it as an example for how to use an overlay.

 The `restrict` directive is actually the preferred method of restricting operations. The `denyop` overlay was intended primarily as an example for other overlay authors.

Overlays are configured in the `slapd.conf` file. Typically there are three steps to configuring an overlay:

1. Load the dynamic object with the moduleload directive
2. Add the overlay to the *database section* with the `overlay` directive
3. Add any overlay-specific directives to the database section

Let's look at each step in detail.

Loading the module

The first task is to load the module containing the overlay. This part is not always necessary. Some versions of OpenLDAP have all of the modules statically compiled in, which means they are loaded along with the server. More often though, SLAPD is compiled to dynamically load modules that are loaded when SLAPD starts, and almost all overlays are implemented as modules.

 See Appendix A for a further discussion of the difference between these two ways of building OpenLDAP.

The `moduleload` directive should go near the top of the configuration file, before the first `database` directive. To load the `denyop` dynamic object we need to add the following highlighted line:

```
modulepath /usr/lib/ldap
moduleload back_hdb
moduleload denyop
```

When SLAPD starts it will search for the denyop object in its module path, and load it if it finds it.

 If you need to load a module not in the module path you can specify the full path to the module. For example /usr/local/libexec/openldap/my_module.

If SLAPD fails to find the module on startup it will fail to start, exiting with an error like this:

```
lt_dlopenext failed: (/tmp/lastmod) /tmp/lastmod.so: cannot open
                         shared object file: No such file or directory
```

This indicates that the module, lastmod, was not found in the given module path, which in this case was erroneously set to /tmp.

Make sure that the module is in one of the directories listed in modulepath, or that the full path to the module is correct.

Adding the Overlay

The next step is to add the overlay to the overlay stack. Since there are no overlays already specified, this will be the first of three items on the stack. The glue overlay is automatically applied, though it does nothing unless a subordinate directive is present. The backend processing of the operation (the actual directory lookup) is always the last item on the stack.

To add our overlay we need to put the directive in the appropriate database section of the slapd.conf file. In a situation where there are multiple backends, the same overlay directive can be repeated in each database section to load the overlay for each database. The new directive is highlighted in the following example:

```
database hdb
suffix "dc=example,dc=com" "o=My Company,c=US"
rootdn "cn=Manager,dc=example,dc=com"
rootpw secret
directory /var/lib/ldap
overlay denyop
```

Now, we are ready for the third step.

Adding Overlay-Specific Directives

An overlay may have its own special directives. These directives are usually documented in the man page for that overlay.

There is only one directive supported by the `denyop` overlay, and it is the eponymous `denyop` directive. Like the `restrict` directive that we looked at earlier, the `denyop` directive takes a list of operations. Clients will be disallowed from performing any operation in this list.

Earlier in this chapter we used the `restrict` directive to prevent clients from performing `add`, `delete`, and `rename` operations:

```
restrict add delete rename
```

We can implement the same thing with the `denyop` directive:

```
denyop add,delete,modrdn
```

There are a few minor differences between the two directives:

- `denyop` takes a comma-separated list of operations
- `denyop` uses the `modrdn` name instead of using the term `rename`

If a client attempts to perform one of the disallowed operations `denyop` will stop SLAPD from performing the operation, and the client will be returned an `Unwilling to perform` error.

The `denyop` overlay is simple and, due to the restrict directive, not likely to enjoy much use in a production server. But the next overlay that we will look at provides useful features, though the accompanying directives are slightly more complex.

Referential Integrity Overlay

The second overlay we will examine is the RefInt (Referential Integrity) overlay. RefInt is designed to handle cases where the modification or deletion of a record may render attribute values in other records inaccurate.

LDAP groups provide a good context for illustrating the problem that the RefInt overlay is designed to address. In Chapter 3 we created an LDAP group that looked like this:

```
dn: cn=Admins,ou=Groups,dc=example,dc=com
objectClass: groupOfNames
cn: Admins
ou: Groups
member: uid=matt,ou=users,dc=example,dc=com
member: uid=david,ou=users,dc=example,dc=com
```

This group has two members, `uid=matt`, and `uid=david`. These two member attributes refer to other records (identified by their respective DNs) that are also located in the directory. For example, here is the record for `uid=david`:

```
dn: uid=david,ou=Users,dc=example,dc=com
cn: David Hume
sn: Hume
uid: david
ou: Users
objectClass: person
objectClass: organizationalPerson
objectClass: inetOrgPerson
```

What would happen to the `cn=Admins` group if we deleted this record for `uid=david` from the directory information tree? Nothing! The `cn=Admins` group would still contain a member attribute with the DN for `uid=david`. By default, SLAPD does not do any searching for references to a modified or removed DN. Why? The assumption has generally been that such tasks are the responsibility of the applications that access and modify the directory.

But keeping a directory free of invalid references is not a job that everyone wants to leave to external applications. For that reason the OpenLDAP developers created the RefInt overlay, which makes the task of maintaining referential integrity the responsibility of SLAPD.

There are two cases when the RefInt overlay kicks into action:

- When a DN is modified (via a `modrdn` operation): The RefInt overlay does a search of the directory (searching only the values of the attributes specified in the configuration), and replacing any occurrences of the old DN with the newly modified DN
- When a record is removed (with a `delete` operation): The RefInt overlay searches the directory (looking for the specified attributes only), and deletes any references to the DN that it finds

We will look at examples of these, but first let's configure the overlay.

Configuring the Overlay

The first step to configuring the overlay is to make sure the module is loaded. This is done (as always) by adding a `moduleload` directive in the basic section of the `slapd.conf` file, before the first database section:

```
modulepath /usr/lib/ldap
moduleload back_hdb
moduleload denyop
moduleload refint
```

This example builds on our earlier `moduleload` example. Only the highlighted line has been added.

Next, we want to add the overlay to the stack, and configure it for operation. These configuration directives go in each database section for which we want to use the overlay:

```
overlay refint
refint_attributes member uniqueMember seeAlso
refint_nothing cn=EMPTY
```

The first line, the `overlay` directive, adds RefInt to the overlay stack. Remember, it's position relative to other `overlay` directives will determine its position on the overlay stack.

On the next line is the `refint_attributes` directive. This directive takes a list of attributes (separated by whitespace characters) that will be searched whenever a `modrdn` or `delete` operation is performed. We want to include all of the attributes that we want SLAPD to maintain referential integrity for.

Since we have records that are `groupOfNames` and `groupOfUniqueNames` object classes, we want the RefInt overlay to check the `member` and `uniqueMember` attributes. The `seeAlso` attribute, which is an attribute allowed for `organization`, `organizationalUnit`, and `person` objects (all of which are used in our directory information tree), takes a DN for a value, so we want RefInt to check it as well.

The seeAlso Attribute

The `seeAlso` attribute, which allows only values that are DNs, is used to indicate a connection between the record that contains the `seeAlso` attribute, and the record or records that the `seeAlso` attribute points to. There are other attributes, such as the `manager` attribute for `inetOrgPerson` objects, which also take DN values.

The last directive, `refint_nothing`, is used in special cases when RefInt is responding to a `delete` operation.

Sometimes it is not possible for RefInt to delete an attribute value. This happens when a record must (according to the schema) have at least one such attribute value. For example, any `groupOfNames` object must have at least one `member` attribute value. The schema does not allow groups with no members.

But what if deleting an entry would require RefInt to remove the only `member` attribute from a group? We wouldn't want RefInt to try to violate the server's schema constraints.

RefInt avoids the problem this way: RefInt adds the DN in `refint_nothing` as a value for that attribute, and then deletes the other attribute. Effectively, it replaces the deleted value with a known placeholder value.

In the previous example we have set the `refint_nothing` DN to be `cn=EMPTY`. There is no entry in our directory information tree named `cn=EMPTY` (though if there were, it would cause no problems).

Modifying the Records

Now, we will add two records to our directory:

```
dn: uid=marcus,ou=users,dc=example,dc=com
uid: marcus
sn: Tullius
cn: Marcus Tullius
givenName: Marcus
ou: users
objectclass: person
objectclass: organizationalperson
objectclass: inetOrgPerson

dn: cn=Public Relations,ou=Groups,dc=example,dc=com
objectclass: groupOfNames
cn: Public Relations
ou: Groups
member: uid=marcus,ou=users,dc=example,dc=com
```

The first record is for a new `inetOrgPerson` with the UID `marcus`. The second record defines the `cn=Public Relations` group which currently has one member, `uid=marcus`. What happens to the `member` attribute of `cn=Public Relations` if we delete the record for `uid=marcus` by using the following command?

```
$ ldapdelete -U matt uid=marcus,ou=users,dc=example,dc=com
```

Now, we search for the `cn=Public Relations` group:

```
$ ldapsearch -U matt -LLL '(cn=Public Relations)'
```

The record looks like this:

```
SASL/DIGEST-MD5 authentication started
Please enter your password:
SASL username: matt
SASL SSF: 128
```

```
SASL installing layers

dn: cn=Public Relations,ou=Groups,dc=example,dc=com
objectClass: groupOfNames
cn: Public Relations
ou: Groups
member: cn=EMPTY
```

As the last line of the code illustrates, there is still one member (the `groupOfNames` schema requires that there be one) but, thanks to the RefInt overlay, it no longer points to the deleted `uid=marcus` record. Instead it points to the DN we specified in `refint_nothing`.

Usually, though, the record will have more than one member attribute, like the `cn=Admins` example earlier. In such a case when one of those DNs is deleted, the attribute value is completely removed. Consider a modified version of our `cn=Public Relations` group:

```
dn: cn=Public Relations,ou=Groups,dc=example,dc=com
objectclass: groupofnames
cn: Public Relations
ou: Groups
member: uid=david,ou=users,dc=example,dc=com
member: uid=marcus,ou=users,dc=example,dc=com
```

If the record for `uid=marcus` was deleted in this case, then the RefInt overlay would simply delete the second member attribute value, leaving the group looking like this:

```
dn: cn=Public Relations,ou=Groups,dc=example,dc=com
objectclass: groupofnames
cn: Public Relations
ou: Groups
member: uid=david,ou=users,dc=example,dc=com
```

The value of `refint_nothing` is used only when required.

These last two examples have dealt with cases where the `delete` operation is used. But the RefInt overlay also handles changes to DNs made with the `modrdn` operation. For example, what if instead of deleting the record for `uid=marcus` we changed the DN? Using the previous example let's begin with the same two records:

```
dn: uid=marcus,ou=users,dc=example,dc=com
uid: marcus
sn: Tullius
cn: Marcus Tullius
```

```
givenName: Marcus
ou: users
objectclass: person
objectclass: organizationalperson
objectclass: inetOrgPerson


dn: cn=Public Relations,ou=Groups,dc=example,dc=com
objectclass: groupofnames
cn: Public Relations
ou: Groups
member: uid=marcus,ou=users,dc=example,dc=com
```

Let's change the DN of the first record to use Marcus Tullius's better-known name:

```
$ ldapmodrdn -U matt uid=marcus,ou=users,dc=example,dc=com
    uid=cicero
```

In the previous example, we are changing the DN `uid=marcus,ou=users,`
`dc=example,dc=com`, replacing the relative DN portion (`uid=marcus`) with a new
relative DN: `uid=cicero`. Now the first record looks like this:

```
dn: uid=cicero,ou=users,dc=example,dc=com
uid: marcus
uid: cicero
sn: Tullius
cn: Marcus Tullius
givenName: Marcus
ou: users
objectClass: person
objectClass: organizationalPerson
objectClass: inetOrgPerson
```

The `ldapmodrdn` client added a new `uid` attribute value (`cicero`), and then
changed the DN of the entry from `uid=marcus,ou=users,dc=example,dc=com`
to `uid=cicero,ou=users,dc=example,dc=com`. And what about the `cn=Public`
`Relations` group? It now looks like this:

```
dn: cn=Public Relations,ou=Groups,dc=example,dc=com
objectClass: groupOfNames
cn: Public Relations
ou: Groups
member: uid=cicero,ou=users,dc=example,dc=com
```

The RefInt attribute changed the value of the `member` attribute to point to the newly modified DN. Remember, without the RefInt overlay, the `cn=Public Relations` group would point to the now non-existent DN `uid=marcus, ou=users,dc=example,dc=com`.

Drawbacks

Are there any drawbacks of using the RefInt overlay? Performance is one issue. For every deletion or DN modification, the RefInt overlay will check all the values for all of the attributes listed in the `refint_attributes` directive. A large number of deletions or DN modifications can have an impact on system performance. But in most situations, large-scale `delete` and `modrdn` operations are not the norm (and the overlay can always be turned off when doing such operations).

There is one other drawback worthy of consideration. Some applications do handle their own reference checking. It is possible that a poorly-written client might try to delete attribute values that do not exist, generating spurious error messages in the process. Of course, this would not have any negative effect on the directory information tree, but it might alarm the user. However, the vast majority of clients, including many that perform their own integrity checking, should not be hampered by the RefInt overlay.

A Useful Note

When starting up SLAPD after installing a new overlay, it is not uncommon to get the following warning message:

```
WARNING: No dynamic config support for overlay refint.
```

What does this message mean? And is the problem serious?

This warning message can be ignored when configuring OpenLDAP with a `slapd.conf` file. It is simply a notice that the configuration options for this overlay cannot be changed once the server starts. But this is, of course, how all directives in the `slapd.conf` file work.

This warning message applies only to installations that load their configuration into the directory as an LDIF file, and then manage their configuration inside of the directory server (using the `cn=Config` record). This feature is fairly new, and since it does not support all of the OpenLDAP features (such as many overlays), it is not the recommended configuration for most clients.

The Uniqueness Overlay

The last overlay that we will examine in this section is the uniqueness overlay. The uniqueness overlay enforces uniqueness for a configurable set of attributes in the directory. It prevents attributes in different records from containing the same values. This is desirable, for example, when working with the `uid` attribute, where we would clearly not want to have the same UID for multiple users in the system. By default, SLAPD only enforces uniqueness when it comes to DNs—no two DNs may be the same. But other attribute values are unchecked. Using the uniqueness overlay, we can specify which attributes we want SLAPD to ensure uniqueness for.

The first step in configuring the uniqueness overlay is to load the module:

```
modulepath      /usr/local/libexec/openldap
moduleload      back_hdb
moduleload      denyop
moduleload      refint
moduleload      unique
```

In the *Basics* section of `slapd.conf`, we add one more `moduleload` directive. The module we want to load is named `unique`.

Next we want to add this overlay, along with a few specific directives, to the relevant database sections:

```
overlay unique
unique_base dc=example,dc=com
unique_attributes uid
```

This is a very basic configuration for the uniqueness overlay. The `unique_base` directive indicates which parts of the directory information tree we want to enforce uniqueness in. For our exercise we want to enforce uniqueness across our entire directory tree, `dc=example,dc=com`.

The `unique_attributes` directive takes a whitespace-separated list of attributes that the uniqueness overlay will enforce uniqueness constraints. In this example we just want to enforce uniqueness on the UID attribute.

 The behavior of the uniqueness overlay is expected to change in the next version of OpenLDAP (version 2.4). In particular, it will support multiple bases inside a single database.

Thus, according to our configuration, no two UID values for any records in the `dc=example,dc=com` directory information tree should be identical.

Now let's see how this overlay works in practice.

In the discussion of the RefInt overlay, we created the following record:

```
dn: uid=cicero,ou=users,dc=example,dc=com
uid: marcus
uid: cicero
sn: Tullius
cn: Marcus Tullius
givenName: Marcus
ou: users
objectClass: person
objectClass: organizationalPerson
objectClass: inetOrgPerson
```

Note that this record has the UID marcus, even though this attribute is not used in the DN. Now let's try to add the following record:

```
dn: uid=marcus,ou=users,dc=example,dc=com
uid: marcus
sn: Aurelius
cn: Marcus Aurelius
givenName: Marcus
ou: users
objectclass: person
objectclass: organizationalperson
objectclass: inetOrgPerson
```

This record also uses the UID marcus. Without the uniqueness overlay, SLAPD would allow both records to have the same UID. This, of course, will cause problems for applications that assume that a Unique ID is really unique — only zero or one results will be returned for a search on the UID attribute.

But with the uniqueness overlay, as we have configured it, SLAPD will prevent clients from adding a UID value that matches an existing UID value. The uniqueness overlay does this by checking the attributes in add, modify, or modrdn operations. If we try to add the given record for uid=marcus, we get an error:

```
$ ldapadd -U matt -f unique-example.ldif
SASL/DIGEST-MD5 authentication started
Please enter your password:
SASL username: matt
SASL SSF: 128
SASL installing layers
```

```
adding new entry "uid=marcus,ou=users,dc=example,dc=com"
ldap_add: Constraint violation (19)
            additional info: some attributes not unique
```

SLAPD sends back a **Constraint violation** error because the uniqueness overlay will not allow a duplicate UID attribute value. To work around this, we would have to either delete the extra UID attribute from the `uid=cicero` record or use a different UID for Marcus Aurelius's record.

The example configuration we have just seen represents the most typical use of the uniqueness overlay. There are two additional uniqueness directives that provide more complex configurations:

The first is the `unique_ignore` directive. Typically, this is used *instead* of `unique_attributes`.

 While you can use both `unique_attributes` and `unique_ignore`, it is not recommended because it can cause unexpected behavior. See the man page for more detail: `man slapo-unique`.

The `unique_ignore` directive takes a whitespace-separated list of attributes that *should not* be tested for uniqueness. There are attributes, such as `ou`, `sn`, and `objectclass`, that are likely to be legitimately used more than once in a directory. For example, it is perfectly possible for multiple people in an organization to have the same surname, and thus have identical `sn` attribute values.

But when `unique_attributes` is not specified, then by default all *non-operational attributes* are assumed to require uniqueness. Consider this example configuration:

```
overlay unique
unique_base dc=example,dc=com
unique_ignore objectclass sn ou description
```

According to this configuration, all of the attribute values in the directory information tree except `objectclass`, `sn`, `ou`, and `description` will be required to have unique values. Obviously, this configuration is far more restrictive than our first example and it should be used with care.

 Operational parameters — those intended for internal SLAPD use — are not automatically added to the uniqueness list under any circumstances. Doing so might cause hard-to-debug errors that would prevent SLAPD from functioning properly.

Finally, there is one additional directive for the unique overlay. The `unique_strict` directive, which takes no parameters, can be used to turn on "strict" uniqueness enforcement.

By default, the uniqueness overlay allows multiple attributes to have empty (null) values. For example, if we enforce uniqueness on the `uid` attribute, SLAPD would still allow multiple records to have a UID attribute with an empty value. But this is not always desirable. Under some circumstances, it might be necessary to ensure that no more than one attribute has an empty value. The `unique_strict` directive is used for this purpose.

When the `unique_strict` directive is present, the uniqueness overlay will not allow a client to set an attribute value to empty (null) if another instance of the same attribute already exists and already has an empty value.

At this point, you should have a good idea of how to use overlays. We have looked at three different overlays but in the coming chapters we will look at several more.

Summary

The focus of this chapter has been on advanced configuration of the SLAPD server. We began by taking a second look at the `slapd.conf` file. Then we added an additional database to our directory server, supporting a second directory information tree. From there we looked at some ways of improving SLAPD's performance using directives in the `slapd.conf` file, and also tuning the Berkeley DB's `DB_CONFIG` file. In the last section we looked at SLAPD's overlay engine, touring three specific overlays.

By now you should feel comfortable working with the `slapd.conf` file as well as using overlays.

In the next chapter we will examine LDAP schemas, adding a few schemas for new overlays, and then creating our own schema. Later, in Chapter 7, we will expand upon some of the themes in this chapter when we look at the ways to configure multiple OpenLDAP servers to work together.

6
LDAP Schemas

The focus of this chapter will be LDAP Schemas. Schemas are the standard way of describing the structure of objects that may be stored inside the directory. The first few sections are designed to provide foundational knowledge of what schemas do and how they work — a foundation necessary for our work, later in this chapter, using and implementing schemas. But we will continue on from there to a number of more practical topics, including adding pre-defined schemas and defining our own custom schemas.

We will begin with a general examination of schemas. From there, we will look at schema hierarchies. Like the directory information tree itself, schemas are organized into hierarchies. Next, we will examine some of the basic schemas that are included with OpenLDAP. We will also look at two overlays that require their own schemas. Finally, we will create a custom schema consisting of a pair of new object classes, each with new attributes. The main topics we will discuss in this chapter are:

- The basics of schema definitions
- The three types of object classes
- Using different schemas in OpenLDAP
- Configuring the Accesslog and Password Policy Overlays
- Obtaining and using an Object Identifier (OID)
- Creating new schemas by hand

Introduction to LDAP Schemas

We have already looked at a variety of attributes and object classes used in OpenLDAP. For example, we created entries for our users using the `person`, `organizationalPerson`, and `inetOrgPerson` object classes and, in so doing, we used attributes like `cn`, `sn`, `uid`, `mail`, and `userPassword`. We also created groups using the `groupOfNames` and `groupOfUniqueNames` object classes, paying special attention to the `member` and `uniqueMember` attributes. We even looked briefly (in Chapter 3) at object classes and attributes for describing documents and collections of documents (`document` and `documentCollection` respectively).

Each of these object classes and attributes has a strict definition. The definitions of attributes and object classes are bundled together into larger collections called schemas. OpenLDAP applications use these schemas to determine how records should be structured and where (in the hierarchical structure) each entry can be located.

Why Do They Look So Complicated?

LDAP schemas have a bad reputation. They are viewed as complex, arcane, hyper-technical, and difficult to implement. The goal of this chapter is to overcome this perception.

It is understandable why this reputation persists though. I think there are a few aspects of LDAP schemas that are daunting to the neophyte.

First, LDAP schemas are based on generations of technical specifications coming out of the complex X.500 system. Because of this heritage, LDAP schemas make frequent use of equipment that is not particularly human-friendly, such as object identifier numbers that look like this: `1.3.6.1.4.1.1466.115.121.1.25`. However, a little bit of background knowledge can overcome this hurdle.

Second, the LDAP schema definition language is notably different from the sorts of definition languages (DDL) familiar to SQL developers. This is largely due to the different nature of the backend database. LDAP is not inherently tabular as relational databases are, while it does make frequent use of concepts like inheritance (a rarity in SQL DDL languages, though some do support the idea). Finally, while SQL DDL takes the form of a SQL command, LDAP schema definitions are purely descriptive.

But the LDAP schema language is actually quite compact and typically only two directives (`attributetype` and `objectclasstype`), each with a handful of arguments, are needed in order to create custom schemas. For this reason, the learning curve is short, and by the end of this chapter you should be able to comfortably create your own schemas.

Typically schemas are written in plain-text files and stored in a subdirectory of the OpenLDAP configuration folder. In Ubuntu these files are located at `/etc/ldap/schema`. If you built from source the schema files are located by default at `/usr/local/etc/openldap/schema`.

SLAPD does not automatically use all of the schemas in the schema directory. When SLAPD starts up, it loads only the schemas specified in the `slapd.conf` file.

 There is an exception to this rule: certain vital LDAP schema components, like `objectclass`, are hard-coded into OpenLDAP, since they are fundamental to the operation of the server.

Usually schemas are included using the `include` directive. In Chapter 2 we included three schema files in our `slapd.conf` file. The include section, near the top of the file, looks like this:

```
include /etc/ldap/schema/core.schema
include /etc/ldap/schema/cosine.schema
include /etc/ldap/schema/inetorgperson.schema
```

The first line imports the core schema, which contains the schemas of attributes and object classes necessary for standard LDAP use. The second imports a number of commonly used object classes and attributes, including those used for storing document information and DNS records. The `inetorgperson.schema` file includes the inetOrgPerson object class definition and its associated attribute definitions.

In the coming sections we will look at the format of these files, implementing some existing schemas, and finally creating our own schema.

Schema Definitions

LDAP schemas are used to formally define attributes, object classes, and various rules for structuring the directory information tree. The term **schema** refers to a collection of (conceptually related) schema definitions. The `inetOrgPerson` schema, for example, contains the definition of the `inetOrgPerson` object class, as well as all of the extra (non-core) attributes that are allowed or required by the `inetOrgPerson` object class.

A **schema definition** is a special type of directive that provides information about how a particular entity in SLAPD is to be structured. There are four different types of schema definition that can be included in `slapd.conf` (or an included schema definition):

- **Object class definitions**: This defines an object class, including its unique identifier, its name, and the attributes it may or must have.
- **Attribute definitions**: This defines an attribute, including its unique identifier, its name or names, the rules for what types of content will be allowed as values, and how matching operations are performed.

- **Object identifiers**: This attaches a string name to a unique identifier. It is primarily used to expedite creating schemas.

- **DIT content rules**: This specifies rules for what additional (auxiliary) object classes an entry with a particular structural object class may have.

In addition to these four, there are other schema definitions that are not typically placed in a schema. Instead, most of these are generated by OpenLDAP code. Here is a brief description of what each does (for more information see RFC 4512, which defines the LDAP schema language):

- **Matching rule definitions**: These define a rule used for matching operations. Searches may use matching rules (such as equality and substring matching) to find specific attribute values. For example, the `distinguishedNameMatch` matching rule (with unique identifier `2.5.13.1`) defines the matching rule for exactly matching DNs. This rule is used by attributes like `member` (for group membership) and `seeAlso`. Searching with this rule will return successful results only if an attribute's value matches the given DN. The matching rules for any attribute determine what indexes can be created for that attribute.

- **Matching rule uses**: These map attributes to matching rules, and is usually created dynamically by SLAPD. Based on this definition, a client can tell which attributes a particular matching rule can be applied to. It can be used, for example, to find out all of the attribute values that support exact DN matches (the `distinguishedNameMatch` matching rule). The schema definition for a matching rule use (`matchingRuleUse`) contains a unique identifier, the matching rule name, and all of the attributes that this matching rule applies to.

- **LDAP syntaxes**: These describe the syntax allowed for the content of an attribute value. The exact type and syntax of data for an attribute value can be specified when an attribute is defined. There are a number of supported syntaxes (`ldapSyntaxes`) defined for SLAPD, including a syntax for the DN structure, one for binary data, several for kinds of plain text data, and so on. We will talk about supported syntaxes more when we look at attribute definitions.

- **Structure rules**: These define where in a directory information tree a given entry can be located. It is based on the structural object class of the entry. Structural object classes and the object class hierarchy are discussed later in the section *The Object Class Hierarchy* section.

- **Name forms**: These specify what attributes may or must be used in the RDN portion of an entry's DN (based on the entry's structural object class).

SLAPD builds this part of the schema in code. For example, matching rule uses are generated based on what matching rules exist and what attributes implement those matching rules. Like the rest of the schema, matching rules, LDAP syntaxes, structure rules, and name forms can all be accessed over the LDAP protocol. See the *Retrieving Schemas from SLAPD* section for more information.

For the time being though, we will focus primarily on the four schema definitions that can be included in the `slapd.conf` file. In particular, we will focus on creating new object classes and attributes.

Object Classes and Attributes

There are two different types of schema definition that we need in order to extend the types of information that our directory server will store:

- **Attribute type definition**: An attribute type definition defines an attribute, including what attribute names it may have (for example, `cn` and `commonName`), what sort of values an attribute may contain (numbers, string, DNs, and so on), what rules to use when trying to match values, and whether it may have more than one value.

  Any given attribute may require that its value or values be composed of certain characters or data types. For example, the `description` attribute allows long strings of characters, which makes it possible to include a sentence or two of information as a value to a description field.

- **Object class definition**: An object class definition specifies the name of the object class, what attributes it must have, what attributes it may have, and what kind of object it is.

We will look at each of these in turn. To start, let's take another look at one of the schemas introduced in Chapter 3. Here is a graphical representation of the `person` object class:

Person

Required:
    cn
    sn
Allowed:
    userPassword
    telephoneNumber
    seeAlso
    description

The `person` object class has two required attributes (`cn` and `sn`) and four more attributes that are allowed, but not required: `userPassword`, `telephoneNumber`, `seeAlso`, and `description`.

A new record that is of object class `person` (and has no other object classes) might look like this:

```
dn: cn=Thomas Reid, dc=example,dc=com
objectclass: person
cn: Thomas Reid
sn: Reid
userPassword:: DSFSUYJKHGH=
telephoneNumber: 555-555-5555
seeAlso: uid=david,ou=users,dc=example,dc=com
description: A basic user.
```

This record contains all, and only, the attributes in the `person` object class. Attempting to add a different attribute type not mentioned in the schema would lead to an error. Similarly, trying to remove all values for the `cn` or `sn` attributes would also lead to an error since their presence is required.

But how does OpenLDAP know which attributes are required and which are allowed? This information is stored in the schema definition for the `person` object class.

Object Class Definitions

The schema definition is stored in the `core.schema` (and also in `core.ldif`) file at `/etc/ldap/schema` (or `/usr/local/etc/openldap/schema` if you compiled from source). Have a look at this:

```
objectclass
  (
  2.5.6.6
  NAME 'person'
  DESC 'RFC4519: a person'
  SUP top STRUCTURAL
  MUST ( sn $ cn )
  MAY ( userPassword $ telephoneNumber $ seeAlso $ description )
  )
```

This is a simple object class definition. It begins with a descriptor, `objectclass`, which tells the schema interpreter what type of definition is being made. The rest of the definition is enclosed in parentheses. Extra whitespace characters, including line breaks, are generally ignored (unless enclosed in a quoted string), but remember that since `objectclass` is a directive in the `slapd.conf` file format, every line other than the first must start with a whitespace character.

The first field within the definition is the numeric identifier for the object class: `2.5.6.6`. This unique identifier is called an **Object IDentifier** (**OID**). Every schema definition has a unique OID that distinguishes that definition from any other definition in the world. Because this OID is supposed to be globally unique there is an official procedure for giving a definition a unique identifier. This will be described later in the chapter. For now it is sufficient to note that these OIDs must be universally unique.

Any LDAP application may refer to a definition by its OID. Object classes, attributes, matching rules, and many other LDAP entities have OIDs.

The Root DSE record is a good example of how LDAP clients can learn important information about a server's capabilities based on the OIDs that the server presents to the client. See Appendix C for an example.

The second field in the definition is the NAME field. While an OID is easily used by a computer, it is not so easily used by humans. So, in addition to an OID, server-unique names (in character strings) may be specified. The above object class only has one name: `person`. Multiple names can be given to a single object class, but usually a single one will suffice.

In a schema definition, the string names should always be enclosed in single quotation marks. In a list of string values, each value must be enclosed in single quotes and the entire list must be enclosed in parentheses. For example, if the person definition specified two names, `person` and `humanBeing`, the NAME field would look like this:

```
NAME ( 'person' 'humanBeing' )
```

Note also that spaces are not allowed in the values of the NAME field, so `'human being'` would be an illegal name.

In attribute definitions, it is more common to give attributes a long name and an abbreviated name. For example, `cn` and `commonName` are both names for the attribute with OID `2.5.4.3`.

Most of the time object classes and attributes are referred to by the values in the NAME field rather than by OID.

By convention, names that consist of multiple words are concatenated by capitalizing the first letter of each word after the first. For example, commonName is composed of two words: common and name. Only the second word is capitalized. Underscores, dashes, and other special characters are typically not used to concatenate words. Thus, you should not use names like common_name or common-name.

The DESC field is a brief description of what this schema definition is to be used for. In this case the description field refers to an RFC (RFC 4519) that gives a detailed explanation of the object class. Of course it is not necessary to create an RFC to formally define your schemas, though if you plan on distributing the schema widely writing an RFC is a good idea.

The next field, SUP, which is short for 'superior,' indicates what the parent object class of this object class is. The parent of the person object class is the object class called top. Object classes, like directory information trees, are organized in hierarchies. The top object class is at the top of the object class hierarchy. The STRUCTURAL keyword also pertains to how this schema definition fits into the schema hierarchy. We will discuss schema hierarchies in the next part.

The last two fields are less mysterious. They define which attributes a person object must (MUST) contain, and which attributes an object may (MAY) contain.

The syntax for the MUST and MAY fields is straightforward. Each description takes a list of attributes:

```
MAY ( userPassword $ telephoneNumber $ seeAlso $ description )
```

The list of attribute values (designated either by OID or by an attribute name) is enclosed in parentheses. Values are separated with the dollar sign ($). The example above indicates that the four values, userPassword, telephoneNumber, seeAlso, and description, are all attributes that a person object is allowed to have.

An attribute should be specified in only one of the two lists. There is no need to put an attribute in both a MAY and a MUST list.

Of course, the names can be replaced with OIDs instead. Thus, the following two lines are equivalent:

```
MUST ( sn $ cn )
```

and

```
MUST ( sn $ 2.5.4.3 )
```

The OID for the cn attribute is 2.5.4.3, and either identifier will work.

There are a few fields that may be present in an object class definition but which are not present in the previous code. The first is the OBSOLETE keyword, which appears after the DESC field. This is used to designate an object class as obsolete but still (temporarily) supported.

The second is the extensions section, which is used for providing implementation-specific extensions to a schema. At the end of the schema one or more extensions may be specified. An extension is a keyword followed by a list enclosed in parentheses. By default, none of the schemas included in OpenLDAP's schema/ directory have any extensions.

In summary then, an object class definition begins with the objectclasstype directive, and can contain the following fields:

- A unique OID to identify this object class (example: 2.5.6.6).
- A NAME field with a unique name (NAME 'person').
- A DESC field with a brief description of the purpose of the object class (DESC 'RFC4519: a person').
- Optionally, it may contain an OBSOLETE tag if the class is obsolete and should not be used.
- A SUP line, indicating what object class is the parent (superior) of this one. Also, this line should specify the type of object class (STRUCTURAL, ABSTRACT, or AUXILLIARY). Example: SUP top STRUCTURAL. Abstract classes do not have superiors. When defining an abstract class SUP can be omitted.
- A MUST field with a list of attributes that must be specified for an instance of this object class. Example: MUST (sn $ cn).
- A MAY field with a list of attributes that can optionally be added to records of this object class. Example: MAY (userPassword $ telephoneNumber $ seeAlso $ description).
- One or more extensions.

Object class definitions are an important part of schemas and we will look back at these concepts several times in this chapter. After covering other definition types, we will take a detailed look at the object class hierarchy. As we do that the role of the SUP line will become clearer.

Further on we will look at some specific object classes and we will also write our own custom object class. But before we move on to those things we will look at the other schema definitions. Next, we will look at attribute definitions.

Attribute Definitions

The `person` object class that we examined now can have six different
attributes—the two necessary `sn` and `cn` attributes, and the optional `userPassword`,
`telephoneNumber`, `seeAlso`, and `description` attributes. Just as the object class
was defined in the schema, so each attribute is also defined. The syntax for attribute
definitions is similar though the fields allowed in the definition are different and
more numerous.

The schema definition for the `telephoneNumber` attribute is a good example of a
basic attribute definition:

```
attributetype
    (
    2.5.4.20
    NAME 'telephoneNumber'
    DESC 'RFC2256: Telephone Number'
    EQUALITY telephoneNumberMatch
    SUBSTR telephoneNumberSubstringsMatch
    SYNTAX 1.3.6.1.4.1.1466.115.121.1.50{32}
    )
```

The attribute definition begins with an `attributetype` directive. The rest of the
definition is enclosed in parentheses.

The first field in the definition is the unique OID for this attribute. As with all OIDs,
this identifier must be globally unique. The OID `2.5.4.20` should only be used to
refer to a `telephoneNumber` attribute. Later in this chapter, in the section *Getting an
OID*, we will discuss getting and using a base OID.

After the OID comes the NAME field that associates one or more names with
the attribute.

> The names given in the NAME field are usually called *attribute descriptions*
> (see the discussion of the search operation in Chapter 3). This term is
> confusing when talking about schema definitions because the attribute
> schema definition has a description field, and that field is not the
> attribute description.

It is not uncommon for attributes to have two names—a long name (such as
`commonName` or `surname`) and an abbreviated name (`cn` or `sn` respectively). When an
attribute has multiple names, the list of names should be enclosed in parentheses. As
an example, consider the NAME field for the `fax` attribute:

```
attributetype
    (
    2.5.4.23
```

```
NAME ( 'facsimileTelephoneNumber' 'fax' )
DESC 'RFC2256: Facsimile (Fax) Telephone Number'
SYNTAX 1.3.6.1.4.1.1466.115.121.1.22
)
```

Note the syntax of the highlighted line. Each name in the list of names is enclosed in single quotes (') and the entire list is enclosed in parentheses.

 SLAPD will refer to attributes by the first name. Thus, if you search for the fax attribute SLAPD will return the matching attributes as facsimileTelephoneNumber not as fax.

The DESC field provides a brief description of the purpose of the attribute. In the telephoneNumber attribute definition, the value of this field is 'RFC2256: Telephone Number', indicating that the attribute is defined in RFC 2256.

One important aspect of defining an attribute is specifying how an application should test two attribute values to see if they match. Do TEST and test match? In some cases we might want them to, while in others we might not. Does t*st match test? Again, in some cases, this is desirable while in others it is not.

We can determine, in the attribute definition, which matching rules should be used to test whether one value matches another. When we discussed the search operation in Chapter 3 we saw four different comparison operators that could be used in search filters:

- The equality operator (=)
- The approximation operator (~=)
- The greater-than-or-equal-to operator (>=)
- The less-than-or-equal-to operator: (<=)

In addition to these we looked at using regular expression characters, such as the asterisk (*), to match portions, or substrings, of an attribute value. The behavior of each of these is determined, to a large degree, by the matching rules in the attribute definition.

When the LDAP server processes a comparison (during operations like binding, comparing, and searching) it uses the schema to determine how to handle these comparisons. The schema specifies which matching rules should be used. There are three different sorts of matching rules that can be assigned in a schema:

- The equality rule, EQUALITY
- The ordering rule, ORDERING
- The substring matching rule, SUBSTRING

An attribute schema may specify rules for one, two, or all three of these. The value of each can be either the OID or the name of a matching rule. In the telephoneNumber schema, EQUALITY and SUBSTRING are used:

```
EQUALITY telephoneNumberMatch
SUBSTR telephoneNumberSubstringsMatch
```

When an equality test for a telephone number is requested, such as the evaluation of the filter (telephoneNumber=+1 234 567 8901), the telephoneNumberMatch rule is used. Note that the plus sign (+) is part of the telephone number, not part of the operator. If the filter includes a wild-card match, such as (telephoneNumber=+1 234 567*), then the telephoneNumberSubstringsMatch rule is used instead.

[With no ORDERING rule defined, SLAPD will not process matching tests for >= or <= operators. Any comparison will return false.]

How do these two matching rules perform? Let's look at an example. When we defined the user with UID matt, we assigned that user a telephone number. Here, we will search for that entry, requesting only the telephoneNumber attribute:

```
$ ldapsearch -LL -U matt '(uid=matt)' telephoneNumber
```

And the search result is as follows:

```
SASL/DIGEST-MD5 authentication started
Please enter your password:
SASL username: matt
SASL SSF: 128
SASL installing layers
version: 1
dn: uid=matt,ou=Users,dc=example,dc=com
telephoneNumber: +1 555 555 4321
```

The telephoneNumber attribute has the value +1 555 555 4321. Now let's perform a search using the telephone number:

```
$ ldapsearch -LL -U matt '(telephoneNumber=+1 555 555 4321)' uid \
    telephoneNumber
```

And the search result is as follows:

```
SASL/DIGEST-MD5 authentication started
Please enter your password:
SASL username: matt
SASL SSF: 128
```

```
SASL installing layers
version: 1
dn: uid=matt,ou=Users,dc=example,dc=com
uid: matt
telephoneNumber: +1 555 555 4321
```

As expected a search using the exact phone number returned a result. This looks no different from what we would expect a string matching rule to do. Using the special `telephoneNumberMatch` rule in the schema has some advantages though. When using this matching rule, SLAPD will ignore certain telephone number formatting characters. Here's an example using a substring search:

```
$ ldapsearch -LL -U matt '(telephoneNumber=+1 555-555-43*)' uid \
    telephoneNumber
```

Here is the result:

```
SASL/DIGEST-MD5 authentication started
Please enter your password:
SASL username: matt
SASL SSF: 128
SASL installing layers
version: 1
dn: uid=matt,ou=Users,dc=example,dc=com
uid: matt
telephoneNumber: +1 555 555 4321
```

The filter in this example uses dashes (-) where the previous filter used spaces. Using the `telephoneNumberSubstringMatch` rule, SLAPD ignored the dashes. With the `telephoneNumberMatch` and `telephoneNumberSubstringMatch` rules, the numbers `+15555554321`, `+1 555 555 4321`, `1-5-5-55554-3-2-1`, and `+1 555-555-4321` are all treated as identical matches.

This illustrates the virtue of being able to specify matching rules in the schema. For attributes such as `cn`, `sn`, or `mail` (email address), we certainly wouldn't want dashes to be treated the same as white space characters. We wouldn't want `Dan Forth` to match `Danforth`. But it is certainly a desirable feature when matching phone numbers. The LDAP answer to this problem is to assign matching rules fitting to the type of information stored in the attribute.

 Other attributes, like `homePhone`, `pagerTelephoneNumber`, and `mobileTelephoneNumber` (all defined in `cosine.schema`) all use the `telephoneNumberMatch` and `telelphoneNumberSubstringMatch` matching rules too. Since they all share the same format there is no need to assign each a different specialized matching rule.

Matching Rules and Indexes

Some backends, such as BDB and HDB, support indexes (using the `index` directive in `slapd.conf`). The index supported is determined by the matching rules defined for an attribute. For example, an attribute with an equality matching rule can have an equality (`eq`) index. Likewise, one with a substring matching rule supports `sub` indexes.

The last field in the `telephoneNumber` matching scheme is the SYNTAX field. This relates to the type and structure of the data stored in values for `telephoneNumber` attributes.

```
SYNTAX 1.3.6.1.4.1.1466.115.121.1.50{32}
```

The value of the SYNTAX parameter has two parts. The first is the OID (or the name) of the LDAP syntax, and the second, set off in curly braces ({ and }) is the maximum length (usually the number of characters) for the field. The length specifier is optional, and the server is not obligated to enforce the maximum length.

The OID mentioned earlier, `1.3.6.1.4.1.1466.115.121.1.50`, is the telephone number syntax. This indicates that attribute values for instances of the `telephoneNumber` attribute are to contain the characters (integers, dashes, spaces, and so on) that a phone number would require. SLAPD will reject attempts to add phone numbers that contain letters and other special characters. Later in this chapter, in the *Creating a Schema* part, we will look at the list of common LDAP syntaxes that OpenLDAP supports.

As far as complexity goes the `telephoneNumber` attribute is about average. However, many attribute definitions are much shorter, taking advantage of the fields set in similar attributes. Thus, there are many attributes that, because they inherit most of their features from their superior (parent) attribute, have only an OID, a NAME field, and a DESC field. The schema definition for the ever popular `cn` attribute looks like this:

```
attributetype
    (
    2.5.4.3
    NAME ( 'cn' 'commonName' )
    DESC 'RFC2256: common name(s) for which the entity is known by'
    SUP name
    )
```

In this case, the SUP name field indicates that the name attribute is the parent of the cn attribute. Attributes, like object classes, can be organized hierarchically. A superior attribute is the parent or prototype for this attribute and certain properties, if left unspecified in the schema definition, are inherited from the superior. Syntax and matching rules, for example, can be inherited from a parent.

In the previous example no matching rules and no LDAP syntax were specified. Therefore, the cn attribute type inherits these values from its superior. The name attribute uses the caseIgnoreMatch EQUALITY matching rule and the caseIgnoreSubstringMatch SUBSTR rule, and uses the Directory String LDAP syntax (1.3.6.1.4.1.1466.115.121.1.15). A directory string is a UTF-8 encoded string intended to store text.

There are a handful of other fields that the previous examples do not make use of. These are OBSOLETE, SINGLE-VALUE, COLLECTIVE, NO-USER-MODIFICATION, USAGE, and the extension area. Let's briefly look at those.

The OBSOLETE flag, which usually appears after the DESC field, plays the same role in attribute definitions as it does in object class definitions. It labels an attribute obsolete. While obsolete attributes are still supported and can be used for records in the directory information tree, they are to be treated as deprecated, subject to removal in future versions of the schema or software. OBSOLETE takes no parameters.

The SINGLE-VALUE flag indicates that the defined attribute can only have one attribute value. Typically, an attribute can have an arbitrary number of values. But any attribute whose schema includes the SINGLE-VALUE flag can have no more than one. The domain component (dc) attribute that we looked at in Chapters 3 and 4 is an example of this. An object that has a dc attribute can only assign one value to that attribute. SINGLE-VALUE takes no parameters.

The COLLECTIVE flag indicates that this attribute is a collective attribute. Entries can be grouped, with collective attributes, into an **entry collection**.

Collectives are implemented in OpenLDAP via the collect overlay, which is not compiled or installed by default, though it can be found in the servers/slapd/overlays directory of the source code. The schemas necessary for collective support are also not included by default in the OpenLDAP distribution, and must be copied from another source (such as RFC 3671).

Here's a rough idea of how entry collections work:

1. One record is the collection record, and must use the `collectiveAttributeSubentry` object class. This becomes the authority for that collective attribute. All other subordinate records then inherit the attribute (and its value) and the attribute is visible (though read-only) as an attribute of each of these records. For more information on collectives see RFC 3671 (`http://www.ietf.org/rfc/rfc3671.txt`).

2. The `NO-USER-MODIFICATION` flag is used to indicate that the attribute is an operational attribute (used by SLAPD or an overlay), and cannot be modified by an LDAP client. This is not usually used in user-defined schemas. Use it only when writing a custom overlay that will make use of its own operational attributes.

3. The `USAGE` field provides SLAPD with information about what will use the attribute. There are four possible values. The first three, `directoryOperation`, `distributedOperation`, and `dSAOperation`, all indicate that SLAPD itself uses the attribute. The last, `userApplication`, is the default and it indicates that the attribute is primarily intended to be used by client applications. Since most schemas are intended for client application use, the default is usually what is desired and the `USAGE` field is rarely used.

4. Finally, `attributetype` definitions can also use extensions, though there are no extensions used in the main schemas included in OpenLDAP. The syntax for extensions is the same for attribute types as it is for object class definitions.

In summary, an attribute schema definition begins with the `attributetype` directive which is followed by a schema definition enclosed in parentheses. The following fields are allowed in attribute definitions:

*   A unique OID number, which is required. Example: `2.5.4.15`.

*   A `NAME` field, with one or more names for the attribute. Example: `NAME 'businessCategory'`.

*   A `DESC` field containing a description of the attribute type. Example: `DESC 'RFC2256: business category'`.

*   A `DEPRECATED` tag, if the attribute is deprecated.

*   A `SUP` field with the name or OID of the superior attribute type. Example: `SUP postalAddress`.

*   An `EQUALITY` matching rule OID or name. Example: `EQUALITY caseIgnoreMatch`.

*   An `ORDERING` matching rule OID or name.

- A SUBSTR matching rule OID or name. Example: SUBSTR caseIgnoreSubstringsMatch.

- A SYNTAX field with an LDAP syntax OID, and an optional length. Example: SYNTAX 1.3.6.1.4.1.1466.115.121.1.15{128}.

- The SINGLE-VALUE flag, if the attribute can only have one value.

- The COLLECTIVE flag, if the attribute is a collective attribute.

- The NO-USER-MODIFICATION flag, if the attribute is an operational attribute that client applications should not be able to modify.

- The USAGE field, together with one of the four keywords (userApplication, directoryOperation, distributedOperation, or dSAOperation) used to indicate what the attribute is to be used for.

- Any extensions that the attribute definition requires.

At this point we have looked at both object class definitions and attribute definitions. When creating your own custom schemas it is most likely that these are the only two types of schema definitions that you will need to use.

We have discussed the basics of schemas and seen a few examples in the text. Later in this chapter we will look at some other specific examples. But if you want to take a look at more examples of attribute and object class schemas peruse the files in the schema directory for OpenLDAP (/etc/ldap/schema or /usr/local/etc/openldap/schema). The best place to start is with the core.schema schema, which defines the standard LDAPv3 schemas.

> While reading core.schema you might notice that several very important object classes and attribute types are commented out. Why? Because they are included in the **system schema**, which is hard-coded into OpenLDAP. This schema is found in the OpenLDAP source code in slapd/schema_prep.c.

The cosine.schema file contains many other commonly used schemas and is also a good place to look. The inetOrgPerson.schema schema is a good example of what a user-defined schema file ought to look like. Or, for a shorter example of a user-defined schema, see openldap.schema.

While attributetype and objectclass are the two primary directives used in schema creation there are a few others which we will cover, albeit more briefly, in the next two sections.

Object Identifier Definitions

The object identifier directive (`objectidentifier`) is an extension to the standard definition language. While it doesn't provide additional functionality to the schema language, it serves as a time-saving (and human-friendly) utility.

The `objectidentifier` directive is used to assign a string alias to an OID. When SLAPD processes OID fields for `attributetype`, `objectclasstype`, and `ditcontentrule` directives, if it encounters a string instead of an OID, it will check to see if this string is an alias to an OID and, if so, it will use the value of the OID. The `telephoneNumber` schema we examined in the last section provides a good example:

```
attributetype
  (
  2.5.4.20
  NAME 'telephoneNumber'
  DESC 'RFC2256: Telephone Number'
  EQUALITY telephoneNumberMatch
  SUBSTR telephoneNumberSubstringsMatch
  SYNTAX 1.3.6.1.4.1.1466.115.121.1.50{32}
  )
```

Instead of using the OID for the telephone number equality and substring matching rules (`1.3.6.1.4.1.1466.115.121.1.50` and `1.3.6.1.4.1.1466.11` `5.121.1.58`, respectively), the schema refers to the names of the matching rules: `telephoneNumberMatch` and `telephoneNumberSubstringMatch`. This later form is much easier for humans to read.

The `objectidentifier` directive makes it easy to define such aliases for OID numbers, in whole or in part. Here is a simple example of assigning a name to an OID:

```
objectidentifier exampleComDemo 1.3.6.1.4.1.8254.1021.3.1
```

Using a directive like this at the top of a schema makes it possible to refer to the OID using the name `exampleComDemo` later.

> The given OID is valid and is registered to the author. If you are developing your own LDAP schemas, you should register your own OID (see the *Getting an OID* section). While you are free to use this OID when recreating these examples, do not use it to write your own extensions. Otherwise, there will be no way to ensure that such OIDs are globally unique which defeats the purpose of the OID.

For example, we could create a schema like this:

```
objectclass
  (
   exampleComDemo
   NAME 'myPersonObjectClass'
   DESC 'My Person Object Class'
   SUP inetOrgPerson STRUCTURAL
  )
```

Note that instead of using the OID number for the object, we used the `exampleComDemo` alias. But, generally, we would not assign one alias per object class. It would be more convenient to alias a common root OID and then append just the last part of the OID number. For example:

```
objectidentifier exampleComOC 1.3.6.1.4.1.8254.1021.1
objectclass
  (
   exampleComOC:1
   NAME 'myPersonObjectClass'
   DESC 'My Person Object Class'
   SUP inetOrgPerson STRUCTURAL
  )
```

In this example we used the `objectidentifier` directive to create an alias for the OID base that will be used for all of my object class definitions. Thus, when SLAPD encounters the name `exampleComOC`, it will expand it to `1.3.6.1.4.1.8254.1021.1`. The object class definition for `myPersonObjectClass` should have the OID `1.3.6.1.4.1.8254.1021.1.1` (note the extra `.1` at the end). Rather than writing out the entire number we use the `exampleComOC` alias and append a colon (`:`) and then the numeric suffix for the object class.

When SLAPD encounters `exampleComOC:1` it will expand it to `1.3.6.1.4.1.8254.1021.1.1`. Likewise, if I were to create a second object class with the desired OID `1.3.6.1.4.1.8254.1021.1.2`, I could use `exampleComOC:2` instead of typing out the entire long OID.

 Using the `objectidentifier` attribute can not only save typing, but reduce typos in an area particularly prone to typos (and with typos particularly difficult to spot).

For more examples of the `objectidentifier` directive, see `openldap.schema` in the schema directory for OpenLDAP.

DIT Content Rules

The last schema directive we will look at is the `ditcontentrule` directive which is used for creating **DIT Content Rules**.

 DIT stands for Directory Information Tree. This abbreviation is a frequently used bit of LDAP parlance.

A DIT content rule identifies a particular structural object class, and indicates which auxiliary object classes are allowed (or not allowed) to be included in entries that use that object class.

For an example, let's use a few of the object classes introduced in Chapter 3. In the *Anatomy of an LDIF File* section we created an entry representing a document. It implemented the `document` object class, whose schema (located in `cosine.schema`) looks like this:

```
objectclass
    (
    0.9.2342.19200300.100.4.6
    NAME 'document'
    SUP top
    STRUCTURAL
    MUST documentIdentifier
    MAY ( commonName $ description $ seeAlso $ localityName $
          organizationName $ organizationalUnitName $
          documentTitle $ documentVersion $ documentAuthor $
          documentLocation $ documentPublisher )
    )
```

This is a structural object class. Also in Chapter 3, in the *Adding System Records* section we added the entry for `uid=authenticate,ou=System,dc=example,dc=com`. This entry implemented the `simpleSecurityObject` object class. Here is the schema for `simpleSecurityObject`:

```
objectclass
    (
    0.9.2342.19200300.100.4.19
    NAME 'simpleSecurityObject'
    DESC 'RFC1274: simple security object'
    SUP top
    AUXILIARY
    MUST userPassword
    )
```

This object class is an auxiliary object class, meaning that it can be added to entries that already have a structural object class, the result being that the attributes of the auxiliary object class are now available for that entry.

 For more discussion on the different sorts of object classes and how they function, see the discussion in Chapter 3 and the section in this chapter called *The Object Class Hierarchy*.

According to default OpenLDAP settings, if we had an entry with the document structural object class, we could give this document a password (for binding to the directory) by adding objectclass: simpleSecurityObject to the record, and then adding a userPassword attribute. This would give us a record looking something like this:

```
dn: documentIdentifier=011,uid=david,ou=Users,dc=example,dc=com
documentIdentifier: 011
documentTitle: Treatise on Human Nature
userPassword:: c2VjcmV0
objectClass: document
objectClass: simpleSecurityObject
```

This entry is essentially a document that has the ability to log in! A client that used this record's DN and the correct password could log in as this document.

Perhaps there are cases where this is desirable, but for the sake of this example, let us suppose that this is a configuration that we do not want to allow.

Normally, decisions about which entries have which object classes are left to external applications. But what if we wanted to make sure that no application could give document a userPassword attribute?

The best method for solving this problem is to create a DIT content rule that disallows adding the userPassword attribute to any entry that has the document object class. This is done with the ditcontentrule directive:

```
ditcontentrule
  (
  0.9.2342.19200300.100.4.6
  NAME 'noPWForDocs'
  DESC 'Do not allow passwords for documents'
  NOT userPassword
  )
```

The form of the ditcontentrule directive should be familiar by now. Like the objectclass and attributetype directives, this directive encloses the DIT content rule definition inside of parentheses.

The first field is an OID. But unlike the other schema definitions, this OID is not the OID for this definition. Instead, it is the OID of the structural object class that we are targeting.

In this case, the OID `0.9.2342.19200300.100.4.6` is the OID for the `document` object class. You can verify this with a glance at the document schema listed a few pages back or by browsing the cosine schema.

The `NAME` field should contain a unique name used for referencing this rule. For the most part, the value of this field is used in reporting references to this rule in the log file, and in responses to the client.

The `DESC` field contains a short-text description of what the rule does.

The `NOT` field contains a list of OIDs or names of attributes that should be disallowed. The name `userPassword` comes from the `NAME` field in the `userPassword` attribute definition.

With this content rule in place, what will happen if we try to add a `userPassword` attribute to a document? Here is an example using `ldapmodify`:

```
$ ldapmodify -U matt
SASL/DIGEST-MD5 authentication started
Please enter your password:
SASL username: matt
SASL SSF: 128
SASL installing layers
dn: documentIdentifier=011,uid=dave,ou=users,dc=example,dc=com
changetype: modify
add: objectclass
objectclass: simpleSecurityObject
-
add: userPassword
userPassword: secret
modifying entry
        "documentIdentifier=011,uid=dave,ou=users,dc=example,dc=com"
ldap_modify: Object class violation (65)
        additional info: content rule 'noPWForDocs' precluded
        attribute 'userPassword'
```

The highlighted portion in this example is the attempted modification. We attempted to add the `simpleSecurityObject` object class and the `userPassword` attribute to the record. But the server responded with an **Object class violation** error, giving the following reason:

```
content rule 'noPWForDocs' precluded attribute 'userPassword'
```

Our custom DIT content rule did its job—it prevented the addition of the `userPassword` attribute to the `document` entry.

This DIT content rule we created above is a negative rule—it defines what attributes an entry *cannot* have. But `ditcontentrule` can also be used to create positive rules: rules that specify which attributes (or auxiliary object classes) are allowed.

For example, we could write a rule that says that every entry that is an `inetOrgPerson` must have a `userPassword`:

```
ditcontentrule
  (
    2.16.840.1.113730.3.2.2
    NAME 'reqPassword'
    DESC 'Require userPassword for inetOrgPerson'
    MUST userPassword
  )
```

The OID used in this rule is the OID for the `inetOrgPerson` object class. The MUST field indicates that any entry with the structural object class `inetOrgPerson` must also have the `userPassword` attribute set.

Because of this rule, an attempt to add a new `inetOrgPerson` entry without a `userPassword` would result in an error similar to the one we looked at earlier:

```
$ ldapadd -U matt
SASL/DIGEST-MD5 authentication started
Please enter your password:
SASL username: matt
SASL SSF: 128
SASL installing layers
dn: uid=Johann,ou=users,dc=example,dc=com
uid: johann
ou: users
cn: Johann Fichte
cn: Johann Gottlieb Fichte
sn: Fichte
givenName: Johann
objectclass: person
objectclass: organizationalPerson
objectclass: inetOrgPerson
adding new entry "uid=Johann,ou=users,dc=example,dc=com"
ldap_add: Object class violation (65)
        additional info: content rule 'reqPassword' requires attribute
        'userPassword'
```

The record being added (highlighted) is a valid `inetOrgPerson` entry, according to the `inetOrgPerson` object class definition. But, because of the DIT content rule, adding the record failed because there is no `userPassword` attribute value specified.

Now let's expand this rule to take advantage of the AUX field. The AUX field may be used to explicitly state which auxiliary classes can be combined with this structural object class.

In our newly revised DIT content rule we will make it so that only the `pkiUser` and the `labeledURIObject` auxiliary object classes can be added to an `inetOrgUser` record.

 The `pkiUser` object class is an auxiliary object class designed to indicate that an entry is capable of performing **public key infrastructure (PKI)** secure transactions. It has one attribute, `userCertificate`, that contains the user's cryptographic certificate. See the Wikipedia page for a quick introduction to PKI: `http://en.wikipedia.org/wiki/Public_key_infrastructure`.

The `labeledURIObject` object class allows an additional attribute, `labeledURI`, which takes a URI (such as a URL) and a plain text description:

```
labeledURI: http://aleph-null.tv Home Page
```

The URI is separated from the label by a white space. So the URI is `http://aleph-null.tv` and the label is `Home Page`. The `labeledURIObject` is defined in RFC 2079 (`http://www.ietf.org/rfc/rfc2079.txt`).

Also, we will change the NAME and DESC elements to reflect the fact that our rule now does more than just require a `userPassword`. The DIT content rule now looks like this:

```
ditcontentrule
  (
  2.16.840.1.113730.3.2.2
  NAME 'inetOrgPersonRules'
  DESC 'Restrictions for entries with inetOrgPerson object class'
  MUST userPassword
  AUX ( labeledURIObject $ pkiUser )
  )
```

Note the syntax of the AUX field. To list multiple values in a field it is necessary to enclose the list of values, separated by a dollar sign ($), inside of parentheses.

Using this DIT content rule, we can successfully add a URL (using the `labeledURIObject` auxiliary object class) to my record:

```
$ ldapmodify -U matt
SASL/DIGEST-MD5 authentication started
Please enter your password:
SASL username: matt
SASL SSF: 128
SASL installing layers
dn: uid=matt,ou=users,dc=example,dc=com
changetype: modify
add: objectclass
objectclass: labeledURIObject
-
add: labeledURI
labeledURI: http://aleph-null.tv Home Page
modifying entry "uid=matt,ou=users,dc=example,dc=com"
```

The entry, highlighted above, was added successfully because the `labeledURIObject` (which allows the `labeledURI` attribute) is allowed by the content rule. But if I try to add a different auxiliary object class—one not explicitly allowed in the DIT content rule – the change request will be denied:

```
$ ldapmodify -U matt
SASL/DIGEST-MD5 authentication started
Please enter your password:
SASL username: matt
SASL SSF: 128
SASL installing layers
dn: uid=matt,ou=users,dc=example,dc=com
changetype: modify
add: objectclass
objectclass: userSecurityInformation
modifying entry "uid=matt,ou=users,dc=example,dc=com"
ldap_modify: Object class violation (65)
        additional info: content rule 'inetOrgPersonRules' does not
        allow class 'userSecurityInformation'
```

The DIT content rule prevented the addition of an auxiliary object class because this class is not specified in the AUX field of the rule.

Like the other definitions, the `ditcontentrule` directive also allows the OBSOLETE flag.

In summary, the `ditcontentrule` directive takes a definition of a DIT content rule enclosed in parentheses. The following fields are supported:

- The OID of the structural object class to which this rule applies.
- The NAME field, which provides a short name used to identify the rule.
- The DESC field, which contains a description of the rule.
- The OBSOLETE flag to mark this rule as obsolete.
- The AUX field, which contains the names or OIDs of all auxiliary classes that the entries of this object class are allowed to implement.
- The MUST field, which contains a list of all of the (not already mandatory) attributes that entries of this object class must have.
- The MAY field, which lists all of the fields that a member of this object class may have. As of OpenLDAP 2.3.30, this is not exclusive. Attributes not in this list but allowed by object class schema definitions are still allowed. In other words, MAY does not impose any restrictions.
- The NOT field, which contains a list of attributes that an entry of this object class cannot have. This cannot be applied to attributes that are required by the object classes schema definition.

Now we have looked at the four different schema definition directives allowed in the `slapd.conf` file (or included files). With this information you should be able to read through and understand any of the schemas defined in OpenLDAP.

Next we will take a quick look at how to get schema information out of a SLAPD server using the LDAP protocol.

Retrieving the Schemas from SLAPD

When SLAPD loads the schemas, it stores them in a special part of the directory information tree, along with the Root DSE record; a special entry holds schema information. Having this information is useful for debugging, but more importantly it provides a way for client applications to find out about what types of objects and attributes may be stored in this directory server.

Obtaining the information from the directory is as easy as issuing an `ldapsearch` command.

The schema information is stored in a special record called the **subschema subentry**. You can access the subschema subentry using `ldapsearch`:

```
$ ldapsearch -U matt -b 'cn=subschema' -s base +
```

Access to the `cn=subschema` record is governed by global ACLs (ACLs that appear before the database section). For example, to grant access to the subschema to users only, you can use a rule like this: `access to dn.exact="cn=subschema" by users read`.

This will retrieve the entire schema specification from the server including not only the attribute and object class definitions, but also definitions of matching rules, matching rule uses, structure rules, name forms, and LDAP syntaxes.

But, as with any other record in an LDAP server, we can use search filters to get just the values of specific attributes. For example, we can find out what all of the existing DIT content rules are:

```
$ ldapsearch -LL -U matt -b 'cn=subschema' -s base ditcontentrules
SASL/DIGEST-MD5 authentication started
Please enter your password:
SASL username: matt
SASL SSF: 128
SASL installing layers
version: 1
dn: cn=Subschema
dITContentRules: ( 0.9.2342.19200300.100.4.6 NAME 'noPWForDocs' DESC
        'Do not allow passwords for documents' NOT userPassword )
dITContentRules: ( 2.16.840.1.113730.3.2.2 NAME 'inetOrgPersonRules'
        DESC 'Restrictions for inetOrgPerson object class.'
        AUX ( labeledURIObject $ pkiUser )
        MUST userPassword )
```

This search returns all of the DIT content rules currently included in the schema definitions for this server. Of course, the only two there are the ones we created in the last section.

The following schema-related attributes are included in the `cn=Subschema` record:

- `ldapSyntaxes`: This attribute has one value for every LDAP syntax supported in the directory. Example: `ldapSyntaxes: ( 1.3.6.1.1.16.1 DESC 'UUID' )`.

- `matchingRules`: This attribute has one value for every matching rule in the directory. Example: `matchingRules: ( 2.5.13.14 NAME 'integerMatch' SYNTAX 1.3.6.1.4.1.1466.115.121.1.27 )`.

- `matchingRuleUse`: This attribute has one value for every matching rule use, which pairs matching rule OIDs with a list of all of the attributes that implement that matching rule. Example: `matchingRuleUse: ( 2.5.13.27 NAME 'generalizedTimeMatch' APPLIES ( createTimestamp $ modifyTimestamp ) )`.

- `attributeTypes`: This attribute has one value for every attribute definition in this directory. Example: `attributeTypes: ( 2.5.4.3 NAME ( 'cn' 'commonName' ) DESC 'RFC2256: common name(s) for which the entity is known by' SUP name )`.

- `objectClasses`: This attribute contains one value for every object class definition. Example: `objectClasses: ( 2.5.6.2 NAME 'country' DESC 'RFC2256: a country' SUP top STRUCTURAL MUST c MAY ( searchGuide $ description ) )`.

- `dITContentRules`: This attribute contains one value for every DIT content rule defined.

Other standard attributes, such as `cn`, `objectclass`, and the basic operational attributes, are also part of the record.

Examining schemas this way is an alternative to simply reading the schema files. While it has less documentation (since there are no comments), using filters can be helpful. Also, information not in the standard schemas (such as schema definitions for operational attributes) is also available in this record.

Later in the chapter we will begin implementing schemas in SLAPD, first by including some already written schemas, then by writing our own. But next we will take a quick look at one more theoretical component of schemas: the schema hierarchy.

The ObjectClass Hierarchy

Object classes and attributes in LDAP can be organized into hierarchical relationships. A hierarchical relationship is one in which one entity stands in a parent or superior relationship to one or more subordinate entities.

Attribute hierarchies tend to be simple, and require only a short explanation. Object classes, on the other hand, use a more complicated hierarchical model and will be the focus of this part of the chapter.

In the cases of both attribute and object class hierarchies, the mechanism for creating the hierarchy is the schema definition. Schema definitions for both attributes and object classes use the `SUP` field to indicate a relationship to a parent, or superior.

We will start out with a brief discussion of attribute hierarchies, and then move on to the more complicated object class hierarchies.

Attribute Hierarchies

Attribute hierarchies are simple relationships wherein one attribute can, through its subordinate relationship to another attribute, inherit certain features, such as matching rules and LDAP syntaxes.

The simplicity of attribute hierarchies manifests itself in a few ways:

- There is no requirement that an attribute have any relation to other attributes. In other words, there is no requirement that attributes be part of a hierarchy. Many, such as the telephoneNumber attribute we looked at in the previous part, stand on their own.

- Attribute hierarchies do not play a significant role in how attributes are used. Attribute hierarchies exist primarily to keep attribute schema definitions clean and succinct, minimizing repetition.

The name attribute, which is conventionally not used directly in any object class, is a good example of the use of superior/subordinate relationships in attribute definitions. Thirteen attributes in the core schema list name as their superior. The cn attribute is one example.

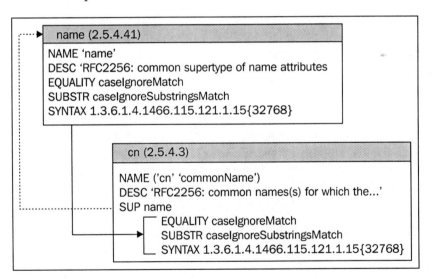

The schema definition for cn uses only the NAME, DESC, and SUP fields, with SUP indicating that the name attribute is the superior of cn.

Since the `cn` attribute definition does not specify any matching rules or an LDAP syntax, these are inherited from the name attribute. Hence, `cn` is assigned the equality and substring matching rules defined in `name`, as well as the LDAP syntax and length.

But there is not much more that can be done with attribute hierarchies. Other than matching rules and syntax nothing else is automatically inherited from the superior, and there are no other benefits in using attribute hierarchies.

Subordinate Attributes and Searching

There is one interesting effect that results from attribute hierarchies. A request for a superior attribute may return subordinate attributes as matches. For example, here is a search requesting just a single attribute: `name`:

```
$ ldapsearch -LL -U matt '(uid=matt)' name
SASL/DIGEST-MD5 authentication started
Please enter your password:
SASL username: matt
SASL SSF: 128
SASL installing layers
version: 1
dn: uid=matt,ou=Users,dc=example,dc=com
ou: Users
cn: Matt Butcher
sn: Butcher
givenName: Matt
givenName: Matthew
title: Systems Integrator
st: Illinois
l: Chicago
```

According to the search parameters, the search should return any `name` attribute values for records with `uid=matt`. But the record returned (highlighted) has more than that. In addition to the DN, which is always returned, the record also has `ou`, `cn`, `sn`, `givenName`, `title`, `st`, and `l` values.

Why is this? This happens simply because all of those attribute types have `name` as the superior.

Such behavior extends to search filter behavior, as well. For example, a search filter like (name=Marcus) will result in a search being performed against all attributes that use name as a superior:

```
$ ldapsearch -LL -U matt '(name=Marcus)'
SASL/DIGEST-MD5 authentication started
Please enter your password:
SASL username: matt
SASL SSF: 128
SASL installing layers
version: 1
dn: uid=cicero,ou=Users,dc=example,dc=com
uid: marcus
uid: cicero
sn: Tullius
cn: Marcus Tullius
givenName: Marcus
ou: users
objectClass: person
objectClass: organizationalPerson
objectClass: inetOrgPerson
```

The record for uid=cicero matched because the givenName field has the value Marcus. As can be seen in the attribute type definition, the givenName attribute has name as a superior attribute type:

```
attributetype ( 2.5.4.42 NAME ( 'givenName' 'gn' )
    DESC 'RFC2256: first name(s) for which the entity is known by'
    SUP name
```

While this feature can cause some unexpected behavior for those unfamiliar with schemas, it can prove quite useful at times.

For the most part, attribute hierarchies are fairly simple. Object class hierarchies are more complex though. And we will now take a look at them.

Object Class Types: Abstract, Structural, and Auxiliary

Like attributes, object classes can be organized into hierarchies. Typically, there is one major object class hierarchy. But while the hierarchical organization of object classes plays an important part in the structure of the directory, not all object classes are part of the hierarchy. To understand why this is we must begin by examining the different types of object classes.

There are three types of object class: abstract, structural, and auxiliary as follows:

- An **abstract object class** holds a place at the top of the object class hierarchy. It may set required and allowed attributes for all object classes beneath it in the hierarchy, but no record can be an instance of that object class only. Further, any parent of an abstract object class must also be abstract.

- A **structural object class** also holds a place in the hierarchy, and is a subordinate of (or, to phrase it differently, inherits from) either another structural object class or an abstract object class. An entry in the directory is an instance of a structural object class. When one structural object class subclasses another structural object class, the parent class is treated as if it were abstract. So, operationally speaking, for any given record it has only one structural object class — the structural object class is lowest on the object class hierarchy.

- An **auxiliary object class** is not required to be part of the object class hierarchy, though it can be. An auxiliary object class is intended to allow extra attributes to be defined for a record that already has a structural object class. For example, a record that describes a system account may not be in the person part of the hierarchy but may still need a password. The simpleSecurityObject is an auxiliary object class that can be added to other structural object classes to allow (and, in fact, require) that a userPassword attribute be set.

Abstract and structural object classes are organized into a hierarchy, with abstract classes at the top, and structural object classes as subordinates of those. In core schema (core.schema), there is only one abstract object class: top. This object class marks the top of the object class hierarchy — the ancestor (the highest superior) of all object classes.

The Object Class Hierarchy: An Overview

The hierarchy begins with the abstract object class top. Beneath it are any number of structural object classes, all of which are either direct or indirect subordinates. A direct subordinate is one that lists top as its superior object class (in the SUP field of the schema definition). An indirect subordinate is farther down the object class hierarchy. It lists another abstract or structural object class as its superior, but that superior either itself refers to top as its superior, or refers to another indirect subordinate.

In other LDAP references, a superior class is sometimes called a **superclass**, while a superior attribute (in the attribute hierarchy) is called a **supertype**. Likewise, the terms **subclass** and **subtype** can be used to indicate the subordinate relationships in classes and attributes.

Structural object classes have either an abstract object class or another structural object class as their superior.

Auxiliary object classes may or may not be in the object class hierarchy. They can have superiors, but they are not required to.

Here is a pictorial representation of a simple object class hierarchy (consisting of four object classes) and a pair of records in the directory information tree that we created in Chapter 3:

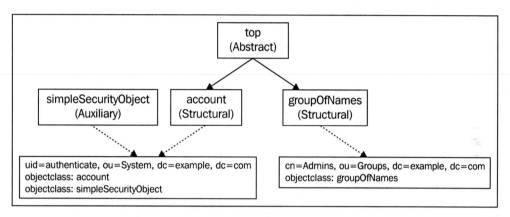

The `account` and `groupOfNames` structural object classes both have `top` listed as their superior (as indicated by the solid lines). `simpleSecurityObject`, an auxiliary object class, has no superiors.

Beneath the object class hierarchy are two records, with the DN and object class attributes displayed. The dotted lines indicate which schemas these entries implement. Each of the two records (the `uid=authenticate` user and the `cn=Admins` group) are related to a different part of the object class hierarchy. `cn=Admins` is a `groupOfNames`, while `uid=authenticate` is an account that also has the attributes of a `simpleSecurityObject`.

This representation of the object class hierarchy is designed to show how the organization of schemas is related to the entries within the directory.

It is important to keep in mind that there are two different hierarchies in play here. The two entries above are part of the directory information tree hierarchy. Their position in that hierarchy is indicated by their DNs. The `uid=authenticate` entry, for example, is a child of the `ou=System` entry, which in turn is a child of the `dc=example,dc=com` entry (the root entry for our directory information tree).

But by their object classes, the entries can also be related to the object class hierarchy, as is illustrated. For the time being it is only this second hierarchy — the object class hierarchy — that we are interested in.

Let's take a look at each of the three types of object classes. Understanding the differences between the three, and the respective role each plays, will illuminate the concepts at play in the object class hierarchy.

Abstract Classes

The first of the three types that we will examine is the **abstract class**. While abstract classes are only rarely used, they play a major role in the development of the object class hierarchy.

We have already talked about the special `top` object class. The most commonly used LDAP schemas do not use any other abstract object classes beside `top`. The `top` object class definition looks like this:

```
objectclass
  (
   2.5.6.0
   NAME 'top'
   DESC 'RFC2256: top of the superclass chain'
   ABSTRACT
   MUST objectClass
  )
```

It requires only one attribute: `objectclass`. All structural object classes should be related, either directly or indirectly, to `top`. And any abstract object class that will have structural object classes subordinate to it must also be related to `top`. While it is possible to create an abstract class without a superior class, effectively starting a new tree of object classes, this is rarely done.

Abstracts without Superiors

The main circumstance for defining abstract classes without superiors is when all of the classes that inherit from that abstract class will be auxiliary object classes. Structural object classes, according to RFC 4512, must be related (directly or indirectly) to the `top` object class.

But `top` is not the only abstract object class in frequent use. There are a few common schemas included with OpenLDAP, notably the `java.schema` and `corba.schema`, which make use of abstract object classes whose superiors are `top`. If an abstract object class has a superior, it must be an abstract superior.

Abstract object classes can have lists of attributes in the MUST and MAY fields of their definition. The top object class, as we just saw, requires the objectclass attribute. Any entry that implements a structural object class subordinate to this abstract object class inherits the MUST and MAY constraints of the parent.

For example, in the java.schema the class javaObject is abstract. Here is its definition:

```
objectclass
    (
    1.3.6.1.4.1.42.2.27.4.2.4
    NAME 'javaObject'
    DESC 'Java object representation'
    SUP top
    ABSTRACT
    MUST javaClassName
    MAY ( javaClassNames $ javaCodebase $
          javaDoc $ description )
    )
```

According to the SUP field, this object class is subordinate to top. It requires that any entry that implements javaObject has a javaClassName attribute. It also defines several attributes—javaClassNames, javaCodebase, javaDoc, and description—that entries may include.

The Java schema is used to store serialized Java objects in a directory server. It is defined in RFC 2713.

There are no structural object classes subordinate to javaObject. However, there are a couple of auxiliary object classes that are subordinate to javaObject: javaSerializedObject and javaMarshalledObject. Here is the javaSerializedObject schema definition:

```
objectclass
    (
    1.3.6.1.4.1.42.2.27.4.2.5
    NAME 'javaSerializedObject'
    DESC 'Java serialized object'
    SUP javaObject
    AUXILIARY
    MUST javaSerializedData
    )
```

Only one attribute is required in this class: javaSerializedData. There are no optional attributes specified in this definition.

If some entry uses the `javaSerializedData` object class what fields *must* it have? And what fields *may* it have?

It must have a `javaSerializedData` attribute. We can see that from the `javaSerializedObject` schema. But it also must have the `javaClassName` attribute because that is required in the object class of the superior `javaObject` object class. And a `javaSerializedData` entry may have any of the attributes listed in the MAY field of the `javaObject` schema: `javaClassNames`, `javaCodebase`, `javaDoc`, and `description`.

This example illustrates the use of the abstract object class as a way of organizing object classes into hierarchies, grouping similar object classes (here, `javaSerializedObject` and `javaMarshalledObject`) under a common (and more generic) ancestor, `javaObject`. The `javaObject` abstract object class is then used to specify the common attributes that both of the subordinate object classes need included.

Thus, one of the major uses of abstract object classes is to collect common attributes that should be (or may be) included in object classes that are defined as subordinate to it.

Abstract classes are rare. In contrast, the most commonly used object class type is the structural object class.

Structural Object Classes

As we have seen in a number of examples, every record has a DN and one or more object classes. From there, what other attributes it has depends on the object classes. But there are constraints on which object classes an entry has. One major factor that determines what object classes an entry may have is the structural object class hierarchy.

Every record in the directory must have at least one structural object class. The structural object class determines what type of entry a record is. For example, an entry with the structural object class `organization` is an `organization` entry.

Once an entry has been created in the directory, its structural object class cannot be changed. Adding and removing auxiliary object classes is allowed, but the structural object class is unalterable (as is, *ipso facto*, the chain of superior object classes).

An entry may implement more than one object class, and not all the object classes that it implements need be structural. Let's take a look at the organization record we created in Chapter 3:

```
dn: dc=example,dc=com
description: Example.Com, your trusted non-existent corporation.
dc: example
o: Example.Com
objectClass: top
objectClass: dcObject
objectClass: organization
```

There are three object classes for this entry:

- top — an abstract object class

- dcObject — an auxiliary object class

- organization — a structural object class

 The top object class is not strictly necessary in this entry. SLAPD implicitly includes top in all entries, since all structural object classes derive from it.

How do we know which object classes are of which type? The schema definitions for these object classes are the primary source of such information.

The structural object class locates this entry in the hierarchy of object classes, a hierarchy composed of abstract and structural object classes.

An entry may have more than one structural object class as long as they are all related by superior/subordinate relationships.

In the case where there are multiple structural object classes in one record, the most subordinate object class (the one farthest from the root object class, top) will have all of the rest of the structural object classes as ancestors. That is, for the object class farthest from top in the object class hierarchy, all other structural object classes must be superior to it. This lowest object class is then treated as the structural object class.

For example, in Chapter 3 we created a record for the user barbara:

```
dn: uid=barbara,ou=Users,dc=example,dc=com
ou: Users
uid: barbara
sn: Jensen
cn: Barbara Jensen
givenName: Barbara
```

```
displayName: Barbara Jensen
mail: barbara@example.com
userPassword: secret
objectClass: person
objectClass: organizationalPerson
objectClass: inetOrgPerson
```

This user belongs to four object classes. Three of these were explicitly stated earlier: `person`, `organizationalPerson`, and `inetOrgPerson`. All three of these happen to be structural object classes. The fourth, the `top` object class, is implicitly included.

All four of these object classes are related in the hierarchy. The `top` abstract object class sits at the top of the object class hierarchy. The `person` object class is directly subordinate to top. That is, the `person` object class definition lists `top` as its parent:

```
objectclass
  (
  2.5.6.6
  NAME 'person'
  DESC 'RFC2256: a person'
  SUP top
  STRUCTURAL
  MUST ( sn $ cn )
  MAY ( userPassword $ telephoneNumber $ seeAlso $ description )
  )
```

While `person` points to `top` as its superior, `organizationalPerson` points to `person`. And `inetOrgPerson` points to `organizationalPerson` as its superior. Thus, we get a hierarchy of object classes:

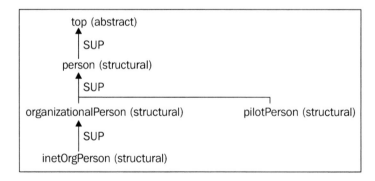

So, according to this hierarchy, any entry that is an `inetOrgPerson` must also abide by definitions of all of its superiors: `organizationalPerson`, `person`, and `top`. Any required attributes of any of those object classes will be required for an `inetOrgPerson` entry, and any optional attributes for any of those classes is optional for an `inetOrgPerson` entry.

Thus, the required fields for `inetOrgPerson` are `sn` and `cn`, both of which it gets from the `person` object class, and the `objectclass` attribute, which it inherits from `top`.

 For a complete list of fields required by and allowed by `inetOrgPerson`, see the subsection *Adding User Records* in Chapter 3.

In the previous figure, the `pilotPerson` object class is also included, which represents another branch of the hierarchy. Like `organizationalPerson` and `inetOrgPerson`, `pilotPerson` describes a person within an organization, but it includes a number of attributes not present in `organizationalPerson` and `inetOrgPerson`, including the `favouriteDrink` and `janetMailBox` attributes.

While `pilotPerson` is not officially obsolete, it is not usually used; `inetOrgPerson` is typically used instead. But like `organizationalPerson`, `pilotPerson` lists `person` as its superior. Thus, it inherits the attributes of `person` and `top`. However, it is not related, directly or indirectly, to `organizationalPerson` or `inetOrgPerson`, and thus inherits none of their attributes.

Because `pilotPerson` is not related to `organizationalPerson` or `inetOrgPerson`, and because all of these are structural object classes, SLAPD will not allow any record to implement the `pilotPerson` object class and `organizationalPerson` or its subordinates. For example, if we try to add a record with all four of the person-describing object classes, we will get an error:

```
$ ldapadd -U matt
SASL/DIGEST-MD5 authentication started
Please enter your password:
SASL username: matt
SASL SSF: 128
SASL installing layers
dn: uid=charles,ou=users,dc=example,dc=com
uid: charles
ou: users
cn: Charles Sanders Peirce
sn: Peirce
gn: Charles
objectclass: person
objectclass: organizationalPerson
objectclass: inetOrgPerson
objectclass: pilotPerson

adding new entry "uid=charles,ou=users,dc=example,dc=com"
```

```
ldap_add: Object class violation (65)
        additional info: invalid structural object class chain
        (inetOrgPerson/pilotPerson)
```

When the client requests that the record above be added, SLAPD responds with an **Object class violation** error, indicating that the chain of object classes is not correct. This is because `pilotPerson` is not related to `organizationalPerson` or `inetOrgPerson`.

Returning to our record for `uid=barbara`, that entry lists three object classes:

```
objectClass: person
objectClass: organizationalPerson
objectClass: inetOrgPerson
```

As we saw in the previous figure, `inetOrgPerson` is the lowest object class on the hierarchy — the far most from `top`. That means that SLAPD considers this object class to be the structural object class for the record. It even sets a special operational attribute, `structuralObjectClass`, that stores this value. Thus, you can get information on the structural object class through `ldapsearch`:

```
$ ldapsearch -LL -U matt '(uid=barbara)' structuralObjectClass
```

Here is the information:

```
SASL/DIGEST-MD5 authentication started
Please enter your password:
SASL username: matt
SASL SSF: 128
SASL installing layers
version: 1
dn: uid=barbara,ou=Users,dc=example,dc=com
structuralObjectClass: inetOrgPerson
```

When handling operations and evaluating rules, such as DIT content rules, SLAPD will treat this record as an `inetOrgPerson` record.

Within this discussion of structural object classes we have covered the gist of the object class hierarchy. An entry's place in the hierarchy is determined by its structural object class. But not all object classes affect a record's placement in the object class hierarchy. Let's turn to the third type of object class: auxiliary object classes.

Auxiliary Object Classes

Auxiliary object classes provide a mechanism for adding one or more attributes to an entry with an existing structural object class. Think of it as a modular system for defining a collection of related attributes that can be attached to otherwise (conceptually) unrelated object classes.

To get an idea of how this works let's take another look at the `uid=authenticate` entry:

```
dn: uid=authenticate,ou=System,dc=example,dc=com
uid: authenticate
ou: System
description: Special account for authenticating users
userPassword:: c2VjcmV0
objectClass: account
objectClass: simpleSecurityObject
```

The structural object class for this entry is `account`. The `simpleSecurityObject` object class is auxiliary.

The `account` schema, found in `cosine.schema`, looks like this:

```
objectclass
  (
    0.9.2342.19200300.100.4.5
    NAME 'account'
    SUP top STRUCTURAL
    MUST userid
    MAY ( description $ seeAlso $ localityName $
          organizationName $ organizationalUnitName $ host )
  )
```

This entry, according to the COSINE standard (RFC 4524), is to define a system account on a computer.

For whatever reason, the creators of the standard did not include the attributes necessary to give the account a password. This makes sense. It is probably not typical that a system account would need to authenticate against LDAP. However, the system account we have created needs to perform directory operations and so we need this account to have a `userPassword` attribute.

One way to achieve this is to create a new structural object class subordinate to account, but which requires a `userPassword` attribute. But there is also an object class in `core.schema` designed specifically for the purpose of giving non-person entries in the directory a `userPassword` to allow them to bind. In other words, there is an existing object class that provides exactly the functionality we require: the `simpleSecurityObject` object class.

The `simpleSecurityObject` is also defined in the COSINE schema.

The `simpleSecurityObject` schema looks like this:

```
objectclass
  (
  0.9.2342.19200300.100.4.19
  NAME 'simpleSecurityObject'
  DESC 'RFC1274: simple security object'
  SUP top
  AUXILIARY
  MUST userPassword
  )
```

This schema definition adds one required attribute to any implementing entry, `userPassword`. Effectively then, the `simpleSecurityObject` object class can be added to an entry in order to allow it to bind to the directory (assuming the ACLs allow).

Given the combination of the structural object class, `account`, and the auxiliary object class, `simpleSecurityObject`, our `uid=authenticate` record now has three required fields:

- `objectclass`, inherited from `top`
- `uid`, from the `account` structural object class
- `userPassword`, from the `simpleSecurityObject` auxiliary object class.

This example illustrates how the auxiliary object class can be used to add additional attributes to an entry that already belongs to a structural object class.

Rather than creating new structural object classes for each set of attributes you want an entry to have, the auxiliary object class mechanism makes it possible to define a modular collection of add-on attributes that can be attached to entries as needed.

By default, any auxiliary object class can be added to a record regardless of the structural object class of that record.

In other words, by default it is legal to take an entry with a `person` structural object class (an entry obviously intended to represent a human being) and attach to it the `javaSerializedObject` auxiliary object class (an entry intended to describe a stored representation of a Java binary class).

Historically, the responsibility for judiciously choosing which auxiliary object classes ought to be added to an entry has been left to LDAP client applications and users. However, you can use DIT content rules (see the previous part of this chapter) to formalize which auxiliary object classes an entry of a given structural object class is allowed to have.

Moving Onward

Up to this point, this chapter has focused on the details of the LDAP schema system, and has focused as much on theoretical points as it has on practice.

In these pages, I have tried to provide a condensed explanation of LDAP schemas, focusing on the aspects most applicable to the goals of this book. This material should provide the necessary background knowledge for reading schema definitions, wisely selecting which schemas to use for your own directory needs, and writing custom schemas.

However, if you intend to work on the OpenLDAP code, write overlays or modules, or even write schemas intended for public standardization, you ought to read the LDAP RFCs, particularly RFC 4512, which defines the LDAP schema language.

Now we are ready to move on to more practical matters. In the next section, we will implement a few overlays that require extra schemas. As we configure those overlays we will examine the schemas and the role those schemas play in the functioning of the overlay.

After that, we will create our own short schema.

Schemas: Accesslog and Password Policy Overlays

In the last chapter we saw OpenLDAP's overlay technology, and we implemented a few simple overlays. In this chapter we have seen how LDAP schemas work. Now we are going to take a look at a few overlays that require custom schemas.

The two overlays that we will examine are the `accesslog` overlay and the `ppolicy` (Password Policy) overlay.

Because they require their own schemas, and because each provides a robust feature set, these two overlays have a more complicated configuration. However, since the basic concepts are familiar already, we will move quickly.

Logging with the Accesslog Overlay

The Access Logging overlay (`accesslog`) extends the logging abilities of the SLAPD server. First, it makes it possible to track client access to the directory server. Second, it stores this logging data within the directory, making it possible to retrieve access logs from any authorized LDAP client.

Since it stores information inside of the directory server, and since the format for access log entries is not already described in any of the familiar schemas, the access logging overlay needs its own schema.

The access log schema is still considered experimental, and has not yet been finalized. Nor is it included in the schema directory (`/etc/ldap/schema` or `/usr/local/etc/openldap/schema`). The object classes are defined in the man page (`man slapo-accesslog`).

However, the access log overlay automatically loads its own schema, so there is no manual schema configuration to be done.

The process of installing the `accesslog` is of four steps:

1. Load the `accesslog` module
2. Configure the `accesslog` backend section
3. Create a database to store the access log
4. Configure the directory backend to log to the new database

Loading the accesslog Module

By now, this step should be familiar. Along with the other `moduleload` statements at the top of `slapd.conf`, we need to add one to load the `accesslog` module:

```
modulepath      /usr/local/libexec/openldap
moduleload      back_hdb
moduleload      denyop
moduleload      refint
moduleload      unique
moduleload      accesslog
```

When SLAPD is restarted the `accesslog` module, which contains the `accesslog` overlay, will be loaded.

Configuring the Access Log Backend

The `accesslog` overlay needs a location within the directory server to write the access information. We will create an extra database backend that will hold the logging data.

There is nothing particularly special about this backend. It functions just like any other, and we will use the standard set of configuration directives. But there is one catch to implementing `accesslog`: the database where the access logs are stored must appear in `slapd.conf` *before* the database that it is going to record access data about.

We want to log access to our first database (the one with suffix dc=example,dc=com), so we need to insert the configuration directives for the access log before the dc=example,dc=com database. Here's the beginning of the original Example.Com database definition:

```
###############################
# BDB Database Configuration #
###############################
# Database 1: Example.Com

database        hdb
suffix          "dc=example,dc=com" "o=My Company,c=US"
rootdn          "cn=Manager,dc=example,dc=com"
```

We will insert our access log configuration above the `database` directive in the previous example:

```
###############################
# BDB Database Configuration #
###############################
# Database 1: Logging DB

database hdb
suffix cn=log
rootdn          "cn=Manager,cn=log"
rootpw          secret
directory       /var/lib/ldap/accesslog
#directory      /usr/local/var/openldap-data/accesslog
index reqStart eq

###############################
# Database 2: Example.Com
database        hdb
suffix          "dc=example,dc=com" "o=My Company,c=US"
```

The highlighted section is the definition for the access log database.

As with the other databases, this one uses the HDB backend. The suffix for our logging directory will simply be cn=log.

Each logging event will be stored as an LDAP record, and each entry in the logging directory will have a DN composed of two attributes. The RDN is the reqStart attribute (which contains the timestamp indicating when the request started), and ends with the suffix which, in our case, is cn=log.

This database also has its own manager account and password (rootdn and rootpw). The Berkeley DB files will be stored at /var/lib/ldap/accesslog—a directory we will create on the file system in the next step.

Finally, the index directive configures an equality (eq) index for the reqStart attribute, which is the attribute SLAPD uses to create DNs. It uses this attribute when performing maintenance operations, so it is a good idea to have this attribute indexed.

There are a few more things to do in slapd.conf. But before doing those, we will create a directory for the Berkeley DB files.

Creating A Directory for the Access Log Files

Like the other HDB databases, this new database needs a location on the server's file system to store Berkeley DB database files. In the earlier configuration, we pointed SLAPD to the directory /var/lib/ldap/accesslog. Now, we need to create that directory and configure it for a Berkeley DB environment.

The first thing to do is create the new directory. From a shell this can be done easily:

```
$ sudo mkdir /var/lib/ldap/accesslog
```

From there, all we need to do is copy the DB_CONFIG to the new accesslog/ directory:

```
$ sudo cp /var/lib/ldap/DB_CONFIG /var/lib/ldap/accesslog/
```

Depending on the traffic on your server and the amount of data you are logging, you may want to increase or decrease the cache size allocated in DB_CONFIG. See the discussion in the previous chapter for more information on tuning the DB_CONFIG file.

Check the DB_CONFIG files

The DB_CONFIG file we created in the last chapter did not have any absolute references to locations on the file system. But some directives in the DB_CONFIG file (like set_lg_dir) might have absolute path references, which could result in two databases using the same log. That would have catastrophic consequences. Make sure you adjust the DB_CONFIG file accordingly.

Make sure that the new accesslog/ directory is readable and writable for the user account that runs the SLAPD process, and also make sure that that user can read the DB_CONFIG file.

Enabling Logging for the Main Backend

Now we have the logging environment set up. The next thing to do is configure our dc=example,dc=com backend to start using the new logging backend.

Back in slapd.conf, we need to add some new overlay-specific directives inside of the dc=example,dc=com backend. These directives must come after the database definition for the Example.Com database:

```
###############################
# Database 1: Example.Com
database          hdb
suffix            "dc=example,dc=com" "o=My Company,c=US"
# ... a dozen lines omitted ...
overlay accesslog
logdb cn=log
logops all
logold (objectclass=person)
logpurge 7+00:00 2+00:00
logsuccess TRUE
```

The first directive, overlay accesslog, loads the access logging overlay within the context of this particular database. The next five directives are the accesslog-specific directives.

The logdb directive is the only one required by the accesslog overlay. All the rest are optional.

The logdb directive specifies which database will be treated as an access log. In our case we want to use the cn=log database. For a site hosting multiple directory information trees, separate logging databases could be set up for each suffix.

The `logops` directive is used to specify exactly which LDAP operations should be logged. In this example, the keyword `all` indicates that all operations will be logged. But the following options are supported:

- Any operation can be specified by name: `add`, `delete`, `modify`, `modrdn`, `search`, `compare`, `extended`, `bind`, `unbind`, and `abandon`.
- There are a few special keywords that include a collection of operations. These are:
    - `read` (search, compare)
    - `write` (add, delete, modify, modrdn)
    - `session` (bind, unbind, abandon)
- There is the `all` keyword, which includes all operations.

More than one value can be placed on a `logops` line. Values should be separated by an empty space. For example, `logops modify modrdn` will log all modify and modrdn operations.

The `logold` ("log old") directive takes a search filter. When a delete or modify operation is successfully executed, then `accesslog` will check to see if the record matches the filter. If it does match, then `accesslog` will store a complete record of the change, including what attributes were added, and what attributes were changed or removed. For example, when I modified a user with the `ldapmodify` command-line tool, an entry detailing the changes was written to the accesslog directory information tree:

```
dn: reqStart=20070117022818.000002Z,cn=log
objectClass: auditModify
reqStart: 20070117022818.000002Z
reqEnd: 20070117022818.000003Z
reqType: modify
reqSession: 4
reqAuthzID: uid=matt,ou=users,dc=example,dc=com
reqDN: uid=barbara,ou=users,dc=example,dc=com
reqResult: 0
reqMod: objectClass:+ labeledURIObject
reqMod: labeledURI:+ http://example.com Home Page
reqMod: entryCSN:= 20070117022818Z#000001#00#000000
reqMod: modifiersName:= uid=matt,ou=users,dc=example,dc=com
reqMod: modifyTimestamp:= 20070117022818Z
reqOld: objectClass: person
reqOld: objectClass: organizationalPerson
reqOld: objectClass: inetOrgPerson
```

```
reqOld: entryCSN: 20061228230549Z#000000#00#000000
reqOld: modifiersName: cn=Manager,dc=example,dc=com
reqOld: modifyTimestamp: 20061228230549Z
```

The reqMod values show the new modifications, while the reqOld attribute values show the old lines. Note that two lines were added (the object class and the labeledURI), and two were changed (modifiersName, modifyTimestamp).

Why use logold? It may not be particularly useful for log evaluation but, when combined with SyncRepl, synchronization between SLAPD servers can be done more efficiently. (This form of SyncRepl is called **Delta-SyncRepl**.) If you are not using SyncRepl, you probably won't want to use logold at all. We will discuss SyncRepl (and Delta-SyncRepl) in detail in the next chapter.

The logpurge directive directs SLAPD to periodically check the access log and delete old entries. It takes two parameters that provide the following information: how old an entry must be before it is a candidate for being purged, and how long of an interval should pass between checking for entries to remove.

The format of the two parameters is the same:

```
[<number of days>+] <hours>:<minutes>[:<seconds>]
```

Where number of days and number of seconds are optional fields. Our logpurge parameter looked like this:

```
logpurge 7+00:00 2+00:00
```

This indicates that logs seven days old are to be considered for deletion. And after running a check, SLAPD will wait the indicated amount of time—two days—before checking for new deletions.

The last parameter is logsuccess. By default, accesslog records all attempted operations, whether successful or not. To log only the operations that are successfully completed set logsuccess to TRUE.

That's all there is to configuring accesslog. SLAPD will need to be restarted for the new overlay to be added.

The Log Records

Now that we have our new logging overlay running, let's test it out. The first step is to generate some logging data. Since we are logging all operations (logops all), any LDAP operation will do.

Here is a simple `ldapsearch`:

```
$ ldapsearch -x -W -D 'uid=matt,ou=users,dc=example,dc=com' \
    '(uid=matt)' mail gn sn
```

This uses a simple bind, and searches for my own record (`uid=matt`), retrieving the values for the `mail`, `gn` (given name) and `sn` attributes.

With a search like this, what is written to the access log? To find out, we can use `ldapsearch`:

```
$ ldapsearch -LL -U matt -b 'cn=log'
```

The output for this command, even with the results of only one command, is surprisingly large:

```
SASL/DIGEST-MD5 authentication started
Please enter your password:
SASL username: matt
SASL SSF: 128
SASL installing layers
version: 1
dn: cn=log
objectClass: auditContainer
cn: log
dn: reqStart=20070117044539.000000Z,cn=log
objectClass: auditBind
reqStart: 20070117044539.000000Z
reqEnd: 20070117044539.000001Z
reqType: bind
reqSession: 0
reqAuthzID:
reqDN: uid=matt,ou=users,dc=example,dc=com
reqResult: 0
reqVersion: 3
reqMethod: SIMPLE
dn: reqStart=20070117044539.000002Z,cn=log
objectClass: auditSearch
reqStart: 20070117044539.000002Z
reqEnd: 20070117044539.000003Z
reqType: search
reqSession: 0
reqAuthzID: uid=matt,ou=Users,dc=example,dc=com
reqDN: dc=example,dc=com
reqResult: 0
```

```
reqScope: sub
reqDerefAliases: never
reqAttrsOnly: FALSE
reqFilter: (uid=matt)
reqAttr: mail
reqAttr: gn
reqAttr: sn
reqEntries: 1
reqTimeLimit: 3600
reqSizeLimit: 500
dn: reqStart=20070117044540.000000Z,cn=log
objectClass: auditObject
reqStart: 20070117044540.000000Z
reqEnd: 20070117044540.000001Z
reqType: unbind
reqSession: 0
reqAuthzID: uid=matt,ou=Users,dc=example,dc=com
```

There are four different entries returned from the `ldapsearch` and each one has a different structural object class. We will look at each in turn.

The first LDIF entry it displays is the base record for `cn=log`:

```
dn: cn=log
objectClass: auditContainer
cn: log
```

The `auditContainer` object class is designed as a sort of general-purpose object class for the access log. It's schema looks like this:

```
objectClass
  (
  1.3.6.1.4.1.4203.666.11.5.2.0
  NAME 'auditContainer'
  DESC 'AuditLog container'
  SUP top
  STRUCTURAL
  MAY ( cn $ reqStart $ reqEnd )
  )
```

The base record only uses the optional `cn` attribute.

In the `accesslog` schema there are object classes defined for each LDAP operation: `auditAbandon`, `auditAdd`, `auditBind`, `auditCompare`, `auditDelete`, `auditModify`, `auditModRDN`, `auditSearch`, and `auditExtended`. In addition, there is a special object class called `auditObject` that describes general events.

In fact (in the current version) all of the operation object classes listed are subordinates to the `auditObject` object class. Because it is the parent of these other object classes, we will begin by looking at the `auditObject` schema definition.

The `auditObject` object class definition looks like this:

```
objectclass
  (
  1.3.6.1.4.1.4203.666.11.5.2.1
  NAME 'auditObject'
  DESC 'OpenLDAP request auditing'
  SUP top
  STRUCTURAL
  MUST ( reqStart $ reqType $ reqSession )
  MAY ( reqDN $ reqAuthzID $ reqControls $ reqRespControls $
        reqEnd $ reqResult $ reqMessage $ reqReferral )
  )
```

The three required attributes are:

- `reqStart`:A timestamp indicating the starting time of the operation
- `reqType`: A string indicating the operation being executed
- `reqSession`: The connection ID number used (internally) by SLAPD

In addition to these required attributes, there are eight optional attributes:

- `reqDN`: This records the DN of the record the operation is currently operating on.
- `reqAuthzID`: This records the DN of the user performing the operation. If the user is Anonymous the value is left blank.
- `reqControls` and `reqRespControls`: If the client sets any controls, they are indicated here.
- `reqEnd`: This stores the timestamp indicating when the operation was completed.
- `reqResult`: This contains the numeric error code if an error was encountered. If the operation is successful this returns `0`.
- `reqMessage`: If the error code is accompanied by a text message, the message is put in this attribute.
- `reqReferral`: If the operation returned a referral, the referral is noted here.

The second entry returned in the search records the client's bind operation:

```
dn: reqStart=20070117044539.000000Z,cn=log
objectClass: auditBind
reqStart: 20070117044539.000000Z
reqEnd: 20070117044539.000001Z
reqType: bind
reqSession: 0
reqAuthzID:
reqDN: uid=matt,ou=users,dc=example,dc=com
reqResult: 0
reqVersion: 3
reqMethod: SIMPLE
```

This first entry records the bind operation, and is an instance of the `auditBind` object class. The `auditBind` object class is a subordinate of `auditObject`:

```
objectClass
    (
    1.3.6.1.4.1.4203.666.11.5.2.6
    NAME 'auditBind'
    DESC 'Bind operation'
    SUP auditObject
    STRUCTURAL
    MUST ( reqVersion $ reqMethod )
    )
```

It adds two required attributes: `reqVersion`, which records the version of LDAP used for the connection and `reqMethod`, which indicates what method was used in binding.

Looking at the bind entry, we can see that it records the details of a successful bind operation. The start and end times are recorded in `reqStart` and `reqEnd` respectively. The `reqType` indicates that the operation performed is a bind operation. The `reqSession` indicates the internal ID of the request (which happens to be zero because this is the first operation run since we started SLAPD, and connection IDs increment starting at 0).

Since the bind was performed by the anonymous user, the `reqAuthzID` attribute is present, but has no value. The `reqDN` indicates that the client was attempting to bind as `uid=matt,ou=users,dc=example,dc=com`, and the `reqResult` of 0 indicates that the bind operation was completed successfully. The bottom two attributes are the attributes that belong to the `auditBind` object class. The `reqVersion` attribute indicates that the client used the LDAPv3 protocol and, according to `reqMethod`, the bind was a simple bind.

So, the first operation performed in this LDAP session was a bind. The second operation is the search:

```
dn: reqStart=20070117044539.000002Z,cn=log
objectClass: auditSearch
reqStart: 20070117044539.000002Z
reqEnd: 20070117044539.000003Z
reqType: search
reqSession: 0
reqAuthzID: uid=matt,ou=Users,dc=example,dc=com
reqDN: dc=example,dc=com
reqResult: 0
reqScope: sub
reqDerefAliases: never
reqAttrsOnly: FALSE
reqFilter: (uid=matt)
reqAttr: mail
reqAttr: gn
reqAttr: sn
reqEntries: 1
reqTimeLimit: 3600
reqSizeLimit: 500
```

Since it describes a search operation, this entry uses the auditSearch object class, which has the following schema definition:

```
objectClass
   (
   1.3.6.1.4.1.4203.666.11.5.2.11
   NAME 'auditSearch'
   DESC 'Search operation'
   SUP auditReadObject
   STRUCTURAL
   MUST ( reqScope $ reqDerefAliases $ reqAttrsonly )
   MAY ( reqFilter $ reqAttr $ reqEntries $ reqSizeLimit $
        reqTimeLimit )
   )
```

Note that auditSearch is a subordinate not of auditObject but of auditReadObject, another structural object class that is itself subordinate to auditObject. In other words, auditSearch is an indirect subclass of auditObject. The auditReadObject (as of OpenLDAP 2.3.30) does not add any additional attributes.

For the most part the attributes inherited from `auditObject` perform in the same capacity here as they did in the entry for the bind operation. The `reqAuthzID` in this case is the authenticated user's DN, instead of empty, and the `reqDN` shows the base DN for the search operation.

The next set of attributes provide detailed information about the nature of the search request.

- `reqScope` indicates the scope of the search. `reqDerefAliases` indicates that aliased entries (entries mapped to other entries elsewhere in the directory, a concept similar to symbolic linking in Linux file systems) are never dereferenced during searches. The `reqAttrsOnly` flag indicates that the search did not request that only the attribute names be returned. Instead, the names and values were to be returned.

- `reqFilter` contains the LDAP search filter. This is the filter we specified on the command line when running the `ldapsearch` command.

- `reqAttr` has three values, `mail`, `gn`, and `sn`, corresponding to the three attributes I requested in the `ldapsearch` command. And `reqEntries` indicates the total number of matching records found in the directory.

- `reqTimeLimit` and `reqSizeLimit` indicate the (soft) size and time limits requested in the search.

Taken as a whole, this entry provides a detailed record of what my LDAP search was and, from this record alone, it would be trivial to replicate the exact search.

There is one final (short) entry left, the entry that records the client's unbind.

```
dn: reqStart=20070117044540.000000Z,cn=log
objectClass: auditObject
reqStart: 20070117044540.000000Z
reqEnd: 20070117044540.000001Z
reqType: unbind
reqSession: 0
reqAuthzID: uid=matt,ou=Users,dc=example,dc=com
```

Since there are no paramters to the unbind operation (just the closing of a connection), there is no specific object class to model this event. Instead, the `auditObject` object class is used as the structural object class for this entry.

When clients perform other kinds of LDAP operations, such as additions and modifications, different object classes will be used. The object class definitions (and attribute definitions) can be found in the `cn=sucbschema` record. See the earlier section *Retrieving the Schema from SLAPD* for information on how to do this.

Now we have finished looking at the `accesslog` overlay. This overlay can come in use not only for record keeping but for debugging troublesome issues, discovering which attributes would most benefit form indexing, and even adding performance-enhancing functionality to directory replication. In the next section, we will look at the password policy overlay.

Implementing a Complex Overlay: Password Policy

One of the proposed extensions to LDAP is a standardized method for implementing password policies in an LDAP directory. The Password Policy (`ppolicy`) overlay implements the "Password Policy for LDAP Directories" IETF draft, which is likely to soon become an RFC.

A password policy provides account aging, password expirations, password strength checking, grace logins, and a variety of other password maintenance services.

How does this work in OpenLDAP? Password policy information is stored inside of the directory information tree in records described by a specialized schema. The `ppolicy` overlay monitors connections, updating password information and enforcing the password policy as appropriate.

 Password policies operate on the `userPassword` attribute. That means that if you use SASL and store the passwords outside of the directory information tree (in a place such as the `sasldb`), then the `ppolicy` overlay will not function. In this chapter we will be using simple binding.

The password policy schema defines the object class, `pwdPolicy`, that is implemented by password policy entries. There are no object classes for user records. Instead, operational attributes (attributes used internally by SLAPD) are used to store password policy information in user records. These operational attributes are used to store internal information (such as when a user last changed the password), and usually managed solely by the `ppolicy` overlay.

The password policy extension has many features, all documented in the man page, as well as in the IETF draft standard. Since the draft has not been finalized, and is still in a state of change, this module is marked as experimental. New features may be added, or current features altered or even removed, as the standard changes. But the experimental categorization does not reflect on the stability of the code. Administrators of large systems have reported this module to be production quality.

Because of the wealth of features, the ppolicy overlay is not a quick and easy install. It will require the following steps:

1. Include the password policy schema and load the module
2. Create a password policy
3. Configure the ppolicy overlay

Once the password policy overlay is implemented, we will do some testing.

Setting the Global Directives in slapd.conf: Schema and Module

The first thing we need to do is configure the global (basic) section of the slapd.conf file. As with the other overlays we will need to load the ppolicy module. And since we are using a new schema—one stored in the schema/ directory—we will need to include that too.

Since the directives are close together, we can look at both additions at once:

```
include /etc/ldap/schema/core.schema
include /etc/ldap/schema/cosine.schema
include /etc/ldap/schema/inetorgperson.schema
include /etc/ldap/schema/ppolicy.schema

#pidfile /var/run/slapd/slapd.pid
#argsfile /var/run/slapd/slapd.args
pidfile /usr/local/var/run/slapd.pid
argsfile /usr/local/var/run/slapd.args
loglevel none

modulepath /usr/lib/ldap
# modulepath /usr/local/libexec/openldap
moduleload back_hdb
moduleload denyop
moduleload refint
moduleload unique
moduleload accesslog
moduleload ppolicy
```

The two highlighted lines show the necessary changes:

1. The highlighted include directive imports the ppolicy.schema file into the configuration
2. The moduleload directive loads the ppolicy module

In step 3 we come back to the `slapd.conf` file and make a few more changes, but next we need to create a password policy and load it into the directory. That will require restarting SLAPD to pick up the new schema definitions:

```
$ sudo invoke-rc.d slapd restart
```

Creating a Password Policy

This step is more demanding than the previous. Our goal is to load a new password policy into the directory. To do this, we will need to get acquainted with the `pwdPolicy` object class in the `ppolicy` schema, create the requisite LDIF entries for our directory information tree, and then load these into the directory with `ldapadd`.

The `pwdPolicy` object class contains a number of attributes that can be used for storing information about a password policy. A password policy is a set of conditions determining what constraints will be placed on password usage within the LDAP server.

Here is the schema for the `pwdPolicy` object class:

```
objectclass
  (
  1.3.6.1.4.1.42.2.27.8.2.1
  NAME 'pwdPolicy'
  SUP top
  AUXILIARY
  MUST ( pwdAttribute )
  MAY ( pwdMinAge $ pwdMaxAge $ pwdInHistory $ pwdCheckQuality $
        pwdMinLength $ pwdExpireWarning $ pwdGraceAuthNLimit $
        pwdLockout $ pwdLockoutDuration $ pwdMaxFailure $
        pwdFailureCountInterval $ pwdMustChange $ pwdAllowUserChange
        $ pwdSafeModify )
  )
```

This object class is an auxiliary object class so, when we create an entry to hold the policy, it will need a structural object class.

There is only one required attribute for `pwdPolicy`: `pwdAttribute`. The value of this attribute should be set to the OID of the attribute used for password storage. Since the schema is part of a proposed standard, the purpose of this attribute is to make it possible for different directory servers to all use the same schema (since different directory server implementations use different attributes for storing password values). However, for OpenLDAP's SLAPD, the only attribute that can be used here is the OID for `userPassword`, which is `2.5.4.35`.

The `authPassword` attribute, defined in RFC 3112, is a candidate for replacing `userPassword` in future versions of OpenLDAP. However, at this time it is not completely implemented.

The remaining attributes, all of which are optional, are used to store policy information. Here is a brief explanation of what each attribute is used for:

- `pwdMinAge`: This specifies how much time must pass (in seconds) between the last time the password was changed and the next time SLAPD will allow the password to be changed. Setting this prevents an account from having the password changed multiple times in rapid succession.

- `pwdMaxAge`: This specifies how long (in seconds) a password will be considered good. This is calculated from the time when the password was last changed. After the elapsed time, the password will be marked as expired.

- `pwdInHistory`: If you store your passwords in plain text (unencrypted) in the directory then the `ppolicy` overlay can be configured to maintain a password history and prevent users from re-using passwords. This attribute is used to specify the maximum number of passwords that `ppolicy` will maintain for each user. Unless this attribute is set, and to a value greater than zero, no history will be maintained.

- `pwdCheckQuality`: There are two quality checks done by `ppolicy` if `pwdCheckQuality` is set to check passwords. The first is length checking (discussed next). The second is running a custom quality checking function. It is possible (using the `pwdCheckModule` object class and some custom C code) to add your own password quality checking module to SLAPD, and then use it to check password quality. This attribute takes one of three integer values: 0, 1, and 2. Now we have three cases:

  - If the value is 0 (the default), then `ppolicy` will not attempt to do any quality checking.

  - If 1, then `ppolicy` will attempt checking, but if the password is encrypted and certain checking functions cannot be performed, it will return successful.

  - If 2, then if the password checking function cannot run, it will return an error message.

- `pwdMinLength`: If `pwdCheckQuality` is set to 1 or 2, then `ppolicy` will make sure that new passwords meet a minimum length requirement. This attribute, which takes a positive integer, can be used to set the minimum acceptable length for a password.

- `pwdExpireWarning`: When a password approaches its expiration date (set in `pwdMaxAge`), `ppolicy` can provide a warning to the user when the user logs in. This attribute takes the time, in seconds, prior to when the password expires that it should start warning the user. In other words, at `pwdMaxAge` − `pwdExpireWarning` from when the password was set − the user will start getting warning messages. If this is set to `0` (the default) then no expiration warning will be sent.

- `pwdGraceAuthNLimit`: By default (or if this attribute is set to `0`), when a password expires the account is locked and the user can no longer bind to the directory server. But using this attribute we can allow grace logins. The value of this attribute should be a non-negative integer, which will specify how many grace logins a user with an expired password will be allowed before the account is locked.

- `pwdLockout`: This attribute allows you to turn on password lockouts. If this is turned on, then when a user fails to bind a certain number of times (`pwdMaxFailures`) in a row, then the account will be locked for some duration of time (`pwdLockoutDuration`). To turn on `pwdLockout`, which is off by default, set the value of this attribute to `TRUE`.

- `pwdLockoutDuration`: This attribute specifies the amount of time, in seconds, that an account will be locked out if `pwdLockout` is set to `TRUE` and the user fails to log in too many times (the number set in `pwdMaxFailures`). If this is set to `0` or is not set, then the account will be locked until an administrator re-enables it.

- `pwdMaxFailures`: This specifies the number of times in a row that a user can fail a login before being locked out. `pwdLockout` must be set to `TRUE` before this constraint will be enforced though.

- `pwdFailureCountInterval`: This attribute can be used to fine-tune the timing involved in password lockouts. By default (or when this attribute is set to `0`), failed login attempts are stored until a successful login is made. But the value of this attribute can be set to a number of seconds that `ppolicy` will wait before clearing the password failure count.

- `pwdMustChange`: This determines whether or not a user must change their password after an administrator sets it. By default, the user is not prompted to change a password. But if this is set to `TRUE`, if an administrator changes (or initially sets) a password, the user will be prompted to reset the password.

- `pwdAllowUserChange`: By default, users are allowed to change their own passwords. But if this is set to `FALSE`, users under this policy will not be allowed to change their own passwords. Since different policies can be assigned to different groups of users, this allows finer-grained control of write permissions to a password than ACLs do.

- `pwdSafeModify`: By default, once a user has successfully performed a bind operation, the user can change passwords without having to re-send the original password. But if `pwdSafeModify` is set to `TRUE`, then the user will have to send both the old password and the new password in order to change the password value. This adds an extra level of security to the password changing process.

Some of the policy attributes — primarily the password checking functions and password history — require that the password be stored in cleartext within the directory. This is the case simply because comparison functions do not work on encrypted values. Two identical password values, if using different salt sequences, will result in different ciphertexts. Two different hashing algorithms (like MD5 and SHA) will generate different hashes for the same password even if the same salt is used. Likewise, given certain hashing algorithms, two different strings could generate the same ciphertext (though the possibility of this happening to a particular user is negligible).

Most of the other features though, work regardless of how the values are stored in the directory.

Now we are ready to create an LDIF file to hold our policy. By convention, password policies are usually located in a separate OU in the directory information tree. We will add a new OU for that purpose.

And for our policy we will use the majority of the possible attributes:

```
dn: ou=Policies,dc=example,dc=com
ou: Policies
description: Directory policies.
objectclass: organizationalUnit

dn: cn=Standard,ou=Policies,dc=example,dc=com
cn: Standard
description: Standard password policy.
pwdAttribute: 2.5.4.35
pwdMinAge: 60
# 30 days: 60 sec * 60 min * 24 hr * 30 days
pwdMaxAge: 2592000
pwdCheckQuality: 1
pwdMinLength: 7
# Warn three days in advance
pwdExpireWarning: 259200
pwdGraceAuthNLimit: 3
pwdLockout: TRUE
pwdLockoutDuration: 1200
pwdMaxFailure: 3
```

```
pwdFailureCountInterval: 1200
pwdMustChange: TRUE
pwdAllowUserChange: TRUE
pwdSafeModify: TRUE
objectclass: device
objectclass: pwdPolicy
```

The first entry is for our organizational unit. The second is our password policy. Since the `pwdPolicy` object class is auxiliary we have to give the entry another object class, a structural object class. The `device` object class is typically used (based on the testing schema used in the source distribution of OpenLDAP).

Why is pwdPolicy Auxiliary?

There are a few reasons why the creators of the password policy specification might have made such a choice. First, according to RFC 4512, a structural object class must represent a physical entity. Second, making the class auxiliary makes it possible to integrate this schema with other existing schemas. For us, though, this presents the minor difficulty that there are no good candidates for a structural object class.

We can now add this LDIF with `ldapadd`. We have the above LDIF saved in a file called `ppolicy.ldif`, so we can add it with the following command:

```
ldapadd -x -W -D 'uid=matt,ou=users,dc=example,dc=com' -f ppolicy.ldif
```

This adds our two new entries to the directory.

Make sure you have restarted the server since adding the schema. If the ppolicy schema has not been loaded, the above will not work.

Now that we have our entries loaded it is time to return to `slapd.conf` and configure the overlay.

Configure the Overlay Directives

In the first step of setting up the password policy overlay, we added directives to `slapd.conf` to include the `ppolicy` schema definitions and load the `ppolicy` module. Now we will look at the backend configuration for the overlay.

As with the other overlays, all of the configuration directives are backend specific. Also, since the `ppolicy` overlay does a lot of writing to the directory information tree, not all features work on read-only databases.

While this overlay is sophisticated, there are only three directives for the overlay, and these are all straightforward. The relevant section in our `slapd.conf` file, in the `dc=example,dc=com` directory tree, looks like this:

```
overlay ppolicy
ppolicy_default cn=Standard,ou=Policies,dc=example,dc=com
ppolicy_use_lockout
ppolicy_hash_cleartext
```

Once the overlay is applied to this database using the `overlay` directive, there are three overlay-specific directives.

The first, `ppolicy_default`, points to the DN of the entry in the directory information tree that is to be treated as the default password policy entry. As we will see shortly different entries can use different policies. But the one indicated by `ppolicy_default` is the one that `ppolicy` will use when another is not explicitly set. For our example above, it is set to the DN of the entry that we created in the previous step.

The second directive is `ppolicy_use_lockout`. This directive alters how SLAPD reports error messages due to account lockouts. When a user's account is locked by the password policy overlay the user is not allowed to bind again. By default (when this directive is not included), the client is notified that the bind failed because of invalid credentials (the generic LDAP error) but no additional information is given. When this directive is present though, then SLAPD sends the *Account Locked* error code.

> While this extra error message might be helpful to the user, it could have negative consequences. An attacker might be able to determine, based on this information, that the server is using the password lockout features. Such an attacker could then perform a denial of service attack against known accounts on the server simply by attempting to login on each known account until the account was locked.

The last `ppolicy` directive, `ppolicy_hash_cleartext`, modifies the way SLAPD handles changes to the password. In short, if this directive is present, then SLAPD will automatically hash cleartext passwords when they are changed using the LDAP modify operation (as opposed to the LDAP password modify extended operation).

To understand what this means, let's look at an example. In our directory we have the following record (created in Chapter 3):

```
dn: uid=adam,ou=Users,dc=example,dc=com
cn: Adam Smith
sn: Smith
```

```
uid: adam
ou: Users
objectClass: person
objectClass: organizationalPerson
objectClass: inetOrgPerson
```

This user does not yet have a password. One way to set such a password would be to use the ldappasswd too, which (as we saw in Chapter 3) uses the LDAP password modify extended operation. This is the best way to change passwords as the server handles the password encryption. Here's an example of setting a password with ldappasswd:

```
$ ldappasswd -U matt -s secret 'uid=adam,ou=users,dc=example,dc=com'
```

This sets the password for uid=adam to secret. What will the record look like now? Like this:

```
dn: uid=adam,ou=Users,dc=example,dc=com
cn: Adam Smith
sn: Smith
uid: adam
ou: Users
objectClass: person
objectClass: organizationalPerson
objectClass: inetOrgPerson
userPassword:: elNTSEF9WlFzZWdrVUdpT3JKNUgwYXFFRdisxQ0dpaTNYUFdkMjA=
```

The userPassword value is base64 encoded. Its decoded value is this:

```
{SSHA}ZQsegkUGiOrJ5H0aqQv+1CGii3XPWd20
```

SLAPD performed the SSHA hashing of the value.

There is a second way of modifying the password and this is with the LDAP modify operation (as used by the ldapmodify client). When a userPassword value is changed with LDAP modify it is assumed that the client is sending the password value in the form in which it should be stored. In fact, the LDAP standard states that this is how the server should act when performing a modification of an attribute value. Thus, SLAPD will not encrypt the password.

Here's an example of using ldapmodify to set the password:

```
$ ldapmodify -x -W -D 'uid=matt,ou=users,dc=example,dc=com'
Enter LDAP Password:
dn: uid=adam,ou=users,dc=example,dc=com
changetype: modify
replace: userPassword
userPassword: secret
modifying entry "uid=adam,ou=users,dc=example,dc=com"
```

The highlighted portion above is the LDIF information to be modified. The value of the userPassword attribute was set to secret — the same password used in the ldappasswd example. But this time, if we look at the entry, the userPassword value is not encrypted:

```
dn: uid=adam,ou=Users,dc=example,dc=com
cn: Adam Smith
sn: Smith
uid: adam
ou: Users
objectClass: person
objectClass: organizationalPerson
objectClass: inetOrgPerson
userPassword:: c2VjcmV0
```

The password is not hashed. Instead, it is just base64 encoded. The decoded value is secret.

Including the ppolicy_hash_cleartext directive modifies this behavior. During modifications the ppolicy overlay checks to see if the modified attribute is userPassword and if the value is in cleartext. If the value is in cleartext then ppolicy hashes it.

 In effect, turning on this feature causes SLAPD to perform in a nonstandard way, but for the sake of additional security.

For example, we can re-run the same ldapmodify:

```
$ ldapmodify -x -W -D 'uid=matt,ou=users,dc=example,dc=com'
Enter LDAP Password:
dn: uid=adam,ou=users,dc=example,dc=com
changetype: modify
replace: userPassword
userPassword: secret
modifying entry "uid=adam,ou=users,dc=example,dc=com"
```

But this time, since ppolicy_hash_cleartext is on, the password is encrypted:

```
dn: uid=adam,ou=Users,dc=example,dc=com
cn: Adam Smith
sn: Smith
uid: adam
ou: Users
objectClass: person
objectClass: organizationalPerson
objectClass: inetOrgPerson
userPassword:: e1NTSEF9Q0M3QUdSQUlPMG4vYy8rbVZZiRE95bC9aYnpqNHcxdlQ=
```

The userPassword value, decoded, is {SSHA}CC7AGRAIOOn/c/+mVbDOyl/Zbzj4w1wT. When hashing cleartext is enabled, LDAP modify operations (for the userPassword attribute only) behave more like LDAP password modify extended operations.

We've now configured the overlay completely. It will take a restart for SLAPD to pick up the changes to slapd.conf though. Now we are ready to test some of these features.

Test the Overlay

As it is configured now, SLAPD will enforce policy controls on any entry with a userPassword attribute. Let's do a little testing to see how the password policy works.

The Administrator

As I work through the examples I use the uid=matt account as a managing account. This account is allowed (by the ACLs) to perform administrative tasks. But it is also subject to the constraints of the ppolicy overlay.

The root DN account (cn=manager,dc=example,dc=com on this server) is treated differently. For example, the manager can set a password for a user without having to know the user's old password, even if pwdSafeModify is on.

First, let's see how the policy responds to some password changes. And let's start this examination with an ldapmodify attempt:

```
$ ldapmodify -x -W -D 'uid=matt,ou=users,dc=example,dc=com'
Enter LDAP Password:
dn: uid=adam,ou=users,dc=example,dc=com
changetype: modify
replace: userPassword
userPassword: new_password

modifying entry "uid=adam,ou=users,dc=example,dc=com"
ldap_modify: Insufficient access (50)
        additional info: Must supply old password to be changed as
        well as new one
```

The modification attempt fails because the the pwdSafeModify is set to TRUE. There is no way to satisfy this requirement with ldapmodify. Instead we will have to use ldappasswd to change the password and we will have to set it to supply the server with the old password. This is what we will get:

```
$ ldappasswd -x -W -D 'uid=matt,ou=users,dc=example,dc=com' \
  -s new_password -a secret 'uid=adam,ou=users,dc=example,dc=com'
Enter LDAP Password:
Result: Success (0)
```

The `-s` flag is used to specify the new password, while the `-a` flag is used to provide the old password (and then `ldappasswd` prompts for the password of the DN that is binding too). With both of these set we meet the requirements of `pwdSafeModify`.

Since we have password checking turned on we should be able to test password length:

```
$ ldappasswd -x -W -D 'uid=matt,ou=users,dc=example,dc=com' \
  -s short -a new_password   'uid=adam,ou=users,dc=example,dc=com'
Enter LDAP Password:
Result: Constraint violation (19)
Additional info: Password fails quality checking policy
```

In this case the new password, `short`, is (as the name implies) too short. The `pwdMinLength` of the policy states that the password must be seven characters long, and when the password quality checking function is performed (which it will since `pwdCheckQuality` is set to 1), the server returns an error noting that it failed. Unfortunately for the user the message does not indicate the precise reason.

Next, let's look at password expiration warnings and password expirations. This will require some minor changes to our policy for the sake of testing—namely we will want to set the values for `pwdMaxAge` and `pwdExpireWarning` to lower values (values that would normally be too low for a production environment). Let's set the password to expire every ten minutes, and the expiration message to come up for the last nine minutes:

```
$ ldapmodify -x -W -D 'uid=matt,ou=users,dc=example,dc=com'
Enter LDAP Password:
dn: cn=Standard,ou=Policies,dc=example,dc=com
changetype: modify
replace: pwdMaxAge
pwdMaxAge: 600
-
replace: pwdExpireWarning
pwdExpireWarning: 540
modifying entry "cn=Standard,ou=Policies,dc=example,dc=com"
```

Now, when `uid=adam` binds, the following message is logged in the LDAP log:

```
ppolicy_bind: Setting warning for password expiry for
              uid=adam,ou=users,dc=example,dc=com = 536 seconds
```

Unfortunately, no message is sent to the client so the user does not see the message. This may be due to the fact that the draft specification doesn't require that the messages be sent to the client. Expiry warnings then, are useful mainly to administrators.

After ten minutes the userPassword value will be past the expiration point and, the next time the user logs in, SLAPD will mark the password as expired. Again, the user gets no explicit warning of this fact. An entry in the log file indicates the expiration of the account:

```
ppolicy_bind: Entry uid=adam,ou=Users,dc=example,dc=com
              has an expired password: 3 grace logins
```

But in addition to this log entry, a new operational attribute is added to the user's record. The pwdGraceUseTime attribute is added to the user's record, and the time stamp there indicates the last time the user performed a bind operation:

```
$ ldapsearch -LL -x -W -D 'uid=matt,ou=users,dc=example,dc=com' \
 '(uid=adam)' pwdGraceUseTime
Enter LDAP Password:
version: 1
dn: uid=adam,ou=Users,dc=example,dc=com
pwdGraceUseTime: 20070121172107Z
```

Each time a DN with an expired userPassword binds to the directory, a new value is added to the pwdGraceUseTime attribute. So after uid=adam has performed three binds after the password expiration date, the user's record will contain three pwdGraceUseTime attribute values:

```
$ ldapsearch -LL -x -W -D 'uid=matt,ou=users,dc=example,dc=com' \
 '(uid=adam)' pwdGraceUseTime
Enter LDAP Password:
version: 1
dn: uid=adam,ou=Users,dc=example,dc=com
pwdGraceUseTime: 20070121172107Z
pwdGraceUseTime: 20070121173638Z
pwdGraceUseTime: 20070121174603Z
```

After the number of pwdGraceUseTime values reaches the number in the pwdGraceAuthNLimit attribute of the policy, the account will be treated as locked, and that DN (uid=adam, in this case) will not be allowed to bind anymore. If uid=adam attempts to bind he will get an error message:

```
$ ldapsearch -x -W -D 'uid=adam,ou=users,dc=example,dc=com' \
 '(uid=adam)'
Enter LDAP Password:
ldap_bind: Invalid credentials (49)
```

Furthermore, a message is added to the log noting the problem:

```
ppolicy_bind: Entry uid=adam,ou=Users,dc=example,dc=com
               has an expired password: 0 grace logins
```

At this point an administrator will have to take steps to enable the account again.

Password Policy Operational Attributes

In the previous section we tested several different features of the password policy. Now we will look at performing administration operations on accounts.

The ppolicy overlay stores information about a user's adherence to a password policy in that user's record. The information is stored in operational attributes.

Unlike regular attributes, operational attributes are not returned to clients unless the client explicitly requests them (either by name, or with the special plus (+) attribute specifier, which matches any operational attribute). And SLAPD can prevent clients from being able to modify operational attributes.

To begin we will look at an example of what happens when password lockout (pwdLockout) is turned on, and an account gets locked out. The ppolicy overlay uses operational attributes to store information about failures and lockouts.

In our policy, when a user fails to authenticate correctly three times in a row (according to pwdMaxFailure), they will be locked out of their account for some period of time (determined by pwdLockoutDuration).

One of the other users in our directory is uid=dave,ou=users,dc=example,dc=com. This user has failed to authenticate three times. The next time the user attempts to authenticate, even if he uses the right password, he will be disallowed from binding:

```
$ ldapsearch -x -W -D 'uid=dave,ou=users,dc=example,dc=com'\
    '(uid=dave)'
Enter LDAP Password:
ldap_bind: Invalid credentials (49)
```

A few operational attributes in that user's record indicate what the problem is:

```
$ ldapsearch -LL -x -W -D 'uid=matt,ou=users,dc=example,dc=com' \
    '(uid=dave)' +
Enter LDAP Password:
version: 1

dn: uid=dave,ou=Users,dc=example,dc=com
structuralObjectClass: inetOrgPerson
entryUUID: efbf8838-c734-102a-935c-57e457da105f
```

```
creatorsName: cn=Manager,dc=example,dc=com
createTimestamp: 20060823205147Z
pwdChangedTime: 20070121180110Z
pwdFailureTime: 20070121180139Z
pwdFailureTime: 20070121180140Z
pwdFailureTime: 20070121180142Z
pwdAccountLockedTime: 20070121180142Z
entryCSN: 20070121180142Z#000000#00#000000
modifiersName: cn=Manager,dc=example,dc=com
modifyTimestamp: 20070121180142Z
entryDN: uid=dave,ou=Users,dc=example,dc=com
subschemaSubentry: cn=Subschema
hasSubordinates: TRUE
```

Note that the `ldapsearch` in the example is for all of (and only) the operational attributes for entries that match the filter — that's what the plus sign (+) does.

The highlighted lines show the attributes in which we are interested: `pwdFailureTime` and `pwdAccountLockedTime`.

The `pwdFailureTime` operational attribute has a timestamp for every time the user failed a login. When a user has a successful login, the values of `pwdFailureTime` are cleared, so having three values indicates that three logins in a row have failed.

The `pwdAccountLockedTime` indicates what time the password was locked. According to our configuration, the lockout should only last for twenty minutes, after which the user will be allowed to try again.

If the user succeeds the `pwdFailureTime` and `pwdAccountLockedTime` attributes will be removed from the user's record:

```
$ ldapsearch -LL -x -W -D 'uid=matt,ou=users,dc=example,dc=com'
'(uid=dave)' +
Enter LDAP Password:
version: 1
dn: uid=dave,ou=Users,dc=example,dc=com
structuralObjectClass: inetOrgPerson
entryUUID: efbf8838-c734-102a-935c-57e457da105f
creatorsName: cn=Manager,dc=example,dc=com
createTimestamp: 20060823205147Z
pwdChangedTime: 20070121180110Z
entryCSN: 20070121182203Z#000000#00#000000
modifiersName: cn=Manager,dc=example,dc=com
modifyTimestamp: 20070121182203Z
entryDN: uid=dave,ou=Users,dc=example,dc=com
subschemaSubentry: cn=Subschema
hasSubordinates: TRUE
```

In such cases administrators do not have to make any special changes to a user's entry. But what if the user gets locked out? This can happen if `pwdLockDuration` is set to `0` and the user fails to login too many times. It can also happen, as we saw in the example, if the user's password has expired and the user has exhausted the allowed grace logins.

Once the account has been locked, the user will not even be allowed to change his or her password. That means that the manager will need to intervene on the user's behalf and change the password using `ldappasswd`, `ldapmodify`, or another similar tool.

In rare cases, it may be desirable to modify the operational attributes directly. For example, `pwdAccountLockedTime`, `pwdReset`, and `pwdPolicySubentry` can be modified by the manager:

```
$ ldapmodify -x -W -D 'cn=manager,dc=example,dc=com'
Enter LDAP Password:
dn: uid=adam,ou=users,dc=example,dc=com
changetype: modify
add: pwdReset
pwdReset: TRUE
modifying entry "uid=adam,ou=users,dc=example,dc=com"
```

In this example, the `pwdReset` flag for the `uid=adam` account was set to `TRUE`. This will require the user to change the password the next time a bind is performed.

But SLAPD may not allow the other operational attributes to be modified by the standard LDAP modification. This is because the `ppolicy` schema sets the `NO-USER-MODIFICATION` flag on these schema definitions.

Can these operational attributes ever be modified? Using a special control, the **Relax Rules control** (formerly called ManageDIT), managers can change the values of operational parameters that usually do not allow such changes. However, the Relax Rules control is not yet officially released and is not enabled by default in OpenLDAP. We would have to build the development version of OpenLDAP to enable the control.

Summary of ppolicy Operational Attributes

We have looked at a few more operational attributes that `ppolicy` can attach to a record used for bindng. Here's a list of all of the possible attributes along with a brief description of each:

- `pwdChangedTime`: This contains a timestamp indicating when the password was last changed. There can only be one value for this attribute. Passwords in entries that do not have this attribute will never expire.

- `pwdAccountLockedTime`: This attribute is added to an entry when the entry is locked. It contains a timestamp indicating at what time SLAPD marked the account as locked. We saw this used when a user failed to authenticate too many times in a row.

- `pwdFailureTime`: A `pwdFailureTime` attribute value is added to a record every time a user tries to bind, but fails to supply the right password. A successful login clears all `pwdFailureTime` attributes.

- `pwdGraceUseTime`: If a user's account has expired, and the policy allows grace logins, a new `pwdGraceUseTime` value will be added every time the user logs in with an expired password. Resetting the password clears all `pwdGraceUseTime` values.

- `pwdHistory`: If password history tracking is turned on then every time a user changes passwords, the old password is stored in a `pwdHistory` attribute value. Only the number of password specified in the policy are retained in the history

- `pwdPolicySubentry`: This attribute, which allows only one value, takes the DN of the password policy that this record should use. If this attribute is not found, SLAPD uses the default policy (as specified by the `ppolicy_default` directive in `slapd.conf`).

- `pwdReset`: This attribute takes a boolean value. When a manager changes the password the flag is set to TRUE. If the policy also has `pwdMustChange` set to TRUE then the user will have to change her or his password on the next bind (using `ldappasswd`).

At this point we are done working with the Password Policy overlay. Next we will move on to create our own schema.

Creating a Schema

Up to this point we have taken an in-depth look at schema definitions and then implemented a few overlays that made use of custom schemas. By now you should be comfortable working with and reading schemas. Here we are going to create our own schema.

Our goal in this section is to create a small schema for adding blog information to our directory. We want to be able to store a record in the directory to represent a blog, and also link existing entries to these blogs, indicating, for example, that a particular user maintains a particular blog.

To do this we are going to add two object classes — one structural and one auxiliary — and a handful of new attributes. The structural object class, `blog`, will describe an individual blog. It will contain the necessary attributes to describe a blog.

The auxiliary class `blogOwner`, will be used to add blog ownership information to a particular entry. Since the information about the blog will be stored in a `blog` entry, the `blogOwner` object class will only need one attribute that can be used to point to the appropriate `blog` entry.

The first thing we will do is walk through the process of obtaining an OID. Then we will create our object classes. After the object classes are created we will define our new attributes. Finally, we will try out our new schema.

Getting an OID

As we have seen so far the OID (Object Identifier) plays an important role in defining a schema.

An OID is a sequence of integers separated by dots (.). But OIDs are not arbitrary combinations of digits. They are structured to represent the pedigree of an object. As we will use them here, for creating a new schema, we will treat the OID as being composed of three parts:

- The base OID
- The type number
- The item number

The base part of an OID number is assigned by a naming authority. We will get ours from the **Internet Assigned Numbers Authority (IANA)**.

IANA is not the only naming authority. Each country may have its own registry. For instance, in the United States the **American National Standards Institute (ANSI)** also has a registry.

IANA maintains a registry of OIDs for private enterprises. It allocates numbers free of charge and all that is necessary is a one-time registration. However, IANA only gives one number to each enterprise so, if your organization has one already, you should use the existing one. You can view the registry at `http://www.iana.org/assignments/enterprise-numbers`.

To obtain a number go to `http://iana.org/cgi-bin/enterprise.pl` and complete the form there. You will then be assigned an OID looking something like this: 1.3.6.1.4.1.?, where the question mark is replaced with an integer. This OID serves as the basis for the OIDs we use when creating schemas. By appending your own series of digits and dots to this string you can create your own OID numbers, and as long as you take care to keep your OIDs unique within your own domain, you can assume that these OIDs are also globally unique (for you are the only one with the exact base OID).

In these examples I am using the OID registered to me. These OIDs may be used to replicate the examples herein, but do not use my OID to create your own schemas. The practice of using someone else's OID is called **OID hijacking**, and is frowned upon because it compromises the assumption that OIDs are globally unique.

While this series of digits has some semantic meaning (it means, roughly, that the owner is a private enterprise operating within IANA's namespace), there are no constraints on how you decide to structure your OIDs. You could, for example, just append a new set of random digits to the base OID each time you needed to create a new OID:

```
1.3.6.1.4.1.8254.78.45146762
1.3.6.1.4.1.8254.57.483729598
```

But it is often more manageable to come up with some semantic scheme for organization. A version derived from the OpenLDAP foundation's scheme is recommended. From the base OID, create a segment to be used just for LDAP OIDs:

```
1.3.6.1.4.1.8254.1021
```

Now we have just one portion of the namespace that will be used only for LDAP OIDs. From here we will use a simple subcategory identifier. Starting with the OID arc 1.3.6.1.4.1.8254.1021, we will create OIDs of the form:

```
1.3.6.1.4.1.8254.1021.x.y
```

Where x indicates the type of object and y indicates the specific object we are identifying. The OpenLDAP Foundation uses the following types:

- LDAP syntaxes (1)
- Matching rules (2)
- Attribute types (3)
- Object classes (4)
- Supported features (5)
- Protocol mechanisms (9)
- Controls (10)
- Extended operations (11)

We are only going to create object classes and attributes, so the value of x for our classes will be 3 for OIDs attached to attributes and 4 for OIDs attached to object classes.

For the y value, we will just start with the digit 1 and increment each time we define a new object of that type. For example, our first object class will have the OID:

```
1.3.6.1.4.1.8254.1021.4.1
```

And for our second object class we will just increment the last value from 1 to 2:

```
1.3.6.1.4.1.8254.1021.4.2
```

Again, this is just one convention and different organizations use different conventions. While I advocate this convention you are free to choose another if you find that it is better for your needs.

There are two things to keep in mind though. First, you need to ensure that the OIDs are unique across your arc. That means you should maintain a registry of them in a place accessible to all people in your organization who work with the OIDs. Second, adding meaning to the numbers can provide tremendous utility, as it can help you recall or derive what an otherwise arbitrary string of numbers represents.

Now we are ready to begin creating our schema.

Giving Our OID a Name

Our schema definitions are all going in a file called `blog.schema`, which we will later reference in an `include` statement in `slapd.conf`.

Most usually once the base OID for LDAP objects is defined, it is convenient to use the `objectidentifier` directive in `slapd.conf` to make the OIDs more readable, and make the process of creating schema definitions less error prone.

We can do this in the first few lines of our schema file:

```
objectidentifier blogSchema 1.3.6.1.4.1.8254.1021
objectidentifier blogAttrs blogSchema:3
objectidentifier blogOCs blogSchema:4
```

The first line maps the name `blogSchema` onto the OID `1.3.6.1.4.1.8254.1021`. Now we can refer to that long OID as `blogSchema`, which is much easier to remember.

The second and third `objectidentifier` directives add a few more aliases. The second one sets the name `blogAttrs` refer to the OID `blogSchema:3` (which is `1.3.6.1.4.1.8254.1021.3`). Thus, when we define attributes we can use the shortcut `blogAttrs:1` instead of typing the whole thing out as `1.3.6.1.4.1.8254.1021.3.1`.

Similarly, `blogOCs` alias (short for "blog object classes") can be used to refer to the `1.3.6.1.4.1.8254.1021.4` arc.

With this mechanism in place we have implemented the organizational strategy explained in the previous section, and our OID naming from here on should be a simple matter of incrementing the last integer of an OID.

Creating Object Classes

We will be starting with our object classes, and then use these defined object classes to guide the creation of our attributes. This is typically the way creation of schemas is done, but it does have one counter-intuitive result: object classes must be defined after the attributes that they contain. In effect then, we are jumping to the end of our schema file to add object classes, and will later add attribute definitions between the object identifiers and the object classes.

The first object class to describe is the `blog` class. This object class will define the attributes necessary to define a blog. For our purposes we are going to create a very simple object class, though there are many more attributes that could be attached.

We want the class to have the following attributes:

- `blogTitle`: The title of the blog
- `blogUrl`: The URL (Uniform Resource Locater) of the main page for the blog
- `blogFeedUrl`: The URL for the RSS or Atom feed of the URL
- `description`: A brief text description of the blog

Of these, the `blogUrl` and `blogTitle` attributes should be required. `blogUrl` is an essential component of a blog. Without this, an entry describing a blog would be of little value. And the `blogTitle` attribute is necessary to give us a naming component to use in DNs.

For the sake of clarity of meaning, here we have prepended the `blog` string to any new attributes so that they can be immediately distinguished from other similar attributes.

Naming Object Classes and Attributes

If your object classes or attributes are designed for internal use, or for application-specific use, it is advised that the name of the organization or application be prepended to the attribute and object class names. That helps to make the purpose of the defined items explicit.

Fortunately for us, `description` is already defined. While we could use the `title` attribute, as defined in `core.schema`, this could introduce confusion, as that attribute is used to refer to the title of a person in an organization. To avoid any confusion then, we will avoid reusing that attribute.

Already we have said that this object class is going to be structural, and we have a scheme for determining an OID number. There are no similar object classes so we will create a class whose superior is `top`. We now have all the information we need to create our schema definition:

```
objectclass
  (
    blogOCs:1
    NAME 'blog'
    DESC 'Describes an online blog accessible by URL.'
    SUP top
    STRUCTURAL
    MUST ( blogUrl $ blogTitle )
    MAY ( blogFeedUrl $ description )
  )
```

In the OID field we used the object identifier we assigned in the last section. And we started with 1, our first object class.

The `blogOwner` object class is to be marked auxiliary so that we can attach it to a variety of different entries, regardless of the structural object class. For example, regardless of whether the blog is a corporate blog, or is maintained by an organizational unit, or is simply an individual's, we can add this object class to the desired entry.

We want to use the `blogOwner` object class to insert a pointer from an entry to the appropriate `blog` entry in the directory information tree. Since that is all we need, a single attribute will suffice for these purposes:

- `blogDN`: The DN describing the `blog` that this entry is affiliated with.

This object class then, turns out to be even simpler than the previous one:

```
objectclass
  (
    blogOCs:2
    NAME 'blogOwner'
    DESC 'Indicates that this entry is responsible for a blog.'
    AUXILIARY
    MUST ( blogDN )
  )
```

This OID number differs from the first only in that the last value has been incremented. This follows the scheme we defined in the previous section.

Since this is an auxiliary object class, there is no need for a superior. And since we want this class to be used to point to a `blog` entry elsewhere in the directory, the `blogDN` attribute is required.

Now we have our two object classes. In creating them we have referred to four attributes that currently do not exist. It is time to create them.

Creating Attributes

As we created the `blog` and `blogOwner` object classes, we tentatively defined (in our text) four attributes: `blogTitle`, `blogUrl`, `blogFeedUrl`, and `blogDN`. Now we will define each of these, beginning with `blogTitle`.

In order to define our attribute we want to decide on the syntax of the attribute and also the matching rules that SLAPD will use for this attribute. The `blogTitle` will contain values that are strings of text data. So the syntax we want is one that supports this. The **Directory String syntax**, defined in RFC 4517, is intended for just such a purpose. And it supports internationalization, storing characters in UTF-8.

When performing searches, we do not want the case of the text (upper or lower) to make a difference. In other words, we want "My Blog" and "my blog" to be treated as matches. So we need to find the matching rule that will best support this. There are over three dozen matching rules supported in OpenLDAP (you can see a list by searching the `cn=Subschema` entry). We want to implement string-based equality and substring matching on our `blogTitle` attribute, so the pair of matching rules we will want to use are `caseIgnoreMatch` and `caseIgnoreSubstringsMatch`.

Now, we have all of the information necessary for creating a new attribute type:

```
attributetype
  (
  blogAttrs:1
  NAME 'blogTitle'
  DESC 'Title of a blog.'
  EQUALITY caseIgnoreMatch
  SUBSTR caseIgnoreSubstringsMatch
  SYNTAX 1.3.6.1.4.1.1466.115.121.1.15{256}
  )
```

The OID field is `blogAttrs:1`, indicating that this is our first attribute.

The LDAP syntax OID is the OID for a **Directory String**. At the end of the OID, the {256} suggests that the maximum length of the title be constrained to 256 characters.

 The characters are in UTF-8, so this might take up as much as 512 bytes of space if each of the 256 characters is two bytes.

The next two attributes, `blogUrl` and `blogFeedUrl`, are similar and we can take advantage of that as we define them.

The first thing to examine is the LDAP syntax of these attributes. Unlike `blogTitle`, we do not want the values of `blogUrl` and `blogFeedUrl` to be in the Directory String syntax, because (according to RFC 3986 and the previous URL standards) URLs are to use a subset of the ASCII character set.

 For more on URLs and internationalization, see the W3C's *Web Naming and Addressing* page: `http://www.w3.org/Addressing/`. Links to information as well as pertinent RFCs can be found there.

Instead of using Directory String syntax, we should use the **IA5 String syntax** which describes an extended ASCII character set. The OID for this syntax is `1.3.6.1.4.1.1466.115.121.1.26`.

Similarly, when we specify matching rules, we want to use the IA5 matching rules. And since URLs are case-sensitive, we want exact matches. We do not want the case to be ignored. So for matching rules we want `caseExactIA5Match` and `caseExactIA5SubstringsMatch`.

Now we can define both attributes:

```
attributetype
  (
  blogAttrs:2
  NAME 'blogUrl'
  DESC 'Uniform Resource Locator (URL) for a blog.'
  EQUALITY caseExactIA5Match
  SUBSTR caseExactIA5SubstringsMatch
  SYNTAX 1.3.6.1.4.1.1466.115.121.1.26{512}
  )

attributetype
  (
  blogAttrs:3
```

```
NAME 'blogFeedUrl'
DESC 'URL to an XML feed for a blog.'
SUP blogUrl
)
```

Since the `blogUrl` field contains the matching rules and syntax that `blogFeedUrl` uses, and since there is an obvious similarity in usage between the two, it makes sense to treat `blogUrl` as the supertype of `blogFeedUrl`. So, `blogFeedUrl` inherits the LDAP syntax and matching rules from `blogUrl`.

Finally, we need to define our `blogDN` field, which will hold a DN. There is syntax and specific matching rules for DNs, and we will use those. The **Distinguished Name syntax**, defined with the OID `1.3.6.1.4.1.1466.115.121.1.12`, is used for values that are DNs. And the `distinguishedNameMatch` matching rule is used for performing exact matches on DNs. There are no substring or ordering matches for DNs.

Our last attribute then, looks like this:

```
attributetype
    (
    blogAttrs:4
    NAME 'blogDN'
    DESC 'DN of a blog entry in the directory.'
    EQUALITY distinguishedNameMatch
    SYNTAX 1.3.6.1.4.1.1466.115.121.1.12
    )
```

Now we have our entire schema defined. We are ready to test it.

Loading the New Schema

As with all other schemas, in order to load this schema, we must include it in `slapd.conf`.

```
include /etc/ldap/schema/core.schema
include /etc/ldap/schema/cosine.schema
include /etc/ldap/schema/inetorgperson.schema
include /etc/ldap/schema/ppolicy.schema
include /etc/ldap/schema/blog.schema
```

It is assumed here that `blog.schema` is located in the `/etc/ldap/schema` directory (which is a good place to put the schema). If you choose to locate the schema elsewhere, adjust the path accordingly.

The highlighted line in the code is the only addition necessary (the rest should be there already). Note that our schema is only dependent on `core.schema`. The other three are not necessary to make our schema work.

Restarting SLAPD will load the schema.

Troubleshooting Schema Loading

If there is an error in the schema SLAPD will not start, failing instead with an elaborate error message like this:

```
/etc/schema/blog.schema: line 89: Unexpected token before
                         MUST ( blogDN ) )
ObjectClassDescription = "(" whsp
    numericoid whsp   ; ObjectClass identifier
    [ "NAME" qdescrs ]
    [ "DESC" qdstring ]
    [ "OBSOLETE" whsp ]
    [ "SUP" oids ]   ; Superior ObjectClasses
    [ ( "ABSTRACT" / "STRUCTURAL" / "AUXILIARY" ) whsp ]
                      ; default structural
    [ "MUST" oids ]   ; AttributeTypes
    [ "MAY" oids ]    ; AttributeTypes
    whsp ")"
slapd stopped.
connections_destroy: nothing to destroy.
```

This error was triggered when we misspelled AUXILIARY—a cause not easily divined by this error message. But it illustrates the fact that the process of writing a schema definition takes patience and precision.

The best strategy for dealing with such failures is to carefully read the errant schema definition over, hunting for errors. Sometimes simplifying a definition can help eliminate other possible errors too. Finally, checking the definition against the specification in RFC 4512 can help you spot any nondescript syntactical errors.

A New Record

Now we can use `ldapadd` to add a new `blog` entry to our directory information tree. We will add information about the official corporate blog of Example.Com:

```
$ ldapadd -U matt
SASL/DIGEST-MD5 authentication started
Please enter your password:
SASL username: matt
```

```
SASL SSF: 128
SASL installing layers
dn: blogTitle=Example.Com News,dc=example,dc=com
blogTitle: Example.Com News
blogUrl: http://example.com/blogs/main
blogFeedUrl: http://example.com/rss/main
description: The Official Example.Com Blog.
objectclass: blog

adding new entry "blogTitle=Example.Com News,dc=example,dc=com"
```

The highlighted portion above is the new entry we are adding. The last line, returned by SLAPD, indicates that the entry has been added successfully.

Our user uid=barbara is responsible for maintaining this blog so we can indicate this relationship by adding the blogOwner object class and blogDN attribute to her record with ldapmodify:

```
$ ldapmodify -U matt
SASL/DIGEST-MD5 authentication started
Please enter your password:
SASL username: matt
SASL SSF: 128
SASL installing layers
dn: uid=barbara,ou=users,dc=example,dc=com
changetype: modify
add: objectclass
objectclass: blogOwner
-
add: blogDN
blogDN:  blogTitle=Example.Com News,dc=example,dc=com

modifying entry "uid=barbara,ou=users,dc=example,dc=com"
```

The record for uid=barbara now looks like this:

```
dn: uid=barbara,ou=Users,dc=example,dc=com
ou: Users
uid: barbara
sn: Jensen
cn: Barbara Jensen
givenName: Barbara
displayName: Barbara Jensen
mail: barbara@example.com
objectClass: person
objectClass: organizationalPerson
```

```
objectClass: inetOrgPerson
objectClass: labeledURIObject
objectClass: blogOwner
blogDN: blogTitle=Example.Com News,dc=example,dc=com
```

We have just successfully created and implemented a new schema including new attributes and object classes.

Summary

The focus of this chapter has been the schema. We began with a theoretical look at what makes up a schema and how schemas are defined. Then we looked at the organization of schemas in the directory, focusing on the different types of object class and how they work together to compose a hierarchical directory. From there we turned to more practical material. We looked at the `accesslog` and `ppolicy` overlays, each of which requires its own schema. Finally, we ended by creating our own custom schema, creating a pair of object classes, and a handful of attributes.

In the next chapter we will discuss working with multiple directories, focusing particluarly on directory replication, the process of keeping two or more directory servers synchronized with the same content.

7
Multiple Directories

In the previous chapters we were focused on using a single directory server. But in a networked environment, you may need to configure multiple directory servers to interoperate. In this chapter we will be looking at different ways of getting directory servers to interoperate over a network.

While the focus of this book is OpenLDAP, many of the strategies presented here can be adopted to integrate OpenLDAP with other LDAP directory servers, such as The Apache Directory Server, Fedora DS, Microsoft's Active Directory, and the Novell Directory Server (NDS).

The two main processes we will look at are replication (creating a mirror of a directory information tree on another directory server) and proxying (allowing one directory server to act as an intermediary between an LDAP client and another directory server). In this chapter we will cover:

- The basics of synchronizing and replicating directories
- Directory replication with SyncRepl
- Proxying with the ldap backend
- Adding caching with the Proxy Cache overlay
- Using the transparency overlay to create a hybrid cache

In this chapter we will be working with two servers—one that will host the authoritative copy of the directory, and another that will synchronize itself over the network with the authoritative copy.

Replication: An Overview

Sometimes it is desirable to have multiple identical copies of a directory server. This can be particularly effective in cases where LDAP servers sustain large volumes of traffic, where fail-over protection is required, or in cases where LDAP clients are geographically dispersed, and having local copies of a directory would greatly expedite service. These are cases where LDAP replication can provide a solution.

Replication is the process of configuring two or more directories to contain the same directory information tree (or portion of the directory tree), and to keep the multiple copies of the directory data synchronized over time. This has been a central feature of the OpenLDAP suite since its inception. In fact its predecessor, the University of Michigan LDAP Server, implemented replication early on and, because of this, replication has long been considered a standard task for an LDAP server.

In the standard LDAP model, replication is done in a hierarchy. One server is considered the **master server** (or the **master DSA** (Directory Server Agent), sometimes called the **provider**). This server is responsible for maintaining the canonical version of the directory information tree.

Beneath the master server are one or more **shadow servers** (sometimes called **consumer**, **replica**, or **slave servers**). A shadow server holds a replica of the master server's directory information tree, and clients can connect to the shadow server and perform searches of the directory information tree (DIT). Let's have a look at the following figure:

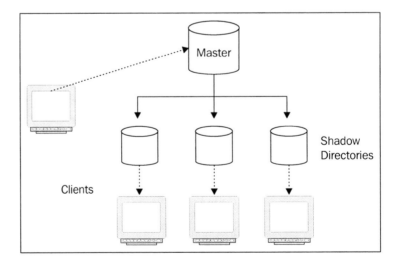

For all practical purposes, shadow servers have read-only features. While the shadow servers can handle many LDAP operations, shadow servers are not allowed to alter the records in the replicated directory information tree. When add, modify, or delete operations are received, for instance, the shadow server will return a **referral** to the client, directing it to contact the master server instead. A referral is a special type of response that directs the client to contact another server to perform that operation. Configuring a referral to point from a shadow server to a master server is a simple matter of adding a `referral` directive to the `slapd.conf` file.

When a client receives a referral it has the information it needs to re-try the operation on the correct server.

Why not allow writing to the slaves? Allowing multiple servers to accept all the modifications, additions, and deletions makes it possible for the directory information tree to taken on inconsistent states. What happens if two directory servers change an attribute at the same time? Or if one modifies a record that another is simultaneously deleting? By allowing write operations only on the master server, it is much easier to keep the many replicas consistent.

> In the 2.4 release of OpenLDAP, it will be possible to configure **multimaster** which will allow multiple servers to act as masters. As with all multimaster configurations, there will be risks that certain inconsistencies arise, but these risks should be minimized.

In OpenLDAP there are two different ways to implement replication. The first is by configuring the master server to keep the shadow servers updated. This is called the *push* method. The second is to configure the slaves to periodically check the master for changes, and update itself accordingly; this is called the *pull* method.

Until OpenLDAP 2.2, the first model was the only model supported in OpenLDAP, and it was done through a stand-alone server called SLURPD. But SLURPD suffered from a number of problems and inefficiencies, and is now deprecated. It will be removed from OpenLDAP 2.4. If you are interested in using it to retain backward compatibility see the *OpenLDAP Administrator's Guide* at http://openldap.org.

As SLURPD aged the OpenLDAP developers began working on a better, more robust way of replicating directories. The result was the new Syncrhonization-Replication (SyncRepl) model, which uses the LDAP synchronization protocol to keep shadow directories synchronized with a master server.

SyncRepl

In OpenLDAP 2.2, the developers released a new, experimental form of replication called **LDAP Synchronization-Replication**, or **SyncRepl** for short. This method was both more reliable and more configurable, and it was further refined and designated stable when OpenLDAP 2.3 was released. It is now the preferred way of handling replication for OpenLDAP servers.

Unlike the SLURPD replication process, SyncRepl does not require a second daemon process. The SLAPD server implements the shadow server portion of the code, and the provider services (for the master server) are provided in an overlay. SyncRepl can use either a shadow-from-master pull or a hybrid pull/push method.

In the pull scenario (called the **refresh-only operation**), the shadow server periodically connects to the master server and requests all changes since the last time it checked. The master then sends the shadow all changed records (or, in the case of deletions, the DN of the deleted record).

SynRepl's second method (called **refresh and persist**) is a hybrid of the push features exemplified in the SLURPD model and some of the pull features discussed above (therefore it is not a *true* push method).

In this scenario, the shadow server makes an initial connection to the master and pulls some initial updates. But it leaves the connection open. When the master modifies its copy of the directory information tree, it pushes information to the shadow server using that open connection. If the shadow server gets disconnected, the master server does nothing. The next time the slave server connects though, it requests all new changes (like in the pull method), and the master sends them.

 For more detailed information about LDAP content synchronization and the SyncRepl implementation included in OpenLDAP, see RFC 4533 (`http://www.rfc-editor.org/rfc/rfc4533.txt`) and the *OpenLDAP Administrator's Guide* at `http://openldap.org`.

The SyncRepl model has some distinct advantages over SLURPD:

1. Since the shadow server initiates connections and handles updates, a network outage does not cause problems with the reliability of the directory information tree. The next time the slave can get back on line it will retrieve all of its updates.

2. There is rarely any need to interrupt service on the master server. When a new shadow server first connects to the master it downloads the entire directory information tree, so there is no need to dump the data from the master server and send it to the shadow (though that method is still supported, and it might be expedient in cases where there is a large directory information tree and a slow network connection).

3. The flexibility in choosing between the refresh-only and refresh-and-persist operations gives you the ability to choose a model that will best match your needs.

Each mode of replication has its advantages. In highly distributed networks, the refresh-only replication tends to work better as it doesn't require keeping a constant connection open across a large and unpredictable network. But since the shadow server only checks the master periodically, there can be a lag between when the master is updated and when the shadow picks up the changes. Most times this does not cause any problems.

On a reliable LAN, the refresh-and-persist (refreshAndPersist) replication may be a better choice — especially if it is important that changes get from the master to the shadow in a minimal amount of time. As soon as the master is changed, it will send the updates to the shadow server. This means that there is less waiting time.

 Even in the refresh-and-persist (refreshAndPersist) operation, a network outage is not catastrophic. The shadow server will simply attempt to re-connect to the master server, retrieving updates as soon as it successfully connects.

These comments are intended to serve as general guidelines. Since it is fairly easy to try both, you may want to experiment to see what works best for you. Generally, on a LAN, refresh-and-persist is the best choice, while on slower links, refresh-only is better. In the next section we will cover the process of configuring SyncRepl between a master and a shadow copy.

Configuring SyncRepl

The SLAPD server comes with all of the functionality necessary for implementing a shadow server, and the `syncprov` overlay provides the functionality for implementing a master server.

SyncRepl was introduced in OpenLDAP 2.2, but configuration was significantly different. SyncRepl should be avoided in production environments running OpenLDAP 2.2.

Getting SyncRepl running requires configuration on both the master and the shadow server. The configuration directives for both are added to the backend sections of the `slapd.conf` files.

Configuring the Master Server

The first thing we will do is configure one server as a master. This server will listen for replication requests from our shadow server and will send updates as requested. Throughout this book we have been configuring a SLAPD server. Now we will use that server as the master.

The functionality of the master server is implemented in an overlay called `syncprov` (which is short for **Synchronization Provider**). We need to load and configure that overlay.

Since our SLAPD server is built using modules, the first step is to add a module-loading instruction near the top of the `slapd.conf` file:

```
modulepath      /usr/local/libexec/openldap
moduleload      back_hdb
moduleload      refint
moduleload      unique
moduleload      accesslog
moduleload      syncprov
```

When the directory server is restarted the `syncprov` module will be loaded. Now we need to make some changes to the configuration section for database that we are going to replicate. The main portion of this directory configuration looks something like this:

```
database  hdb
suffix  "dc=example,dc=com"
rootdn  "cn=Manager,dc=example,dc=com"
rootpw  secret
directory  /var/lib/ldap
#directory  /usr/local/var/openldap-data
index  objectClass  eq
index  cn  eq,sub,pres,approx
index  uid  eq,sub,pres
index  sn  eq,sub,approx
index  member  eq
```

Now we want to set this database up for SyncRepl.

The first thing to add is a few additional indexes. These indexes will track a pair of operational attributes that are frequently accessed in the SyncRepl process: the `entryCSN` attribute, and the `entryUUID` attribute.

The `entryCSN` attribute is used to store a **Change Sequence Number (CSN)** in each record. The value of `entryCSN` is basically a fine-grained time stamp that indicates when the attribute was last modified. The `entryUUID` attribute, the second attribute, contains a (universally) unique identifier for that entry, and can be used to quickly identify corresponding entries on master and shadow servers. Like any other attributes, these attributes can be retrieved through an LDAP search:

```
$ ldapsearch -LLL -U matt "(uid=matt)" entryCSN entryUUID
SASL/DIGEST-MD5 authentication started
Please enter your password:
SASL username: matt
SASL SSF: 128
SASL installing layers

dn: uid=matt,ou=Users,dc=example,dc=com
entryUUID: bec1eb70-c5b0-102a-81bf-81bc30f92d57
entryCSN: 20070122003136Z#000000#00#000000
```

When SyncRepl searches for these attributes it does equality checking, so we should configure an index for performing equality tests:

```
index entryCSN,entryUUID eq
```

This `index` directive, which configures two equality indexes — one for each attribute — can be added to the `slapd.conf` file just beneath the other `index` directives.

Next we need to load and configure the `syncprov` overlay. There are only two configuration directives generally used by this overlay, so our complete overlay configuration for the master server looks like this:

```
overlay syncprov
syncprov-checkpoint 50 10
syncprov-sessionlog 100
```

The first line loads the `syncprov` overlay. The second line specifies how often SyncRepl information ought to be written to the database. Just as with the BDB and HDB backends, SyncRepl is tuned to perform operations as fast as possible. Writing to the underlying database is costly, so streamlining the process can improve performance.

The `syncprov-checkpoint` directive instructs the overlay to only write changes to the database when a new write request comes in and either a certain number of writes have already occurred (`50` in this case), or a certain number of minutes (`10`) has elapsed.

The second directive, `syncprov-sessionlog`, specifies how many modifications and deletions ought to be stored in the session log. The master uses information in this log to determine what information needs to be sent to the shadow servers. In this case, it will store the latest 100 modifications and deletions.

Our finished configuration looks something like this:

```
##############################
# Database 1: Example.Com

database        hdb
suffix          "dc=example,dc=com"
rootdn          "cn=Manager,dc=example,dc=com"
rootpw          secret
directory      /var/lib/ldap
#directory       /usr/local/var/openldap-data
index    objectClass      eq
index    cn           eq,sub,pres,approx
index    uid          eq,sub,pres
index    sn           eq,sub,approx
index    member   eq
index    entryCSN,entryUUID        eq

overlay syncprov
syncprov-checkpoint 50 10
syncprov-sessionlog 100
```

Once modifications to `slapd.conf` are finished it is a good idea to run `slaptest` to make sure the configuration file can be parsed, and then (for good measure) run `slapindex` to update the index files.

Creating a SyncRepl User

The last thing we need to do to prepare the master server is create a special account for synchronization. The shadow server will connect to the master using this account.

We will create an account similar to the one we use for performing authentication:

```
dn: uid=syncrepl,ou=System,dc=example,dc=com
uid: syncrepl
ou: System
userPassword: secret
```

```
description: Special account for SyncRepl.
objectClass: account
objectClass: simpleSecurityObject
```

We can load this record with the `ldapadd` client:

```
$ ldapadd -U matt -f syncReplUser.ldif
```

In order for the replication account to work, it will also need permissions to update the requisite entries in the directory. This means that the ACLs must grant this user the permissions. While we could spell out detailed ACLs as we did in Chapter 4, for the sake of expedience we will just add the new SyncRepl user to the cn=LDAP Admins group with `ldapmodify`:

```
$ ldapmodify -U matt
SASL/DIGEST-MD5 authentication started
Please enter your password:
SASL username: matt
SASL SSF: 128
SASL installing layers
dn: cn=LDAP Admins, ou=Groups, dc=example,dc=com
changetype: modify
add: uniqueMember
uniqueMember: uid=syncrepl,ou=system,dc=example,dc=com
modifying entry "cn=LDAP Admins, ou=Groups, dc=example,dc=com"
```

Now, the `uid=syncrepl` user is a member of the LDAP administrators group, and the ACLs that apply to that group will also apply to our new user.

That is all there is to configuring the directory to act as a master. Next, we will configure the shadow server.

Configuring the Shadow Server

We will configure our shadow server to use `refreshOnly` replication, where the slave server periodically checks the master for updates and, if it finds any, retrieves the changes and loads them into its own directory tree.

Our shadow server will be a fresh instance of SLAPD, running on another server on the same LAN. Let's start with a basic `slapd.conf` file. We will change this file as we configure SyncRepl:

```
# slapd.conf - Configuration file for LDAP SLAPD
##########
# Basics #
```

```
##########
include   /etc/ldap/schema/core.schema
include   /etc/ldap/schema/cosine.schema
include   /etc/ldap/schema/inetorgperson.schema
include   /etc/ldap/schema/blog.schema

pidfile  /var/run/slapd/slapd.pid
argsfile  /var/run/slapd/slapd.args
loglevel none

modulepath /usr/lib/ldap
moduleload back_hdb

############################
# BDB Database Configuration #
############################
# Database 1: Example.Com

database  hdb
suffix   "dc=example,dc=com"
rootdn   "cn=Manager,dc=example,dc=com"
#rootpw   secret
directory  /var/lib/ldap
index   objectClass,member eq
index   cn,uid,sn  eq,sub
index   entryCSN,entryUUID eq
#include  /usr/local/etc/openldap/acl.conf
```

This should look familiar, based on the configuration we assembled in Chapters 2 and 3. There are a few things to note though:

- All of the schemas that the master uses must be loaded on the shadow server too.

- In this case we are going to replicate the entire master directory onto this shadow SLAPD server, so we want the suffix to be the same, dc=example,dc=com.

- We do not want a root password for this instance. All updates will come from the master, and we do not want any changes to be made locally.

- There is no requirement that the indexes be the same on the master and the shadow server (in fact, there is no requirement that the master and shadow server even run the same database backends), but we do want to make sure that objectclass, entryCSN, and entryUUID are all indexed, since those are important for SLAPD's performance.

This basic `slapd.conf` file should be capable of running a stand-alone server. But we don't want to run a stand-alone server; we want it to get its information from, and stay synchronized with, the master server.

The syncrepl Directive

When a shadow SLAPD server performs its synchronization operations, it acts like a special sort of LDAP client. It binds to the master server and performs LDAP operations—usually the special LDAP synchronization operation defined in RFC 4533.

It should come as no surprise then, to find that configuring a shadow server to act like a SyncRepl consumer is similar to configuring other LDAP clients. Most of the configuration has to do with providing information about how the shadow should bind to the master and how it should perform searches.

The majority of the configuration work for implementing a shadow server is done with one `slapd.conf` directive: `syncrepl`. This directive takes a number of parameters, in `name=value` format, that specify how the shadow server is to behave. Here is a `syncrepl` directive that contains all of the parameters necessary to perform basic synchronization. In the `slapd.conf` file, this directive goes in the database configuration section for our `example.com` backend:

```
syncrepl rid=001
  provider=ldap://directory.example.com
  type=refreshOnly
  interval=00:00:05:00
  searchbase="dc=example,dc=com"
  binddn="uid=syncrepl,ou=system,dc=example,dc=com"
  credentials=secret
```

This directive provides the minimum configuration necessary to make SyncRepl work. The directive has seven name/value parameters: `rid`, `provider`, `type`, `interval`, `searchbase`, `binddn`, and `credentials`.

The first parameter is `rid`, the **Replica Identifier (RID)**. This three-digit number must be unique among all of the shadow servers that use the same master server. The master SLAPD instance uses the RID to track which consumer servers are contacting it. Typically, it is best start with a low RID number and increment it for each shadow server. Thus, `rid=001` indicates that this is the first shadow server. If we were to add a second shadow copy it would be `rid=002`.

In earlier versions of OpenLDAP the master had to contain a list of all RIDs for its consumer servers. That is no longer necessary.

The provider parameter should contain the LDAP URL for the master. Either `ldap://` or `ldaps://` protocols can be used. The host portion can be either a host name or an IP address, and an optional port can be added to the end, separated by a colon. For example, to connect to a master using LDAPS over a non-standard port you could use a provider like this: `ldaps://10.0.1.34:6868`. Note that only this simple form of LDAP URL can be used. The complete LDAP URL syntax, such as containing a base DN, search filter, and so on, is not supported here.

Using StartTLS instead of SSL/TLS

You can configure the shadow server to connect over LDAP (unencrypted) and then issue a StartTLS command to begin TLS encryption between it and the master server. To do this, add `starttls=yes` (or `starttls=critical` if failure to finish TLS negotiation should stop the transaction).

The `type` parameter determines which of the two replication modes the shadow server will use when connecting to the master. The only acceptable values are `refreshOnly` and `refreshAndPersist`.

In our example we used the `refreshOnly` option. In a refresh-and-persist configuration the `interval` parameter will be ignored.

Otherwise, there are no significant differences between configuring refresh-only and refresh-and-persist.

The `interval` parameter indicates how long the shadow server will wait before checking the master for updates. This applies to the `refreshOnly` mode where the consumer server connects, checks for updates, and then disconnects. It will then wait the period specified by `interval` before checking again.

The syntax for the `interval` parameter is `dd:hh:mm:ss`, where `dd` is number of days to wait, `hh` is hours, `mm` is minutes, and `ss` is seconds. If this parameter is not specified it defaults to one day (`01:00:00:00`). A shorter interval is often desirable especially if it is important for shadow servers to provide up-to-date information right away. In the previous example the shadow server will wait five minutes (`00:00:05:00`) between checks.

> If it is very important for shadow servers to stay closely synchronized, and the shadow is on the same LAN as the master, the `refreshAndPersist` mode is probably a better fit.

One potential difficulty with the `refreshOnly` mode arises in the case where the master server becomes unavailable (for example, because of a network outage or a server failure). How should the shadow server behave? In addition to the interval parameter, there is an additional parameter that allows tuning of the refresh interval but this option takes effect only when the master server cannot be reached.

This parameter, `retry`, provides information about what should be done when the shadow server cannot contact the master server. It looks like this: `retry="120 10"`. This instructs the shadow server to retry the connection every `120` seconds up to `10` times when the master server becomes unavailable.

> **Using the retry Parameter**
>
> It is a good idea to set the `retry` parameter in both refresh-only and refresh-and-persist configurations. This will ensure that a brief network failure does not disturb replication.

This parameter can take multiple pairs. For example, we can configure it to check a couple of times in short intervals, then (if it still cannot connect) to test again at longer intervals for a longer period of time: `retry="30 10 600 20"`. This time, if the shadow server cannot connect to the master it will try to reconnect every `30` seconds `10` times in a row. If the master still cannot be connected, then it will wait ten minutes (600 seconds), and try again. It will repeat this process twenty more times. But after these attempts the shadow server will give up trying to reach the master.

To configure the shadow server to test indefinitely — to keep trying until it connects — the special + (plus) symbol can be inserted in lieu of a retry count. For example, the parameter `retry="60 +"` would instruct the shadow SLAPD to try connecting to the master once a minute until it finally succeeds, in which case it will return to its regular timing as set in the `interval` parameter.

After the interval parameter is the `searchbase` parameter. This indicates what the base DN for the synchronization request will be. Generally, `searchbase` should be the same as the database `suffix` directive for the shadow server.

A shadow server need not replicate the entire directory information tree of the master server. For example, we could have configured the shadow server to just replicate the `ou=users` branch with a database configuration like this:

```
database    hdb
suffix      "ou=users,dc=example,dc=com"
rootdn      "ou=users,dc=example,dc=com"
directory   /var/lib/ldap
index    objectClass,member eq
index    cn,uid,sn   eq,sub
index    entryCSN,entryUUID eq
include /etc/ldap/acl.conf
syncrepl rid=001
  provider=ldap://directory.example.com
  type=refreshOnly
  interval=00:00:05:00
  searchbase="ou=users,dc=example,dc=com"
  binddn="uid=syncrepl,ou=system,dc=example,dc=com"
  credentials=secret
```

Again, note that `suffix` and `searchbase` are the same.

The `searchbase` directive is one of several that compose the search specification. We could also use `scope`, `filter`, `attrs`, `attrsonly`, `sizelimit`, and `timelimit` parameters to construct a more complex search specification. Leaving these parameters off though, we have simply accepted the default which performs a search like this:

- `scope` is set to `sub`
- The `filter` is set to `(objectclass=*)`.
- The `attrs` field is set to `*,+`, which will request all regular and operational attributes
- No `attrsonly` flag is included so both attributes and values are returned
- The `sizelimit` and `timelimit` parameters are both set to `unlimited`

The sixth and seventh parameters in the `syncrepl` directive are `binddn` and `credentials`. These are used to perform a simple bind to the directory.

When configuring the master server we created the `uid=syncrepl` account. Now we will use that same DN to connect from the shadow server to the master. As was noted before, the master server does not automatically grant this account any special privileges; the ACLs on the master will be applied to this account.

Also, size and time limits will be applied to this user. A frequently made mistake when configuring SyncRepl is to inadvertently subject the SyncRepl user to a size or time limit that is too low. The result of this is that the shadow server may only get part of the directory information tree that it is supposed to have, and will not be able to provide clients with complete directory information.

If system resources allow, you will typically want to allow the SyncRepl user unlimited time and request size.

The `credentials` parameter, in the case of a simple bind, holds the password.

 Our basic configuration uses a simple bind and an unencrypted (plain LDAP) connection. This is not secure. Using StartTLS, SSL/TLS, or an appropriately strong SASL mechanism would provide increased security.

Simple binding is not the only type supported for SyncRepl. SASL authentication can also be turned on, though this may require additional parameters:

- `bindmethod=sasl`: By default, the bind method is set to simple. To enable SASL authentication this parameter must be manually set.

- `saslmech=<SASL Mechanism>`: This should be set, for example, to DIGEST-MD5 to do MD5 hashing of the password prior to transmitting it. See the SASL section in Chapter 4 for more information.

- `authcid=<uid>`: This should be set to the SASL ID of the account that will be used to authenticate. The (similar) `authzid` parameter can be used to configure an alternate authorization account.

- `credentials=<SASL Credentials>`: The `credentials` field is used, in SASL authentication, to pass credential information to the SASL subsystem. In the DIGEST-MD5 mechanism, for example, `credentials` holds the account's password.

- `realm=<SASL Realm>`: Realm information (see Chapter 4) can be passed with this parameter.

- `secprops=<SASL Security Props>`: Additional SASL security properties can be passed with this parameter.

Finally, it should be noted that by default, during a SyncRepl operation, the shadow server does not perform schema checking on the records that it receives from the master. In other words, if the master sends the shadow server a record that violates schema constraints, the shadow server will simply store the errant record, making no attempt to validate or reject it.

Usually, it is desirable to have schema checking disabled. Since the master server should always be doing schema checking a second set of identical checks is redundant, and it slows down the replication process. However, on rare occasions it may be desirable to have that extra layer of evaluation. Schema checking of replicated records can be enabled in the `syncrepl` directive by adding the `schemachecking=on` parameter.

Configuring a Referral

Operations that write to a replicated directory information tree can only be done on the master server. You cannot, for example, change an attribute by connecting to a shadow server and performing an LDAP add operation. In other words, shadow servers are effectively read-only.

If a client attempts to modify an entry on a shadow server, that server will respond that it will not perform the modification:

```
$ ldapmodify -x -W -D "uid=matt,ou=users,dc=example,dc=com" -H \
    ldap://localhost
Enter LDAP Password:
dn: uid=matt,ou=users,dc=example,dc=com
changetype: modify
replace: description
description: testing modify against shadow.

modifying entry "uid=matt,ou=users,dc=example,dc=com"
ldap_modify: Server is unwilling to perform (53)
    additional info: shadow context; no update referral
```

In this example, when we tried to modify the description attribute value for our own record, the server responded with `unwilling to perform` error.

While a shadow server cannot allow updates of its own data, it can be configured to redirect the client to the master server. This is done by adding an additional directive to the database section (typically just below the `syncrepl` directive) to indicate what server requests should be redirected to. The directive looks like this:

```
updateref ldap://directory.example.com
```

Now, when a client attempts to perform a write operation, instead of receiving an error, it will receive a referral:

```
$ ldapmodify -x -W -D "uid=matt,ou=users,dc=example,dc=com" -H \
    ldap://localhost
Enter LDAP Password:
dn: uid=matt,ou=users,dc=example,dc=com
changetype: modify
replace: description
description: testing modify against shadow.

modifying entry "uid=matt,ou=users,dc=example,dc=com"
ldap_modify: Referral (10)
  referrals:
    ldap://directory.example.com/uid=matt,ou=users,dc=example,dc=com
```

Many clients can be configured to do what is called **referral chasing**. That is, when they receive a referral they can automatically follow the referral. In a case like the given one, the client would automatically attempt the modification operation against the master server at `directory.example.com`.

Starting Replication

At this point we have taken a close look at both the master and shadow configuration options for SyncRepl. Now we are ready to turn things on.

Once the master server is configured it must be restarted for the configuration changes to take effect. Once the `syncprov` overlay is loaded, SLAPD will be functioning as a master. This should all be done before starting up the configured consumer server, otherwise the shadow server will try to fetch information from the master, but the master will not have the necessary LDAP operation available.

After the master is running again the shadow server can be started. For a small to medium-sized directory on a network with decent bandwidth, there is no reason to manually load any directory data into the shadow server. Instead, when the shadow server initially contacts the master, it will fetch a fresh copy of the directory information tree (to the extent that the master's ACLs allow) and store it all locally.

Within a few minutes, the shadow server should have a correct and complete replica of the information stored in the master server.

For Larger Directories...

The automatic download of the directory information tree from master to shadow is definitely easy to do, but with a large directory information tree with gigabytes of information, performing the update over the network (using the LDAP protocol for every transaction) can be unduly time-intensive as well as resource-intensive.

In such cases, it is often better to use `slapcat` on the master to dump the directory contents (no need to stop SLAPD to do this), and then transfer the LDIF file to the shadow server and import it with `slapadd`.

[Appendix C contains instructions on using `slapcat` and `slapadd` to dump and load SLAPD databases.]

Since the `slapcat` and `slapadd` programs do not incur the overhead of the LDAP network protocol, they can outperform SyncRepl on adding new records. And on networks where bandwidth cannot be devoted to such large-scale data transfers, LDIF files can be transported via alternate (offline) media.

Once the directory databases have been populated with `slapadd`, you can start the shadow server.

Delta SyncRepl

By default, when the master sends a shadow server a modified or added record, it sends *the entire record*, not just the changes. This is done because the master does not keep track of what information has been sent to the shadow server.

But the `accesslog` overlay does keep track of what information is sent to the shadow servers. By configuring SLAPD to use the `accesslog` overlay to provide logging information for the the `syncprov` overlay the replication process can be streamlined, sending only the changed information instead of the whole record. This is called **Delta SyncRepl**. In modification-heavy networks or directories that contain very large records, this streamlining can result in noticeable performance improvements.

> **Delta SyncRepl** is an advanced configuration. As it involves the cooperation of a couple of overlays, as well as some fairly-complicated configuration, it may not be the best solution for all configurations. My own experience with small and medium-sized directories replicating over LAN and WAN links has been that regular SyncRepl is sufficient, and Delta SyncRepl is not necessary.

Configuring Delta SyncRepl requires a few changes on the master server, and a small change on the shadow server.

The Master Server's Configuration

The master server must be running the `accesslog` overlay, which we implemented in Chapter 5. We will start off by setting up the logging database for that overlay. This configuration is very similar to the one created in Chapter 5:

```
# Database 1: Logging DB
# This is used by the access
# log overlay
database hdb
suffix cn=log
rootdn          "cn=Manager,cn=log"
rootpw          secret
directory       /var/lib/ldap/accesslog
index reqStart,objectclass,entryCSN,reqResult eq
overlay syncprov
syncprov-nopresent TRUE
syncprov-reloadhint TRUE
```

This section creates a new logging database, named `cn=log`, into which access log information will be written.

Only a few lines in this section differ from the configuration in Chapter 5. First, the index directive now builds indexes on `reqStart`, `objectclass`, `entryCSN`, and `reqResult`. While `reqStart` and `entryCSN` are used internally, the SyncRepl consumer will make heavy use of `objectclass` and `reqResult` attributes, so indexing these will speed up the replication process.

The last four directives are new. The `syncprov` overlay must be added to the accesslog database configuration in order to configure the accesslog for SyncRepl. These two flags, `syncprov-nopresent` and `syncprov-reloadhint`, both must be turned on (TRUE) for the Delta SyncRepl to work. In fact, the `syncprov-nopresent` flag should *only* be turned on when doing Delta SyncRepl.

> **Setting Limits and ACLs**
>
>
>
> Depending on your `sizelimit` and `timelimit` settings, you may need to explicitly grant the `uid=syncrepl` user unlimited time and size limits on the `cn=log` database. Also, make sure the ACLs for this database grant `read` access to `uid=syncrepl`. See Chapter 4 for more on ACLs, and Chapter 5 for more on `limit` directives.

Finally, we want to give the `syncrepl` user unlimited search time and result size with the `limit` directive introduced in Chapter 5.

Next, we need to slightly reconfigure the database that we are going to replicate. In the `slapd.conf` file, this should be placed directly beneath the given accesslog definition:

```
###############################
# Database 2: Example.Com
database        hdb
cachesize       500
idlcachesize    1500
suffix          "dc=example,dc=com"
rootdn          "cn=Manager,dc=example,dc=com"
rootpw          secret
directory       /var/lib/ldap
index   objectClass     eq
index   cn          eq,sub,pres,approx
index   uid         eq,sub,pres
index   sn          eq,sub,approx
index   member  eq
index   entryCSN,entryUUID      eq
```

```
overlay syncprov
syncprov-checkpoint 50 10
syncprov-sessionlog 100
overlay accesslog
logdb cn=log
logops writes
# Purge logs for entries one week old, check once every two days.
logpurge 7+00:00 2+00:00
logsuccess TRUE
```

The highlighted section marks the new addition to the database section of the replicated backend database. The `accesslog` overlay here is configured to use the `cn=log` database defined previously. The only operations we need to record are those that write to the database (add, modify, delete, and modrdn).

 Depending on your size and time-limit settings, you may also need to add an explicit limits directive granting `uid=syncrepl` unlimited time and result size to finish operations.

These are the only changes that need to be done on the master. Now we will look at the changes to the shadow server's `slapd.conf` file.

The Shadow Server's Configuration

On the consumer (shadow server) side, enabling Delta SyncRepl requires the addition of a couple of parameters in the `syncrepl` directive:

```
syncrepl rid=001
  provider=ldap://10.21.77.100
  type=refreshOnly
  interval=00:00:02:00
  searchbase="dc=example,dc=com"
  binddn="uid=syncrepl,ou=system,dc=example,dc=com"
  credentials="secret"
  syncdata=accesslog
  logbase="cn=log"
  logfilter="(&(objectclass=auditWriteObject)(reqResult=0))"
```

The new portion of the `syncrepl` directive consists of the addition of the three highlighted lines at the end of the given example. These lines instruct the shadow server to consult the master's accesslog database to get information about synchronization.

The `syncdata` parameter indicates what source SyncRepl should use to get information about the records which need updating. This should be set to `accesslog` to indicate that we are using an accesslog backend.

The `logbase` directive should be set to the base DN of the access-log on the master server. In the previous section we set this to `cn=log`.

Finally, the `logfilter` parameter defines what filter ought to be used when searching the master server's accesslog. When it comes to replication, we want information about any changes to the database—adds, modifies, modRDNs, or deletes. These are all writing operations and will be recorded in the accesslog with the `auditWriteObject` object class. Further, we only want to synchronize transactions that were done successfully (remember, accesslog records failed attempts to change the directory and we don't want to replicate those). In cases where writes are successful the `reqResult` flag will be set to `0`. So we add that to our filter too.

> For a complete set of configuration files doing Delta SyncRepl, see the following Tech Note on the Connexitor blog: `http://www.connexitor.com/forums/viewtopic.php?t=3` (Connexitor is Symas's commercially-supported distribution of OpenLDAP).

Now both the master and the shadow servers are configured. When starting things up for the first time you may want to delete the old shadow database (see the instructions earlier in this chapter) and start over. Again, restart the master server before starting the consumer.

That's all there is to configuring Delta SyncRepl. Next, we will take a look at some strategies for debugging replication problems.

Debugging SyncRepl

One of the frustrating factors of configuring a network-based server-to-server setup like SyncRepl is the difficulty in debugging. Here are a few tips for making SyncRepl debugging easier.

Starting Over

Sometimes a first shot at configuring replication fails. It is possible, and in fact quite easy, to wipe out the entire database for the shadow server and then start over again from scratch.

If you are using the BDB or HDB backends, all you need to do is delete all of the data files in the database directory:

```
$ sudo /etc/init.d/slapd stop
$ cd /var/lib/ldap
$ rm -f *.bdb __db.* log.*
```

> Warning: Make sure you do not delete the DB_CONFIG file!

The next time you restart SLAPD it will rebuild the data files from scratch.

Similar steps can be taken to migrate databases, fix corrupted backends, and so forth. But these cases require a little more care. For more detailed instructions, see Appendix C.

Strategic Logging

Another way of debugging replication is to run the shadow SLAPD instance in the foreground and turn on the sync log level:

```
$ sudo slapd -d sync
```

This will print verbose information on the synchronization process.

Increasing log information on the master server may also be helpful. The acl logging level can be useful for evaluating how access rules are applied to the SyncRepl user's requests. For harder issues, the trace debug level can also be very helpful.

A Few Common Mistakes

There are a few common mistakes made when configuring SyncRepl.

Limits and ACLs: I have already mentioned the time- and size-limit issue: sizelimit and timelimit directives apply to the SyncRepl user just as they do to any other non-manager account. If the database has more entries than the maximum size limit, or the connection takes a long time to replicate, then the replication from master to shadow may end prematurely, resulting in an incomplete synchronization.

ACLs too can have surprising results in replication. If an ACL denies access to the SyncRepl user, it will not be able to synchronize that information. That, too, can result in incomplete synchronization. Fortunately, SLAPD will attempt to automatically bridge as many of these inconsistencies as it can. Unfortunately, that may keep the problem invisible for a longer period of time.

Untuned DB_CONFIG: In Chapter 5, we looked at the DB_CONFIG file, a special configuration file for tuning the BDB/HDB database backend. When configuring a shadow server it is important to put a DB_CONFIG file in the database directory (/var/lib/ldap). If the DB_CONFIG file is absent or poorly tuned, the database environment will be much slower. While that may not be noticeable to clients performing brief occasional searches, this can have detrimental effects on replication. Larger transactions (like the initial update or transferring of significant modifications) can be many times slower than they would be with a well-tuned database environment.

Sometimes, this just increases delay times in updating the database, but when combined with time limits, it can result in truncated synchronizations.

Failed SASL Authentication: SASL configurations can sometimes cause confusion when implementing SyncRepl (or SLURPD, for that matter). If you typically use SASL for authentication, and the SASL information is not stored in the directory information tree, then you will also need to make sure the external SASL data is synchronized.

In Chapter 4 we configured SASL to do DIGEST-MD5 authentication using the external /etc/sasldb2 file for storing passwords. If we are to use SASL DIGEST-MD5 authentication on our shadow servers, we will need to make sure that they each have the same /etc/sasldb2 file, which will require using some other non-OpenLDAP tool, like **rsync** (http://samba.anu.edu.au/rsync/).

One method of working around this is to store cleartext SASL passwords inside of the directory, instead of in the sasldb2 file. This is done simply by using the {CLEARTEXT} password hash instead of {SSHA} or some other mechanism. See Chapter 3 for more information. The OpenLDAP Administrator's Guide (http://openldap.org) also explains this configuration.

Simple binding (by DN and user password) should work just fine with replication, as should the SASL EXTERNAL authentication we configured in Chapter 6.

Configuring an LDAP Proxy

Sometimes, instead of replicating a directory information tree, it is desirable to proxy the communication with an LDAP directory. In this scenario a SLAPD server is configured to stand between clients and another LDAP server elsewhere on the network, and respond to client requests with directory information retrieved from the other LDAP server.

OpenLDAP supports a couple of different ways of configuring SLAPD to serve as a proxy.

Using the LDAP Backend

One way of setting up proxying between two servers is to configure one server to use the `ldap` backend (instead of BDB or HDB). The `ldap` backend listens for requests and, when it gets them, transparently forwards the request to another LDAP server. For example, say we have two servers, directory.example.com, which stores the database, and proxy.example.com which uses the `ldap` backend to proxy requests to the directory.example.com server.

From the client's perspective, when the client connects to proxy.example.com, it appears to get results from proxy.example.com. All network traffic moves between the client and the proxy, and there is nothing in the returned results that indicates that the result were fetched from another server. In addition, the `ldap` backend follows referrals automatically, rather then requiring the client application to do referral chasing.

From the perspective of directory.example.com, the connection comes from proxy.example.com.

At the protocol level, the `ldap` backend transparently forwards all requests from the client on to the other server. In other words, when the client binds, it is not binding to proxy.example.com but to directory.example.com.

> This too is configurable, and more advanced binding configurations can be achieved. Such features are discussed in the section *Using Identity Management Features*.

Every client gets its own connection from the proxy to the directory, with one exception. All the clients that connect as the anonymous user are proxied through the same connection to the remote server.

> TLS connections go from the client to the proxy. The proxy can be configured to use TLS between it and the remote server either when the client requests TLS, or every time the proxy connects to the remote server. This is done with the `tls` directive for the `ldap` backend.

Configuring the `ldap` backend to act as a proxy is very simple. Here is a complete `slapd.conf` configured for the `ldap` backend:

```
# slapd.conf - Configuration file for LDAP SLAPD
##########
# Basics #
##########
```

```
include   /etc/ldap/schema/core.schema
include   /etc/ldap/schema/cosine.schema
include   /etc/ldap/schema/inetorgperson.schema
include   /etc/ldap/schema/blog.schema

pidfile  /var/run/slapd/slapd.pid
argsfile /var/run/slapd/slapd.args
loglevel none

modulepath /usr/lib/ldap
moduleload back_ldap

###############
# LDAP Backend #
###############

database ldap
uri "ldap://directory.example.com"
suffix "dc=example,dc=com"
```

The significant points of this example are highlighted.

Once the back_ldap module has been loaded, the backend is defined in just three directives. The database directive points to the ldap backend (instead of the hdb backend we have been using in previous chapters).

The uri directive takes as a value a space-separated list of LDAP URLs. In this case there is only one. Having more than one URL comes in handy when one of the servers goes down. When there is a list, the ldap backend will try to connect to the servers in order. If the first server is down, it will move on to the second URL, and so on until it either runs out of servers or finally makes a connection.

The suffix directive indicates which suffix or suffixes this backend serves. This should contain the base DN or DNs that the remote directory provides. It is possible to use the proxy to make available only a branch or two of the remote server using this method. For example, the remote server might provide access to dc=example,dc=com. But we could set the suffix on this proxy to ou=users, dc=example,dc=com, and users of this server would then only be able to search that part of the directory information tree through this proxy.

> A number of OpenLDAP users have reported successfully implementing the ldap backend to proxy requests to other directory servers, such as Microsoft's Active Directory.

There are a handful of other configuration options available for the ldap backend, all of which are document in the slapd-ldap man page: man slapd-ldap. But we will only look at one subset: the identity management features.

Using Identity Management Features

There are more sophisticated things that can be done with the ldap backend. You can, for instance, separate the authentication and authorization tasks, authenticating as the DN supplied by the client but then performing all work as a different user.

This feature, called **ID assertion**, allows you to set up a proxy (perhaps accessible on a less secure network) that can allow users to bind as themselves, but then use an account with lower permissions (such as a system account whose permissions are restricted by ACLs) to get only a limited subset of information from the directory.

Configuring ID assertion requires only a few additional directives. On the proxy, you will need to add two directives to the ldap database configuration: idassert-bind and idassert-authzFrom.

The idassert-bind directive specifies how the proxy server ought to authenticate to the remote directory server. Here's an example configuration:

```
idassert-bind
    bindmethod=simple
    binddn="uid=authenticate,ou=system,dc=example,dc=com"
    credentials="secret"
    mode=none
```

This directive defines the account (and authentication style) that the proxy will use to connect to the remote directory in order to authenticate the client.

The supported values of bindmethod are simple (to do a simple bind), sasl (to do SASL binds), and none. If none is used then ID assertion is not done (which achieves the same effect as not using this directive at all).

The binddn and credentials parameters specify the DN and password for connecting to the remote directory.

The mode parameter specifies whose identity will be asserted to the remote server. In the given example we set the mode to none, which means that the proxy will assert the DN specified in binddn as its identity. In other words, the proxy will perform all operations on the remote server as the DN in binddn.

For a more complicated proxy, you can set mode to anonymous (which asserts the anonymous identity to the remote directory) or self (which asserts the identity sent by the client). These implement the **Proxied Authorization (proxyAuth) Control** defined in RFC 4370 (http://www.rfc-editor.org/rfc/rfc4370.txt).

For `anonymous` or `self`, you may also need to set the `authz-policy` directive in `ldap.conf`, and add `authzFrom` or `authzTo` entries to the proxy's or client's DN (respectively). For more information see the man pages for `slapd.conf` and `slapd-ldap`.

The `idassert-authzFrom` directive is used to authorize which clients can make use of the proxy. For example, we could set a rule that allows users to use the proxy if their DNs are in the `ou=users` subtree:

```
idassert-authzFrom dn.subtree="ou=users,dc=example,dc=com"
```

Like other directives that make use of the `dn` specifier, this one supports the regular list of modifiers, like `dn.subtree`, `dn.one`, and `dn.regex`. See the discussion of limits in Chapter 5 for an explanation of these modifiers.

Turning the Simple Proxy into a Caching Proxy

As we have configured the proxy so far, every request to the proxy is relayed to the remote directory server. No results are retained on the proxy. So when the same request is performed several times, the proxy connects to the remote directory server each time and forwards the request. It is possible, however, to use the `pcache` (**Proxy Cache**) overlay to add caching to the proxy, storing a subset of the remote directory on the proxy. This can significantly speed up performance in some cases.

Proxy Cache works by storing a subset of frequently-accessed information in a database on the proxy SLAPD instance. When the proxy receives a request for information stored in the cache, it will return the cached data instead of fetching the records from the remote server.

Records are stored in an **LRU (Least Recently Used)** cache, which means that once the cache fills up, the records that were accessed *least recently* are removed to make way for new entries. Additionally, an entry is only served out of the cache for a certain period of time (called Time To Live, or TTL) before the proxy once again connects to the remote directory to fetch a fresh copy of the entry. This keeps the proxy from serving stale or out of date information that has changed in the main directory since the last time the proxy accessed the records.

Binding is not cached by `pcache`. Every client connection must still bind, and the behavior of the bind operation depends on the configuration of the `ldap` backend. It can use ID assertion, or pass authentication through to the remote host.

The `pcache` overlay is configured in the proxy's `slapd.conf` file. The first few steps of implementing the `pcache` overlay are familiar. Near the top of our configuration file we need to add the `moduleload pcache` line to load the correct module.

In the database section we need to add the `pcache` overlay with the usual `overlay` directive. Then, there are several directives necessary to configure the `pcache` overlay. Here is the entire database configuration section for an `ldap` database with the proxy cache overlay:

```
database ldap
uri "ldap://10.21.77.100"
suffix   "dc=example,dc=com"
rootdn "cn=Manager,dc=example,dc=com"
idassert-bind
   bindmethod=simple
   binddn="uid=authenticate,ou=system,dc=example,dc=com"
   credentials="secret"
   mode=none
idassert-authzFrom "dn.subtree:dc=example,dc=com"
overlay pcache
proxycache bdb 1000 1 50 1200
directory /var/lib/ldap/cache
index objectclass eq
index uid,mail eq,sub
index queryid eq
proxycachequeries 100
proxyattrset 0 uid mail cn sn givenName
proxytemplate (uid=) 0 600
```

The beginning of the file does not differ much from the identity assertion configuration we used in the previous section. One difference however, is the addition of the `rootdn` directive which is required by the database-backed `pcache` overlay. It is never used for authentication purposes so using the base DN of the directory is fine.

Once the overlay has been added to the overlay stack using `overlay pcache`, the first proxy cache directive appears:

```
proxycache bdb 1000 1 50 1200
```

This directive handles the core configuration of the proxy cache engine. It has five different parameters:

- The database type: `pcache` needs a place to store the cached data, and it can use one of the underlying database mechanisms such as `bdb`, `hdb`, or `ldif`. If you want an efficient storage system, `bdb` or `hdb` are the best choices. Later in the configuration, we will have to set some directives for the database.

- The maximum number of entries in the cache: You can set an upper limit on the number of entries that will be cached. You can estimate how many entries you need based on the number of records in this database and the type of use that this proxy will get.

- The number of attribute sets to store: The proxy cache stores a subset of information from the remote directory. Which attributes are cached is controlled by defining **attribute sets**. This parameter should be set to the number of attribute sets defined. We will initially define one, so the value above is `1`.

- The maximum number of entires per search result. Some searches can return a large number of entries, and this takes up a lot of space on the proxy (and introduces inefficiency if this particular large search is not frequently performed). To avoid such a problem, this parameter specifies the maximum number of entries that a search can have if its results are to be cached. A search that returns more than the max (`50` in this case) will not be cached.

- The consistency check interval. This specifies the number of seconds to wait between checking records for expired TTLs. If a record's TTL has passed, then the record is considered stale and is removed from the cache.

The first field in the `proxycache` directive is the database type, specifying what database backend will be used to store cached data. Now we need to add a few directives to configure that database backend:

```
directory /var/lib/ldap/cache
index objectclass eq
index uid,mail eq,sub
index queryid eq
```

The `directory` directive (a familiar one we used when configuring the HDB backend in Chapter 3) points to the directory where the BDB files will be stored.

If you set `directory` to a location that doesn't exist yet, make sure to create that directory on the file system: `mkdir /var/lib/ldap/cache`. You should also put a copy of the `DB_CONFIG` file in the `cache/` directory, or else the default Berkeley DB settings will be used, and those usually result in poor performance.

After the database directive, there are several index directives which specify which indexes ought to be created and what types of searches each should support. As usual, these index files can be used to expedite performance.

There are two indexes that should definitely be included: an equality index on `objectclass`, and an equality index on `queryid`. The `queryid` index is specific to the `pcache` backend which uses `queryid` to identify queries cached in the database. Other indexes should be specified where they will increase lookup speeds for the queries defined in the proxy cache templates (which we will examine in a moment).

You can also use other directives (like `cachesize`) that are defined for the BDB backend. See the discussion in Chapter 5 and the man page for `slapd-bdb` for more detail.

Now we have a few more pcache-specific directives to examine:

```
proxycachequeries 100
proxyattrset 0 uid mail cn sn givenName
proxytemplate (uid=) 0 600
```

The `proxycachequeries` directive specifies how many queries (not entries) should be cached.

The `proxyattrset` directive indicates what attributes ought to be cached. The proxy cache stores a subset of the remote directory. That subset is not merely a subset of the total entries, but also a subset of the attributes for each entry. In the example here, this `proxyattrset` specifies that only the `uid`, `mail`, `cn`, `sn`, and `givenName` attributes (and their values) should be cached. A request for any other attribute will be proxied to the remote server.

The `proxyattrset` directive has two parts:

- The first is an integer identifier, `0` for the first `proxyattrset`, `1` for the second, and so on
- The second part is the list of attributes (separated by spaces) that will be stored in the cache

There can be more than one `proxyattrset`, but the total number of `proxyattrset` directives must be explicitly specified in the `proxycache` directive. In our configuration, we only have one `proxyattrset` directive, so the third parameter (the number of attribute sets) in the `proxycache` directive is set to `1`.

The last directive is the `proxytemplate` directive. A **filter template** specifies what sort of searches will be stored in the cache, and indicates which attributes will be stored for records that match the search filter. The directive has three parameters:

- A filter template
- The `proxyattrset` directive to use
- The TTL for entries that match this template

A filter template is a variation on a regular LDAP filter. A regular filter might look like this: `(uid=m*)`, or `(&(ou=users)(objectclass=person))`. A filter template is a filter without the asserted value; that is, it is a template with nothing on the right-side of the equals sign. `(uid=)` and `(&(ou=)(objectclass=))` are filter templates for the two search filters.

If an incoming search's filter matches the filter template (and it doesn't return more than the maximum number of results) then it will be handled by the cache. For example, the filters `(uid=*)`, `(uid=mat*)` and `(uid=dave)` all match the filter template `(uid=)`. They can be handled by the cache, but `(&(uid=*)(ou=system))` cannot as it doesn't match a defined filter template.

The second parameter is the numeric identifier for the `proxyattrset` directive that should be used. In our example we set this to `0`, which uses `proxyattrset 0`. Thus, this filter template caches the values of the `uid`, `mail`, `cn`, `sn`, and `givenName` attributes.

The `proxyattrset` directive is used to determine whether to serve incoming searches from the cache or by connecting to the remote directory. If the request matches a search filter template, and the attributes list supplied by the client has only attributes in `proxyattrset`, then results may be served out of the proxy cache. For example, if a request comes in with the search filter `(uid=m*)` (which matches the `(uid=)` template) and requests the `uid`, `mail`, and `sn` attributes, these results can be served out of the cache. On the other hand, if the attributes list is `uid`, `mail`, and `telephoneNumber`, then the cache will be skipped and the proxy will fetch the information from the remote server. Why is this? Simply because one of the attributes, `telephoneNumber`, is not stored in the cache at all, and so the `pcache` overlay cannot fulfill the entire request.

The third parameter for the `proxytemplate` directive is the TTL. This specifies how many seconds an entry can be in the cache before it is considered stale and removed or refreshed.

There is a special fourth parameter that can be used too: the so-called **Negative TTL**. By default, the proxy cache caches only successful requests. That is, if a search request is made, and the remote directory returns zero records, no information is cached.

Sometimes, however, it might be useful to cache a "miss," so that if the same query comes in again it can be immediately served from the cache, instead of requiring another trip to the remote directory—a trip likely to result in the same empty result set. The negative TTL parameter allows you to turn on caching of misses, and also set the number of seconds that a negative result (a record of a miss) should be retained in the cache.

Notes on the Attribute Sets and Templates

One of the potentially confusing things about the proxy cache overlay is the relationship between attribute sets and filter templates (and the `proxycache` directive's count of attribute sets).

Every attribute set should be referenced by at least one filter template. But multiple filter templates can use the same attribute set. For example, the following is legitimate:

```
proxycachequeries 100
proxyattrset 0 uid mail cn sn givenName
proxytemplate (&(mail=)(objectclass=)) 0 600
proxytemplate (uid=) 0 600
```

In this case, both filter templates refer to the same attribute set (the one with the ID number 0).

The same template can be used with different attribute sets. Here's what happens under such circumstances. Consider the following:

```
overlay pcache
proxycache bdb 1000 2 50 1200
# ... skipped a few lines...
proxyattrset 0 uid mail cn sn givenName
proxyattrset 1 uid description
proxytemplate (uid=) 0 600
proxytemplate (uid=) 1 600
```

The above is legal and works but has interesting results.

 Notice that the third parameter of `proxycache` is now 2 instead of 1. This reflects the fact that there are now two `proxyattrset` directives defined.

If a search is done for `(uid=m*)` requesting `uid` and `mail`, a cache entry will be generated for the first attribute set.

But if a search is done for (uid=m*) requesting uid and description, then an entry is generated for the second attribute set.

If a search is done for (uid=m*) requesting mail and description, it will *miss* both caches and results will be retrieved from the remote server.

The proxy cache overlay can turn the ldap backend into more than just a simple proxy. By tuning the attribute sets and templates to match frequently used queries, you can use pcache to improve the responsiveness of the proxy and reduce the amount of traffic to the remote directory.

A Translucent Proxy

Consider the following situation. A remote directory contains the basic information that you need. You want to create an LDAP proxy to that directory but there are a few values that you want to modify on the proxy (but not on the remote directory).

This can be done with the translucent overlay, which proxies requests to a remote directory, but also allows attributes to be locally modified and stored while not modifying the remote directory information tree. This sort of hybrid proxy is called a **translucent proxy**.

We will briefly take a look at configuring a translucent proxy.

As usual, near the top of the slapd.conf file of the proxy, we will need to load the translucency module. We will also need the LDAP and BDB module, since both backends will be used:

```
moduleload back_ldap
moduleload back_bdb
moduleload translucent
```

Now we can skip ahead in the configuration file to the database section.

For a translucent proxy we will need to configure it to store some information locally, but also act like a proxy and retrieve information from a remote directory server. Here is a sample configuration for the transparent overlay:

```
database bdb
directory /var/lib/ldap/transparent
suffix "dc=example,dc=com"
rootdn "uid=authenticate,ou=system,dc=example,dc=com"
rootpw secret
index objectclass eq
index uid eq,sub
lastmod off
```

```
overlay translucent
uri "ldap://10.21.77.100"
idassert-bind
    bindmethod=simple
    binddn="uid=authenticate,ou=system,dc=example,dc=com"
    credentials="secret"
    mode=none
idassert-authzFrom "dn.subtree:dc=example,dc=com"
```

The `transparent` overlay uses a database (in this case the `bdb` backend) to store information locally, and then implicitly uses the `ldap` backend to connect to the remote directory. As with the `pcache` overlay, it is best to use BDB or HDB for the backend data storage mechanism.

For the `bdb` backend configuration, we need the usual directives: `directory`, `suffix`, `rootdn`, `rootpw`, and one or more `index` directives (we should at least have an equality index on `objectclass`).

We also turn off modification timestamps (`lastmod off`) so that SLAPD doesn't automatically generate the corresponding `modifiersName` and `modifyTimestamp` operational attributes. You can remove this line if you want that information to be stored in the proxy's database but, when a client requests a record from the proxy, it will see different modification information than it would see if connecting to the remote directory.

The `rootdn` and `rootpw` password play a special role in a translucent proxy. This DN is the *only* user that can add new records to the proxy's database. And any LDAP modification, add, or modRDN operations that come from this user will change *only* the local copy of the data.

> The root DN can only access values on the remote server that it is allowed to access, but it can add or modify any record on the local translucent database. This means, effectively, that it may be able to write entries into branches of the directory tree that it cannot access (because of ACLs on the remote directory).

Now we have the backend database configured. Next, we want to configure the `translucent` overlay.

After the `overlay` directive, inserting `translucent` into the overlay stack, we need to supply the `translucent` overlay with information about the remote directory.

Since the `translucent` overlay uses the `ldap` backend, any `ldap` backend parameters can be used here:

```
overlay translucent
uri "ldap://10.21.77.100"
idassert-bind
  bindmethod=simple
  binddn="uid=authenticate,ou=system,dc=example,dc=com"
  credentials="secret"
  mode=none
idassert-authzFrom "dn.subtree:dc=example,dc=com"
```

The `uri` directive is used to point the translucent proxy to the remote server. And again we use the identity assertion discussed earlier in this chapter to handle authorization to information from the remote server.

Now let's examine a few examples of the translucent proxy in action. First, we can grab a record proxied from the remote server:

```
$ ldapsearch -x -W -D 'uid=matt,ou=users,dc=example,dc=com' \
    -H ldap://proxy.example.com -b 'dc=example,dc=com'
      -LLL '(uid=manny)'
Enter LDAP Password:
dn: uid=manny,ou=Users,dc=example,dc=com
sn: Kant
uid: immanuel
uid: manny
ou: Users
objectClass: person
objectClass: organizationalPerson
objectClass: inetOrgPerson
givenName: Manny
cn: Manny Kant
```

In this example we use `ldapsearch` to connect to the proxy (`ldap://proxy.example.com`) and retrieve the record with `uid=manny`.

This operation causes the proxy to retrieve the record from the remote server. It then compares that record to the information in its own database of modifications and, if any local modifications to that record apply, they will be inserted into the resulting record.

Let's say that we want to add a `description` field to Manny's record, but we only want that field to exist on the proxy not on the remote directory. We can accomplish this by using `ldapmodify`, and authenticating as the root DN for the proxy (`uid=authenticate,ou=system,dc=example,dc=com`):

```
$ ldapmodify -x -W \
    -D 'uid=authenticate,ou=system,dc=example,dc=com'\
     -H ldap://proxy.example.com
Enter LDAP Password:
```

dn: uid=manny,ou=users,dc=example,dc=com

changetype: modify

add: description

description: This was added only to the proxy.

```
modifying entry "uid=manny,ou=users,dc=example,dc=com"
```

This modification simply adds the description attribute along with the message: **This was added only to the proxy.**

> Note that in this example we bind as the DN listed as the rootdn for the translucent database. That is because this is the only DN that can write to the translucent (local) database.

Now the modification should have been written only to the translucent database. As a result we should be able to repeat our search before against the proxy and see the new description field:

```
$ ldapsearch -x -W -D 'uid=matt,ou=users,dc=example,dc=com' \
    -H ldap://proxy.example.com -b 'dc=example,dc=com' -LLL \
     '(uid=manny)'
Enter LDAP Password:
```

```
dn: uid=manny,ou=Users,dc=example,dc=com
sn: Kant
uid: immanuel
uid: manny
ou: Users
objectClass: person
objectClass: organizationalPerson
objectClass: inetOrgPerson
givenName: Manny
cn: Manny Kant
```
description: This was added only to the proxy.

When the proxy receives this search operation, it requests the entire record for
uid=manny from the remote directory. That record looks something like this (plus the
operational attributes, which are not shown):

```
dn: uid=manny,ou=Users,dc=example,dc=com
sn: Kant
uid: immanuel
uid: manny
ou: Users
objectClass: person
objectClass: organizationalPerson
objectClass: inetOrgPerson
givenName: Manny
cn: Manny Kant
```

The translucent proxy then compares that record with its own, which looks like this:

```
dn: uid=manny,ou=users,dc=example,dc=com
description: This was added only to the proxy.
```

The two records are then merged, with changes to the translucent database taking
precedence over those from the remote directory. The result is the appending of the
description attribute to the end of the returned record.

> The translucent database can be dumped with the slapcat tool, and
> backups can be loaded with the slapadd tool.

But how do we know that this modification wasn't written to the remote directory?
We can run a search on that directory and see the unchanged record:

```
$ ldapsearch -x -W -D 'uid=matt,ou=users,dc=example,dc=com' \
    -H ldap://directory.example.com -b 'dc=example,dc=com' -LLL \
      '(uid=manny)'
Enter LDAP Password:
dn: uid=manny,ou=Users,dc=example,dc=com
sn: Kant
uid: immanuel
uid: manny
ou: Users
objectClass: person
objectClass: organizationalPerson
objectClass: inetOrgPerson
givenName: Manny
cn: Manny Kant
```

A transparent proxy can be used to provide local modification of entries that are otherwise controlled externally. Like the other forms of proxying, there is no OpenLDAP-specific remote directory, the transparent proxy can use any standards-compliant LDAP v3 directory as a remote directory.

Summary

In this chapter we have examined several strategies for configuring LDAP servers to work cooperatively. We first looked at synchronizing and replicating a directory information tree from a master directory to one or more shadow (subordinate) directory servers using SyncRepl.

After looking at replication we turned to proxying, and looked at three different proxy configurations: the simple proxy, a caching proxy, and a transparent proxy.

This chapter concludes our detailed look at the OpenLDAP server suite. Next we will turn to the tasks of integrating LDAP and extending applications to make use of directory data. Most of the applications we will examine use the OpenLDAP libraries to implement their LDAP functionality.

8
LDAP and the Web

The book thus far has been focused on the LDAP services themselves. In this chapter we will look at integrating LDAP with other services. The focus of this chapter will be on integrating OpenLDAP and LDAP-enabled web services. The goal is not only to provide some concrete examples of certain web services, but also to give a general idea as to the common features of LDAP-enabled applications. We will make use primarily of the Apache web server, and of the phpLDAPadmin tool. In this chapter, we will cover the following topics:

- The basics of LDAP-enabled applications
- Using OpenLDAP for Apache authentication
- Other features of Apache's LDAP module
- Installing and configuring phpLDAPadmin
- Managing a directory server through the web interface

We will conclude with some general guidance on integrating OpenLDAP and LDAP-aware applications.

The LDAP-Aware Application

What does it mean to say of an application that it is LDAP-aware? An LDAP-aware application is an application that can make use of directory information by contacting a directory server over the LDAP protocol and performing LDAP operations.

While the most common use of directory services is authentication, it is certainly not the only thing LDAP can be used for. Some DNS servers use a directory server to store zone information. Sendmail and Postfix can use LDAP to store information on mail routing. Mozilla Thunderbird, Microsoft Outlook, and many other mail clients treat LDAP servers as address books. All of these applications are rightly considered LDAP-enabled applications.

While there are many LDAP-aware applications, not all of them support the LDAP v3 protocol in spite of the fact that LDAP v3 has been around for a decade (see RFC 2251). Many LDAP-aware applications still use version 2 of the LDAP protocol, which lacks some important features, like StartTLS support and SASL binding.

The common feature of an LDAP-enabled application is the ability to connect to and bind to a directory server. And this is the feature that most often requires configuration. For that reason, most LDAP-enabled applications will need at minimum the following pieces of information:

- A DN that will be used to bind to the directory.

- A password to use when binding.

- Information about the location of the LDAP server. This may be in the form of an `ldap` URL (`ldap://directory.example.com:389`) or a host and port pair (`host=directory.example.com, port=389`).

Some applications may need additional info, such as a search filter or a list of attributes to request.

If the DN is for the Anonymous user (which is an empty string), then password must not be set.

Of course, asking users to remember a full DN when they are normally accustomed to remembering only a login ID might not be a successful strategy. For this reason, many LDAP-enabled applications will use the traditional two-stage authentication, consisting of performing two simple binds.

Such an application will prompt a user for a login ID (usually mapped to the `uid` attribute in OpenLDAP) and a password. Then, the application will bind as an initial DN (often this DN will be anonymous), and then perform a search for the specified login attribute, in order to get the full DN. Then, the application will rebind with the newly-located DN and the user's supplied password.

In Chapter 5, we covered the different methods of binding to OpenLDAP.

In this case, the application itself is not doing the password verification. It sends the password to the directory server, and the directory server does the appropriate authentication.

In rarer cases, applications may attempt a SASL bind instead of a simple bind. Then the application will not need the full DN. Instead, it will just need the SASL-specific information for the user (such as login ID and password for DIGEST-MD5, or an X.509 certificate for the SASL EXTERNAL mechanism).

Applications that just use LDAP for authentication usually only need to perform the bind operation (or operations). Once the application knows that the user can successfully bind, the application has found out all it needs to know from the LDAP server.

Other applications (such as an address book or a DNS server) may continue to interact with the LDAP server to perform searches, or even to change the directory information tree.

In this chapter we will first look at the Apache web server's ability to use OpenLDAP as an authentication source. Then we will move on to services that perform more substantial interactions with the directory server.

Apache and LDAP

The Apache web server (`http://httpd.apache.org`) is the most frequently used web server on the Internet. It runs on most of the major operating systems, and is known for its stability and rich feature set. Almost every Linux distribution includes Apache as a supported package.

At the time of writing, Apache 2.2 is the version distributed with Ubuntu. But Apache 2.0 is still widely in use. Since configuration of LDAP between these two versions is slightly different, I will focus on Apache 2.2 but include tips on configuring the older Apache 2.0.

A Short Guide to Installing Apache

Apache has an excellent manual, and the basic configuration provided with Ubuntu (and most other distributions, as well) is ready for basic use with very little configuration. So in this section, I will provide a very basic guide to getting started with Apache.

To learn more, you may want to consult the Apache website (`http://httpd.apache.org`), the Ubuntu Apache configuration documentation (`https://help.ubuntu.com/7.04/server/C/httpd.html`), or one of the many guides, online and in print, on configuring Apache.

To install apache on Ubuntu, you will only need to run one command:

```
$ sudo apt-get install apache2
```

Installation of Apache will likely require that several other dependencies be installed, but apt-get will resolve the dependencies and merely prompt us to allow these to be installed.

 If you built OpenLDAP from source, you may be prompted to install another (possibly older) version of the LDAP libraries to satisfy package dependencies. Doing so will not harm your current LDAP applications.

In the previous version of Apache, version 1.3, an extra module (mod_ldap) needed to be installed in order to get LDAP support, but from Apache 2.0 onwards, LDAP support is included in the core Apache distribution. Later, we will install the PHP module to gain web server support for the PHP language, but for now we need no additional packages.

The Apache configuration files are located, in Ubuntu, in the /etc/apache2 directory. The directory layout looks like this:

```
$ ls -1
apache2.conf
conf.d/
envvars
httpd.conf
magic
mods-available/
mods-enabled/
ports.conf
README
sites-available/
sites-enabled/
ssl/
```

The important ones, as far as we are concerned here, are highlighted.

The apache2.conf file contains the basic settings for Apache. Apache can perform virtual hosting, where one server instance can host multiple different websites (on different IP addresses or host names). The apache2.conf file contains configuration information that applies to the core server and all hosted sites.

Like OpenLDAP, Apache's code is modular. Apart from the basic functionality of the server, features can be implemented in separate modules and loaded into the server at startup. When a module is installed, the module's configuration files are put in the mods-available/ directory. To turn on a module one need only create a symbolic link in the mods-enabled/ directory to the module's configuration files at mods-available/ and, when Apache restarts, it will load the desired module. To further simplify this process there are two tools, `a2enmod` and `a2dismod`, that can be used (respectively) for enabling and disabling Apache modules.

 The method described here applies to Ubuntu, Debian, and a few other Apache distributions, but is not universal. Consult your system documentation for specific notes on how to enable or disable modules on your server. It is usually as simple as adding a line or two to one of the Apache configuration files.

Finally, the virtual-host (or site-) specific configuration files are located at `sites-available/`. Such configuration files contain parameters that are specific to the particular virtual host, but not to the server generally. For example, say we want to host two websites on our Apache instance: `www.example.com` and `www.anothersite.com`. Each of these two sites would have a separate configuration file (usually eponymously called `www.example.com` and `www.anothersite.com`) in the `sites-available/` directory.

But simply having sites in the `sites-available/` folder is not enough to enable the site. As with modules, Apache checks the sites-enabled directory to see what sites it should activate at startup. Enabling a site takes nothing more than adding a symbolic link from the desired configuration file at `sites-available/` in the `sites-enabled/` directory. Again, the Apache utilities `a2ensite` and `a2dissite` can be used to manage those links.

Ubuntu comes configured out of the box with a default website. The configuration file is at `sites-available/default`, and it is already linked to `sites-enabled/`. We need not change this configuration file to have a basic web server running. All we need to do to get Apache going is start it up:

```
$ sudo /etc/init.d/apache2 start
```

You should now be able to browse the default website by pointing a web browser to the IP address of the server, for example `http://192.168.0.211`.

Configuring LDAP Authentication

The HTML files that this website serves are located at `/var/www/`. Let's create a new directory in this folder, and then add password protection to it:

```
$ sudo mkdir /var/www/private
```

Inside of this new directory, let's create a new XHTML page called `index.html`:

```
<!DOCTYPE html PUBLIC "-//W3C//DTD XHTML 1.0 Transitional//EN"
    "http://www.w3.org/TR/xhtml1/DTD/xhtml1-transitional.dtd">
```

```
<html xmlns="http://www.w3.org/1999/xhtml">
<head>
  <title>Insiders Only</title>
</head>
<body>
  <p>This page is private, and only authenticated users should
     be able to access it.</p>
</body>
</html>
```

This is just a simple, no-frills webpage that will set the title to `Insiders Only` and display the message: `This page is private, and only authenticated users should be able to access it.`

Granting Permissions

Apache runs as the user `www-data`. In order to serve the page to clients, Apache will need to be able to read the directory and the page. You may need to set the correct file system permissions with `chmod`. Directories will need to have read and execute permissions for `www-data`, and HTML files will need read access.

At this point you should be able to access this page by appending the directory name to the URL we accessed. In our example, the website URL was `http://192.168.0.211`. To access the `private/` directory's index page, we should be able to use the URL `http://192.168.0.211/private`.

Of course, since we have not yet configured authentication for this directory, we will be able to see the page without first logging in.

Now that we have our new folder and HTML page, we can go about securing it from prying eyes. To do this, we will configure Apache to load the LDAP modules and then add a few lines to the `sites-available/default` file to turn on LDAP authentication for that folder and its contents.

Loading the Modules

The LDAP features for Apache are all implemented as Apache modules. By default, they are not turned on though they are installed. That is, the code is present on the server, and the default configuration files are located at `/etc/apache2/mods-available`, but no symbolic links to those files are present at `/etc/apache2/mods-enabled`.

Between Apache 2.0 and Apache 2.2, the names of these modules changed to better reflect what they are used for.

To enable the correct modules in Apache 2.2, run the `a2enmod` command:

```
$ sudo a2enmod authnz_ldap
```

This will add a link in `mods-enabled` to `mods-available/auth_ldap.load`.

In the older Apache 2.0, we will need to run a similar command:

```
$ sudo a2enmod auth_ldap
```

Why the Difference?

One of the major improvements introduced in Apache 2.2 is the reworking of the "Authentication, Authorization, and Access Control" features. The result of this reworking is a cleaner separation of **authentication (AuthN)** from **authorization (AuthZ)**. This separation is reflected in module names.

Next, we will need to restart the server so that it will load and configure the module:

```
$ sudo /etc/init.d/apache2 restart
```

Once that has been done we are ready to move on to the site's configuration file and add some protection to the new `/var/www/private` directory.

Editing the default Configuration File

The `default` configuration file is around 45 lines long. It contains all of the configuration directives necessary for running a rudimentary web server.The Ubuntu documentation explains the directives in this file.

We are interested in creating a portion of the configuration file with this structure:

```
<Directory "/path/on/file/system">
    Parameter Value
    Parameter2 Value
    #...
</Directory>
```

A `<Directory>` section indicates that the configuration directives enclosed within the tag apply specifically to the named directory (`/path/on/file/system` in the given example) and its contents.

The path that is contained inside the `<Directory>` tag is the file system path, not the relative path component from the URL. That is, our `private/` directory is located at `/var/www/private/` on the file system, but it's URL is `http://192.168.0.211/private` (and its relative URL, the part of the URL after the server section, is `/private/`). In the `<Directory>` tag, we would use `/var/www/private/`.

Since the parameters between the `<Directory>` and `</Directory>` tags apply only to the contents of that directory, a directory section can fine-tune permissions, features, and services at the directory level. We will create our own `<Directory>` section to add LDAP authentication to the `private/` directory.

To set this up we will need a mixture of parameters from the Apache's `mod_auth` and `mod_access` modules, which provide basic authentication and authorization services and are loaded by default, and the `ldap_auth` module, which we just loaded in the last section.

Again, there is a difference between the Apache 2.0 configuration and the Apache 2.2 configuration. We will first take a close look at the Apache 2.2, and also provide a brief example of an Apache 2.0 configuration.

The Directory Section—Apache 2.2

Now we are ready to create a new `<Directory>` section that will apply to the `/var/www/private` directory. We will add the following just above the `</VirtualHost>` line in the `default` configuration file:

```
<Directory "/var/www/private">
  AuthType Basic
  AuthName LDAP
  AuthBasicProvider ldap
  Require valid-user
  AuthzLDAPAuthoritative off
  AuthLDAPBindDN "uid=authenticate,ou=system,dc=example,dc=com"
  AuthLDAPBindPassword "secret"
  AuthLDAPURL ldap://localhost/ou=Users,dc=example,dc=com?uid?? \
      (objectclass=inetOrgPerson)
</Directory>
```

The `<Directory>` section applies to our newly-created `private/` directory, and the directives specified in this section will force web users to authenticate when they try to access the `private/` directory or anything in it.

The first two parameters are part of Apache's built-in `mod_auth_basic` module.

The first parameter in the `<Directory>` section is `AuthType`. This parameter controls how the password information is sent from the client to the server and there are two possible values: `Basic` and `Digest`. If `Basic` is specified then passwords will be sent to the server in cleartext. Unfortunately, many HTTP clients only support `Basic`. `Digest` is more secure (setting it will instruct the client to hash the password before sending), but it is not as widely supported. Since this module uses an LDAP simple bind, the password must be sent unencrypted, which means that only `Basic` is currently supported.

Encrypting HTTP Traffic

The best way of securing this authentication process is by configuring Apache to use SSL/TLS when communicating with the client. The Ubuntu Apache documentation and the official Apache project documentation both cover this.

The value of the `AuthName` field is sent to the browser as a way of indicating what the authentication is for. For example, when a web browser tries to access a file inside the `private/` directory, the user will be prompted for authentication information with a dialog box that looks something like this:

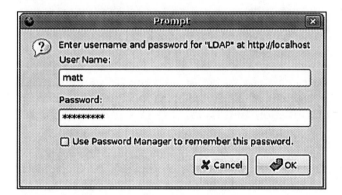

The `AuthName` appears in the first line of the dialog: **Enter username and password for "LDAP" at http://localhost**. In general, the value of `AuthName` ought to be a hint to indicate to the user what she or he is logging in to.

Moving on to the next line in the `<Directory>` section, `AuthBasicProvider` specifies which service will be used for basic authentication. Along with LDAP, Apache supports flat files, hash-style databases, relational databases and other sources.

We want to use LDAP authentication. In Apache 2.2, LDAP authentication (AuthN) and Authorization (AuthZ) services are provided by the module `mod_authnz_ldap`. To use the `mod_authnz_ldap` authentication source, the `AuthBasicProvider` parameter should have the value `ldap`. This means that when the client attempts to authenticate to the web server, an LDAP source will be used to process the authentication tokens. In other words, username and password will be verified against the directory.

Once authentication has successfully occurred, the next phase is *authorization*. During this phase the web server determines whether the authenticated user can access the requested resource. The next two parameters apply to the authorization process.

The `Require` directive specifies what requirements must be met for a user to be granted access to the requested resource. Later, we will examine ways to require that the user have a particular attribute or be a member of a particular group in the directory information tree. But in our example the requirement, `valid-user`, requires only that the user exists in the specified source (the directory in this case) and that the user can successfully authenticate.

`AuthzLDAPAuthoritative` indicates whether LDAP alone ought to be used as a source of authorization information. By default this is on, which will cause Apache to use one of the `ldap-*` `Require` values. But in the previous example all we want to do is make sure that the user is a valid user — that is, that the user successfully authenticated. That alone is sufficient authorization for us. Validity checking, in this way, is provided outside of the `mod_authnz_ldap` module, so we need to turn off the `AuthzLDAPAuthoritative` flag:

```
AuthzLDAPAuthoritative off
```

In order to use the `valid-user` value for the `require` parameter, we need to turn `AuthzLDAPAuthoritative` off so that another module (`mod_auth_basic`) can be used to handle authorization. In this case, LDAP will only do the authentication step.

The next three directives are LDAP-specific:

```
AuthLDAPBindDN "uid=authenticate,ou=system,dc=example,dc=com"
AuthLDAPBindPassword "secret"
AuthLDAPURL ldap://localhost/ou=Users,dc=example,dc=com?uid?? \
    (objectclass=inetOrgPerson)
```

`AuthLDAPBindDN` and `AuthLDAPBindPassword` specify what DN and password Apache should use to perform a simple bind to the LDAP server. When a new authentication request comes in, Apache will bind to SLAPD with this DN and password and then search the directory information tree to get the DN of the user who is trying to authenticate. In other words, the bind DN and password are used for the first phase of the two-stage authentication discussed in the first part of this chapter.

If `AuthLDAPBindDN` and `AuthLDAPBindPassword` are omitted, Apache will bind as the Anonymous user.

For this application, the `uid=Authenticate` system account will be used to access the directory. This provides a degree of security (since we don't have to allow anonymous binding and searching), and it can also provide a better audit trail of who accessed what in the directory.

 Your SLAPD ACLs will need to be configured in such a way as to allow this DN to bind from the Apache server or else the first stage of authentication will fail.

The third `mod_authnz_ldap` directive is `AuthLDAPURL`. This parameter takes as its value an LDAP URL, complete with a base DN, a search type, a search pattern, and the attributes to be returned.

In the previous example we used this LDAP URL: `ldap://localhost/ou=Users,dc=example,dc=com?uid??(objectclass=inetOrgPerson)`. Apache uses this URL to extract all of the information it will need to search for the DN of the user.

When a user logs in, as seen in the login dialog box a few pages back, Apache will get a username and a password. The username should map to the `uid` attribute of that user's LDAP record, and the password should match the value of the `userPassword` attribute (after SLAPD hashes it of course).

Once it has received this information, Apache will bind as the DN in `AuthLDAPBindDN`, and execute a search based on the LDAP URL above, with the goal of getting the DN for the user who is trying to log in.

 Note that it is Apache that does all of the LDAP communication, not the browser. At no point does the web browser connect directly to the LDAP server. This means that the directory can be secured behind a firewall. As long as Apache can contact it, LDAP authentication can be used.

While LDAP URLs are covered in more detail in Appendix B, we will take a brief look at the one we have just seen to understand its function. The protocol section says that Apache is to make an unencrypted LDAP connection:

```
ldap://localhost/ou=Users,dc=example,dc=com?uid?? \
    (objectclass=inetOrgPerson)
```

An SSL LDAP connection can be made by using `ldaps://` instead of `ldap://`. (And you may also need the `LDAPTrustedGlobalCert` parameter to indicate where the certificate authority file for the LDAP certificate is located.)

>
> **Using StartTLS instead of LDAPS**
>
> StartTLS (rather than LDAPS) is the preferred way of making an SSL/TLS connection to the directory. To use StartTLS in Apache 2.2 add the directive `LDAPTrustedMode TLS` to the `<Directory>` section. Again, you may need the `LDAPTrustedGlobalCert` parameter or other SSL/TLS parameters.

After the protocol section of the URL comes the host:

```
ldap://localhost/ou=Users,dc=example,dc=com?uid?? \
    (objectclass=inetOrgPerson)
```

In this case, SLAPD is running on the same server as Apache, so `localhost` (or `127.0.0.1`) will cause Apache to use the loopback interface to connect to SLAPD.

The next section is the base DN, the DN where SLAPD will start its search for the user:

```
ldap://localhost/ou=Users,dc=example,dc=com?uid?? \
    (objectclass=inetOrgPerson)
```

Since our users are all under the `ou=Users,dc=example,dc=com` branch, that is what we will use for our base DN.

The rest of the parameters are all separated by question marks (?) instead of slashes. After the base DN comes the attribute that SLAPD will search for:

```
ldap://localhost/ou=Users,dc=example,dc=com?uid?? \
    (objectclass=inetOrgPerson)
```

In this case, the name that the user sent to the directory should be her or his UID, so we want to look for the `uid` attribute. Similarly, you can use `cn` or any other attribute provided that you know it will return no more than one match.

For Apache authentication to work an identifying attribute must return a unique DN. The operating principle for this is as follows: if a search for an entry were to return more than one, Apache would have no way of knowing which of the records was the appropriate one for the authenticating user. Therefore, if a search returns with multiple DNs Apache will consider the authentication attempt to have failed, and will not allow the user to access the site.

After `uid` comes an empty parameter, indicated by the presence of two separators in a row (`??`) `??`:

```
ldap://localhost/ou=Users,dc=example,dc=com?uid?? \
    (objectclass=inetOrgPerson)
```

This section, which is left blank, can be used to specify the search scope. By leaving this empty, we are accepting the default scope, which is `sub` (subtree). A subtree scope instructs SLAPD to look for any records that appear in or subordinate to the base DN. Other options are `base`, `one`, and `children`.

The last field is the filter:

```
ldap://localhost/ou=Users,dc=example,dc=com?uid?? \
    (objectclass=inetOrgPerson)
```

This indicates that only records with the `inetOrgPerson` object class should be searched. When Apache processes the URL, it will construct a search filter that combines the username search with the given filter. The result is something like this: `(&(uid=matt)(objectclass=inetOrgPerson))`, where `matt` is the name of the user trying to log in.

Against our directory information tree, the search should return one DN, `uid=matt, ou=users,dc=example,dc=com`. When the DN is returned to Apache it will then perform a second bind, this time as `uid=matt,ou=users,dc=example,dc=com` with the password submitted by the user. If this bind succeeds then Apache will grant the user access.

With these parameters in the `<Directory>` section, we have now configured Apache to only allow web users to see information in the `private/` directory if they exist in the directory information tree and can supply the information necessary to successfully bind.

Changes in Apache 2.0

To get basically the same behavior in Apache 2.0, we need to make a few minor changes to the configuration:

```
<Directory "/var/www/private">
    AuthType Basic
    AuthName LDAP
    Require valid-user
    AuthLDAPBindDN "uid=authenticate,ou=system,dc=example,dc=com"
    AuthLDAPBindPassword "secret"
    AuthLDAPURL ldap://localhost/ou=Users,dc=example,dc=com?uid?? \
        (objectclass=inetOrgPerson)
</Directory>
```

This file differs from the Apache 2.2 configuration only in that it is missing the `AuthBasicProvider` and the `AuthzLDAPAuthoritative` parameters.

Other Features of the Require Parameter

In the previous section we used the `Require valid-user` parameter to enforce the authorization requirement that any user that tried to access that section of the site be present in the directory information tree and be able to successfully bind.

But there are other options that the `Require` parameter will take. We will briefly see each. Apache 2.0 used different names for these and I have put them in parentheses after the name that Apache 2.2 uses:

- `valid-user`: This requires that the user is present in the directory and can bind. This option is the same in both 2.0 and 2.2.

- `ldap-user` (`ler`): This requires that the user be in the list of users. For example, `Require ldap-user matt dave` would only allow users who are valid and who have the UID `matt` or the UID `dave`.

- `ldap-dn` (`dn`): This requires that the DN be an exact match to the one in the `Require` parameter. For example, `Require ldap-dn uid=matt,ou=users,dc=example,dc=com` would require that the user be valid and have the DN `uid=matt,ou=users,dc=example,dc=com`.

- `ldap-group` (`group`): This requires that the user be valid and a member of the specified group. We will look at this directive more closely later.

- `ldap-attribute`: This parameter is named the same in both 2.0 and 2.2. For a user to gain access if this is used in a `Require` parameter, the user must be valid and must have the attribute as asserted in this parameter. For example, `Require ldap-attribute departmentNumber=001` will only grant access to users who are valid, and also have the attribute `departmentNumber` with the attribute value `001`.

- `ldap-filter` (*new in Apache 2.2*): This takes an LDAP filter and grants access if a user is valid and if the user's record is returned when an LDAP search is executed with that filter.

Configuring group-based access can be slightly more complicated than the other `Require` directives. A basic use of this requirement looks like this:

```
Require ldap-group cn=Admins,ou=groups,dc=example,dc=com
```

[In Apache 2.0, `ldap-group` should be replaced by `group`.]

According to this directive, in order to authenticate, the user must be a member of the group `cn=Admins,ou=groups,dc=example,dc=com`. When a web user attempts to log in, Apache will bind as the user in `AuthLDAPBindDN`, do its search for the user's DN, bind as that user, and then (again as the user in `AuthLDAPBindDN`) check to make sure that that user is in the `cn=Admins` group.

In order to allow this group search to operate correctly, the user in `AuthLDAPBindDN` must have access to group entries. (Our ACLs in Chapter 4 did not allow this.) You might need to add a rule like this to your ACLs:

```
## Allow anyone to read the groups branch. (Needed for group auth)
access to dn.subtree="ou=groups,dc=example,dc=com"
        by * read
```

This will allow anyone (including the Anonymous user) the ability to read entries in the `ou=groups` subtree.

How does Apache know what type of group attribute to look for? The `groupOfNames` object class uses the `member` attribute, while the `groupOfUniqueNames` object class uses the `uniqueMember` attribute. Both are standard LDAP object classes.

Apache checks both `member` and `uniqueMember` attributes. But the case may arise where you need to treat another attribute as a member attribute. `seeAlso`, `owner`, and `roleOccupant` are all standard attributes that could be so treated, and you can also define another one in a custom schema. In such cases, you can use the `AuthLDAPGroupAttribute` parameter in the `<Directory>` section to indicate to Apache what attribute it should treat as a membership attribute.

phpLDAPadmin

We have configured Apache to use its built-in LDAP modules to perform authentication with the help of a directory server. Now we are going to turn to a more complex web-based application, **phpLDAPadmin**. phpLDAPadmin is an application, written in PHP, designed to help manage a directory server. While it is known to work on other directory servers, it was developed against OpenLDAP.

Prerequisites

Before we can install phpLDAPadmin, we will need to install a few other packages. In the first part of this chapter we looked at Apache. This (or some other web server) is required to run phpLDAPadmin. Additionally, some recent version of PHP (we will use PHP 5) is needed, along with the PHP LDAP module.

For example, to install PHP 5, we would run the following command:

```
$ sudo apt-get install libapache2-mod-php5 php5-ldap
```

Installing PHP may require the satisfaction of several other dependencies, but `apt-get` will take care of the heavy lifting for you.

> If you built OpenLDAP from source, you may be prompted to install another (possibly older) version of the LDAP libraries to satisfy package dependencies. Doing so will not harm your current LDAP applications.

Once PHP is installed, you can restart Apache, and then move on to installing phpLDAPadmin.

Installing phpLDAPadmin

The easiest way to install phpLDAPadmin is to use the package in the Ubuntu repository.

phpLDAPadmin is included in the *universe* repository in Ubuntu. This means that as long as you have the universe repository enabled in your sources (see `/etc/apt/sources.list`), you can install it with a simple `apt-get` command:

```
$ sudo apt-get install phpldapadmin
```

phpLDAPadmin will be installed on the file system at `/usr/share/phpldapadmin`, and Apache is configured to direct requests for `http://hostname/phpldapadmin` to the phpLDAPadmin application. The Apache configuration is located at `/etc/phpldapadmin/apache.conf`.

> It is also easy to install phpLDAPadmin from the source distribution available at `http://phpldapadmin.sourceforge.net`. Once the web server and PHP are installed, it is simply a matter of unpacking the source code into a folder under the web server's web root directory (for example `/var/www/`). For complete instructions, see the installation guide on the official phpLDAPadmin documentation wiki: `http://wiki.phpldapadmin.info/tiki-index.php?page_ref_id=6`.

Once phpLDAPadmin is installed, we can move on to configuration.

Is Your Package Broken?

Some versions of the Ubuntu phpLDAPadmin (notably `phpldapadmin_0.9.8.3-7`) shipped with a missing configuration file. Because of this, during the installation, you may see an error like this:

```
* Forcing reload of web server (apache2)...
grep: /etc/apache2/conf.d/phpldapadmin: No such file or directory
apache2: Syntax error on line 195 of /etc/apache2/apache2.conf: Could
not open configuration file /etc/apache2/conf.d/phpldapadmin: No such
file or directory
[fail]
invoke-rc.d: initscript apache2, action "restart" failed.
```

The problem is that the file `/etc/phpldapadmin/apache.conf` (which is linked to `/etc/apache2/conf.d/phpldapadmin`) is missing.

Fortunately, we can create a suitable one-line `apache.conf` file in the `/etc/phpldapadmin` directory. The purpose of this configuration file is to map a suitable URI for phpLDAPadmin to the absolute path on the file system where the phpLDAPadmin scripts are.

To create this mapping, we need to put only the following line in the `/etc/phpldapadmin/apache.conf` file:

```
Alias /phpldapadmin /usr/share/phpldapadmin/htdocs
```

After saving this change simply restart the web server:

```
$ sudo invoke-rc.d apache2 restart
```

Apache should then restart without an error.

Configuring phpLDAPadmin

The phpLDAPadmin configuration file is at `/etc/phpldapadmin/config.php`. phpLDAPadmin uses a config file format that, while common in PHP and Perl applications, may seem daunting to one who is used to editing the typical name/value parameter files that most UNIX applications use.

There are two major ways in which this configuration file differs from the standard type:

- The way default configuration options are handled
- The form of a configuration parameter

Regarding the first, phpLDAPadmin has two configuration files, one that stores all of the default settings (`/usr/share/phpldapadmin/lib/config_default.php`), and one intended for administrators to edit (`/etc/phpldapadmin/config.php`). Administrators should only change this second config file. The `config_default.php` file should not be altered.

When phpLDAPadmin attempts to access a setting, it will first check to see if there is a custom setting in the custom settings file (`config.php`). If one is found, that setting will be used. If one is not found, the value of the default setting is used.

The advantage of this technique is that upgrades to phpLDAPadmin need not make any changes to the custom configuration file. Only the default file is modified. The downside is that sometimes new parameters are added, but go unnoticed, since the administrator's configuration file remains unchanged.

The second difference, the form of the configuration parameter, is based in part on the first. Instead of using a simple text file to store parameters, phpLDAPadmin uses PHP variables to store information. In this sense, the `config.php` configuration file is actually a piece of code.

There are some clear advantages in doing this:

- All of the built-in PHP features can be used in the configuration file (including dynamically evaluated scripts)
- No special configuration file parser is needed, making code size smaller and run time faster

But there are definitely some drawbacks to this method, and the main one is that readability of the file can be greatly diminished. The default configuration file, for example, is almost 400 lines long and contains code (though only a smattering) mixed with configuration parameters.

Another drawback is that straightforward configuration of the application will still require some knowledge of the PHP language.

As we look at the configuration file, I will not assume working knowledge of PHP, and will explain some of the constructs in the configuration file.

A Basic Look at Configuration Parameters

The configuration parameters in phpLDAPadmin can look daunting at first. In this section, I will explain the format of each type of configuration parameter. Each section gives a very brief example of what the parameter form looks like, followed by a more lengthy description of what is going on.

If you are not a programmer, don't get discouraged if not all of this makes sense. The important thing is that you understand the structure of each of the configuration directives.

 Since this is not a PHP tutorial, I will only briefly introduce the concepts that are necessary to understand what we are doing when we set parameters. For more information on PHP, the PHP team maintains a very good online manual that can be accessed at http://www.php.net/manual/en/.

Configuration parameters in phpLDAPadmin's `config.php` file take one of three forms: a variable setting, a function call, or an array setting.

Setting a variable

Setting a variable is the simplest of the three. In brief, a variable assignment looks like this:

```
$variable_name = 'value';
```

This is how variable definitions work.

In PHP, all variable names are prefixed with a dollar sign ($). The equals sign (=) is used to assign a value to a variable. String values should be enclosed in single quotes (') or double quotes ("). Numbers (integers or floating point) need not be enclosed in quotation marks of any sort. Every line should end with a semi-colon (;). Here are two examples:

```
$name = 'Matt';
$favorite_number = 7;
```

The first sets the value of the `$name` variable to the string `Matt`. The second sets the value of the `$favorite_number` variable to the integer `7`.

There are only a few of these simple configuration parameters in `config.php`. Most take the form of the more complex PHP statements.

Calling a function

The second form of a configuration parameter in phpLDAPadmin's configuration file uses a function call. Briefly, a function call looks like this:

```
$object->function('parameter one', 'parameter 2');
```

A function may have zero or more parameters, and the number is determined by the programmer.

Functions can be attached to objects. An object, roughly speaking, is a container for data and functions. phpLDAPadmin is an object-oriented program, meaning that it makes frequent use of objects to organize the functional units of the source code.

To call a function that is attached to the object, you will need to use the arrow (access) operator (->), which is composed of a dash (-) and a greater-than sign (>). This indicates that the function is a *member* of the object. Here's an example taken from the phpLDAPadmin configuration file:

```
$i = 0;
$ldapservers = new LDAPServers;
$ldapservers->SetValue($i,'server','name','My LDAP Server');
```

The first line takes the variable named $i, and assigns it the value 0.

The second line creates a new LDAPServers object, and assigns it to the variable $ldapservers. Now, anytime we work with the variable $ldapservers we are actually working with an object that has all of the member functions and variables defined in the LDAPServers class. The LDAPServers class describes the servers that phpLDAPadmin will connect to.

You can think of a class as defining all of the parts of a machine, and the object as an instance of that machine. Once we have our copy of our LDAPServers machine, we can access the data stored in the machine, and also use the machine's functions to perform certain tasks.

According to the class definition for this object, it has a handful of member functions, including the SetValue() function. This function stores data in the $ldapservers object. So the third line in the given example sets some information about the LDAP server:

```
$ldapservers->SetValue($i,'server','name','My LDAP Server');
```

This line uses the `SetValue()` function of `$ldapservers`. The `SetValue()` function takes four different pieces of information:

- The number for the server (the value of `$i`, in this case)
- A string representing what sort of setting this is (`'server'`)
- A string that names the property being set (`'name'`)
- A string representing the value of the property (`'My LDAP Server'`)

Later we will talk about what each one of these does. For the time being, though, the important thing is to understand the general form of the function: `$object->function( param_1, param_2);`. A function can have as many parameters as the programmer decides upon.

For the most part, the comments in the configuration file will guide us as to what sorts of parameters each function will need. You should not need to look at any other piece of code to figure out what to put in an object.

Now let's take a look at the list kind of directive.

Setting an Array Value

The last sort of configuration parameter in phpLDAPadmin is the array. There are two basic forms of setting an array value:

```
$my_array[0] = 'My Value';
$my_map['Key Name'] = 'Value';
```

An **array** is an organized collection of information. PHP has two different kinds of arrays: an indexed array (where things are stored in a numbered sequence) and a map (where things are stored in name/value pairs).

An indexed array can be created like this:

```
$my_array = array( 'a', 'b', 'c');
```

This creates an array with three items, `'a'`, `'b'`, and `'c'`. The first one, `'a'`, is stored in the first slot of the array and can be accessed by index number:

```
$my_array[0];
```

Note that the first index number is zero, not one. This would return the value `'a'`. The second one can be accessed using the index number of the second item:

```
$my_array[1];
```

This would return 'b'.

In a map-type array, instead of using a number for an index, some string (or other object) can be used. For example, we can create an map this way:

```
$my_map = array( 'First Name' => 'Matt', 'Last Name' = 'Butcher' );
```

This creates an array with two items, one named `First Name` and one named `Last Name`. Now, instead of accessing them by index, I can access them by name:

```
$my_array['First Name'];
```

This would return 'Matt'.

Once an array is created using the `array()` function, you can add elements to an array by assigning a value to an array slot. For an indexed array, this might look like the following:

```
$my_array[3] = 'd';
```

This would put 'd' at the fourth position (0, 1, 2, **3**) in the array.

Likewise, adding a value to a map is similar, except in place of the index number, you use a key name:

```
$my_array['First Name'] = 'Dave';
```

This adds the name 'Dave' to the array item with the key name 'First Name'.

Finally, arrays can be nested inside of each other. Again, here is an example from the phpLDAPadmin config file:

```
$q=0;
$queries = array();
$queries[$q]['name'] = 'User List';
$queries[$q]['base'] = 'dc=example,dc=com';
```

In this example the `$queries` array is an indexed array where each value is a mapped array. So `$queries[0]['name']` and `$queries[1]['name']` represent two different name values. Each name value is stored in a different slot in the indexed array. Think of the array as being structured like this bit of pseudo-code:

```
Queries[0]:
   'name' => 'User List'
   'base' => 'dc=example, dc=com'
Queries[1]:
   'name' => 'Another List'
   'base' => 'dc=demo, dc=net'
```

Now we have two different queries (both stored in the same indexed array): Query 0 and Query 1. Each query has its own name and base.

These are the basic features of arrays—the features that we will be using to configure phpLDAPadmin. Now we are ready to move on to the actual configuration of phpLDAPadmin.

Configuring the LDAP Server Settings

The first thing we need to do is configure phpLDAPadmin to connect to our LDAP server. This is done using the `$ldapservers` object.

In my installation, Apache and OpenLDAP are running on the same server, so I will configure phpLDAPadmin to connect to the local instance.

To begin this part of the configuration we need to locate the `$ldapservers` object in the configuration file. The line we are concerned with looks like this:

```
$ldapservers = new LDAPServers;
```

It is located on line 63 of our default configuration file.

This defines the `$ldapservers` object. The rest of our configuration directives for our LDAP server need to go below this line.

The first thing to do is set up the information about our LDAP connection. We want to giver our LDAP server a name, host and port info, and information on whether we want this connection to be encrypted with TLS:

```
$ldapservers->SetValue($i,'server','name','Example.Com');
$ldapservers->SetValue($i,'server','host','localhost');
$ldapservers->SetValue($i,'server','port','389');
$ldapservers->SetValue($i,'server','tls',false);
```

This names our server `Example.Com`, and sets it up to connect to `localhost` on the default LDAP port `389` without any SSL/TLS encryption.

The `$i` in the given functions indicates the number of the LDAP server that we are configuring. `$i` is set to `0`, indicating that this is the first LDAP server we are configuring. Where we would have to configure a second LDAP server, we would change `$i` to `1` and then continue with a second batch of the same sorts of directives.

The second parameter, `'server'`, indicates that we are setting server parameters. The third parameter (`'name'`, `'host'`, `'port'`, and `'tls'`) indicates the exact server parameter we are setting, and the fourth parameter contains the value to be assigned to the parameter.

Note that the TLS setting is for turning on and off StartTLS (see Chapter 4). If you want to use LDAPS (SSL-based LDAP), then use an LDAP URL, 'ldaps://example.com', in the host setting and set the port to the correct LDAPS port (636 by default).

Next, we need to tell phpLDAPadmin where to store login information. This information is stored in the auth_type parameter:

```
$ldapservers->SetValue($i,'server','auth_type','session');
```

When a user logs into phpLDAPadmin, information used for binding to LDAP gets stored. There are three places where this information can be stored:

- A cookie in the web browser ('cookie')
- A server session variable ('session')
- (The information can be added by hand to) the configuration file ('config')

In general, we should store the information in a session variable (as the given example does). If you should choose cookie-based storage make sure you also set $config->custom->session['blowfish'] to a string of random characters. The string is used as a key for the Blowfish cipher and it must be at least 32-characters long. A longer key is better.

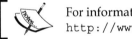 For information on the blowfish cipher, see http://www.schneier.com/blowfish.html.

The next parameter sets the list of naming contexts (base DNs) that phpLDAPadmin should display:

```
$ldapservers->SetValue($i,
    'server','base'(,array('dc=example,dc=com'));
```

This sets up only one context DN: dc=example,dc=com. While this setting is necessary on some LDAP servers, OpenLDAP should not need it. OpenLDAP publishes a list of contexts in the Root DSE record, and phpLDAPadmin can get the information from there. In fact, that is the default configuration for phpLDAPadmin, so the setting can be left off or set to this:

```
$ldapservers->SetValue($i,'server','base',array());
```

This creates an empty list of contexts (array()), and causes phpLDAPadmin to look up the supported contexts in the Root DSE.

There are just two parameters left to look at:

```
$ldapservers->SetValue($i,'login','anon_bind',false);
$ldapservers->SetValue($i,'appearance','password_hash','ssha');
```

Let's see these two settings:

- The first setting disables anonymous binding. This will prevent users from accessing phpLDAPadmin without logging in first. Even if this is allowed though, the ACLs in SLAPD will still prevent such users from modifying the directory information tree.

- The second setting sets the default password hash to be used. Instead of using the LDAP Password Modify extended operation, phpLDAPadmin attempts to directly modify the userPassword attribute. In order to do this it must perform all of the encryption and base-64 encoding before sending the update to SLAPD. This setting tells phpLDAPadmin which hashing algorithm should be used when modifying passwords. OpenLDAP uses SSHA by default, and so we should set phpLDAPadmin to do the same.

  If you set a different value in slapd.conf using the password-hash directive, you should set the same value here.

 Not all of the cipher options in phpLDAPadmin are supported by OpenLDAP (or any other LDAP server, for that matter). You should not use the blowfish cipher for passwords. OpenLDAP does not support that cipher and phpLDAPadmin incorrectly labels it as a crypt hash.

While there are many other configurable parameters in the phpLDAPadmin configuration file, we have the basics configured. We can now test out the phpLDAPadmin tool with our web browser.

A First Look at phpLDAPadmin

With PHP installed, Apache restarted, and phpLDAPadmin configured, we are now ready to connect to phpLDAPadmin. Ubuntu installs phpLDAPadmin so that it is available at the URL http://<hostname or IP address>/phpldapadmin/. In this case I am running the web browser on the same machine as the Apache server, so http://localhost/phpldapadmin points to the phpLDAPadmin tool.

When phpLDAPadmin first loads, it will look something like this:

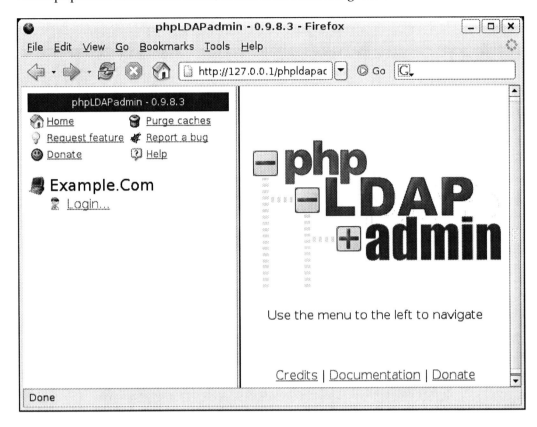

The left-hand frame is the navigation frame for phpLDAPadmin. The computer icon accompanied by the text **Example.Com** indicates the server that we configured. If phpLDAPadmin has been configured with multiple hosts, then the left frame will list them all.

Here is the screenshot:

At the top section, just below the version banner (**phpLDAPadmin – 0.9.8.3**), there are six links. The **Home** link points to this page. **Request feature**, **Donate**, and **Report a bug** all point to various places on the external phpLDAPadmin website. **Help** loads an internal page that in turn points back to the phpLDAPadmin forum website.

Finally, the **Purge caches** link can be used to purge the internal caches of copies of LDAP data that phpLDAPadmin uses to optimize performance. This may be necessary if phpLDAPadmin displays an old copy of some piece of data when it should display a more recent update.

To log in to our server, click on the **Login...** link beneath the **Example.Com** icon. This will load the login screen in the main frame on the right side.

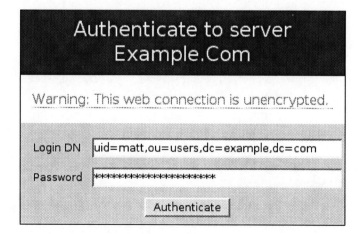

Note that unlike Apache by default, phpLDAPadmin by default requires that you enter your entire DN to log in. It then binds directly as that DN.

> The warning message **Warning: This web connection is unencrypted** indicates that the connection between the browser and the web server is HTTP and not the encrypted HTTPS. For an application like this, it is a good idea to configure Apache to use HTTPS. For more information, see `http://httpd.apache.org/docs/2.0/ssl/`.

If the `anon_bind` parameter in the phpLDAPadmin `conf.php` file is set to `true` instead of `false`, users will also be able to check a box to log in as the Anonymous user:

```
$ldapservers->SetValue($i,'login','anon_bind',true);
```

In that case they will not need to enter either a DN or a password, but phpLDAPadmin will allow them to browse the directory information tree to the extent allowed by the ACLs.

Navigating phpLDAPadmin

Once you have logged in, the navigation frame will display a list of directory information trees hosted on this directory server, as shown in the screenshot:

Beneath **Example.Com**, there is now a list of seven links:

- **schema**: Clicking this displays the entire schema (from `cn=subschema`) that this LDAP server supports.
- **search**: This loads the main search form for performing simple LDAP searches.

- **refresh**: This refreshes the data currently displayed in the tree beneath. If entries get added, but don't immediately show up, clicking **refresh** should do the trick.

- **info**: The **info** link loads the Root DSE information (decoded to make it easier for humans to read) in the main frame. This can be a very useful resource for finding out about the directory server. (See Appendix C for more information about the Root DSE.)

- **import**: This uploads an LDIF file, and then attempts to add the entries to the directory server (via an LDAP add operation).

- **export**: Using this link you can download a copy of the contents of the directory. This too uses the LDAP protocol, which means that it is subject to ACLs and might not export everything. In other words, it is not a replacement for slapcat. It does have the added advantage though, of being able to export to LDIF, DSML (an XML format), CSV (comma separated version), and VCARD.

- **logout**: This link logs the current user out of phpLDAPadmin.

Underneath this list of links are the base entries for the two directory information trees currently hosted on this server, the cn=log tree, which holds the accesslog, and the dc=example,dc=com tree which holds the directory entries we have been creating throughout this book.

Both of these trees show up because the base DN set in config.php looks like this: $ldapservers->SetValue($i, 'server', 'base', array());. This caused phpLDAPadmin to use information from the Root DSE to determine which directory information trees were hosted here. The Root DSE returned two: cn=log and dc=example,dc=com.

Clicking on a plus (+) icon expands that part of the tree, and shows the subordinate entries:

Navigating the directory information tree then, can be done quickly and efficiently through the left-pane navigation.

Each entry in the tree has only the RDN portion of the DN displayed. Through viewing the hierarchy one can build the full DN, but if you wish to display the full DN by default you can set the following parameter in the `config.php` file:

```
$config->custom->appearance['tree_display_format'] = '%dn';
```

Conversely, if you want to show just the value of the RDN, without the `attr=` part, you can set it to `%rdnValue` in the given parameter instead.

Viewing and Modifying a Record

To view an entire record, simply click on the desired entry in the hierarchy view in the left-hand navigation frame. For example, if we click on `cn=Admins` the full record will be displayed in the main frame:

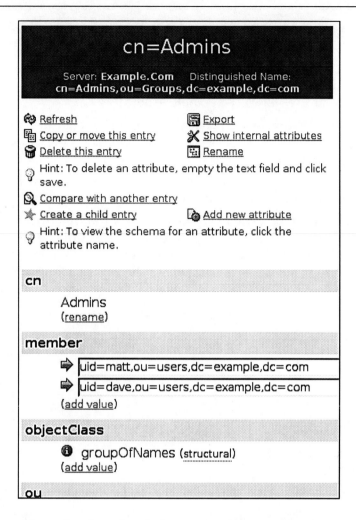

This screen provides a number of tools for manipulating a record, as well as a full display of all of the record's attributes. The tools are as follows:

- **Refresh**: This refreshes the current record. This may be useful in situations where the entry may have changed since the last time this page was loaded.

- **Copy or move this entry**: This can be used to relocate (or make a copy of) the entry to another location in the directory information tree.

- **Delete this entry**: This runs an LDAP delete on the record, removing it from the directory information tree.

- **Compare with another entry**: This shows a side-by-side editable view of two different records in the directory. This can be useful to visually scan two records, or to look at one record as a reference for creating another.

- **Create a child entry**: This creates a new entry that is subordinate to the presently selected one.

- **Export**: This performs the same function as the **Export** link in the left navigation pane except that it selects the present entry by default, instead of requiring the user to select a point to export.

- **Show internal attributes**: This displays the operational attributes for the selected record. Of course, operational attributes cannot be modified by a client application and so these attributes will be read-only.

- **Rename**: This allows you to change the RDN of an entry (such as we have done with the `ldapmodrdn` command line tool).

- **Add new attribute**: Using this, you can add new attributes to an entry. phpLDAPadmin allows you to pick from a list of attributes that the object classes of the current record allows a record to have. In other words, there is no danger of accidentally selecting an attribute that is not allowed for that record.

Beneath this selection of tools is a display of all of the attributes for the current record:

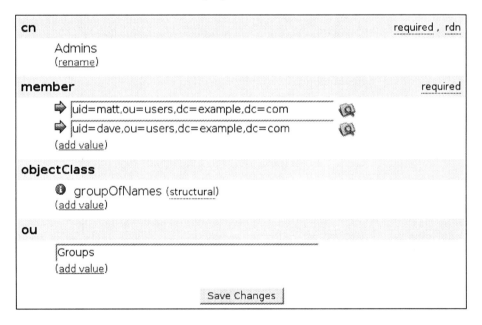

The `cn=Admins` group record has the following (non-operational) attributes: `cn`, `member`, `objectclass`, and `ou`. phpLDAPadmin analyzes the record and presents options that are fitting for the record.

First, cn cannot be modified since it is used in the RDN (as is noted on the far right-hand side). Also, it is labeled as **required**. Clicking on the **rename** link will do the same thing as the **rename** option in the list of tools: it will prompt me to perform a modrdn operation.

Under the member attribute, which is also required, there are two values: the DNs of the users who are members of this group.

The arrows (➡)to the left of the DNs are links pointing to the records of those users. If you click on the link it will load a page similar to this one that allows you to edit the record for that DN.

On the other side of the member DN fields are icons that look like a directory with a magnifying class (🔍). Clicking on this will allow you to navigate the directory tree to find another DN to place in this field.

We will look at that dialog in just a moment. But first, we will look into adding a new group member to our group by adding a new attribute value.

Looking at the **member** section of the record display, we can add a new member by clicking on the **add value** link. This will bring up an attribute editing screen:

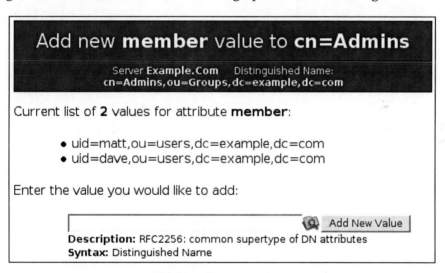

The attribute editing screen is used to add a new attribute to an existing record. At the top of the screen, we can see some basic information about what attribute (**member**) we are adding to which record (**cn=Admins**).

Next, the attribute editor lists the existing values of the attribute (since this group already has two members). Finally, there is a single-text input box to allow us to enter a new member.

phpLDAPadmin examines the schema for this attribute and displays the schema description as well as a human-readable description of the syntax.

Also, since the value of this field is a DN, the find icon (the folder image with the magnifying glass) appears on the right side. We can click that icon to bring up the find dialog, and in that window we can navigate the directory information tree in search of the DN we want to add. This is what it will look like:

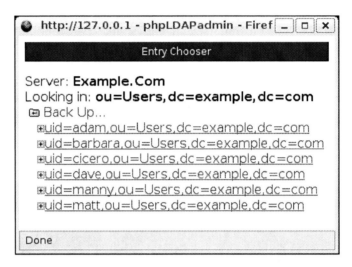

Clicking on a plus sign (+) icon will expand that branch of the tree, while clicking on the DN itself will insert that DN into the field on the attribute editing screen.

 This finding dialog is used frequently in phpLDAPadmin, and provides a simple tree navigation tool for locating entries within the directory information tree.

Now we have the desired value in the new `member` field:

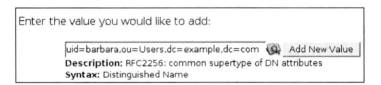

Clicking the **Add New Value** button will provisionally add this attribute to our `cn=Admin` group, and return us to the record view. Our new addition is shwon on the main record view:

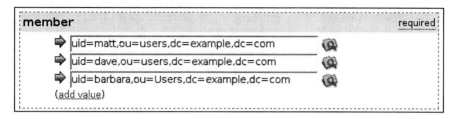

Now we have three members. At the bottom of this page is a button labeled **save changes**. This button saves any changes made directly to fields on this page, but it is not needed to save the new group member—the user uid=barbara has already been added to the group.

Notice that the objectClass field does not allow modification of structural object classes. That is because LDAP does not allow changing an entry's structural object class. However, new object classes (auxiliary ones) can be added using the **add value** link.

Also, next to each object class is an information icon (❶)—a blue circle with a white letter i.

Clicking on this icon will load the schema viewer for that object class, which displays helpful information about an object class:

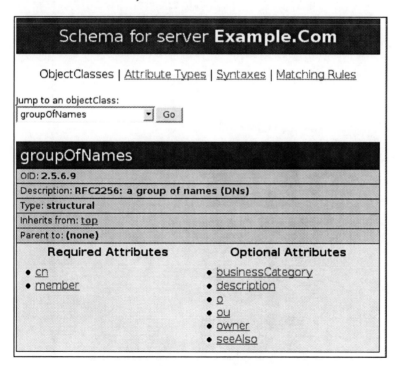

The schema viewer shows all of the information stored in the LDAP schema, but in a much more human-friendly way than the schema files we looked at in Chapter 6. The schema viewer provides an interface to view object classes, attribute definitions, matching rules, and syntax information. In this case it is showing the `groupOfNames` object class. Attributes and superior object classes are linked which makes it much easier to navigate through the schemas. Additionally, there is a **Jump to an objectClass** drop-down list that provides a fast way to look at some of the other object classes.

Adding a New Record

New records can be added from many points in phpLDAPadmin. Anywhere there is a star icon (✳), it denotes a position where a new subordinate record can be added.

Let's add a simple user account. To do this we will use the tree view in the left-hand navigation pane to locate the `ou=Users` branch:

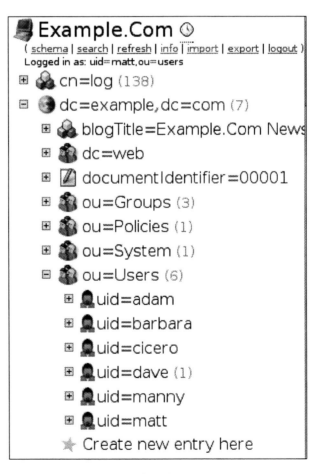

Clicking on the star icon (**Create new entry here**) will load the record creation view into the main frame. From here we can begin defining our new user's entry.

The first thing to do is select a structural object class for our new user. phpLDAPadmin gives us a list to choose from:

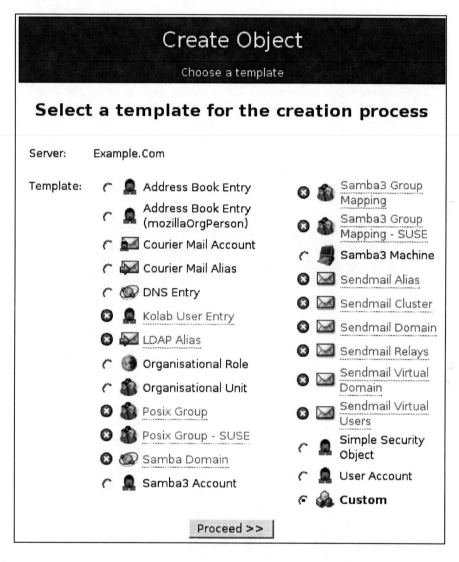

The phpLDAPadmin system has a number of pre-defined templates for adding new entries but our LDAP server is not configured with all of the object classes that phpLDAPadmin supports. (Many of these schemas are defined, though, in the /etc/ldap/schemas/ directory.)

Attempting to add a **User Account** (which uses the `posixUser` object class, as defined in `nis.schema`) will cause problems when you try to create the user.

Those that are defined in phpLDAPadmin but are disabled in the template definition are marked with a white arrow on a black circle; they cannot be selected.

> New custom templates can be created and added easily. Templates are simple XML files stored at `/etc/phpldapadmin/templates/`. To add a new template, just create a new XML file (or copy and modify an existing one), save it in the `templates/` directory, and then use the **Purge cache** tool in phpLDAPadmin to force a reload of the XML files. See the bundle of examples included with this book (available at the Packt website: `http://www.packtpub.com`).

We want to create a new `inetOrgPerson` object. Since there is no pre-defined template for an `inetOrgPerson`, we will use the **Custom** template.

The first thing to do is create the DN and decide on a structural object class:

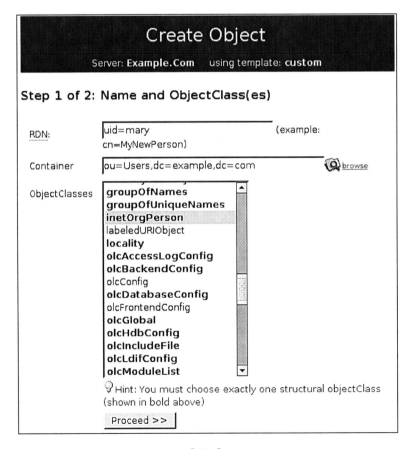

Our new user's UID will be mary and, as always, we will be using uid as the attribute in the RDN. The user will be in the ou=Users organizational unit. And we want to select inetOrgPerson (and person and organizationalPerson) from the list of object classes. Clicking **Proceed >>** will bring us to the next screen, where we can fill out a number of attribute values. Here is the next screen:

The required attributes are at the top of the form. After that, there is a section for selecting multiple optional attributes and giving them values. If you add a userPassword value here, it will be properly encrypted and stored on the directory server.

Scrolling to the bottom of this page there is a button labeled **Create Object**. Clicking that will perform an LDAP add operation on the directory server.

Once the new user is created phpLDAPadmin will display the entry.

Other templates streamline this process by automatically selecting the correct object classes and narrowing down the available attributes to just those used most often.

Searching with phpLDAPadmin

The last task we are going to look at with phpLDAPadmin is **searching**. phpLDAPadmin comes with a set of searching utilities that can be used to find information in the directory information tree.

To get to the search screen, click on **search** in the left-hand navigation frame. This will take you to the basic search screen:

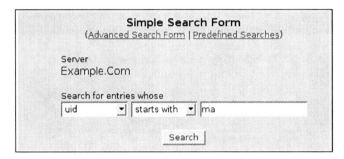

Here, we will search for any entries whose UID starts with the string ma. Pressing the **Search** button will execute the search, which, for our directory, returns four records:

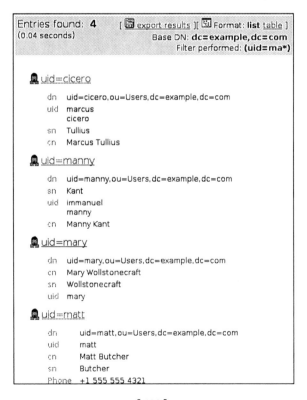

This returned all of the users who had a UID that starts with ma. Note that, by default, the search will check all available directory contexts. That might mean that one directory information tree will have zero search results and another may have a host of matches.

Sometimes it is nice to have more control over the LDAP search though. Clicking the **Advanced Search Form** link at the top of the simple search screen will load a search screen with more options:

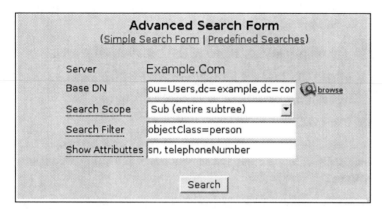

This allows us to explicitly set the base DN, the scope, and the search filter, as well as specify a list of attributes that we want returned. In short, this search form contains the fields we are accustomed to seeing in other LDAP applications, like the ldapsearch command-line client.

This too will return a list of items matching our specification.

The third search option is **Predefined Searches**. This tool is especially helpful for running searches with the same parameters time after time.

The searches are predefined at the bottom of the config.php file in the /etc/phpldapadmin/ directory. The predefined search section begins like this:

```
$q=0;
$queries = array();
```

The first line sets up a query counter and the second line creates a new array of queries. We are going to add configuration directives to the $queries array.

A search definition looks like this:

```
$queries[$q]['name']       = 'Users with Email Addresses';
$queries[$q]['base']       = 'ou=Users,dc=example,dc=com';
$queries[$q]['scope']      = 'sub';
$queries[$q]['filter']     = '(&(objectClass=inetOrgPerson)(mail=*))';
$queries[$q]['attributes'] = 'cn, uid, mail';
```

Each line adds a new name/value pair to the first slot in the `$queries` array (remember, `$q` is `0`, which indicates the first slot of the array). By now, the format of such a filter ought to look pretty familiar:

- `name`: The human-readable name of the pre-defined search.
- `base`: The base DN that the search will start with.
- `scope`: The search scope (base, one, sub, children).
- `filter`: The LDAP filter.
- `attributes`: The list of attributes that should be returned to the user. Note that the attribute list is enclosed by quotes and values are separated by commas.

If we were to create a second filter, we would first increment the `$q` variable, and then define a new set of parameters:

```
$q++;
$queries[$q]['name']       = 'Entries with SeeAlso attributes';
$queries[$q]['base']       = 'dc=example,dc=com';
$queries[$q]['scope']      = 'sub';
$queries[$q]['filter']     = '(seeAlso=*)';
$queries[$q]['attributes'] = 'cn, description';
```

The line `$q++` changes the value of `$q` from `0` to `1`, putting the next five parameters in the next indexed slot of the `$queries` array.

Once we have defined the filters and saved the file, we are ready to test them out. There is no need to restart Apache or SLAPD; phpLDAPadmin reads its configuration file with every new request, and will pick up our changes immediately.

Here is the screen for **Predefined Searches**:

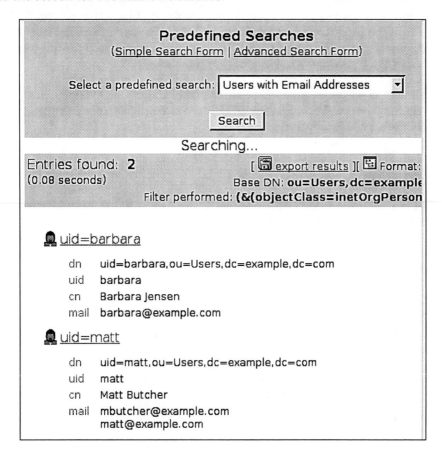

With the predefined search, all we must do to run it is select the desired search from the drop down list at the top of the page and press the **Search** button. Since the filter is stored in the configuration file, phpLDAPadmin doesn't need any additional information from us.

We've now looked at the main features of phpLDAPadmin, a well-developed tool for managing an LDAP directory through a web interface.

phpLDAPadmin is not the only Open Source program for managing directory servers. There are standard desktop tools like GQ (http://gq-project.org), and dozens of other web-based LDAP tools. There are also plugins to bring LDAP support to other popular web-based applications (like Squirrelmail, Joomla, and OpenCms).

There are also tools available to bring LDAP services to other authentication tools. For example, the `libpam-ldap` package provides **PAM (Pluggable Authentication Modules)** with the capabilities for performing LDAP lookups. And **saslauthd**, an SASL daemon that provides authentication services, can also be configured to connect to an LDAP server for authentication purposes.

Finally, there are a whole host of DNS servers, mail servers, file servers, and other packages that can be configured to use LDAP to store and retrieve information, particularly authentication information.

Summary

In this chapter, we have looked at configuring other tools to interoperate with OpenLDAP. We began with the Apache web server, using LDAP as a source of authentication and authorization. Next we installed phpLDAPadmin, a web-based program for managing directory servers. We looked at the main features and did some custom tuning.

Of course, this is only scratching the surface of the applications that are LDAP-enabled. The information presented in this chapter should get you going on implementing any LDAP-enabled application, since they all require the same basic configuration information: host, port, bind information, and search filters.

To find out more about LDAP-enabled applications, you may want to take a look at some of the Open Source package websites like Freshmeat.Net (`http://freshmeat.net`) and Source Forge (`http://sourceforge.net`).

A
Building OpenLDAP
from Source

In this appendix, we will walk through the process of building OpenLDAP from source code. We will begin by configuring our Linux platform to compile OpenLDAP. Then we will configure, compile, and install OpenLDAP. Compiling OpenLDAP might sound daunting, but it is not, and I have attempted to provide instructions straightforward enough that even those without experience of C will be able to quickly compile from source.

Why Build from Source?

Many Linux and UNIX distributions are slow to migrate from one version of OpenLDAP to another. The reasons for this are open to speculation, but one reason may be that distribution maintainers are reluctant to quickly adopt new versions of software when it already performs well, is integrated with other services, and performs a task that is security-sensitive and functionally central to many organizations. OpenLDAP, providing authentication services, is just such a service.

Because of this reluctance, you may not find the latest and greatest version of OpenLDAP included in your Linux or UNIX distribution of choice. If you need (or want) the newest features that OpenLDAP has to offer, you may want to fetch a clean copy of the source code and build from scratch.

Getting the Code

To get the latest version of the code visit the official OpenLDAP website at http://openldap.org. This site is hosted by the **OpenLDAP Foundation**, a non-profit group that governs and oversees the OpenLDAP project.

On the home page you will find a link to the current release in a highlighted box in the lower right-hand corner,as shown in the screenshot:.

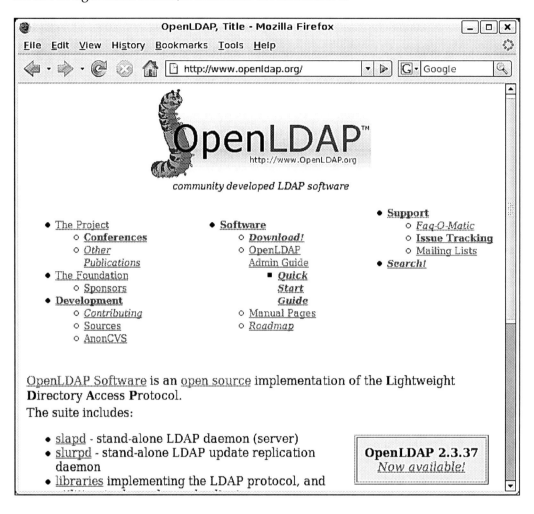

You can download the most recent stable version directly from there, or you can visit the download page (listed as **Download!**) in the center column of the table of links to find other versions (past versions, current experimental and beta versions, and so on).

The Tools for Compiling

Whenever you build an application from source code, you need the right set of tools and libraries. OpenLDAP is no exception. Thankfully, OpenLDAP is a little lighter on requirements than some server applications out there.

Compiling is done on the command line, so you will need to open a terminal or otherwise gain access to the shell.

Build Tools

You will need the standard tool chain for working with C and C++ applications; a C compiler, a linker, and a make program. Fortunately, all of these come as standard with almost every Linux distribution available. You can test your system for the appropriate tools using the `which` command, which will tell you where the tools are located on your filesystem (assuming they are in one of the directories listed in your `$PATH` environment variable).

Here's a quick example of how you can check to see where the tools are and what the current version of each tool is. My system is Ubuntu Linux 6.06. Version numbers on your own system may vary. That's okay. OpenLDAP should compile on all modern Linux distributions, and probably on all modern UNIX distributions as well.

```
$ gcc --version
gcc (GCC) 4.0.3 (Ubuntu 4.0.3-1ubuntu5)
Copyright (C) 2006 Free Software Foundation, Inc.
This is free software; see the source for copying conditions.
There is NO warranty; not even for MERCHANTABILITY or FITNESS FOR A
PARTICULAR PURPOSE.
$ which ld
/usr/bin/ld
$ ld --version
GNU ld version 2.16.91 20060118 Debian GNU/Linux
Copyright 2005 Free Software Foundation, Inc.
This program is free software; you may redistribute it under the terms
of the GNU General Public License.  This program has absolutely no
warranty.
$ which make
/usr/bin/make
$ make --version
GNU Make 3.81beta4
Copyright (C) 2003  Free Software Foundation, Inc.
This is free software; see the source for copying conditions.
There is NO warranty; not even for MERCHANTABILITY or FITNESS FOR A
PARTICULAR PURPOSE.
This program built for i486-pc-linux-gnu
$
```

In each case I used the `which` tool to know where the tool was located. The programs I checked were `gcc`, `ld`, and `make` — the compiler, linker, and make program (respectively). As long as some path is returned, this indicates that the tool is installed. If no command is found, `which` returns without any output. Thus, if I searched for a fake command, `blah`, the output would look like this:

```
$ which blah
$
```

Thus, if you run `which` for any of the programs (`gcc`, `ld`, or `make`), and get no output, it indicates that you do not have the required tool.

> On some UNIX systems, the GCC compiler (`gcc`) may not be present, but another C compiler may exist. The *de facto* name for C compilers is `cc`, and if `which gcc` yields no result, you may want to try `which cc`.

After the `which` command in the given example, I ran each command with the `--version` flag (with *two* dashes before `version`) to tell me which version was installed. The `--version` flag is a GNU standard, but non-GNU programs (such as other versions of `make` or `cc`) may not support it.

The next thing to do is set a couple of environment variables that will provide some basic settings for the given tools. While there are many options that you can provide to your tools through environment variables, here we will just provide the basics for building OpenLDAP.

> Some Linux and UNIX distributions set the necessary environment variables for you. In such cases, it is almost always better to use the already-defined environment variables, which are often optimized specifically for your system, rather than the generic ones we will be setting now.
>
> To find out if you have the necessary environment variables, run the `env` command (with no arguments) and check the output to see if `CC`, `CFLAGS`, and `PATH` are defined.

One way to set environment variables is with the `export` command. When you use the `export` command, the environment variables will be stored for the duration of your shell session (in other words, until you exit from the shell or close the terminal window). Here we will set the necessary environment variables using `export`:

```
$ export CC=gcc
$ export CFLAGS="-O2"
```

The first export sets the $CC environment variable to gcc. The make program will use this to determine which compiler to use. (If you are using the cc compiler instead, then adjust the example to point to cc instead of gcc). Note that when you *set* an environment variable, you do not use the dollar sign ($) before the variable name. When you *reference* the variable however, you will need to include the dollar sign.

The second line sets the $CFLAGS variable. The $CFLAGS variables are the options that get passed to the compiler during compilation. In this case, we are passing it the option -02 (that's a captial letter O, not a zero). This tells the compiler to use level 2 optimization when compiling the code.

The $PATH environment variable should also be set. However, by using the which command to see where our tools were, we have already verified that the necessary directories (that is, the directories that contain our tools) are specified in the $PATH variable.

If you are dealing with a non-standard system or non-standard builds of any of the libraries, or if you are interested in passing some other options to the build tools, you may also have to use some additional environment variables. You can use $CPPFLAGS to pass options to the C preprocessor (cpp, part of GCC). Likewise, you can pass the linker (ld) options with the $LDFLAGS variable. Finally, if you have libraries (compiled modules of code used by other applications) that are stored in non-standard places, you can use the $LIBS variable to specify the location of these libraries. If you need to use the variables you should consult the documentation for the tools and libraries.

At any point you can check your environment variables with some simple commands. The env command (executed with no arguments) will list all of the environment variables currently defined, as well as their values. You can also check an individual environment variable with the echo command. Simply type echo, followed by the name of the environment variable to display the value of that environment variable:

```
$ echo $PATH
/usr/local/sbin:/usr/local/bin:/usr/sbin:/usr/bin:/sbin:/bin:/usr/bin
/X11:/usr/games
```

In this example echo $PATH shows the list of directories the shell searches to find programs. As you may recall the which command, when run, printed out the location of the specified tool. To find tools it searched each of the directories specified in the $PATH variable.

At this point we are ready to move on to the next step: installing the necessary dependencies.

Installing Dependencies

Dependencies are packages that OpenLDAP will require to compile and to run. Installing these dependencies will vary from platform to platform (and from Linux distro to Linux distro). Here, I will use the Debian tools (included in Ubuntu Linux) to install packages.

OpenLDAP requires standard C libraries, regular expression libraries, and the Berkeley DB 4.2 (or later) libraries. These are almost always included in modern Linux distributions. In addition to the libraries, the header files are also required. Often these are stored in separate packages (usually called DEV packages). To install, for example, the Berkeley DB 4.2 development package in Ubuntu, you can execute the following command from the command line:

```
$ sudo apt-get install libdb4.2-dev
```

This will fetch and install the required package.

There are various other packages that are useful to install, and we will need them in order to build all of the features that we use in this book. You will need to install:

- OpenSSL (for SSL and TLS support)
- SASL 2 (for SASL authentication support)

If you are interested in storing your directory in a relational database engine, such as MySQL or Oracle, you might also want to install iODBC2 (for database backend support).

All of these packages are common on modern Linux system. Make sure that the packages are installed, and that the DEV (or -dev) add-ons for each of these is installed as well. In Ubuntu 6.06 these can be installed with one (rather long) command:

```
$ apt-get install libssl0.9.8 libssl-dev libiodbc2 libiodbc2-dev
          libsasl2 libsasl2-dev
```

Other distributions may use different installers, and even different package names, but you should have no problem finding them based on the bullet list of names that have been provided.

 OpenLDAP includes many optional modules that provide additional functionality (such as debugging or integration with other services). These modules are not covered in this book, though you may choose to explore them on your own. Some of these modules require additional libraries. Consult the OpenLDAP documentation included in the source code for more specific information.

At this point you have all the tools and requirements necessary for building OpenLDAP. Now we move onward to the actual compiling process.

Compiling OpenLDAP

In the last section we prepared all of the tools and libraries for building OpenLDAP. In this section we will configure, compile, and test OpenLDAP.

First, we need to get our OpenLDAP server source code moved into a temporary directory for building. Copy the `openldap-2.3.x.tgz` file into the appropriate directory and then unpack the file:

```
$ mkdir build/
$ cp openldap-2.3.37.tgz build/
$ cd build
$ tar -zxf openldap-2.3.37.tgz
```

Here, I created a new directory (called `build/`), copied the OpenLDAP source code archive into the new directory, changed the working directory to `build/`, and then unpacked the file with the `tar` utility (the flags `-zxf` instruct tar to uncompress (z) and extract the contents (x) of the file (f) `openldap-2.3.37.tgz`). Once this is done, the `build/` directory should contain a directory called `openldap-2.3.37`. Use cd to change to that directory: `cd openldap-2.3.37`.

Configuring

Now we need to run the configuration script to prepare the source code for compiling. This script determines how OpenLDAP will be built, and what options will be enabled or disabled by default. OpenLDAP is very configurable, and there are many different options from which to choose. To see the complete list of options, you can run the configuration script with the `--help` flag:

```
$ ./configure --help
```

This command will print out a list of every option available for configuring OpenLDAP. It will also indicate whether or not the option is on by default. For example, the first few lines of the SLAPD database backend section looks like this:

```
SLAPD Backend Options:
    --enable-backends      enable all available backends no|yes|mod
    --enable-bdb           enable Berkeley DB backend no|yes|mod [yes]
    --enable-dnssrv        enable dnssrv backend no|yes|mod [no]
```

We can see that each option has three possible states: yes, no, and mod (which builds the component as a pluggable module instead of building it into slapd). Of those listed, only the flag `--enable-bdb`, which enables the Berkeley DB backend, is on by default.

For the most part, the defaults are good. All of the crucial options are turned on by default. However, there are a few additional modules discussed in this book that are not on by default, and we will want to turn them on manually. They are:

- `--enable-ldap`: Enables the LDAP backend storage mechanism (see Chapter 7)
- `--enable-ppolicy`: Enables the password policy overlay (see Chapter 6)

If you do not plan to use the ODBC database backend, you can add `--enable-sql`, but you will need to make sure that you install the iODBC2 packages discussed in the previous section.

 By default, OpenLDAP will be installed (with the final make install step) into subdirectories at `/usr/local`. This is the recommended place to put applications and libraries that are "local" applications. Packages that are not distributed as standard pre-configured applications (like deb or RPM packages) are considered local packages. If you want to put the package somewhere else, use the `--prefix` and `--exec-prefix` flags.

Now we are ready to run the configuration command:

```
$ ./configure --enable-ldap --enable-sql --enable-ppolicy
```

This will kick off an evaluation process that may take several minutes. The configuration script will systematically evaluate your system settings, determining what tools you are using, how it should build, and whether or not the system has all of the necessary libraries.

If the configure process terminates with an error, it will indicate why it failed. Usually, this failure will indicate that one of the required libraries or tools is not present. For example, if it dies with an error stating that `sql.h` is missing, this indicates that the iODBC2 header files (from `libiodbc2-dev` in Ubuntu) were not found. This usually indicates that they are not installed at all, though it may also indicate that they were installed in a non-standard location.

Some missing libraries will not stop configure from running. Such packages will generate errors instead of warnings. Two examples of this are the OpenSSL libraries and the SASL libraries. Once the configuration script has completed, scroll back through the results and make sure there are no lines that look like this:

```
configure: WARNING: Could not locate TLS/SSL package
configure: WARNING: TLS data protection not supported!
```

or

```
configure: WARNING: Could not locate Cyrus SASL
configure: WARNING: SASL authentication not supported!
```

If you see these you will probably want to make sure the appropriate packages (remember the DEV packages) are installed, and then re-run the `./configure` script.

Once the configuration script has run through, and there are no warnings or errors, you are ready to build OpenLDAP's source code.

Building with make

Building with make is a two-step process. First, the auxiliary libraries must be built, then the main tools and servers must be built. Fortunately, all this hard work can be done in one short command:

```
$ make depend && make
```

This will compile all of the libraries (`make depend`) and then, if the first part was successful, it will run the main build (`make`). Compiling may take a long time.

Usually, the configuration script makes sure everything is in order before the main compilation begins. On rare occasions though, one of the two make commands may fail. If this happens you will have to evaluate the error message and determine what steps to take to fix the problem. In most cases the problem has to do with an unsatisfied dependency—some package or tool that OpenLDAP requires is not installed, and (for one reason or another), this gap was not noticed by the configuration script.

Sometimes the documentation included with OpenLDAP (`README`, `make`, and the documentation in the `docs/`, `libraries/`, and `servers/` directories) will point out possible problems.

> If the make fails and you cannot find the problem, your best bet may be to search the OpenLDAP mailing list archives (visit `http://openldap.org`) or, if all else fails, subscribe to the mailing list and ask about the problem there.

Once the compiling process ends, it is a good idea to run the automated testing procedure to make sure that the code was built correctly. This is also done with `make`:

```
$ make test
```

Because the test includes frequent programmatic delays and performs dozens of tests, this process may take several minutes to complete. When it is done, review the output and make sure there are no errors. Note that some of the test will be skipped because we did not compile OpenLDAP with all of the possible options turned on. Skipped tests are normal and are nothing to worry about.

Now we are ready to install our fresh new OpenLDAP server.

Installation

Installing is done with one additional command:

```
$ sudo make install
```

On some versions of Linux or UNIX, instead of using `su`do, you will need to switch users (`su`) to root and run the make install command as root: `su -c 'make install'`. You will be prompted to enter the password for your account (or, if you use `su` instead of `sudo`, the root password). Once you have correctly entered the password, the necessary OpenLDAP files will be copied to subdirectories of `/usr/local`.

On some systems, the directories that contain local executable files (`/usr/local/bin` and `/usr/local/sbin`) are not included in the `$PATH` environment variable. As a result, simply typing an OpenLDAP command at a command line may return an error. One way to get around this problem is to type in the entire path to the command:

```
$ /usr/local/sbin/slapcat
```

But this can be tedious. You can also append the appropriate paths to your `$PATH` environment variable. Then you will be able to simply issue the command without specifying the absolute path to the command:

```
$ export PATH= /usr/local/bin:/usr/local/sbin:$PATH
$ slapcat
```

In this example the export command re-sets `$PATH` for the current session. So the variable `$PATH` is assigned the values `/usr/local/bin`, `/usr/local/sbin`, and the contents of the current `$PATH` variable (which likely contains `/bin`, `/sbin`, `/usr/bin`, and other directories). Order is important. When the shell is searching for a command (`slapcat`, in the given example), it will search from the first directory in `$PATH` on to the last directory. As soon as it finds a match, it will stop searching. So, for example, if there were two `slapcat` commands, the shell would use the first one it found. In our case, it is best to put the two `/usr/local` directories early in the path just in case an older version of LDAP is installed elsewhere on the file system.

Usually, the `export` command should be added to the shell configuration file (for example ~/.bash_profile) so that the additional path information is automatically added every time you start a shell session.

You are now ready to configure the new version of OpenLDAP.

Building Everything

In the build mentioned in the previous section we compiled only the basics. This gets us what we need to run just the basics. But there are lots of OpenLDAP backends and overlays that can be useful (many of which are covered in this book). In cases where we want to build everything, typically it is best to compile OpenLDAP with module support, and compile all of the overlays and backends as modules. That way we can have all of the extras available, but only the ones needed (and configured in slapd.conf) get loaded at runtime.

> Many of the additional backends and overlays have their own dependencies. For example, the Perl backend requires that the Perl libraries be installed. Most of the necessary dependencies are installed by default in Ubuntu. If you don't have the requisite libraries for a module, the `configure` or `make` programs will let you know what library is missing, and you will have to track down which package contains that library. For this process, you may find the package search on Debian's website useful (http://www.us.debian.org/distrib/packages#search_contents).

Since we are building OpenLDAP with modules, we will need to make sure that libtool and the libtool header files are installed. In Ubuntu, it is not installed by default. Also, since the Perl backend (back_perl) will be installed, we will need to install the Perl development package. You can install all of these with one command:

```
$ sudo apt-get install libtool libltdl3 libltdl3-dev libperl-dev
```

The libltdl3 library is usually installed by default, but the others are also needed to compile OpenLDAP with module support. Now we are ready to build OpenLDAP with modules.

To build OpenLDAP with all of the extra modules, we just need to use the correct flags with `configure`:

```
$./configure --enable-dynamic --enable-modules --enable-backends=mod \
            --enable-overlays=mod
```

To build everything we need only four flags. The first, `--enable-dynamic` enables shared libraries. Second, `--enable-modules` simply tells `configure` that we want to use modules. The next two indicate what backends and overlays we want built: `--enable-overlays`, which is set to `mod` in order to build modules, and `-enable-backends` (also set to `mod`) to build all of the available backends.

Once `configure` completes, you can run `make`:

```
$ make depend && make && make test
```

This will build all the dependencies, then build OpenLDAP (and all of the modules), and then test everything. When you are ready to install, you can follow the instructions in the previous section.

Summary

In this appendix we have briefly examined the process of building OpenLDAP from source. At this point you should have the information necessary for building OpenLDAP from source.

We have looked at a very basic build and also a complete build using modules. But there are many other available options. You can learn more about building OpenLDAP from the documentation included with OpenLDAP.

B

LDAP URLs

To query a directory a client must send the server several different pieces of information. To make it possible to group all of this information together into one standards-based string format, LDAP developers proposed a standard LDAP URL syntax, which follows the URL standard (RFC 3986). In this appendix we will take a look at the format of LDAP URLs.

The LDAP URL

The LDAP URL is composed of eight different parts:

1. The **protocol**, which is usually LDAP (`ldap://`), though the non-standard LDAPS protocol (`ldaps://`) is used.
2. The **domain name** (or IP address) of the server. The default is `localhost`.
3. The **port number** of the server. The default is the standard LDAP port, `389`.
4. The **base DN** for the search.
5. The list of **attributes** to be returned. The default is to return all the attributes.
6. The **scope** specifier. The default is to use the `base` scope.
7. The **search filter**. The default is `(objectclass=*)`.
8. The **extension** field. If the server supports extensions, parameters for those extensions can be passed in the last field.

Combining seven of the eight parts (we will skip the extension field) we can create a URL that looks something like this:

```
ldap://example.com:389/ou=Users,dc=example,dc=com?mail?sub?(uid=matt)
```

This URL is composed of the seven parts in this way:

```
<protocol>://<domain>:<port>/<basedn>?<attrs>?<scope>?<filter>
```

Where we have to use an extension we would simply append a question mark (?) and the extension information to the end of the given URL.

Using this URL to perform an LDAP search, the result would be as follows:

- The client would connect to Example.Com on port 389 using the LDAP protocol.

- The based DN would be set to ou=Users,dc=example,dc=com.

- The client would request the **mail** attributes for all the entries in the subtree of ou=Users,dc=example,dc=com where the UID was matt.

To use LDAPS (the non-standard practice of using LDAP over a dedicated SSL/TLS port), use ldaps:// instead of ldap://.

In many cases it is convenient to shorten the URL and accept the default options. For example, the default domain is localhost (or the IP address 127.0.0.1), the address of the server on which the URL is executed. And the default port is 389 (unless the protocol is ldaps:// instead of ldap://, in which case the default port is the LDAP port 636).

The port can be left off in most cases. But the domain portion of the URL can be omitted too:

    ldap:///ou=Users,dc=example,dc=com?mail?sub?(uid=matt)

Note that there are now three slashes at the beginning, ldap:///. The domain name, which normally appears between the second and third slash, is not specified. If this URL were used, the LDAP application would connect to the localhost (the default host) at port 389 (the default LDAP port), and then proceed to run the search.

Now let's say that instead of wanting the LDAP server to return just the mail attribute, we want it to return all of the standard (non-operational) attributes. To do this, we simply leave the attribute specification empty:

    ldap:///ou=Users,dc=example,dc=com??sub?(uid=matt)

Now, the attribute position has no value, though the two adjacent question marks (??) indicate where the empty attribute position is.

In the previous two examples, when we have omitted specific field values, we have had to leave the designators in the URL, so we have ldap:/// for the domain portion of the URL, and ? without a value for the attribute specification (which looks like ?? in the given example).

But when we drop values from the *end* of the URL we do not need to leave the empty position designators. For example, if we were to drop the filter from the end, we do not need to leave trailing ? at the end of the URL. Here's an example:

```
ldap:///ou=Users,dc=example,dc=com?mail?sub
```

In this example the `mail` attributes for every entry under `ou=Users,dc=example,dc=com` are returned.

Common Uses of LDAP URLs

Throughout this book LDAP URLs have been used for various purposes.

In Chapter 4 we used LDAP URLs to perform searches in the `authz-regexp` directive in `slapd.conf`.

While a full LDAP URL, as we examined, can be a useful way to formulate a search, this is probably not the primary use of LDAP URLs. More commonly the LDAP URL syntax is simplified and used to capture only basic information.

Not all LDAP URLs are for Searching

In Chapter 3 we used LDAP URLs to connect to SLAPD from the `ldapsearch` utility, but we were not using the LDAP URL as a way to specify a search string. In many cases in fact, an LDAP URL may be used simply to provide protocol, host, and port information in one convenient string:

```
ldap://example.com:646
```

In this example the LDAP URL provides sufficient information for a client to use the plain LDAP protocol when connecting to the server `Example.Com` on the non-standard port 646.

Directory referrals, handled in the `slapd.conf` file by the referral directive, also use LDAP URL syntax, but only use the protocol, domain, and port settings.

LDAP URLs then, are used for two main purposes, and the purpose of each determines the form:

- LDAP search URLs follow the sophisticated eight-field format, and can convey all the information needed for an LDAP agent to perform a search

- LDAP connection URLs utilize only protocol, host, and port information, and are used mainly to convey information about how to connect to a directory

There are currently no LDAP URL forms for modifying or deleting LDAP records.

For More Information on LDAP URLs...

The LDAP URL format is described in the standards-track RFC 4516. The RFC is loaded with examples, and covers the use of extensions and encoding of special characters. The RFC is available online at `http://rfc-editor.org/rfc/rfc4516.txt`.

Summary

This brief primer provides an overview of the LDAP URL syntax. LDAP URLs are used in a variety of contexts, to provide connection information, and sometimes (in their more sophisticated form) to provide information necessary for performing an LDAP search.

C

Useful LDAP Commands

In the course of this book we looked at all the command line tools that come in the OpenLDAP distribution. But the scope of this book requires the discussion of each of these tools briefly. There are some advanced uses of these tools that can come in handy at times. In this appendix I have provided examples of such uses.

In this appendix, we will cover

- Getting information about the directory using `ldapsearch`
- Creating backups of the directory using two different strategies
- Rebuilding a BDB/HDB database

Getting Information about the Directory

Many LDAP servers provide information about their configuration and functional abilities. This information is stored in such a way that LDAP clients can directly access it using a search operation. For example, a client can fetch the **root DSE** record to find out the basic capabilities of the server. It can also access the **subschema** of the server and find out what object classes, syntaxes, matching rules, and attributes are supported.

The Root DSE

The **root DSE (DSA-Specific Entry**, where **DSA** stands for **Directory Service Agent**) is a special entry that provides information about the server itself. The DN of the root DSE is an empty string (""). To retrieve it we need a carefully-crafted LDAP search that will set an empty search base and then retrieve that root entry:

```
$ ldapsearch -x -LLL -b '' -s base -W -D \
    'cn=Manager,dc=example,dc=com' '+'
```

Note that the base is set to an empty string, and the search scope is limited to the base record. These parameters combined have the effect of requesting only the record that has an empty DN. Also, since most of the attributes in the root DSE are operational attributes, we need to specify '+' at the end of the search.

The results of running this search look something like this:

```
dn:
structuralObjectClass: OpenLDAProotDSE
configContext: cn=config
namingContexts: dc=example,dc=com
supportedControl: 2.16.840.1.113730.3.4.18
supportedControl: 2.16.840.1.113730.3.4.2
supportedControl: 1.3.6.1.4.1.4203.1.10.1
supportedControl: 1.2.840.113556.1.4.319
supportedControl: 1.2.826.0.1.334810.2.3
supportedControl: 1.2.826.0.1.3344810.2.3
supportedControl: 1.3.6.1.1.13.2
supportedControl: 1.3.6.1.1.13.1
supportedControl: 1.3.6.1.1.12
supportedExtension: 1.3.6.1.4.1.1466.20037
supportedExtension: 1.3.6.1.4.1.4203.1.11.1
supportedExtension: 1.3.6.1.4.1.4203.1.11.3
supportedFeatures: 1.3.6.1.1.14
supportedFeatures: 1.3.6.1.4.1.4203.1.5.1
supportedFeatures: 1.3.6.1.4.1.4203.1.5.2
supportedFeatures: 1.3.6.1.4.1.4203.1.5.3
supportedFeatures: 1.3.6.1.4.1.4203.1.5.4
supportedFeatures: 1.3.6.1.4.1.4203.1.5.5
supportedLDAPVersion: 3
supportedSASLMechanisms: NTLM
supportedSASLMechanisms: DIGEST-MD5
supportedSASLMechanisms: CRAM-MD5
entryDN:
subschemaSubentry: cn=Subschema
```

Among other things, this record gives us information about what controls, features, and extensions are understood by and enabled on the server. For example, there is a `supportedFeature` line that reads:

```
supportedExtension: 1.3.6.1.4.1.4203.1.11.1
```

This line indicates that this LDAP server supports an LDAPv3 extension for **Change Password** operations as defined in RFC 3062 (`http://www.rfc-editor.org/rfc/rfc3062.txt`).

Using this information, a well-crafted LDAP client would be able to perform a server-side Change Password operation instead of changing the password on the client side and then using a Modify operation to send the change to the server.

> The advantage of the Change Password operation is in the server's storage. If the client changes a password through a Modify operation it must know in advance what types of encryption are supported on the server, it must do the encrypting itself, and then submit the encrypted password to the server. Usually, it is better to have the client securely contacting the server (over TLS, for example), and then using a Change Password operation so that the server can do the storage.

The root DSE record also points to the configuration (cn=config) and subschema (cn=subschema) records.

The Subschema Record

The subschema record is stored in cn=subschema. This record contains detailed information about the schemas supported by the server, including what types of matching rules it has available, what sort of syntaxes are allowed in attributes, and what attributes and object classes are recognized by the server.

This information can be used by client applications to correctly craft records or searches, and then correctly interpret the responses.

The subschema record can be retrieved with ldapsearch using the following command:

```
ldapsearch -x -LLL -b 'cn=subschema' -s base -W \
    -D 'cn=Manager,dc=example,dc=com'  '+'
```

In this example we request the desired record by setting the base DN to cn=config, and then requesting a search type of base (-b 'cn=subschema' -s base). This returns the exact record with the DN cn=subschema.

Also, most of the attributes we want are operational attributes, which means they will not be returned in a normal search, so at the end we specify '+' to indicate that we want the operational attributes.

The record returned looks like this:

```
dn: cn=Subschema
structuralObjectClass: subentry
createTimestamp: 20061216235843Z
modifyTimestamp: 20061216235843Z
```

```
    ldapSyntaxes: ( 1.3.6.1.1.16.1 DESC 'UUID' )
    ldapSyntaxes: ( 1.3.6.1.1.1.0.1 DESC 'RFC2307 Boot Parameter' )
    # ... lots of lines removed
    objectClasses: ( 2.16.840.1.113730.3.2.2 NAME 'inetOrgPerson'
      DESC 'RFC2798: Internet Organizational Person'
      SUP organizationalPerson STRUCTURAL
      MAY ( audio $ businessCategory $ carLicense $ departmentNumber $
      displayName $ employeeNumber $ employeeType $ givenName $
      homePhone $ homePostalAddress $ initials $ jpegPhoto $
      labeledURI $ mail $ manager $ mobile $ o $ pager $ photo $
      roomNumber $ secretary $ uid $ userCertificate $
      x500uniqueIdentifier $ preferredLanguage $ userSMIMECertificate $
      userPKCS12 ) )
    objectClasses: ( 1.3.6.1.4.1.4203.666.11.1.4.2.1.2 NAME
      'olcHdbConfig' DESC 'HDB backend configuration'
      SUP olcDatabaseConfig STRUCTURAL
      MUST olcDbDirectory
      MAY ( olcDbCacheSize $ olcDbCheckpoint $ olcDbConfig $ olcDbNoSync
          $ olcDbDirtyRead $ olcDbIDLcacheSize $ olcDbIndex $
          olcDbLinearIndex $ olcDbLockDetect $ olcDbMode $
          olcDbSearchStack $ olcDbShmKey $ olcDbCacheFree ) )
    entryDN: cn=Subschema
    subschemaSubentry: cn=Subschema
```

A subschema record contains all of the schema information and thus, it may be well over a thousand lines.

Subschema records can be particularly useful to learn about what schemas a server supports, or when developing and debugging custom schemas, as discussed in Chapter 6.

The Configuration Record

An experimental feature of OpenLDAP 2.3 (and one that will probably reach production quality in OpenLDAP 2.4) is the ability to store the LDAP configuration inside of the directory. To do this you must first re-create your configuration in LDIF format using a special configuration schema, and instruct SLAPD to read its configuration from this new LDIF file.

The configuration is stored inside of the directory with the DN cn=config. It can be accessed with a search similar to the one used in the previous section:

```
ldapsearch -x -LLL -b 'cn=config' -s base -W \
    -D 'cn=Manager,dc=example,dc=com'  '*'
```

In OpenLDAP 2.3, not all of the overlays and features of OpenLDAP work correctly with this new configuration style, and that is a significant drawback to its use. But improving this alternate configuration mechanism is a priority for development in OpenLDAP 2.4.

What might be the advantages of storing your configuration in the directory? Here are a few:

- Easy access to configuration information through `ldapsearch` and other LDAP clients.
- The ability to edit configuration information through directory tools like `ldapmodify`.
- Replication support for SLAPD configuration. You may be able to use SyncRepl to synchronize directory configurations across the network.

If you would like to implement the new LDAP-based configuration file format, you can learn about it in the LDAP Administrators Guide at the OpenLDAP site: `http://www.openldap.org/doc/admin23/slapdconf2.html`.

Making a Directory Backup

There are two common strategies for backing up the contents of your directory. One is to make a backup of the directory database. The other is to dump the contents of the directory into an LDIF file.

A Backup Copy of the Directory Database

Different backends locate the contents of the directory in different locations. For example, the BDB and HDB backends store data in special Berkeley DB database files. SQL-based backends store the information in a relational database management system. Special backends like the LDAP and Perl backends may not store data at all, but might simply access other sources.

Each of these backends will require a different backup procedure. Here we will just look at backing up BDB and HDB databases—the types we've used throughout the book.

 This method is not portable. BDB/HDB files are version sensitive. Each new release of OpenLDAP (or of Berkeley DB) may use different structures for these databases, so this backup method only works when the backup and the restore are done on the same software versions.

In Ubuntu these database files are located at `/var/lib/ldap`. All of the files in this directory, including the indexes (those that end with the `bdb` extension), the main database files (`__db.???`) and the log files (`log.??????????`). It is also a good idea to make a copy of the `DB_CONFIG` file, though it rarely changes and does not store any directory data.

When backing up these files it is best to stop SLAPD. Here's a very simple example using common shell tools:

```
$ sudo invoke-rc.d slapd stop
$ sudo cp -a /var/lib/ldap/* /usr/local/backup/ldap/
$ sudo invoke-rc.d slapd start
```

This will stop SLAPD and copy all of the files at `/var/lib/ldap/` to `/usr/local/backup/ldap/`. Then, SLAPD will be started again.

An LDIF Backup File

The second, and more portable, strategy for backing up the directory is to dump the contents of the directory to an LDIF file. There are several distinct advantages to this approach:

- There is no need to stop SLAPD
- The output is more portable, and data can be moved from one database backend to another, and from one OpenLDAP version to another

There is less redundant data, so backup files are much smaller than the BDB/HDB files. To make an LDIF backup file of the contents of a directory server with only one database (that is, it has only one directory root), the command is simple:

```
$ sudo slapcat -l /usr/local/backup/my_directory.ldif
```

This command uses `slapcat` to dump the contents of the directory, in the LDIF format, into the file `/usr/local/backup/my_directory.ldif`. It can be loaded back into the directory using the `slapdadd` tool discussed in Chapter 3.

If your directory contains more than one directory information tree, you will need to run the `slapcat` routine once for each server, using the `-b` flag to identify the suffix (base DN) of the directory information tree you want to dump:

```
$ cd /usr/local/backup
$ sudo slapcat -b "dc=example,dc=com" -l example_com.ldif
$ sudo slapcat -b "dc=test,dc=net" -l test_net.ldif
```

In this example we backup each directory into its own LDIF file.

Rebuilding a Database (BDB, HDB)

Sometimes it is necessary to rebuild a backend database. This process differs depending on the database backend. For instance, with a SQL backend, it might entail dumping, dropping, and re-creating tables in the database.

> Moving to a new server and transferring contents to a new slave server are also processes similar to rebuilding a database, and the differences are mentioned within the text here.

The most commonly-used backends for OpenLDAP are the HDB and BDB backends (both based on the Berkeley DB lightweight database). In this section, I want to cover the process of rebuilding these databases.

This process consists of five steps:

1. Stop SLAPD
2. Dump the directory data into a file
3. Delete the old directory files
4. Create a new database
5. Start SLAPD

None of these steps is particularly difficult. In fact, for a small to medium-sized directory, this process can be done in less than ten minutes.

> **Moving from Server to Server**
>
> Moving a directory from one server to another is done by a process very similar to that described here. Only step three, as mentioned later, differs. In this case, instead of deleting directory files, the LDIF file would be transferred from the original server to the new server. Steps one and two would be run on the original server, and steps four and five would be done on the new server.

Step 1: Stop the Server

The purpose of stopping the server is to prevent additional changes to the directory information tree while we are working on it.

If you are just dumping the contents of a master directory to import into a shadow server that will use SyncRepl, you need not stop the server. Any changes that happen after the directory has been dumped will be retrieved by the shadow server during its first LDAP synchronization operation.

This can be done either by killing the server's process ID, or by running the startup script with the stop command:

```
$ sudo invoke-rc.d slapd stop
```

Now that the server is stopped, we can dump the database.

Step 2: Dump the Database

In Chapter 3 I covered the OpenLDAP utilities. One of the tools I discussed was the `slapcat` program, which is a tool for dumping the contents of the directory into an LDIF file. That is the program we will use in this step.

Why use `slapcat` instead of an `ldapsearch`? There are two reasons.

First, `slapcat` preserves all of the attributes (and records for that matter) that the LDAP server uses, including the operational attributes that are stored. (Those operational attributes that are generated at runtime are not generated by `slapcat`, and that is good. We wouldn't want to import those, anyway.)

Second, `slapcat` accesses the database directly, instead of opening an LDAP connection to the server. That means that ACLs, time and size limits, and other by products of the LDAP connection are not evaluated, and hence will not alter the data.

The BDB/HDB database is stored in a small set of files located at `/var/lib/ldap` (or `/usr/local/var/openldap-data` if you built from source). Usually access to those files is restricted to only the ID of the SLAPD user. By default this is `root` or `ldap`. In order to extract information using `slapcat`, you will need to have access to those files.

We have this command:

```
$ sudo slapcat -l /tmp/backup.ldif
```

This command executes `slapcat` as root. The `-l` flag is used to pass in the name of the output file. In this case the file `backup.ldif` will be created in the `/tmp` directory.

You may prefer putting the LDIF file in a folder other than /tmp, especially if you plan on keeping the LDIF file for more than a few minutes.

In most cases the -l flag is the only one you will need. If you have more than one backend and you only want to dump one, you can use the -n flag to specify which backend to dump.

Once the slapcat is complete, we are done with this step.

Before continuing however, you may want to check the contents of the LDIF file to make sure that it is not corrupt. Do this before deleting the database files.

Step 3: Delete the Old Database Files

If you are re-building a database you will want to delete the old database files before building new ones.

 You do not need to do this if you are either migrating from an old server to a new server or configuring SyncRepl shadow servers.

These files are stored at /var/lib/ldap (or /usr/local/var/openldap-data if you built from source). However, not all of the files in that directory should be deleted. We only want to delete:

- The index files: files that end in '.bdb'.
- The main database files: files named __db.???, where the question marks are replaced by numbers in sequence (__db.001, __db.002, and so on).
- The alock file: a file used internally for storing locking information. (Usually, this can be left with no negative consequences, but if SLAPD crashed, this can be left in an unstable state.)
- The BDB log files: files named log.??????????, where the ten question marks are replaced by numbers in sequence: log.0000000001, log.0000000002, and so on.

There is one file we definitely do not want to delete. This is our database configuration file, DB_CONFIG. Deleting it would cause the BDB engine to use its default settings, which are not tuned to our needs, and generally cause OpenLDAP to perform poorly.

So, to delete the files, we can do the following:

```
$ cd /var/lib/ldap
$ sudo rm __db.* *.bdb alock log.*
```

To reduce the risk of data loss, you may want to backup the __db.*, *.bdb, and log.* files before removing them. Or instead of doing an rm, you may use mv to move the files to a different location:

```
$ cd /var/lib/ldap
$ sudo mkdir backup/
$ sudo mv *.bdb log.* alock __db.* backup/
```

Now the database directory has been cleared. We are ready to create new database files.

Step 4: Create a New Database

The new database can be created and populated with the data all in one step, using the slapadd utility that we covered in Chapter 3. Still in the OpenLDAP data directory, run the following command:

```
$ sudo slapadd -l /tmp/backup.ldif
```

This will create all of the necessary files, import the LDIF file, and handle all of the data indexing as well.

> If you are running your LDAP server as a user other than root (and it is a good idea to do so), you will also need to use chown to change the ownership on all of the files at /var/lib/ldap to be owned by the SLAPD userID: sudo chown openldap *.bdb log.* __db.*.

All we need to do now is restart the server.

Step 5: Restart SLAPD

If you stopped the server in step 1 you will need to restart it.

Restart the server in one of the usual ways. Using the init script is usually the best way:

```
$ sudo invoke-rc.d slapd start
```

That's all there is to it. Now you should have SLAPD running with a fresh copy of the database.

Troubleshooting Rebuilds

As long as the LDIF file exported with `slapcat` is good, there is not much that can go wrong in this process. Even if you have to delete and recreate several times, as long as the LDIF file is safe, no important data is at risk.

If SLAPD is running as a user other than `root`, the main problem with importing is usually the permissions on the database files at `/var/lib/ldap`. Permissions on the configuration files in `/etc/ldap` directory may also be the source of SLAPD failures. Make sure they are owned by the appropriate user.

When switching versions of OpenLDAP, occasionally an old LDIF file will not be valid in the new server (this happened between OpenLDAP 2.0 and OpenLDAP 2.2, and again between 2.2 and 2.3; it could happen again in the future). While the standard schemas are fairly stable over time, operational attributes, which are not usually standardized, are more volatile, and do change from release to release.

Often, the fix will be tweaking records in the LDIF file to match the attributes used in new version. One other common issue has to do with starting up the server. Sometimes, when using the init script, you will not be able to get the server to start, but no informative message will be sent to the console or the log files. (One common reason for the failure to start is the permissions issue I noted earlier).

A good first step in solving startup problems is to run `slapd` from the command line, with debugging enabled: `sudo slapd -d trace`.

Summary

In this appendix we looked at a couple of useful commands, including some designed to get detailed information about the directory server itself. Also, we saw two ways of making directory backups, and examined the process of rebuilding a directory database.

Index

Thank you for buying
Mastering OpenLDAP

Packt Open Source Project Royalties

When we sell a book written on an Open Source project, we pay a royalty directly to that project. Therefore by purchasing Mastering OpenLDAP, Packt will have given some of the money received to the OpenLDAP Foundation.

In the long term, we see ourselves and you—customers and readers of our books—as part of the Open Source ecosystem, providing sustainable revenue for the projects we publish on. Our aim at Packt is to establish publishing royalties as an essential part of the service and support a business model that sustains Open Source.

If you're working with an Open Source project that you would like us to publish on, and subsequently pay royalties to, please get in touch with us.

Writing for Packt

We welcome all inquiries from people who are interested in authoring. Book proposals should be sent to authors@packtpub.com. If your book idea is still at an early stage and you would like to discuss it first before writing a formal book proposal, contact us; one of our commissioning editors will get in touch with you.

We're not just looking for published authors; if you have strong technical skills but no writing experience, our experienced editors can help you develop a writing career, or simply get some additional reward for your expertise.

About Packt Publishing

Packt, pronounced 'packed', published its first book "Mastering phpMyAdmin for Effective MySQL Management" in April 2004 and subsequently continued to specialize in publishing highly focused books on specific technologies and solutions.

Our books and publications share the experiences of your fellow IT professionals in adapting and customizing today's systems, applications, and frameworks. Our solution-based books give you the knowledge and power to customize the software and technologies you're using to get the job done. Packt books are more specific and less general than the IT books you have seen in the past. Our unique business model allows us to bring you more focused information, giving you more of what you need to know, and less of what you don't.

Packt is a modern, yet unique publishing company, which focuses on producing quality, cutting-edge books for communities of developers, administrators, and newbies alike. For more information, please visit our website: www.PacktPub.com.

Pluggable Authentication Modules

ISBN: 978-1-904811-32-9   Paperback: 124 pages

A comprehensive and practical guide to PAM for Linux: how modules work and how to implement them

1. Understand and configure PAM

2. Develop PAM-aware applications and your own PAMs using the API and C

3. How to authenticate users in Active Directory, mount encrypted home directories, load SSH keys automatically, and restrict web and rsh services

Designing and Implementing Linux Firewalls and QoS using netfilter, iproute2, NAT and l7-filter

ISBN: 1-904811-65-5   Paperback: 280 pages

Learn how to secure your system and implement QoS using real-world scenarios for networks of all sizes

1. Implementing Packet filtering, NAT, bandwidth shaping, packet prioritization using netfilter/iptables, iproute2, Class Based Queuing (CBQ) and Hierarchical Token Bucket (HTB)

2. Designing and implementing 5 real-world firewalls and QoS scenarios ranging from small SOHO offices to a large scale ISP network that spans many cities

3. Building intelligent networks by marking, queuing, and prioritizing different types of traffic

Please check **www.PacktPub.com** for information on our titles

Printed in the United States
124425LV00003B/11-20/A

9 781847 191021